Read this book online today:

With SAP PRESS BooksOnline we offer you online access to knowledge from the leading SAP experts. Whether you use it as a beneficial supplement or as an alternative to the printed book, with SAP PRESS BooksOnline you can:

- Access your book anywhere, at any time. All you need is an Internet connection.
- Perform full text searches on your book and on the entire SAP PRESS library.
- Build your own personalized SAP library.

The SAP PRESS customer advantage:

Register this book today at www.sap-press.com and obtain exclusive free trial access to its online version. If you like it (and we think you will), you can choose to purchase permanent, unrestricted access to the online edition at a very special price!

Here's how to get started:

1. Visit www.sap-press.com.
2. Click on the link for SAP PRESS BooksOnline and login (or create an account).
3. Enter your free trial license key, shown below in the corner of the page.
4. Try out your online book with full, unrestricted access for a limited time!

Your personal free trial **license key** for this online book is: **pubx-7h6j-tfqm-z8s9**

**Optimizing Sales and Distribution in SAP® ERP:
Functionality and Configuration**

 PRESS

SAP PRESS is a joint initiative of SAP and Galileo Press. The know-how offered by SAP specialists combined with the expertise of the Galileo Press publishing house offers the reader expert books in the field. SAP PRESS features first-hand information and expert advice, and provides useful skills for professional decision-making.

SAP PRESS offers a variety of books on technical and business related topics for the SAP user. For further information, please visit our website: *www.sap-press.com*.

Rajen Iyer
Effective SAP SD
2007, 365 pp.
978-1-59229-101-4

Matt Chudy and Luis Castedo
Practical Guide to Sales and Distribution in SAP ERP
2010, ~425 pp.
978-1-59229-347-6

Hess, Lenz, Scheibler
Sales and Distribution Controlling with SAP NetWeaver BI
2009, 250 pp.
978-1-59229-266-0

Martin Murray
SAP MM – Functionality and Technical Configuration, Second Edition
2008, 588 pp.
978-1-59229-134-2

Ashish Mohapatra

Optimizing Sales and Distribution in SAP® ERP

Functionality and Configuration

Bonn • Boston

Galileo Press is named after the Italian physicist, mathematician and philosopher Galileo Galilei (1564–1642). He is known as one of the founders of modern science and an advocate of our contemporary, heliocentric worldview. His words *Eppur se muove* (And yet it moves) have become legendary. The Galileo Press logo depicts Jupiter orbited by the four Galilean moons, which were discovered by Galileo in 1610.

Editor Meg Dunkerley
Technical Reviewer Paul Warren
Copyeditor Ruth Saavedra
Cover Design Jill Winitzer
Photo Credit Image Copyright Karel Gallas. Used under license from Shutterstock.com
Layout Design Vera Brauner
Production Editor Kelly O'Callaghan
Assistant Production Editor Graham Geary
Typesetting Publishers' Design and Production Services, Inc.
Printed and bound in Canada

ISBN 978-1-59229-329-2

© 2010 by Galileo Press Inc., Boston (MA)
1st Edition 2010

Library of Congress Cataloging-in-Publication Data
Mohapatra, Asislia.
  Optimizing sales and distribution in SAP ERP functionality and configuration / Ashish Mohapatra. — 1st ed.
    p. cm.
  Includes bibliographical references and index.
  ISBN-13: 978-1-59229-329-2 (alk. paper)
  ISBN-10: 1-59229-329-8 (alk. paper)
  1. SAP R/3. 2. Sales management--Computer programs. 3. Physical distribution of goods — Management--Computer programs. I. Title.
  HF5438.35M34 2010
  658.8'10028553--dc22
                                                                           2010005758

All rights reserved. Neither this publication nor any part of it may be copied or reproduced in any form or by any means or translated into another language, without the prior consent of Galileo Press GmbH, Rheinwerkallee 4, 53227 Bonn, Germany.

Galileo Press makes no warranties or representations with respect to the content hereof and specifically disclaims any implied warranties of merchantability or fitness for any particular purpose: Galileo Press assumes no responsibility for any errors that may appear in this publication.

"Galileo Press" and the Galileo Press logo are registered trademarks of Galileo Press GmbH, Bonn, Germany. SAP PRESS is an imprint of Galileo Press.

All of the screenshots and graphics reproduced in this book are subject to copyright © SAP AG, Dietmar-Hopp-Allee 16, 69190 Walldorf, Germany.

SAP, the SAP-Logo, mySAP, mySAP.com, mySAP Business Suite, SAP NetWeaver, SAP R/3, SAP R/2, SAP B2B, SAPtronic, SAPscript, SAP BW, SAP CRM, SAP Early Watch, SAP ArchiveLink, SAP GUI, SAP Business Workflow, SAP Business Engineer, SAP Business Navigator, SAP Business Framework, SAP Business Information Warehouse, SAP inter-enterprise solutions, SAP APO, AcceleratedSAP, InterSAP, SAPoffice, SAPfind, SAPfile, SAPtime, SAPmail, SAPaccess, SAP-EDI, R/3 Retail, Accelerated HR, Accelerated HiTech, Accelerated Consumer Products, ABAP, ABAP/4, ALE/WEB, Alloy, BAPI, Business Framework, BW Explorer, Duet, Enjoy-SAP, mySAP.com e-business platform, mySAP Enterprise Portals, RIVA, SAPPHIRE, TeamSAP, Webflow and SAP PRESS are registered or unregistered trademarks of SAP AG, Walldorf, Germany.

All other products mentioned in this book are registered or unregistered trademarks of their respective companies.

Contents at a Glance

1	Introduction	21
2	Master Data	43
3	Sales	89
4	Pricing	165
5	Credit Risk Management	205
6	Logistics Management	233
7	Billing	289
8	Cross-Functional Customization	345
9	Reporting and Analysis	399
10	Summary and Conclusion	453
A	Customization of Local Layout	457
B	List of SAP Area Menus	473
C	How to Initialize a Material Period	503
D	The Author	507

Contents

Acknowledgments 15
Preface 17

1 Introduction 21

1.1 Introduction to SAP ERP 21
    1.1.1 Applications and Functionalities in SAP ERP 22
    1.1.2 Development, Quality, and Production Servers 23
    1.1.3 SAP ERP Customizing Implementation Guide 24
    1.1.4 SAP ERP Resources 25
1.2 Introduction to SAP GUI 25
    1.2.1 The Typical SAP Screen 27
    1.2.2 SAP Easy Access Menu Paths and Transaction Codes 28
    1.2.3 SAP Icons 29
    1.2.4 Wild Cards 29
    1.2.5 Function Keys 30
1.3 ASAP Methodology 30
1.4 SAP Solution Manager Overview 31
1.5 Organizational Structure in SAP 33
    1.5.1 Importing Organizational Units 33
    1.5.2 Defining Organizational Units 34
    1.5.3 Assigning Organizational Units 38
    1.5.4 Checking for Consistency 39
1.6 Summary 41

2 Master Data 43

2.1 Customer Master Data 43
    2.1.1 Reducing Sales Areas 44
    2.1.2 Defining Customer Account Groups 47
    2.1.3 Customer Master Record Fields 49
    2.1.4 Customer Mass Maintenance 51
2.2 Customer Credit Master Data 58
    2.2.1 Preliminary Settings 59
    2.2.2 Customizing Text IDs 60

7

	2.2.3	Defining Groups and Categories	60
	2.2.4	Authorization Control for Customer Credit Master Record Fields	60
2.3		Material Master – Sales Views	62
	2.3.1	Important Sales-Relevant Material Master Fields	62
	2.3.2	Customizing Material Master Fields	65
2.4		Batch Master Data	70
	2.4.1	Defining Batches	71
	2.4.2	Configuring System Messages	74
	2.4.3	Configuring the Layout of Batch Master Records	74
	2.4.4	Document Management System for Batch Master Records	75
	2.4.5	Configuring Batch Numbers	76
	2.4.6	Configuring Shelf Life Expiration Date (SLED)	77
	2.4.7	Configuring Batch Classification	79
2.5		Overview of Other Master Data	82
	2.5.1	Vendor Master Data	82
	2.5.2	Employee Master Data	84
	2.5.3	General Ledger Master Data	86
	2.5.4	User Master Data	86
2.6		Summary	88

3 Sales — 89

3.1		Principles of Processing Sales Documents	90
3.2		Sales Document Types	91
3.3		Item Categories and Schedule Line Categories	99
	3.3.1	Item Categories	100
	3.3.2	Schedule Line Categories	102
3.4		Create with Reference	103
3.5		Copy Control	107
3.6		Partner Determination	112
3.7		Availability Check and Transfer of Requirements (ATP)	114
	3.7.1	Availability Check	116
	3.7.2	Transfer of Requirements (TOR)	123
3.8		Outline Agreements	124
	3.8.1	Customer Contracts	124
	3.8.2	Scheduling Agreement	128
3.9		Special Business Transactions	128

	3.9.1	Consignment Sale Processing	128
	3.9.2	Returnable Packaging	129
	3.9.3	Make-to-Order Production	130
	3.9.4	Bill of Materials	130
	3.9.5	Third-Party Order Processing	131
	3.9.6	Individual Purchase Order	131
	3.9.7	Configurable Material	131
3.10	Incompletion Control and Its Practical Use		132
	3.10.1	Define Status Groups	133
	3.10.2	Identify Incompletion Groups	133
	3.10.3	Define Incompleteness Procedure	134
	3.10.4	Assign Incompleteness Procedure	135
3.11	Free Goods and Free Items		136
3.12	Material Determination, Listing, and Exclusion		140
3.13	Batch Determination in Sales		142
	3.13.1	Condition Tables	142
	3.13.2	Access Sequence	142
	3.13.3	Strategy Type	143
	3.13.4	Batch Search Procedure	144
3.14	Returns (Complaints) Processing		146
	3.14.1	Free-of-Charge Delivery and Subsequent Delivery	146
	3.14.2	Invoice Correction without Return	147
	3.14.3	Returns	147
3.15	Intercompany Sales Processing		148
3.16	Common Integration Points with Material Management		150
3.17	Outputs in Sales		152
3.18	Foreign Trade		157
	3.18.1	Countries	158
	3.18.2	Currencies	158
	3.18.3	Number Ranges	158
	3.18.4	Commodity Codes and Import Code Numbers	159
	3.18.5	Procedure	159
	3.18.6	Business Transaction Type	160
	3.18.7	Mode of Transport	161
	3.18.8	Customs Offices	161
	3.18.9	INCO Terms	161
	3.18.10	SAP GTS	162
3.19	Summary		163

4 Pricing ... 165

- 4.1 Introduction to Condition Techniques ... 166
- 4.2 Condition Records ... 168
  - 4.2.1 Add Fields to Field Catalog ... 175
  - 4.2.2 Create Condition Tables ... 175
  - 4.2.3 Create Access Sequence ... 175
  - 4.2.4 Create Condition Types ... 176
  - 4.2.5 Create Pricing Procedure ... 180
  - 4.2.6 Assign Pricing Procedure ... 182
  - 4.2.7 Create Condition Records ... 182
- 4.3 Optimizing Price Determination ... 183
- 4.4 Rebate Agreement ... 186
- 4.5 Customized Pricing Report and Price List ... 192
- 4.6 Common External Tax Software Packages ... 197
  - 4.6.1 Defining and Testing the Physical Destination for External Tax Calculation ... 198
  - 4.6.2 Activating the SAP Tax Interface ... 199
  - 4.6.3 Configuring External Tax Documents ... 199
  - 4.6.4 Defining Tax Jurisdiction Codes ... 200
  - 4.6.5 Defining the Tax Category for Different Countries ... 200
  - 4.6.6 Defining Customer Tax Classifications ... 200
  - 4.6.7 Defining Material Tax Indicators ... 201
  - 4.6.8 Setting Tax Codes ... 201
  - 4.6.9 Maintaining Tax Condition Records and Master Data Records ... 202
- 4.7 Summary ... 203

5 Credit Risk Management ... 205

- 5.1 Credit Management ... 205
  - 5.1.1 Prerequisites for Automatic Credit Control ... 206
  - 5.1.2 Customer Credit Master Records ... 211
  - 5.1.3 Automatic Credit Control ... 215
  - 5.1.4 Credit Management Operations ... 219
- 5.2 Blocking and Unblocking Customers ... 223
- 5.3 Payment Guarantee ... 225
  - 5.3.1 Forms of Payment Guarantee ... 225
  - 5.3.2 Payment Guarantee Determination Procedure ... 226

5.4 Common Problems and Their Solutions 230
5.5 Summary 232

6 Logistics Management   233

6.1 Delivery Types and Delivery Item Categories 234
    6.1.1 Delivery Types 234
    6.1.2 Delivery Item Category 238
    6.1.3 Automatic Determination of Delivery Item Category 241
6.2 Picking, Handling Unit Management, Packing, and Goods Issue ... 242
    6.2.1 Picking 242
    6.2.2 Handling Unit Management 244
    6.2.3 Packing 245
    6.2.4 Goods Issue 246
6.3 Delivery Processing Integration with Warehouse Management 247
6.4 Principles of Processing Deliveries Including Delivery Due Lists ... 248
    6.4.1 Profile for Delivery Creation 250
    6.4.2 List Profile 252
    6.4.3 Function Codes Excluded During List Processing 257
    6.4.4 Assign Profile to Scenarios 258
    6.4.5 Maintain Requirement Routines 259
    6.4.6 Modify Layout 259
6.5 Routes and Route Determination 259
    6.5.1 Define Routes 260
    6.5.2 Route Determination 262
    6.5.3 Route Schedule Determination 263
6.6 Scheduling 264
6.7 Stock Transfer Including Intercompany Transfers 266
    6.7.1 Define the Number Range for Stock Transfer Orders 267
    6.7.2 Define the Document Type for Stock Transfer Orders 268
    6.7.3 Create Internal Customers for Receiving Plants 269
    6.7.4 Define Shipping Data for Receiving Plants 269
    6.7.5 Assign Document Type to Plants 270
    6.7.6 Assign Delivery Type and Checking Rule to
           STO Document Type 271
    6.7.7 Create Vendor Master Record for Receiving Plant 272
6.8 Outputs in Shipping 273
6.9 Batch Determination in Deliveries 276

	6.10	Processing Serialized Materials	277
	6.11	Interface with Carrier Software	279
		6.11.1 Customization of the SAP Interface	280
		6.11.2 How to Use External Tax Software	284
	6.12	Common Problems and Their Solutions	285
	6.13	Summary	288

7 Billing 289

	7.1	Principles of Bill Processing	290
		7.1.1 Creating Individual Invoices	290
		7.1.2 Collective Billing Document	292
		7.1.3 Invoice Split	294
		7.1.4 Billing Due List	295
		7.1.5 Invoice List	295
		7.1.6 Cancellation Invoice	296
		7.1.7 General Billing Interface	296
	7.2	Billing Types	298
		7.2.1 Customizing Billing Types	298
		7.2.2 Number Ranges for Billing Types	303
		7.2.3 Check Customized Billing Types	306
	7.3	Complaint Documents	308
	7.4	Billing Plan	310
		7.4.1 Define Billing Plan Types	310
		7.4.2 Define Date Descriptions	312
		7.4.3 Define and Assign Date Categories	312
		7.4.4 Maintain Date Proposals for Milestone Billing	314
		7.4.5 Assign Billing Plan Types to Sales Document Types	315
		7.4.6 Assign Billing Plan Types to Item Categories	315
		7.4.7 Define Rules for Determining Dates	316
	7.5	Revenue Account Determination	317
		7.5.1 Field Catalog for the Account Determination Table	318
		7.5.2 Account Determination Table	318
		7.5.3 Access Sequence	320
		7.5.4 Account Determination Type	321
		7.5.5 Account Determination Procedure	322
		7.5.6 Account Key	323

		7.5.7	Assign General Ledger to Account Determination Types	324
	7.6		Accounts Interface	325
		7.6.1	Revenue Recognition	325
		7.6.2	Reconciliation Account Determination	327
		7.6.3	Cash Account Determination	328
		7.6.4	Data Forwarded to Accounting Document	328
	7.7		Some Billing Related Problems and Their Solutions	329
	7.8		Summary	343

8 Cross-Functional Customization ... 345

	8.1		Text Processing	345
		8.1.1	Text IDs	348
		8.1.2	Text Determination Procedure	349
		8.1.3	Assigning Text IDs to a Text Determination Procedure	350
		8.1.4	Define Access Sequence	351
		8.1.5	Assignment of Text Determination Procedure	352
		8.1.6	Text Determination Analysis	353
	8.2		Message Control	355
		8.2.1	IDoc Interface and EDI	356
		8.2.2	Application Link Enabling	362
	8.3		Web Interface	362
		8.3.1	Creating A Web Interface using the Wizard	364
		8.3.2	Creating a Web Interface Manually	365
		8.3.3	Other Tools for Web Interface	366
	8.4		Batch Management	367
		8.4.1	Batch Where-Used List	368
		8.4.2	Batch Information Cockpit	371
	8.5		ABAP Tools	374
		8.5.1	SD User Exits	375
		8.5.2	Debugging	376
		8.5.3	LSMW	378
	8.6		Numbering Objects	390
		8.6.1	Maintain Number Ranges	392
		8.6.2	Create Number Range Objects	394
	8.7		Summary	398

9 Reporting and Analysis 399

- 9.1 Useful Standard Reports 399
  - 9.1.1 Classification of Standard Reports 400
  - 9.1.2 Features Available in Standard Reports 409
- 9.2 Developing Reports Using Query 410
  - 9.2.1 Create Query 411
  - 9.2.2 Data Source 411
  - 9.2.3 Insert Tables 412
  - 9.2.4 Join Tables 414
  - 9.2.5 Selection and List Fields 416
  - 9.2.6 List Screen Layout 417
  - 9.2.7 Create a Z-Transaction for the Query 421
- 9.3 Sales Information System 423
  - 9.3.1 Standard Analyses 423
  - 9.3.2 Flexible Analyses 427
  - 9.3.3 General Checks for Info-Structure 433
  - 9.3.4 Checks for SIS Info-Structures 437
- 9.4 Business Intelligence and Reporting 439
- 9.5 Developing ABAP Reports 443
  - 9.5.1 Create Program by Specifying Program Attributes 444
  - 9.5.2 Write Program and Activate 446
  - 9.5.3 Change Text Elements 449
  - 9.5.4 Documentation 449
  - 9.5.5 Create Variant 450
  - 9.5.6 Test the Program 450
- 9.6 Summary 452

10 Summary and Conclusion 453

Appendices 457

- A Customization of Local Layout 459
- B List of SAP Area Menus 473
- C How to Initialize a Material Period 503
- D The Author 507

Index 509

Acknowledgments

I would like to sincerely thank my editor, Meg Dunkerley, and all those who approved my proposal, for their trust in me. I rediscovered the meaning of the word *edit* when I got feedback from the developmental editor, Ms. Kelly Harris. I also acknowledge the valuable suggestions made by our technical editor, Mr. Paul Warren and the copyeditor, Ruth Saavedra. I know there are a lot of people at SAP PRESS who directly or indirectly are part of this book. I may never know them personally, but always felt their contributions.

I also acknowledge all my teachers, friends, and colleagues who have a big influence on the way I think, learn, and write. I would like to especially thank my boss, Mr. Nikhil Aggarwal, and my mentor, Mr. Atulya Kumar Panda.

I thank my parents, Sri Madhav Chandra Mohapatra and Smt Sarala Mohapatra, and my elder brothers Mr. Amar Ranjan Mohapatra and Mr. Gyan Ranjan Mohapatra, who in spite of all their financial difficulties, provided me with the best education possible. My wife, Namita, daughter, Dikshya, and son, Tejash are a constant source of love and motivation for me. They inspire me to deliver the best.

Finally, I dedicate this book to Him who needs no acknowledgment, but rather acknowledges us by His blessings.

Preface

Any company selling products or services must have the ability to efficiently fulfill orders and deliver their products and services. An integrated sales and distribution system enables them to create contracts and agreements, acknowledge order receipt, fulfill orders, and provide accurate invoices. In today's competitive environment, the ability to handle these processes cost-effectively is vital. The Sales and Distribution functionality in SAP ERP is such a tool. It is one of the most important and most often implemented SAP logistics functionalities. It provides companies tools for managing the different stages of the order-to-cash process, making the information more manageable and accessible.

Who This Book Is For

The book can help the following groups learn how to customize the Sales and Distribution functionality in SAP ERP and how to integrate it with other systems. The target groups are:

- Consultants
- IT administrators
- Project leads
- Key team members

What Will Be Covered Throughout

Sales and Distribution is a mature functionality in SAP ERP. Over the years, SAP has added a lot of new tools to it. The book is written with SAP ERP users in mind. It's divided into nine chapters, and in the tenth chapter we have summarized the book for you. As you start reading the book, you should also do the steps yourself. This book answers the question, "Now that Sales and Distribution in SAP ERP is implemented, what next?" You'll gain a complete understanding of the Sales and Distribution functionality in SAP ERP and how it can be used to make your business processes more efficient. You'll learn how to improve system performance and get a better return on investment for your SAP ERP implementation. You'll be able to use SAP ERP to fulfill orders and deliver their products and services more effectively.

In **Chapter 1**, Introduction, we'll introduce the general tools and features of SAP ERP. We'll introduce you to the project management tools such as ASAP and SAP Solution Manager. We cover the customization of enterprise structures in this chapter, and you'll be ready with your own organizational units and proper assignments for further use in other chapters.

In **Chapter 2**, Master Data, you'll learn how to do mass maintenance of master data records. We'll cover several kinds of master data records, such as customer master records, material master records, and so on. We'll also cover how to customize master data fields and how to customize layout.

Chapter 3, Sales, is the longest and most important chapter. Most of the processes in the Sales and Distribution functionality in SAP ERP start at this stage and culminate in billing. We'll discuss the customization of orders, items, and schedule line categories, and we'll cover both normal and special business processes such as consignment, or third-party sales. You'll develop a thorough understanding of the copy control technique and use of different routines. This chapter will introduce the condition technique, which is used throughout the SAP system for automatic determination. In this chapter, we'll also discuss automatic determination of free goods, sales output, material listing, material exclusion, partners, and batches, as well as incompletion control. You'll learn about foreign trade and intercompany sales processing, as well as integration with the Materials Management functionality in SAP ERP Operations, especially for availability checks and transfer of requirement.

Chapter 4, Pricing, will again take you through the steps of customization for condition techniques. The condition technique used for automatic determination of pricing is considered the complete demonstration of the tool. You'll also learn how to customize rebate agreements, pricing reports, and the SAP interface for external tax software for sales and use tax.

In **Chapter 5**, Credit Risk Management, the primary topic is the steps to customize automatic credit control. You'll also learn certain operations in credit management, and we'll discuss forms of payment guarantee and how to customize them. We'll conclude the chapter with some problems and their solutions

In **Chapter 6**, Logistics Management, we'll discuss the customization of delivery document types and their item categories. You'll learn about the different processes such as picking, packing, serialization, and goods issue. You'll also learn about the determination process of storage locations, routes, batches, and item categories. We'll discuss the steps needed to customize the SAP interface (SD TPS 4.0) that integrate it with external carrier software, and how to customize a delivery due list. We'll discuss delivery processing, batch determination, scheduling, stock transfer processing, and output processing and conclude with some practical issues and their solutions.

Chapter 7, Billing, covers the customization of billing types, billing plans, and the interface with accounting. The list of practical issues and solutions will be provided at the end.

Chapter 8, Cross-Functional Customization, includes coverage of text processing, message control, Web interface, batch management, ABAP tools, and numbering objects. These are topics that are useful but not fully discussed in earlier chapters. These topics are not exclusive to Sales and Distribution, but are important for you to understand.

Chapter 9, Reporting and Analysis, starts off with a list of standard reports and analyses and their features. We'll also discuss the standard reports and analyses that SAP NetWeaver BW offers. The chapter will discuss three tools for creating customized reports and analyses: the Sales Information System, ABAP queries, and ABAP reporting.

We'll summarize the book in **Chapter 10**, Summary and Conclusion.

This chapter provides perspective to the Sales and Distribution functionality in SAP ERP and reviews the overall SAP ERP solution. You'll learn about the features of the SAP graphical user interface, come to understand the role of ASAP methodology and the SAP Solution Manager, and how to define and assign units of an enterprise structure relevant for Sales and Distribution.

1 Introduction

In this chapter, we'll introduce you to the SAP software that is most important from an optimization point of view: SAP ERP, the SAP Graphical User Interface (GUI), ASAP methodology, and the SAP Solution Manager. We conclude with a discussion of the enterprise structure in SAP systems, covering the organizational units that are most important from the sales and distribution perspective.

1.1 Introduction to SAP ERP

This book discusses how to customize the Sales and Distribution functionality in SAP ERP and provides practical information to help you solve real-life business issues. Before we get into Sales and Distribution, let's discuss the various functionalities in SAP ERP. In this section, we'll discuss four main topics of SAP ERP: its applications and functionalities, its server organization, its Implementation Guide, and the resources available to its users. The first section provides an overview of the functionalities other than Sales and Distribution available in SAP ERP. Our discussion of the server architecture should give you a basic understanding of the different servers in your SAP landscape, so you can understand various roles on different servers, and the role of correction and transportation requests. Finally, the sections on the Implementation Guide and other resources explain how you can expand your learning beyond this book.

1.1.1 Applications and Functionalities in SAP ERP

SAP ERP delivers its software in modular form, which means it consists of several applications and components, each of which has individual functionalities. This structure helps small and mid-size companies adopt specific portions of SAP software and then gradually integrate other specialized modules as they grow.

The SAP ERP solution is primarily divided into three groups of applications: SAP ERP Financials, SAP ERP Operations (logistics), and SAP ERP Human Capital Management (HCM). A few examples of applications and the software within these applications are listed below (please note that this list is not exhaustive):

1. SAP ERP Financials
   - Financial Accounting
   - Controlling
   - Fund Management
   - Asset Management
2. SAP ERP Operations (logistics)
   - Materials Management
   - Sales and Distribution
   - Logistics Execution and Warehouse Management
   - Quality Management
   - Production Planning
   - Plant Maintenance
3. SAP ERP Human Capital Management
   - Personnel Management
   - Payroll

Sales and distribution is also referred to as *order fulfillment* in the SAP Supply Chain Management (SAP SCM) solution.

SAP ERP software is integrated to serve the primary objective of resource planning at the enterprise level. Currently, it's not just the integration of one SAP ERP component or functionality with another that is important, but the integration of SAP and non-SAP solutions. SAP has adopted a process of certification for non-SAP solutions to ensure integration of this nature. Without integration, you must enter the same data again and again in different components, which can often result in data loss (and is otherwise inefficient).

The components of the Sales and Distribution functionality in SAP ERP are given below and discussed throughout this book.

1. Basic Functions (SD-BF)
2. Master Data (SD-MD)
3. Sales (SD-SLS)
4. Foreign Trade (SD-FT)
5. Billing (SD-BIL)
6. Sales Support: Computer-Aided Selling (SD-CAS)
7. Contract Handling for Consumer Product (SD-CH)
8. Electronic Data Interchange (SD-EDI)
9. POS Interface (SD-POS)
10. Information System (SD-IS)

We will also cover the following logistics components:

1. Shipping (LE-SHP)
2. Transportation Planning and Processing (LE-TRA-TP)
3. Batch Management (LO-BM)

1.1.2 Development, Quality, and Production Servers

SAP ERP software is often placed on three different servers: the development, quality, and production servers. The *development server* contains customization information and allows consultants to try out different techniques before implementing them in the system. The *quality server* is a place where consultants can test the scenarios they have implemented in the development server. It's often created by making a copy of the production server (which we discuss in a moment) including master and transactional data. It can also be used for training. Once a scenario has been fully tested in the quality server, it can be moved to the *production server*, which is where data is stored for all SAP ERP users. Developers rarely work on the production server.

1 Introduction

This correction and transport system ensures that users are not affected by new developments and that the SAP system never has to go offline during the implementation of changes and corrections.

1.1.3 SAP ERP Customizing Implementation Guide

The SAP Implementation Guide (IMG) aims to simplify SAP customization by documenting actions that are required with helpful tips and notes. Both online and paper versions of the IMG are available to SAP customers and partners; it's accessed through Transaction SPRO and, as shown in Figure 1.1, is present at every node. Both the SAP Standard IMG (Figure 1.1) and Project IMGs are available. A Project IMG may be developed that contains a subset of the Standard IMG.

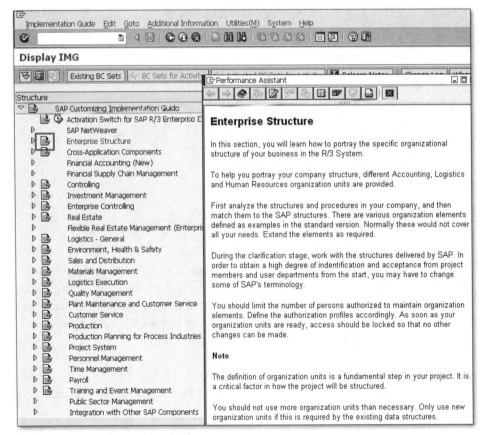

Figure 1.1 SAP Implementation Guide

1.1.4 SAP ERP Resources

SAP has grown beyond a company or software and is now more accurately described as an ecosystem that consists of various entities. These entities include SAP PRESS (*sap-press.com*), SAP Education (*sap.com/services/education*), SAP Service Marketplace (*service.sap.com*), SAP Developers Network (*sdn.sap.com*), and other community forums such as Americas' SAP Users' Group (asug.com), SAP TV (*sap-tv.com*), SAP events (TechEd, SAPPHIRE, and World Tour), and the SAP Help Portal (*help.sap.com*). These, together with the SAP Library and the Implementation Guide, are great resources for learning. SAP also issues Online Support System (OSS) Notes, which are also referred to as *SAP Notes* or *S-Notes*.

1.2 Introduction to SAP GUI

At the mention of the phrase *SAP GUI* (SAP graphical user interface), most users picture the icon you see on your desktop (Figure 1.2), the login screen (Figure 1.3), or the SAP easy access screen (Figure 1.4).

> **Customizing the SAP GUI**
> It's possible to customize the SAP GUI. We discuss this in Appendix A of this book.

Figure 1.2 SAP Logon Pad

1 | Introduction

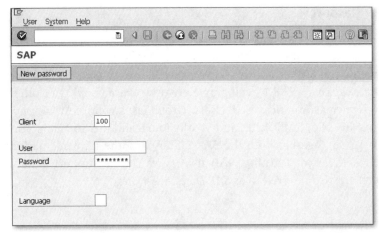

Figure 1.3 SAP Login Screen

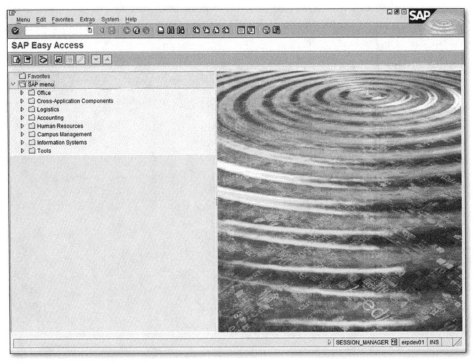

Figure 1.4 SAP Easy Access Screen

However, there's a lot more to the SAP GUI than these elements. In this section, we focus on the following aspects of the SAP GUI:

1.2 Introduction to SAP GUI

- The typical SAP screen
- Menu paths and transaction codes
- Icons
- Wild cards
- Function keys

1.2.1 The Typical SAP Screen

A typical SAP screen has the following components:

- **Menu bar**
  The menu bar contains different menus and submenus that change depending upon the transaction you're using.

- **System function bar**
  This part of the screen is always the same, regardless of which transaction you're using. As you can see in Figure 1.5, it consists of basic actions that allow you to enter and save information and navigate among different screens. (Note: the rightmost icon is used for the customization of the local layout, which we discuss in detail in Appendix A.)

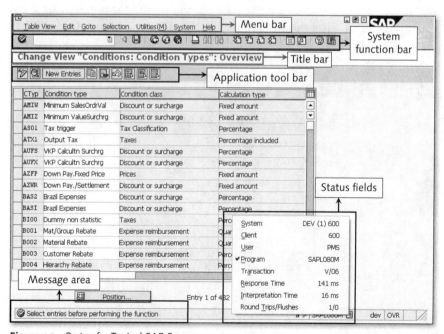

Figure 1.5 Parts of a Typical SAP Screen

▶ **Title bar**
The name of the transaction or program you are currently using appears in the title bar.

▶ **Application toolbar**
The application tool bar contains icons and tabs that change depending on the transaction you're using. Figure 1.5 shows the icons that appear most commonly in transactions.

▶ **Status bar**
The status bar contains two main parts: the message area (which shows you system messages) and the status fields (which show you the system and client you are currently in, the login ID you're using, and the program and transaction code that is currently running in that session, among other things). Because several sessions (or windows) can be open at a time, the information in the status bar can be quite useful.

1.2.2 SAP Easy Access Menu Paths and Transaction Codes

SAP provides two ways to execute any transaction: a menu path (or paths; there can be more than one alternative) and a transaction code. Each transaction can be reached by the menu path or by entering the transaction code in the transaction window and then pressing [Enter]. To display transaction codes in the menu paths, go to EXTRAS • SETTINGS and select the Display Technical Names checkbox (Figure 1.6).

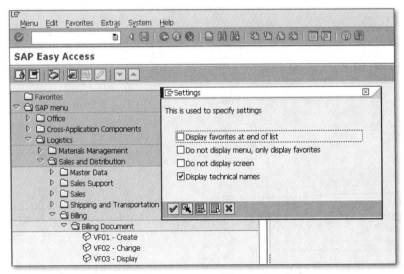

Figure 1.6 Use of SAP Easy Access Menu and Transaction Codes

1.2.3 SAP Icons

SAP systems have been designed to be simple, functional, and smooth, a goal they accomplish with the use of over a thousand self-explanatory icons. (A list of these icons can be downloaded from this book's page on *www.sap-press.com*, or by executing Transaction ICON.) One example of a useful icon is the one shown in the top-left corner in Figure 1.7, which is available even when you're working with a transaction that is taking a lot of time to complete. You can use it to create a new session, which is not possible using the Create New Session icon in such a situation. When you click that icon you get a drop-down menu with Create Session as one option, also shown in Figure 1.7.

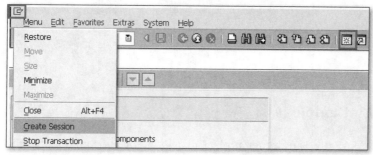

Figure 1.7 Use of System Icon

The icon-based design also improves performance, because they come from the frontend installed on your computer — as opposed to the server — which results in less data exchange between the server and client.

1.2.4 Wild Cards

SAP allows you to use wild card characters. The asterisk (*) is used to replace a string of characters, and the plus sign (+) is used for a single character. These wild cards can be used in the initial screen of any transaction or report when a field can take multiple inputs. Please note that if the input screen is designed so that it can take only one value as input, you cannot use wildcards. For example, if you have named all your company's U.S. subsidiaries using the same naming convention — say, beginning with "US" and four characters long — you can use US* or US++ instead of listing all codes in an initial screen.

29

1.2.5 Function Keys

Some of the function keys on your keyboard can be used consistently for all SAP transactions:

- [F1]: Help
- [F3]: Back
- [F4]: Lists all possible entries of any field
- [F5]: New Entries
- [F6]: Copy As
- [F7]: Select All
- [F8]: Execute
- [F9]: Execute in Background
- [F12]: Cancel

1.3 ASAP Methodology

The objective of ASAP, like any other project management and implementation tool, is timely project completion, within budget, at minimal risk (technical or commercial). It accomplishes this objective by providing templates, methods, tools, and accelerators for successful, quick SAP implementations with optimal usage of resources. It consists of five phases, as shown in Figure 1.8.

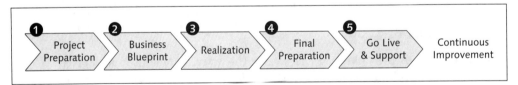

Figure 1.8 Phases of ASAP

❶ Project preparation
   The project team is identified and mobilized, the project standards are defined, and the project work environment is set up.

❷ Blueprint
   The business processes are defined and documented as the business blueprint.

❸ **Realization**
Configuration, unit testing, user acceptance, knowledge transfer, and data migration plans are key components of this phase.

❹ **Final preparation**
Integration, stress, and conversion testing are conducted. End users are trained.

❺ **Go-live and support**
Data migration from the legacy system is completed, the new system is activated, and post-implementation support is provided.

These phases often serve as project milestones and might also used for billing purposes. Tracking progress by using established deadlines helps project managers identify issues that threaten the project and resolve them in a timely manner. An ASAP checklist is used to ensure that each phase is complete and documented before going to the next phase.

Thanks to ASAP, small and mid-sized companies are now often able to implement an SAP system within a couple of months.

1.4 SAP Solution Manager Overview

SAP Solution Manager aims to do the following:

- Optimize the SAP solution environment during deployment, operation, and continuous operation phases
- Improve return on investment (ROI) by lowering cost of ownership
- Support SAP, non-SAP, and future SAP solutions
- Complement ASAP methodology
- Transfer knowledge
- Reduce risk

SAP Solution Manager provides the following advantages:

- **Implementation and upgrades**
  ASAP methodology has become a complementary component integrated into SAP Solution Manager. SAP Solution Manager is seen as the successor of the ASAP methodology. It ensures timely implementation by providing useful content, centralized real-time monitoring, and documentation.

- **Change management**
  SAP Solution Manager controls and tracks all software and configuration changes from the approval stage (for change requests) to the deployment stage. It also allows for post-deployment analysis of changes. Non-ABAP objects are also included in the change and transportation system (for more details on this, refer to SAP Note 1056166. The OSS Note System is explained later).

- **Service desk**
  The service desk of SAP Solution Manager handles user help requests for forwarding to SAP. The organization or the IT service provider can manage the service desk. This system of issue resolution works efficiently and economically.

- **Root cause analysis**
  Performance issues can be due to problems in the system, the server, a database, ABAP code, or SAP NetWeaver. Root cause analysis allows you to identify the source of the problem, enabling you to fix it and avoid similar problems in the future.

- **Monitoring and notification**
  SAP Solution Manager makes centralized, real-time monitoring of the complete SAP landscape (different servers), business processes, intersystem dependencies, and interfaces possible, which reduces cost and risk. Automatic notification through email, SMS, and other communication means ensures fast response and lower risk.

- **Service-level reporting**
  SAP Solution Manager defines and reports service levels, which allows you to have service-level agreements (SLAs) with IT service providers based on measurable parameters.

- **Background job management**
  SAP Solution Manager allows you to schedule background jobs for different components and monitor them for optimum utilization of resources. There is also an enhancement available for this.

- **Services and support**
  SAP Solution Manager suggests and provides SAP support services. These include *SAP Safeguarding* (a remote service), which includes the SAP GoLive Check service; *SAP Solution Management Optimization* (an on-site service), which helps you optimize SAP solutions with the help of SAP staff; and *SAP Empowering (self-service)*, which helps you manage your solutions.

- **System administration**
  SAP Solution Manager makes it possible to centrally execute day-to-day administrative tasks.

- **Value added services**
  Two services that you have to pay for — SAP Central Process Scheduling by Redwood and SAP Quality Center by HP — are enhancements in SAP Solution Manager to optimize background job scheduling and testing, respectively.

1.5 Organizational Structure in SAP

In any implementation project, the first thing you must finalize is the organizational structure (also called enterprise structure). In this section, we explain the elements in the enterprise structure that are relevant for Sales and Distribution.

Below we discuss the four broad steps involved in the customization of an enterprise structure. These steps are:

1. Importing localized sample units
2. Defining required organizational units
3. Assigning organizational units
4. Checking for consistency

1.5.1 Importing Organizational Units

SAP provides sample organizational units customized according to the country, as shown in Figure 1.9. You can access this screen by following the menu path SAP IMG • ENTERPRISE STRUCTURE • LOCALIZE SAMPLE ORGANIZATIONAL UNITS and then clicking on Country Version. It is always advisable to:

- Run this transaction to install these sample units.
- Define the units without preceding zeros. For example, use 100 instead of 001; this is because 001 becomes 1 in Excel, which may cause problems when you transfer data.
- Do not delete the sample organizational units in the development clients.
- Copy the required customized units from these sample units, not from other customized units.

Copying sample units — as opposed to creating them from scratch — not only reduces the time required for customization, but also reduces the chance of errors.

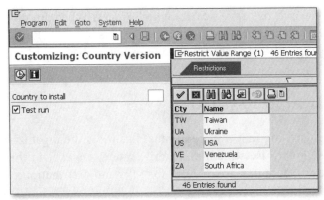

Figure 1.9 Importing Country-Specific Templates of Organizational Units

1.5.2 Defining Organizational Units

In this phase, the enterprise structure of one organization is mapped in the SAP system. The menu path for this is SAP IMG • ENTERPRISE STRUCTURE • DEFINITION. At the Definition node are options such as Financial Accounting, Logistics – General, Sales and Distribution, Materials Management, and Logistics Execution, where you can define different organizational units. Use the FINANCIAL ACCOUNTING component to define the COMPANY CODE and CREDIT CONTROL AREA; LOGISTICS – GENERAL to define the PLANT, VALUATION LEVEL, and DIVISION; SALES AND DISTRIBUTION to define the SALES ORGANIZATION, DISTRIBUTION CHANNEL, SALES OFFICE, and SALES GROUP; MATERIALS MANAGEMENT to define the STORAGE LOCATION; and LOGISTICS EXECUTION to define the WAREHOUSE NUMBER, SHIPPING POINT, LOADING POINT, and TRANSPORT PLANNING POINTS.

In the following subsections, we'll give brief descriptions of each of these organizational units.

Company Code and Company

The *company code* is the level at which balance sheets and profit and loss statements are prepared. The company code is different from the *company*, which refers to a group of companies (or a *holding company*) that is composed of all subsidiary companies represented by the company codes. The company is the highest organizational unit from a Financial Accounting point of view, and all company codes are assigned to one or more companies. Financial Accounting integrates Logistics components at the company code level.

In this book, we refer to the company code as a company, and the company organizational unit as a holding company. The organizational unit company is used primarily for consolidation of financial statements of different company codes and is of little importance in Logistics or for Sales and Distribution.

Credit Control Area

Customers or groups of customers are provided with a *credit limit,* which is a set amount in a specific currency. This credit limit is then used for business with the companies (known as company codes) assigned to the credit control area. The update group for the credit control area defines the total credit exposure of a customer or group of customers. This is the most important organizational unit from a credit management point of view. We discuss credit control areas in more detail in Chapter 5.

Valuation Level

A *valuation level* is the level at which stocks are valuated and is important for inventory management and to determine the cost of a sale. For any specific material, the value is maintained in the material master record (Accounting 1 view). The valuation level is selected only once during customization; once selected, it is available in display mode only. Generally, the recommended valuation area is the plant, as opposed to the company code (a company code valuation level is not even possible in the Production Planning and Controlling components).

Plant

The *plant* usually represents where goods are manufactured and/or stored or where services are rendered. In SAP systems, it can be defined by copying plant 0001 (which is system delivered).

Division

Companies with several products or services group their products and services into different *divisions*. A material or service in an SAP system can only belong to one division; in other words, divisions are mutually exclusive. Thus, if a product is being sold in two divisions —for example, a vacuum cleaner is being sold in both the home care and automobile divisions of a company — the product must have a separate material code for each division. To define a new division, select and copy an existing division, and then make the appropriate changes.

Sales Organization

The organization within a company that is responsible for sales is called the sales organization. There can be more than one sales organization in a company (represented in SAP systems as a company code), but one sales organization cannot be responsible for selling materials or services for two companies (that is, it cannot be assigned to different company codes). New sales organizations are defined by copying sales organization 0001 (predelivered) and making the necessary changes.

Distribution Channel

The *distribution channel* is the means through which a company makes its products and services available to its customers, for example, the wholesale distribution channel, the Internet distribution channel, and the direct sales distribution channel. You create new distribution channels by copying existing ones and making the necessary changes. Only a new key/code and a description for the new distribution channel are required. There is no address or any other fields to be maintained for distribution channels.

> **Sales Area**
>
> The sales area is very important for Sales and Distribution processes, but it's not an independent organizational unit. It's the combination of sales organizations, distribution channels, and divisions.

Sales Office

The *sales office* is the unit responsible for sales to a particular geographical area with one or more customers and is represented by a four-digit alphanumeric key. The geographical areas for different sales offices can overlap. In a standard SAP system, no restriction is imposed on the plant that can serve a sales office and vice versa, except that both should be in the same company code. Any sales document is usually created for a particular sales area, a sales office, and a sales group; the latter two, though optional, are normally present. One customer can be served by different sales offices even when a default sales office is maintained in the customer master record.

Sales Group

A *sales group* is a group of employees attached to one or more sales offices who are responsible for sales pertaining to orders generated by them. More than one sales group can be attached to a sales office. The sales group responsible for a sales order appears at the header level.

Storage Location

The *storage location* in a plant refers to a physical storage location or a logical location. If a New York distribution plant has several warehouses in the city, you might designate them as storage locations (and further assign warehouse numbers in the Warehouse Management functionality in SAP ERP). You can have storage locations such as Sales and Returns to differentiate goods that can be sold to customers from goods that have been returned by customers and thus should not be sold (physically, the different types of stock may be present in the same warehouse). Storage locations are important in delivery and post–goods movement (issue/receipt), because when there is a movement of goods in Sales and Distribution, it's from a storage location. These goods movements have an impact (debit or credit) in Financial Accounting if material is valuated. You can configure the system to automatically determine the storage location during the sale, return, or stock transfer processes.

Warehouse Number

A *warehouse number* is created when the Warehouse Management functionality of SAP ERP is in place. From an integration point of view, you should know that each warehouse is assigned to a plant–storage location combination. Although storage locations may not necessarily mean a physical location, warehouse numbers do refer to a specific warehouse that is physically present. It's important to note from a stock valuation standpoint that material valuation occurs at the Inventory Management level (Plant-Storage Location) and not at the Warehouse Management or bin level.

Shipping Point

A plant can have several shipping points, and one shipping point can serve several plants. A *shipping point* refers to the various exit points of the plant where goods are dispatched to customers or other plants. You can configure your system to automatically propose shipping points during different Sales and Distribution processes including delivery or shipment processing.

Loading Point

Loading points are where goods are loaded and can be automatically proposed in Sales and Distribution. Both loading points and shipping points become very important for the integration of Sales and Distribution with the *Transportation Management* component in Logistics Execution.

Transport Planning Point

A *transport planning point* is the organizational unit responsible for shipping products. Different transport planning points are created for units responsible for shipments of different types; for example, units responsible for rail shipments and air cargo can have two transport planning points.

1.5.3 Assigning Organizational Units

After organizational units are defined, they must be assigned. It is important to understand the guidelines SAP uses for organizational unit assignments; these are listed in Table 1.1.

Step	Assignment	Guidelines
1	Company code to credit control area	One company code can be assigned to more than one credit control area.
2	Plant to company code	One plant can't be assigned to more than one company code.
3	Sales organization to company code	One sales organization can't be assigned to more than one company code.
4	Distribution channel to sales organization	One distribution channel can be assigned to more than one sales organization.
5	Division to sales organization	One division can be assigned to more than one sales organization.
6	Sales area (sales organization, distribution channel, division)	All combinations are possible (maximum possible number of sales areas = number of sales organizations × number of distribution channels × number of divisions), provided all distribution channels and divisions are already assigned to all sales organizations.
7	Sales office to sales area	One sales office can be assigned to all sales areas.

Table 1.1 Guidelines for Organizational Unit Assignments

Step	Assignment	Guidelines
8	Sales group to sales office	One sales group can be assigned to more than one sales office.
9	Sales organizations, distribution channel, plant	One plant can be assigned to all combinations of sales organizations and distribution channels.
10	Sales area to credit control area	One sales area can't be assigned to more than one credit control area.
11	Warehouse number to plant and storage location	One warehouse number can be assigned to several combinations of plants and storage locations, but the plant in all of those combinations must be the same.
12	Shipping point to plant	One shipping point can be assigned to several plants.

Table 1.1 Guidelines for Organizational Unit Assignments (Cont.)

The assignments of different organizational units are done via SAP IMG • ENTERPRISE STRUCTURE • ASSIGNMENTS. Further down this path, you will find the name of the specific functionalities (FINANCIAL ACCOUNTING, SALES AND DISTRIBUTION, and others.). If you want to know where to assign a particular organizational unit (X) to another organizational unit (Y), you must know in which component X was defined. That component is where you'll do the assignment. For example, the assignment of sales organization X to company code Y is done via the menu path SAP IMG • ENTERPRISE STRUCTURE • ASSIGNMENTS • SALES AND DISTRIBUTION, not via SAP IMG • ENTERPRISE STRUCTURE • ASSIGNMENTS • FINANCIAL ACCOUNTING.

1.5.4 Checking for Consistency

SAP offers a consistency check optimizing tool that allows you to check your customization of the enterprise structure in seconds. You can execute this tool by selecting all of the options shown in Figure 1.10. The menu path is SAP IMG • ENTERPRISE STRUCTURE • CONSISTENCY CHECK • CHECK ENTERPRISE STRUCTURE FOR SALES AND DISTRIBUTION.

This tool checks the following:

- Sales organizations
  - Checks whether addresses exist.
  - Checks whether company codes are assigned.

- Checks whether master record conversions are maintained.
- Checks whether sales areas are created.
- Checks whether plants are assigned.
- Checks whether texts exist in the logon language.
- Distribution channels
  - Checks whether master record conversions exist.
  - Checks whether sales areas are created.
  - Checks whether texts exist in the logon language.
- Divisions
  - Checks whether master record conversions exist.
  - Checks whether sales areas are created.
  - Checks whether texts exist in the logon language.
- Sales offices
  - Checks whether sales organizations are assigned.
  - Checks whether addresses exist.
  - Checks whether texts exist in the logon language.
- Sales groups
  - Checks whether sales offices are assigned.
  - Checks whether texts exist in the logon language.
- Shipping points
  - Checks whether all plants are assigned.
  - Checks whether shipping points are assigned.
  - Checks whether addresses exist.
  - Checks whether texts exist in the logon language.
- Plants
  - Checks whether the addresses exist and are complete.
  - Checks whether storage locations are available.

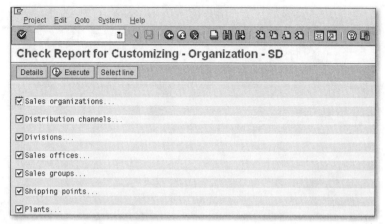

Figure 1.10 Consistency Check

1.6 Summary

In this chapter, we introduced you to the various components of SAP ERP, the SAP IMG, the steps of the ASAP methodology, and the usefulness of SAP Solution Manager. We concluded with a discussion of the organizational units in SAP systems, where we gave basic definitions and took a broad look at the steps involved in establishing an enterprise structure.

In the next chapter, we'll discuss prerequisites for creating important master records in SAP ERP and tools available for the maintenance of master records.

After reading this chapter, you should be able to understand how you can reduce maintenance efforts by creating common distribution channels and divisions, how to customize master data fields, how to modify your screen layout, and how you can carry out specific changes to different master records on a mass scale.

2 Master Data

Master data consists of information that does not change frequently (e.g., addresses) and pertains to customers, employees, SAP system users, materials, batches, condition records (discussed later), vendors, and more. Master data is composed of individual master records; for example, a single customer will have a customer master record, and all of the customer master records together make up the customer master data. Because SAP software was created with the objective of serving almost any company, regardless of its size, industry, or country, predefined master data requires very little customization.

In this chapter, we briefly list the suggested steps for customizing master data fields, focusing specifically on master data relevant for Sales and Distribution and explain how to manage master data post-implementation. Specifically, we go into detail about the following types of master data:

- Customer master data
- Customer credit master data
- Material master data
- Batch management master data

We then conclude with a brief overview of some of the other types of master data. Many of these types are created and maintained in other components, some overview knowledge is helpful for those interested in Sales and Distribution.

2.1 Customer Master Data

In SAP systems, customer master records are broadly divided into three parts: general data, company code data, and sales area data. This data is stored in tables, which consist of fields that are important from a Financial Accounting and Sales and Distribution perspective. General data contains address, communication, control, marketing, payment transaction, unloading point, contact person, and foreign-trade-related information. General data is stored in KNA1, ADRC, ADR2/3/4/5, and other tables. Company code data is stored in Table KNB1 and mainly contains the fields important from a Financial Accounting perspective. Sales area data is stored mainly in Table KNVV and mainly contains the fields important from a Sales and Distribution perspective. The information about partners defined in the customer master record is stored in Table KNVP. There are different transactions that allow you to create, change, and display customer master data based on the combination of areas to be maintained.

> **SAP Tables**
>
> There are close to a hundred thousand standard tables in SAP ERP. These tables store the information (data). Some of them do not store data but pool information from other tables for use or display. All of the tables have columns and rows. Each row is a record. The tables that store the data are available in the Oracle® database that SAP uses. These can be used by non-SAP components as well, but the other types of tables, not available on the Oracle database, are for exclusive use in SAP systems.

In the subsections below, we discuss how to optimize customer master record maintenance using common distribution channels and divisions, how to create customer account groups, how to customize customer master record fields, and how to utilize the tools for mass maintenance.

2.1.1 Reducing Sales Areas

A *sales area* is a combination of sales organizations, distribution channels, and divisions. We represent it by a key that combines all three of these organizational units (for example, a sales area composed of sales organization 1000, distribution channel 10, and division 30 would be referred to as sales area 1000-10-30). The customer master records of one sales area are not available for use by another; thus, if the customer is valid for several sales areas, you must create separate customer records for all of these sales areas. Although this may make the maintenance of customer master records sound difficult, the process is facilitated by the use of a *common distribution channel and division*, which allows you to effectively reduce the number of sales areas for which the customer master record is to be created. We discuss the process of defining common distribution channels and divisions in the subsections below. At the end of the section, we explain how these configurations result in a reduced amount of sales areas and hence a reduction in maintenance effort.

Defining Common Distribution Channels

Common distribution channels are defined using the menu path SAP IMG • SALES AND DISTRIBUTION • MASTER DATA • DEFINE COMMON DISTRIBUTION CHANNEL (Transaction VOR1, Table V_TVKOV_ST), as shown in Figure 2.1. In addition to customer master records, common distribution channels can also be defined for material master records (which we discuss in more detail in Section 2.3). For any distribution channel, another distribution channel can be defined as the common distribution channel. The master data record or condition record maintained for a distribution channel is applicable for all distribution channels for which it is maintained as the common distribution channel.

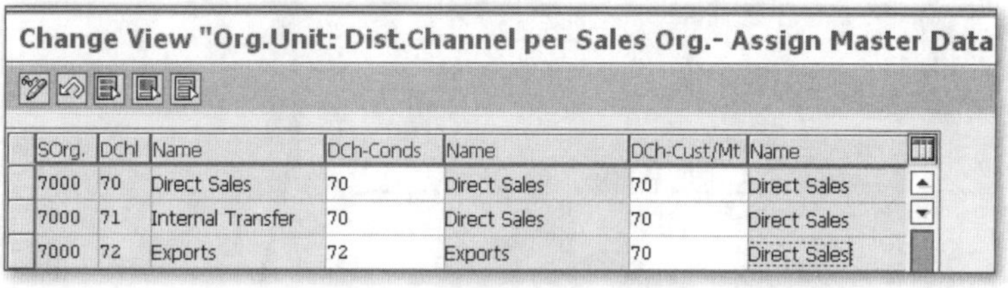
Change View "Org.Unit: Dist.Channel per Sales Org.- Assign Master Data

SOrg.	DChl	Name	DCh-Conds	Name	DCh-Cust/Mt	Name
7000	70	Direct Sales	70	Direct Sales	70	Direct Sales
7000	71	Internal Transfer	70	Direct Sales	70	Direct Sales
7000	72	Exports	72	Exports	70	Direct Sales

Figure 2.1 Defining a Common Distribution Channel

To make one distribution channel a common distribution channel for another distribution channel's condition records, enter the common distribution channel in the DCh-Conds column. As shown in Figure 2.1, distribution channel 70 is a common distribution channel for distribution channels 70 and 71, but not 72.

Similarly, to make a distribution channel common for other distribution channels to share customer and material master records, enter it in the DCh-Cust/Mt column. As shown in Figure 2.1, distribution channel 70 is the common distribution channel for distribution channels 70, 71, and 72. As a result, the customer master record created for sales area 7000-70-10 (where the sales organization is 7000, the distribution channel is 70, and the division is 10) automatically becomes valid for sales areas 7000-71-10 and 7000-72-10.

Note

In addition to customer master records, common distribution channels can be defined for condition records. The common distribution channel for a specific distribution channel defined for reducing the number of required customer master records automatically becomes relevant for material master record creation.

Defining Common Divisions

Common divisions are defined via SAP IMG • SALES AND DISTRIBUTION • MASTER DATA • DEFINE COMMON DIVISION (Transaction VOR2, Table V_TVKOS_ST), as shown in Figure 2.2.

> **Note**
>
> In addition to customer master records, common divisions can also be defined for condition records.

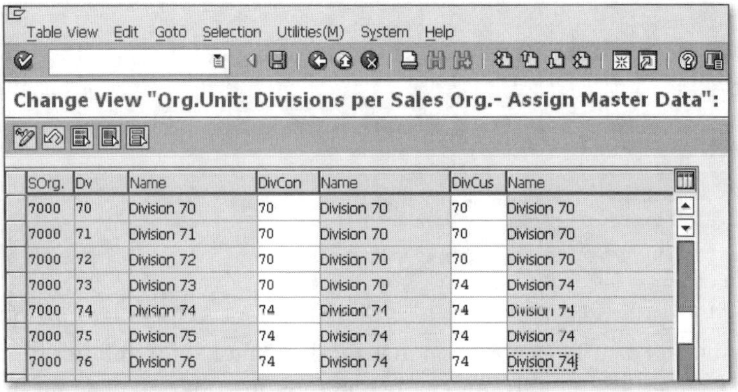

SOrg.	Dv	Name	DivCon	Name	DivCus	Name
7000	70	Division 70	70	Division 70	70	Division 70
7000	71	Division 71	70	Division 70	70	Division 70
7000	72	Division 72	70	Division 70	70	Division 70
7000	73	Division 73	70	Division 70	74	Division 74
7000	74	Division 74	74	Division 74	74	Division 74
7000	75	Division 75	74	Division 74	74	Division 74
7000	76	Division 76	74	Division 74	74	Division 74

Figure 2.2 Defining Common Divisions

The division in the DivCus column is the common division for the division listed in the Dv column and is used for creating and sharing customer master records. As shown in Figure 2.2, division 70 is common for divisions 70, 71, and 72, and division 74 is common for divisions 73, 74, 75, and 76. As a result, customer master records created for sales area 7000-70-70 (where the sales organization is 7000, the distribution channel is 70, and the division is 70) becomes automatically valid for sales areas 7000-70-71 and 7000-70-72.

If you combine the examples shown in Figures 2.1 and 2.2 without a common distribution channel and division, the total number of possible sales areas is 21. If all sales areas are valid for you, and if a customer is valid for all sales areas, you would have to create that customer 21 separate times. However, with the customization of common distribution channels and divisions, even when all sales area are defined and when a customer is valid for all areas, you can drastically reduce the number of times you must create the customer. In this example, you need only create the customer in two sales areas (7000-70-70 and 7000-70-74).

2.1.2 Defining Customer Account Groups

Customer account groups are created primarily to route financial postings to specific SAP General Ledger (GL) accounts; for example, the sales figures for all domestic retail customers may go to the same reconciliation account. All of the foreign customers may be created in a different customer account group, and there is a different reconciliation account (GL) for them. The menu path for creating a customer account group is SAP IMG • Financial Accounting (New) • Accounts Receivable and Accounts Payable • Customer Accounts • Master Data • Preparations for Creating Customer Master Data • Define Account Groups with Screen Layouts (Customers). The transaction code is OBD2.

The steps for creating a customer account group are provided below:

1. Find the standard SAP template that is closest to what you want to create. Copy the selected template using the Copy As ([F6]) icon, as shown in Figure 2.3. The screen shown in Figure 2.4 appears with the message "Specify target entries."

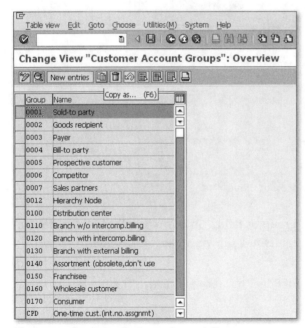

Figure 2.3 Creating a Customer Account Group

2. Enter basic information. Provide the account group name (it does not have to start with Y or Z) and a description for the account group code in the Name field. If the account group is for one-time customers, select the One-Time Account checkbox. If the output determination procedure is the same for all customers in a group, enter it in the Output Determ.Proc. field.

3. Maintain field statuses. The customization of account groups also involves the maintenance of the field status of all customer master fields, also referred to as the maintenance of screen layout. This activity determines how the customer master screens look. Any field can have one of four statuses: *Suppressed, Required Entry, Optional Entry, or Display*. To assign a field status, double-click on General Data, Company Code Data, or Sales Data in the screen shown in Figure 2.4. (We have double-clicked on General Data in our example.)

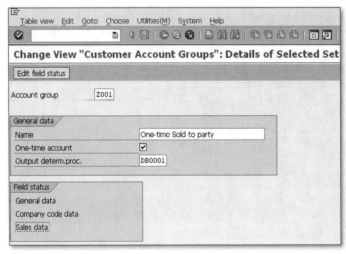

Figure 2.4 Customizing a Customer Account Group

4. Double-click on a particular group of fields. In our example, we have double-clicked on Address (that screen is not shown), which takes you to the screen shown in Figure 2.5.

5. Modify the field status of individual master data fields. The screen for this is shown in Figure 2.5.

2.1 Customer Master Data

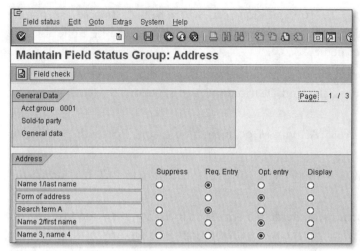

Figure 2.5 Maintain Field Status Group

2.1.3 Customer Master Record Fields

In this section, we discuss how to customize a customer master record field. For most of the fields in customer master records, there are predefined possible entries. You may need to alter the predefined list (by adding, deleting, or modifying text), especially in a post-implementation scenario. Below we provide the steps used as a shortcut for customizing any customer master data field; in our example, we modify the Legal Status field. You can follow these steps to customize other master data record fields as well.

1. Execute Transaction VD02. You can use this transaction for modifying the Legal Status field. Select the Marketing tab in the General Data area. The screen shown in Figure 2.6 appears. You can use Transaction XD02 instead of VD02.

2. Press F1, keeping the cursor on the Legal Status field. The dialog box (Performance Assistance), also shown in Figure 2.6, appears.

3. Click on the Customizing icon highlighted in Figure 2.6. In some cases, this icon will be disabled (for example, for the Terms of Payment field, which is in the Billing tab in Sales Area data). In such cases, click on F4 first, and then F1. The Customizing icon will then be *enabled*. When you click on the enabled Customizing icon, you see a dialog box where you can specify the project name and proceed. (You can also proceed without specifying the project, if authorized.)

This brings you to the configuration icon where you customize the object. If there are multiple locations where the customization can be done, the list appears in an intermediate screen.

4. Select the most relevant option. Your selection should be based on the relevant component (such as Sales and Distribution) and functionality (such as master data).
5. Click on the IMG Activity Documentation icon. Read the available documentation.
6. Click on the IMG-Activity icon (it looks like a clock). This starts the customization.
7. Follow the instructions in the documentation. In many cases, you just have to select an existing item and then click on the Copy As icon (or press [F6]). If only a new key and a description is required, as in the case of the Legal Status field, specify these as the target entries for copying and press [Enter].
8. When copying is complete, save, and transport.

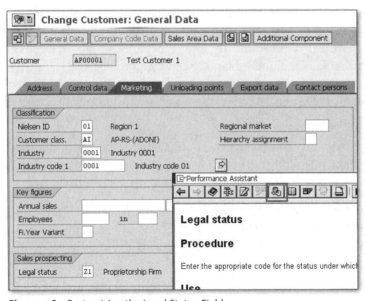

Figure 2.6 Customizing the Legal Status Field

2.1.4 Customer Mass Maintenance

Maintaining master records after implementation is a big task, and manual updating sometimes becomes impossible. When one field in several thousand master records must be changed without error within few minutes, mass maintenance tools are the best option. This section discusses several ways to take care of mass maintenance. In the first two subsections, we focus on using Transactions MASS and SE16N (with the SAP edit function). The last section briefly describes a few alternative options.

Transaction MASS

One way to accomplish customer master data mass maintenance is by using object type KNA1 in Transaction MASS (Menu path: SAP MENU • LOGISTICS • CENTRAL FUNCTIONS • MASS MAINTENANCE • MASS MAINTENANCE • DIALOG PROCESSING), as shown in Figure 2.7.

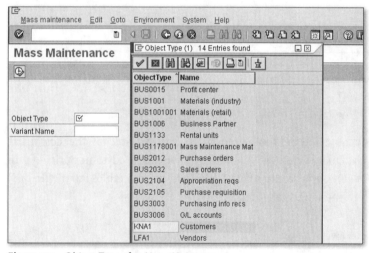

Figure 2.7 Object Types for Mass Maintenance

With Transaction MASS, you can make changes to several fields in several tables simultaneously. By selecting object type KNA1 and executing the transaction, you reach the screen shown in Figure 2.8 (which is the same screen that appears when you execute Transaction XD99; menu path: SAP MENU • LOGISTICS • SALES AND DISTRIBUTION • MASTER DATA • BUSINESS PARTNERS • CUSTOMER MASTER MASS MAINTENANCE). The Tables tab shows a list of tables that can be modified. The Fields tab lists both the name of the table and the fields.

2 | Master Data

> **Note**
>
> You can also use Transaction MASS for the mass maintenance of vendor master data (object type LFA1), GL account master data (object type BUS3006), or material master data (object type BUS1001).

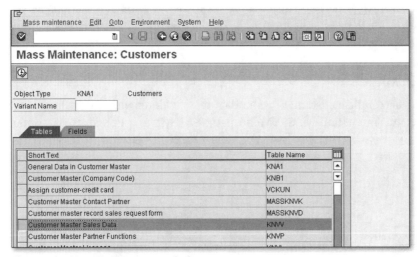

Figure 2.8 Mass Maintenance — Customers

Follow the steps below to use Transaction MASS:

1. Select the specific table and field to be modified. For example, if the customers belonging to a particular region (KNA1-REGIO) have a new customer pricing procedure (KNVV-KALKS), you would select Table KNVV in the Tables tab (Figure 2.8) or KNVV-KALKS in the Fields tab (Figure 2.9).

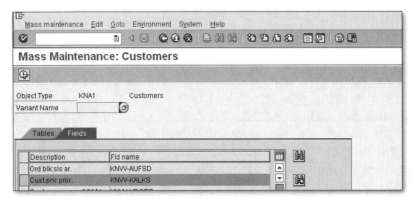

Figure 2.9 Mass Maintenance for Field KNVV-KALKS

52

2. Execute. This action results in the screen shown in Figure 2.10. For our example, because you know that all of the customers of a particular region are to be changed, you can get a list of the customers using Transaction SE16 or SE16N and Table KNA1. Paste the list, press [F8], and select Display All Records. This results in a list of customers with the existing value in the Cust.Pric.Procedure field, as shown in Figure 2.11.

> **Note**
>
> You press the Execution icon (or [F8] key) three times while executing Transaction MASS: first, in the first screen after you select the object (KNA1 for customer master), second, after you specify the table and the field (KNVV-KALKS), and third, after you enter the list or range of customers (or vendor or GLs or others as per the object selected) for which you want the mass change.

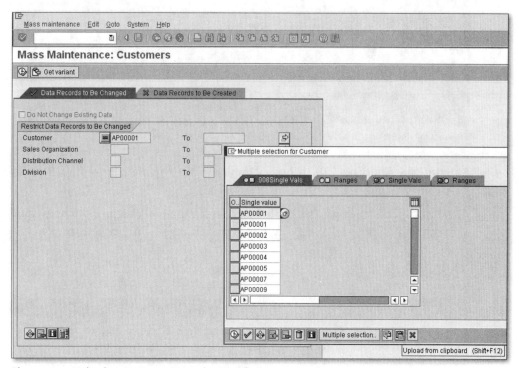

Figure 2.10 Uploading Customer List to be Modified

2 | Master Data

3. If you're using the Tables tab and not the Fields tab in step 1, click on the Select Fields icon. This is the first icon in the task bar shown in Figure 2.11.

4. A new dialog box opens, which is also shown in Figure 2.11. Select Cust.Pric. Procedure (KALKS) and bring it to the Selection Criteria table by clicking on the Choose icon (the black triangle pointing left).

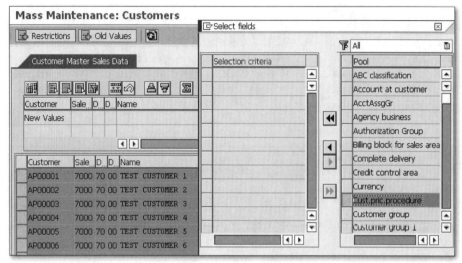

Figure 2.11 Inserting the KNVV-KALKS Field for Mass Maintenance

5. Enter the new value (9, in our example) in the Cust.Pric.Procedure field, as shown in Figure 2.12.

6. Select the column (Cust.Pric.Procedure in our example) to which the new value is to go and click on the Carry Out Mass Change icon (sixth icon from the left).

7. Save.

> **Failed Cases in Mass Maintenance**
>
> It's possible for a few records to fail mass change, for example, if they are locked by a user. Failed cases appear marked red in the results screen. Because there can be a lot of pages of results and very few failed cases, you must carefully check the pages of the result screen.

2.1 Customer Master Data

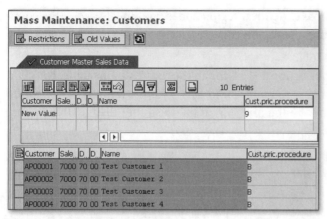

Figure 2.12 Execute the Mass Change

Transaction SE16N with the SAP Edit Function

From ECC 5.0 onward, SAP allows you to directly modify, update, or insert records in any table using Transaction SE16N with the SAP edit function.

> **Warning**
>
> Before using Transaction SE16N with the SAP edit function for several records, you should check it for a single record. Also note that if any info structure or table gets updated when you update the value of a particular field of a table, this does not happen when the field is updated via Transaction SE16N. For updating to happen, you must run an updating program (if such a program is available). We have provided one such example in Chapter 7, Section 7.7, where we discuss how to delete a credit memo request of a cancelled credit memo.

Let's use an example to explain the steps to change (add, delete, or update) table entries using Transaction SE16N with the SAP edit function. In our example, we change the Cust.Pric.Proc field for all customers in a particular region. The steps for this are provided below:

1. Get a list of all customers located in the region for which you are implementing a mass change (Transaction SE16N or SE16).

   For mass changes, you must know the records that need to be modified. You get this list either manually or by using a report or table. For our example, we get it from Table KNA1. Using Transaction SE16N or SE16, get a list of all customers located in the region for which you are implementing a mass change. Because

55

different countries can have identical region codes, you must specify the country code prior to selecting the region code.

2. Restrict Transaction SE16N.

   Instead of executing Transaction SE16N for all the records in the table, restrict it to the cases where changes are required. In our example, we have supplied the list of customers obtained in the first step in the Customer field (KUNNR).

3. Activate the SAP edit function.

   This is done by typing "&SAP_EDIT" in the transaction window and pressing enter when you are still inside Transaction SE16N. This results in the screen shown in Figure 2.13.

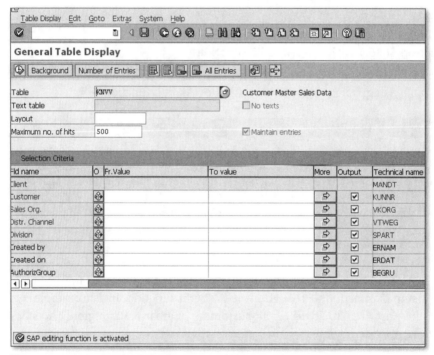

Figure 2.13 Activating the SAP Edit Function (&SAP_EDIT)

4. Execute Transaction SE16N with the SAP edit function active.

   All records appear. Hide all columns except those for which the change is required.

5. Using Excel or other suitable software, provide the new values for the list of records.

   For our example, we have decided to make a new value of 9 for all of the customer pricing procedures (CuPP); currently, the value is B. To do this, we enter the new value 9 in 450 Excel rows (450 is the number of customers to be modified) and then copy it.

6. Open the context menu for the first row of the Customer Pricing Procedure (CuPP) field and select Insert with Overwrite (Figure 2.14).

   The new value should appear in all of the records.

7. Click on the Save icon.

   Clearly, this process takes less time than changing the 450 records one after another using Transaction XD02 or VD02.

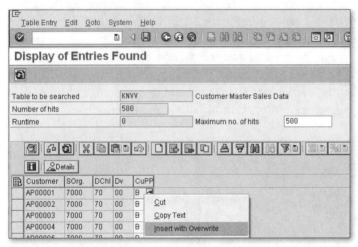

Figure 2.14 Insert with Overwrite to Insert Values from the CuPP Field

Other Methods Used in Mass Maintenance

The Legacy System Migration Workbench (LSMW) and Batch Data Communication (BDC) are also used for the mass maintenance of customer master records (and other master records) and for a variety of other activities (such as creating sales orders and deliveries). In LSMW, you record the steps you follow to modify one record, and then, using the program generated by the LSMW recording, you can make the same modifications for any number of customer master records. We will discuss this as an ABAP tool in Chapter 8. A technical developer writes the

BDC, and it takes values from a local file, which it then uses to make changes in different table fields.

> **Transactions SM30 and SM31**
>
> Transactions SM30 and SM31 are also used for modifying certain standard tables, especially table views used for customization. These transactions cannot be used for maintaining tables that store master data.

2.2 Customer Credit Master Data

Customer credit master data is created and maintained via Transaction FD32 for individual customers and F.34 for mass processing. The screens that constitute the customer credit master record are Overview, Address, Central Data, Status, and Payment History, as you can see in Figure 2.15, which is the initial screen of Transaction FD32. Of these, Address, Status, and Payment History are automatically populated from customer master and transaction data. The fields that must be entered manually are Credit Limit (and its currency), Customer Credit Group, Risk Category, Accounting Clerk, Customer Representative Group, and other data from external rating agencies or internal information and texts.

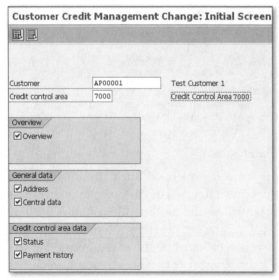

Figure 2.15 Customer Credit Management (Initial Screen)

The four general steps for customizing customer credit master records are:

1. Preliminary setting
2. Customizing text IDs
3. Defining various groups and categories
4. Authorization control for customer credit master fields

We discuss each of these steps in the subsections below.

2.2.1 Preliminary Settings

As shown in Figure 2.16, the first activity is to assign additional credit control areas to the company code. The menu path for this is SAP IMG • FINANCIAL ACCOUNTING (NEW) • ACCOUNTS RECEIVABLE AND ACCOUNTS PAYABLE • CREDIT MANAGEMENT • CREDIT CONTROL ACCOUNT • ASSIGN PERMITTED CREDIT CONTROL AREAS TO COMPANY CODE. In Chapter 1, you learned that a company code can be assigned to only one credit control area but that more than one credit control area can be assigned to a company code. If the latter needs to be done for your company, this is where you should do it. This decision is made at the company level by the finance team.

Figure 2.16 Assign Credit Control Area to Company Code

Now follow the menu path SAP IMG • FINANCIAL ACCOUNTING (NEW) • ACCOUNTS RECEIVABLE AND ACCOUNTS PAYABLE • CREDIT MANAGEMENT • CREDIT CONTROL ACCOUNT • DEFINE PRELIMINARY SETTINGS FOR CREDIT MANAGEMENT (Figure 2.17). In this screen, you must make some basic decisions about how the accounts receivable balance is to be calculated for credit check purposes. You also define the *days of sales outstanding* (DSO) in this step; the DSO is an important key performance indicator (KPI) that your SAP system calculates automatically. DSO is calculated by dividing the total outstanding by the average daily sales for a customer.

2 | Master Data

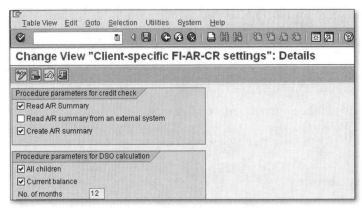

Figure 2.17 Preliminary Settings for Credit Management

2.2.2 Customizing Text IDs

If necessary for your company, you can add text IDs to the text objects KNKK (Credit Management) and KNKA (Credit Management – Central), but there are usually enough text IDs already available in the standard settings. The text IDs are often useful, because qualitative data maintained in text for the customers is as important as quantitative data in Credit Management.

2.2.3 Defining Groups and Categories

You can create different groups and categories and group customers in them while creating customer credit master records. In addition to reporting and analysis, this information is used for monitoring and automatic credit checks. Groups, credit risk categories, credit representative groups, and credit representatives are defined with Transactions OB12, OB01, OB02, and OB51, respectively. We discuss them in more detail in Chapter 5.

2.2.4 Authorization Control for Customer Credit Master Record Fields

You complete authorization control by following the steps below:

1. Define the field groups.
   To do this, execute Transaction OB34 (menu path: SAP IMG • FINANCIAL ACCOUNTING (NEW) • ACCOUNTS RECEIVABLE AND ACCOUNTS PAYABLE • CREDIT MANAGEMENT • CREDIT CONTROL ACCOUNT • DEFINE FIELD GROUPS), as shown in Figure 2.18.

2.2 Customer Credit Master Data

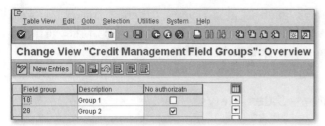

Figure 2.18 Defining Credit Management Field Groups

2. Select the No Authorizatn checkbox, where appropriate.

   If the No Authorization checkbox is selected, there is no authorization check for the fields assigned to the field group. To edit the field groups subjected to authorization checks, you must have *both* overall authorization for changing customer credit master records, and authorization for these specific field groups.

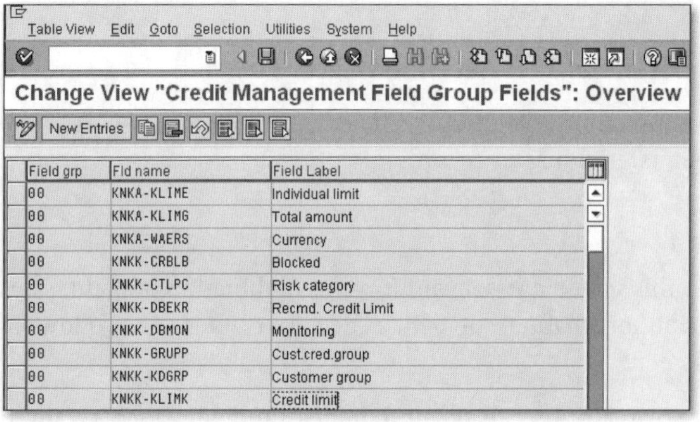

Figure 2.19 Assigning Credit Management Fields to Field Groups

3. Assign different fields to different field groups.

   Use Transaction OB33 (menu path: SAP IMG • FINANCIAL ACCOUNTING (NEW) • ACCOUNTS RECEIVABLE AND ACCOUNTS PAYABLE • CREDIT MANAGEMENT • CREDIT CONTROL ACCOUNT • ASSIGN FIELDS TO FIELD GROUPS) to assign different fields to different field groups based on your requirements. For example, you can create a field group for the field Next Internal Review Date (KNKK-NXTRV). Select the No Authorizatn check-box for that field group. As a result, there will be no additional authorization requirement to change the Next Internal Review Date in any customer credit master record, by any user (provided authorization for Transaction FD32 is given). In Figure 2.19, you can see how the fields of the

61

credit master record are assigned to field groups. Different table fields such as KNKA-KLIME, KNKA-KLIMG, and others, which are fields of the customer credit master record, are shown attached to Field grp 00.

2.3 Material Master – Sales Views

The material master data is considered to be the most important master data in SAP systems and has many screens for storing Materials Management, Financial Accounting, Sales and Distribution, Production Planning, Quality Management, and Controlling information. The Sales and Distribution data is stored in three screens: Sales: Sales Org. Data 1, Sales: Sales Org. Data 2, and Sales: General/Plant Data. In the next two sections, we will discuss important sales-relevant fields in material master records and a few examples of customizing material master fields.

2.3.1 Important Sales-Relevant Material Master Fields

In the following three subsections, we discuss some of the important fields in the three sales views in the material master records.

Sales: Sales Org. Data 1

The fields that make up this screen are relevant for the combination of plant, sales organization, and distribution channel for which they are created. The following fields are part of this screen:

- Base Unit of Measure (e.g., KG, liter) is the unit of measurement (UoM) required for maintaining stock.
- Sales Unit is the unit of measurement in which material is to be sold. It can differ from the base unit of measure.
- The Sales Unit Not Variable checkbox when selected does not allow the user to change the sales unit during document processing.
- The Unit of Measure Group field groups different UoMs.
- The Cross-Distribution Chain Status field specifies the status of the material (e.g., under development, discontinued) for all of the distribution chains (combination for sales organization and distribution channel).

2.3 Material Master – Sales Views

- The Distribution Chain-Specific Status field specifies the status of the material for a distribution chain (as per the organizational data of MMR).
- The Delivering Plant field stores the plant that becomes the default delivery plant in a sales document for the material.
- The Material Group field is customized and used for grouping materials by company- or project-specific criteria.
- The Cash Discount checkbox is selected when a cash discount is allowed for the material.
- Division is used to specify the division to which the material belongs.
- The Tax Classifications field stores the material tax classification indicator for different countries. It is one of the criteria that determines the tax.
- The Minimum Order Quantity field stores the value of the minimum quantity a customer can order.
- The Minimum Delivery Quantity field stores the minimum quantity that can be delivered to a customer.
- Delivery Unit specifies a quantity (e.g., 12) with the UoM. Only multiples of the delivery unit (e.g., 12, 24, 36) are allowed for delivery.
- Rounding Profile is used to derive the delivery quantity for a particular order quantity. For example, when the order quantity is 10 units, the derived delivery quantity can be 12 units based on the rounding profile, especially when the delivery unit is 12.

Sales: Sales Org. Data 2

This screen contains the fields that group the material based on various criteria and attributes. Table 2.1 lists the fields and how they group materials.

Field Name	Group Materials Based On
Material Statistics Group	How they update the Sales information System (SIS) or Logistics Information System (LIS)
Volume Rebate group	Rebate agreement processing
Gen. Item Cat. Group	Item category determination
Pricing Reference Material	Pricing (also refer the following note)
Product Hierarchy	Company- and project-specific criteria

Table 2.1 Fields and Group Materials

Field Name	Group Materials Based On
Commission Group	Commission paid
Material Pricing Group	Pricing
Account Assignment Group	Posting to accounting (GL)
Item Category Group	Item category determination
Material Group 1/2/3/4/5	Company- and project-specific criteria
Product Attributes 1 to 10	Company- and project-specific criteria

Table 2.1 Fields and Group Materials (Cont.)

> **Note**
> Pricing reference material can be used optimally to reduce effort for condition record maintenance. The conditions created for a pricing reference material also become valid for all of the materials that have that pricing reference material.

Sales: General/Plant Data

The values of the fields in this screen are only applicable to the plant for which the material master record is created (base unit of measure and serialization level are two exceptions). For different plants you can have different values (e.g., availability check, transportation group).

- Base Unit of Measure (e.g., KG, liter) is the unit of measurement required for maintaining stock.
- The Gross Weight field is used to note the weight of the material including packaging and other weights.
- The Net Weight field notes the net weight (excluding packaging).
- The Availability Check field is used to group materials for availability checks and transfer to material requirements planning (MRP).
- The Batch Management checkbox is selected for all materials for which creating batches is mandatory.
- The Replacement Part indicator specifies whether the material is a replacement part. If it is, then it specified whether it is mandatory or optional.
- The Qualify for Free Goods Discount indicator is only used for trading goods. While purchasing, this indicator useful to receive the free goods available.

2.3 Material Master – Sales Views

- The Material Freight Group field groups materials based on the fright and/or carrier determination.
- The Transportation Group field groups materials based on transportation and route determination.
- The Loading Group field groups materials with similar loading requirements and is used along with the shipping conditions and delivery plant fields of a sales document for automatic determination of the shipping point.
- Setup time is the time required, if any, to prepare for shipping the material. However, it does not include the actual time for processing the shipment.
- Processing time is the time required to process a specified base quantity.
- Base quantity is required to specify the processing time.
- The Material Group Packaging Materials field groups materials for determining the packaging material.
- The Negative Stock checkbox is selected when a temporary negative stock level is allowed in the plant.
- The Profit Center field specifies the profit center to which the accounting posting should go for the material (in the plant for which the MMR is applicable)
- The Serial No Profile field is filled for the serialized material.
- Serialization Level is left blank if the requirement is to make all of the combinations of material and serial number unique. To make the serial number unique at the client level, set the indicator to 1 for all material master records.
- Distribution Profile is relevant for IS-Retail.

2.3.2 Customizing Material Master Fields

In this section, we discuss the customization of the product hierarchy; material status; material groups 1, 2, 3, 4, and 5; and material commission groups. These are not the only fields that are customized, nor are they the most important; these fields are selected because they have a different customization process than normal.

Product Hierarchy

Product hierarchies are used when materials are grouped in a hierarchical manner, such as for pricing and reporting. In the standard system, the product hierarchy consists of up to three levels; the first and second levels have 5 digits, and the third level has 8. The maximum number of digits is 18, and the maximum number of levels is 9. You can define hierarchy nodes at individual levels of the product hierarchy. The menu path for this is SAP IMG • LOGISTICS – GENERAL • MATERIAL MASTER • SETTINGS FOR KEY FIELDS • DATA RELEVANT TO SALES AND DISTRIBUTION • DEFINE PRODUCT HIERARCHIES (Transaction OVSV).

From this node, as shown in Figure 2.20, you can branch to the following steps:

- **Product hierarchy structure**
  In the Data Dictionary, you can change the structure of the product hierarchy (e.g., the number of levels).

- **Data entry/display**
  Here you define the display of the product hierarchy and the format of the accompanying text.

- **Product hierarchy**
  Here you define your product hierarchies. Refer to the example shown in Table 2.2 to understand how they are defined.

- **Field catalog for pricing**
  Here you make the product hierarchy available for use in pricing.

- **Field catalog for the Logistics Information System**
  Here you make the product hierarchy available for use in the Logistics Information System.

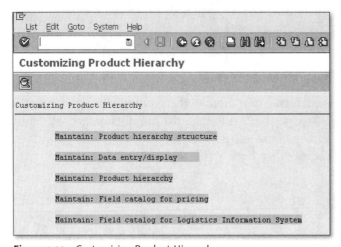

Figure 2.20 Customizing Product Hierarchy

Table 2.2 shows an example of a product hierarchy.

Product Hierarchy	Level No	Description
10000	1	Washing Machine
10000•10000	2	Washing Machine • Semi-automatic
10000•10000•10000000	3	Washing Machine • Semi-automatic • 4 Kg (Capacity)
10000•10000•20000000	3	Washing Machine • Semi-automatic • 6 Kg (Capacity)
10000•20000	2	Washing Machine • Automatic
10000•20000•10000000	3	Washing Machine • Automatic • 5 Kg (Capacity)
10000•20000•20000000	3	Washing Machine • Automatic • 7 Kg (Capacity)
20000	1	Television
20000•10000	2	Television • LCD
20000•10000•10000000	3	Television • LCD • 32"
20000•10000•20000000	3	Television • LCD • 40"
20000•20000	2	Television • Plasma
20000•20000•10000000	3	Television • Plasma • 52"
20000•20000•20000000	3	Television • Plasma • 60"

Table 2.2 Example of Product Hierarchy

Material Status

The material status (also known as the sales status) of any material determines whether the material will be blocked for any particular sales process. The menu path for defining sales statuses is SAP IMG • LOGISTICS – GENERAL • MATERIAL MASTER • SETTINGS FOR KEY FIELDS • DATA RELEVANT TO SALES AND DISTRIBUTION • DEFINE SALES STATUSES. This takes you to the screen shown in Figure 2.21. The steps to customize the material status are below.

1. Select any existing entry. We have selected the first entry (Figure 2.21).
2. Click on the Copy As icon or press F6.
   This takes you to the screen shown in Figure 2.22, with the message "Specify target entries."

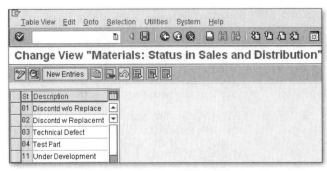

Figure 2.21 Defining Sales Statuses of Materials

3. Change the two-digit status key and description.
4. Assign a status to each of the processes shown in Figure 2.22.

   There are 13 Sales and Distribution processes, for which the status can be defined as a warning (A) or error (B). It's possible to have no message (when neither A nor B is selected) for some processes. For example, in your company or industry, it may be a standard practice to accept an order for a product when it's still under trial, though the delivery is to be made after trial. So even when the status is Under Testing, there is no warning or error while creating the order, but for delivery there can be an error message.

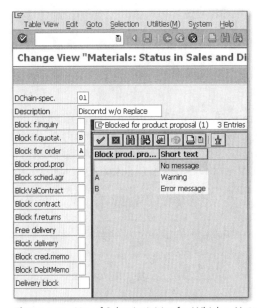

Figure 2.22 List of Sales Activities for Which a Material Can Be Blocked

These statuses are assigned to a material in the material master record in the Sales: Sales Org Data 1 tab, DChain-spec. Status field.

Material Groups 1, 2, 3, 4, and 5

Material groups 1, 2, 3, 4, and 5, which appear in the Sales Org. Data 2 tab of the material master record, are different from the material group (MARA-MATKL), which appears on the Basic Data 1 tab of the material master record. More specifically, material groups 1, 2, 3, 4, and 5 are used for reporting in the Sales and Distribution component, whereas the material group fields of the Basic Data 1 tab are used across all components. The material group (MARA-MATKL) is customized via Transaction OMSF. Material groups 1, 2, 3, 4, and 5 are customized via Transaction OVSU (menu path: SAP IMG • LOGISTICS – GENERAL • MATERIAL MASTER • SETTINGS FOR KEY FIELDS • DATA RELEVANT TO SALES AND DISTRIBUTION • DEFINE MATERIAL GROUPS). As shown in Figure 2.23, any of these material groups can contain several three-digit alphanumeric keys with descriptions; while creating a material master record, you can select one of these fields so that a material will have a value for each material group, from 1 to 5. You can keep one or two of these unused for future usage. These groups can have generic descriptions and can also be used to address one-time reporting requirements.

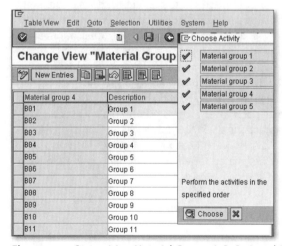

Figure 2.23 Customizing Material Groups 1, 2, 3, 4, and 5

Material Commission Groups

Material commission groups are also used for reporting (and pricing) purposes. In pricing, you can make a material commission group a key field of a pricing condition table for a condition type (price or surcharge). We'll discuss this in Chapter 4. Because the field is used for calculating commission, reports are also prepared using it in the selection screen for that purpose. We'll discuss reporting in Chapter 9. Material commission groups are defined using the menu path SAP IMG • LOGISTICS – GENERAL • MATERIAL MASTER • SETTINGS FOR KEY FIELDS • DATA RELEVANT TO SALES AND DISTRIBUTION • DEFINE COMMISSION GROUPS. As shown in Figure 2.24, you define a material commission group by adding a two-digit alphanumeric key and a description.

Figure 2.24 Defining Material Commission Groups

> **Customer-Material Info Records**
>
> Customer-material info records are a form of master data that are used when the same customers order customer-specific materials. They provide information about a customer's choice of carrier, delivery priority, specific material codes, and other information that is often repeated in their orders. They also permit the customer to order a material (referring their own number) where their material number and your material number differ. During the creation of a sales order for a customer buying a specific material, the information in the customer-material info record overwrites the information that would otherwise flow from customer or material master records. These info records are created, changed, and displayed via Transactions VD51/2/3 (SAP MENU • LOGISTICS • SALES AND DISTRIBUTION • MASTER DATA • AGREEMENTS • CUSTOMER MATERIAL INFORMATION • CREATE / CHANGE / DISPLAY). They can be created for a particular sales organization and distribution channel, and can apply to several materials.

2.4 Batch Master Data

A batch is often used in process industries (oil and gas, concrete, paint, pharmaceuticals, fast-moving consumer goods, and others) or where shelf-life management is a concern (e.g., foods and beverages). A *batch number* is a number associated with a specific storage unit of a material. Products with the same batch number are identical with respect to their most important characteristics, which are often industry-specific (i.e., decided by the industry regulating agency or trade association). The characteristics can vary from company to company. A company dealing with trading goods can decide to give different batch numbers to identify goods sourced from different vendors. Similarly, a manufacturing company can give the same batch numbers to goods that go through the same manufacturing process before being packed in different packages.

A batch master record is created, changed, and displayed via Transactions MSC1N, MSC2N, and MSC3N, respectively. The customization activities you should complete before you create batch master records are defining batches, customizing system messages relevant to batch management, customizing the layout of the batch master record, creating and assigning number ranges for batches, customizing the shelf life expiration date (SLED), and classifying batches. We explain each of these activities below.

2.4.1 Defining Batches

To define a batch, execute Transaction OMCT (menu path: SAP IMG • LOGISTICS – GENERAL • BATCH MANAGEMENT • SPECIFY BATCH LEVEL AND ACTIVE STATUS MANAGEMENT). The activity of defining a batch (Figure 2.25) includes defining the batch level, activating batch status management, and defining the initial status of a new batch. We discuss each of these processes in the following subsections.

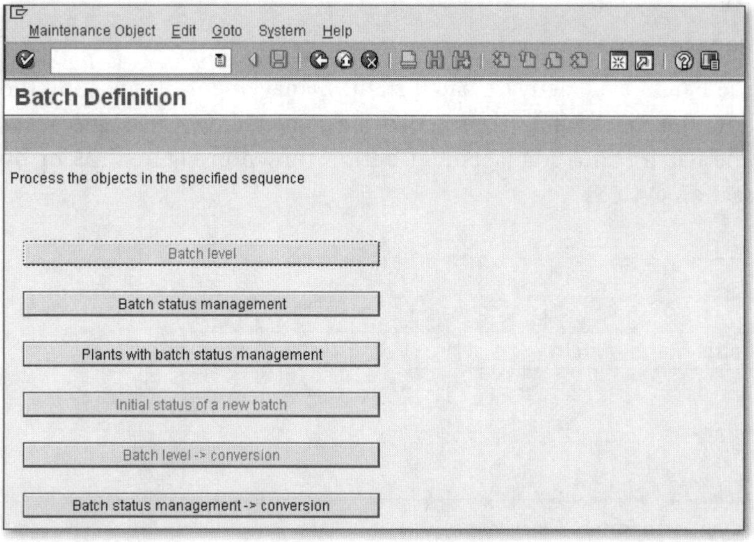

Figure 2.25 Batch Definition (Transaction OMCT)

Batch Level

The batch can be unique at the client, plant, and material level. In a standard SAP system, it's at the material level, as shown in Figure 2.26. You get to this screen when you click on the Batch Level button shown in Figure 2.25 or by executing Transaction OMCE.

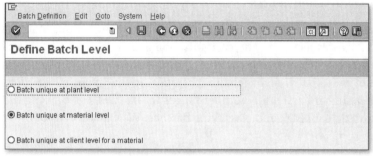

Figure 2.26 Defining the Batch Level

Conversion from one level to another is possible but may be avoided. The conversion program RM07CHDX creates new batch records in Table MCH1 for the new level. If records with the same details already exist in that level, this will create data inconsistency. Refer to SAP Notes 891902 (FAQ: Batch Level) and 533377 (Conversion of Batch Level) if you have to change the batch level. Once you have defined the batch level, you cannot change it through the SAP IMG.

Batch Status Management

After defining the batch level, activate batch status management by selecting the radio button shown in Figure 2.27. You get to the screen shown in Figure 2.27 by clicking on the Batch Status Management button shown in Figure 2.25 or by executing Transaction OMCS.

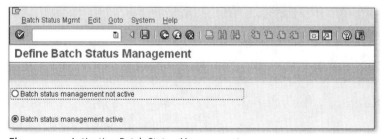

Figure 2.27 Activating Batch Status Management

When the batch is defined at the plant level, you must activate batch status management for each plant (Figure 2.28) using Transaction OMCU.

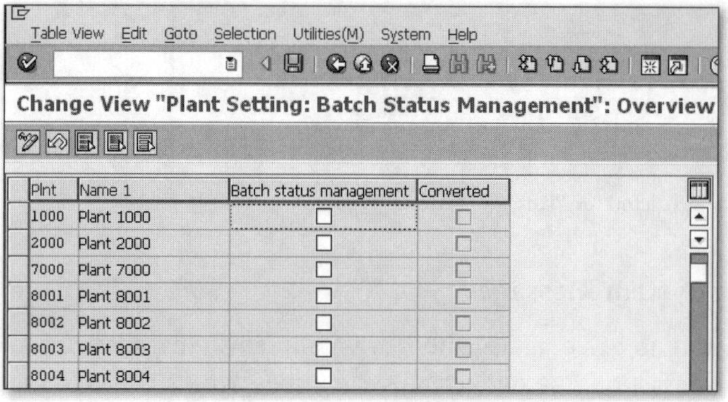

Figure 2.28 Plant Setting: Batch Status Management

Initial Status of a New Batch

As shown in Figure 2.29, you can set the initial status of a new batch for a specific material type to Restricted by selecting the checkbox in the Initial Status column. The screen shown in Figure 2.29 appears when you click on the Initial Status of a New Batch button shown in Figure 2.25 or execute Transaction OMAC.

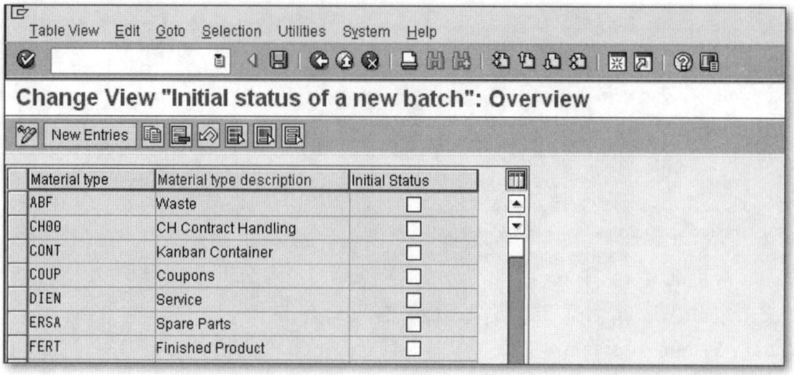

Figure 2.29 Initial Status Restricted for Material Type

When a batch level is defined as a plant, a new batch is made available for restricted or unrestricted use for a combination of plants and material types (Figure 2.30) via Transaction OMAC.

Plnt	Name 1	MTyp	Material type description	Initial Status	Batch stat.mgmt
0001	Werk 0001	DIEN	Service	☐	☐
0001	Werk 0001	ERSA	Spare Parts	☐	☐
0001	Werk 0001	FERT	Finished Product	☐	☐

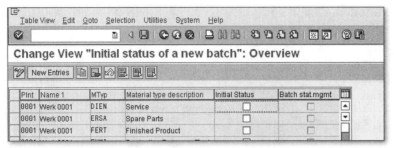

Figure 2.30 Initial Status Restricted for Plant and Material Type

2.4.2 Configuring System Messages

System messages relating to batch management are modified so that they appear when required. The transaction for configuring system messages is OCHS (menu path: SAP IMG • LOGISTICS – GENERAL • BATCH MANAGEMENT • DEFINE ATTRIBUTES OF SYSTEM MESSAGES) and is shown in Figure 2.31. The first column shows the version, the second the application area, and the third a number specific to the message text you see when you encounter it during a transaction. You should be very sure about the category to which any particular message should belong, because messages can enhance or hamper the users' productivity. For example, if a warning appears when it shouldn't (based on the business policy), it might confuse the user; new users may even stop working until the implications are known.

Version	Appl.A.	No.	Message text	Cat
	LB	151	The proportion/product unit & is assigned to a dimension	W
	LB	263	Proportion unit & is assigned to a dimension	E
	LB	264	Product unit & is assigned to a dimension	W
	XU	051	Changed quantity conversion for prop.unit entry qty will be r	W
00	12	003	Date of production/SLED of batch &1 changed to &2/&3 in a	P
00	12	004	Production date of bch &1 (&2) does not match the prod. d	W
00	12	005	SLED of batch &1 (&2) does not match the SLED of the curr	W

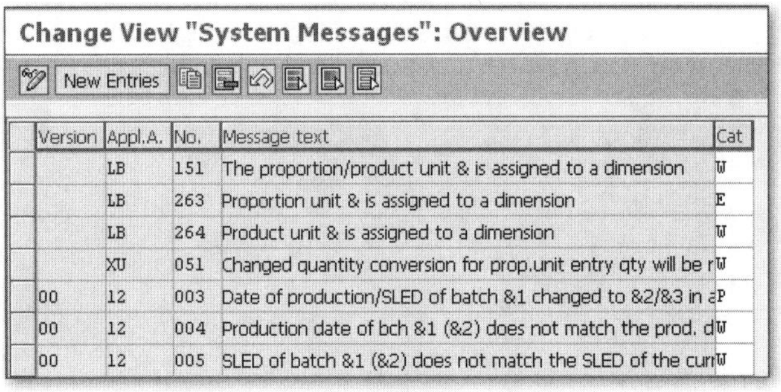

Figure 2.31 Modify System Messages

2.4.3 Configuring the Layout of Batch Master Records

You create, modify, and display batch master records using Transactions MSC1N, MSC2N, and MSC3N, respectively. All fields of batch master records are assigned to a field group (001 to 040), as shown in Figure 2.32. You make the field group mandatory, required, display-only, or hidden by selecting the appropriate radio button (Figure 2.33). Defining a new field group is neither required nor possible.

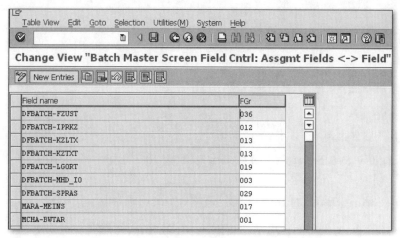

Figure 2.32 Assigning Fields of Batch Master Records to Field Groups

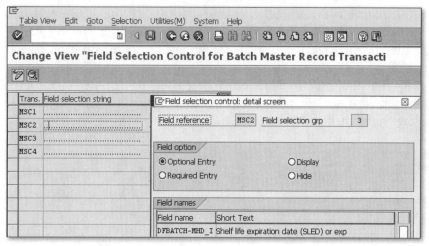

Figure 2.33 Modifying Field Selection Groups

2.4.4 Document Management System for Batch Master Records

It's also possible to activate the document management system (DMS) for batch master records, as shown in Figure 2.34. You can access this screen via Transaction ODOC (menu path: SAP IMG • LOGISTICS – GENERAL • BATCH MANAGEMENT •

ACTIVATE DOCUMENT MANAGEMENT FOR BATCHES). When DMS is activated for the batch master record, a new tab for the document management system appears in the batch master record to the right of the existing tabs.

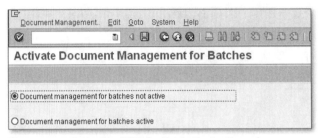

Figure 2.34 Activating DMS for Batch Master Records

2.4.5 Configuring Batch Numbers

Batch numbers, which can be printed on product labels, can be customized for internal and external number ranges, depending upon the requirements. You maintain the numbering object for a batch (BATCH_CLT) using Transaction SNRO or OMAD. As shown in Figure 2.35, the number range 01 is for an internal batch number assignment, and the number range 02 is for an external number assignment (defined by the checkbox in the last column). (You can also have several other number ranges.) Whether the number is generated externally and then fed into the SAP system or generated in the SAP system and then printed on the label doesn't matter; what matters is that the batch number maintained in the SAP system and the one printed on label are the same.

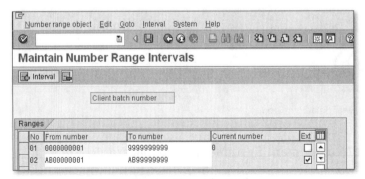

Figure 2.35 Maintaining Number Ranges for Batches

2.4.6 Configuring Shelf Life Expiration Date (SLED)

The unit of measure for counting the expiration date in batch master records can be days, weeks, months, or years, and its format is determined by the *period indicator*. One or more of the four available period indicators can be activated via Transaction O02K (menu path: SAP IMG • LOGISTICS – GENERAL • BATCH MANAGEMENT • SHELF LIFE EXPIRATION DATE (SLED) • MAINTAIN PERIOD INDICATOR), as shown in Figure 2.36. For example, if the period indicator is in days, both the dates are maintained as MM.DD.YYYY; if it's in years, the dates are maintained as YYYY only. If the period indicator is left blank, it will be marked as Day. Table 2.3 lists the internal period indicators and the corresponding external period indicator in English and German, as well as the description in English.

Internal Period Indicator	External Period Indicator		Description
	German	English	
	T	D	Day
1	W	W	Week
2	M	M	Month
3	J	Y	Year

Table 2.3 Standard SAP Period Indicators

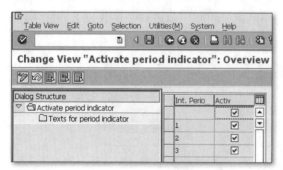

Figure 2.36 Activating Period Indicator

The expiration date restricts the movement of goods, such as stock transfers, goods returned from customers, and goods received from external vendors; these movement types are identified in the system by different keys. It's also possible to keep certain plants free of expiration date checks. As shown in Figure 2.37, plant 0001 has no check for an expired material for a goods receipt; this means the expired material can be received at these plants without any check. You do this is by using

Transaction OMJ5 (menu path: SAP IMG • LOGISTICS – GENERAL • BATCH MANAGEMENT • SHELF LIFE EXPIRATION DATE (SLED) • SET EXPIRATION DATE CHECK) and then selecting the plant.

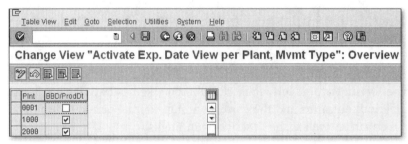

Figure 2.37 Expiration Date Check at the Plant Level

For the receiving plants where the expiration date (SLED) is active, the restrictions are further refined to particular movement types. As shown in Figure 2.38, you define the nature of the check for each movement type using Transaction OMJ5 (menu path: SAP IMG • LOGISTICS – GENERAL • BATCH MANAGEMENT • SHELF LIFE EXPIRATION DATE (SLED) • SET EXPIRATION DATE CHECK) and then selecting the *movement type* option. Movement type defines the nature of the movement when there is any physical or other change in the stock. For example, one movement type may make the stock returned by a customer to available for sale (unrestricted type), whereas another will block it for sale (return type) until quality checks are carried out.

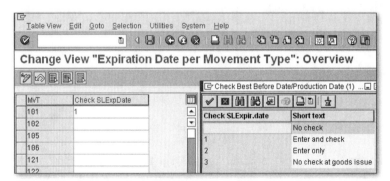

Figure 2.38 Expiration Date Check for Different Movement Types

2.4.7 Configuring Batch Classification

The classification system is a feature not unique to batch management, but part of cross-application components (another example of a cross-application component is DMS). The classification system consists of *classes* and *characteristics* and can also be used to classify materials. It's also used in several components other than Logistics. SAP provides a list of objects for which the class type is predefined, for example, class type 023, Batch. This class type is used for creating classes that classify batches based on different characteristics such as place of manufacturing if the same material is manufactured at several plants. You can create the class in the production client using Transaction CL02 (SAP MENU • CROSS-APPLICATION COMPONENTS • CLASSIFICATION SYSTEM • MASTER DATA • CLASSES). As shown in Figure 2.39, you must use class type 023 to create a class for batch classification.

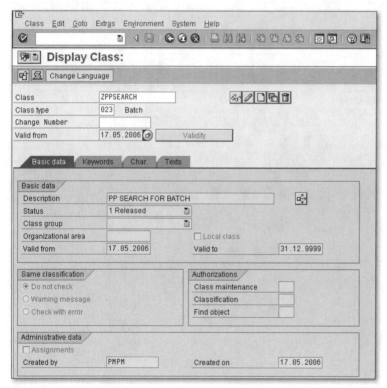

Figure 2.39 Create Class

Characteristics like classes are also master data; as such, they are not transported from the development to the production client, but are created in the production client itself using Transaction CT04 (SAP Menu • Cross-Application Components • Classification System • Master Data • Characteristics). More than one characteristic is often used to define a batch. In Figure 2.40 and 2.41, we show how to make Date of Manufacturing (or Date of Production) a characteristic of the batch. Because the date of manufacturing is to be expressed in terms of a date, the data type is the Date Format; other possible data formats are Character, Numeric, and Currency. The status should be Released, to make the batch available for use. In the Chars Group field, different characteristics can be grouped together and assigned to one characteristics group in the list available. Characteristics groups are defined using the menu path SAP IMG • Cross-Application Components • Classifications System • Characteristics • Define Characteristics Groups. The AuthGrp field (authorization group) is used if the characteristic is to be restricted to specific users.

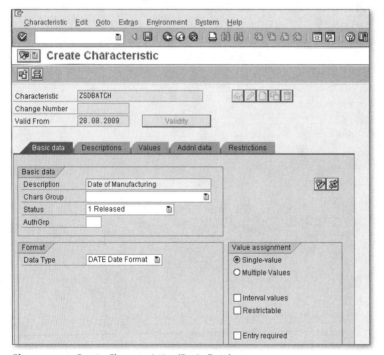

Figure 2.40 Create Characteristics (Basic Data)

When creating a batch where you want to require that the value for the characteristic be entered, select the Entry Required checkbox. The value to be entered can be a single value (as in case of Date of Manufacturing), but you can also allow users to enter multiple values by selecting the Multiple Values radio button. The Interval Values checkbox, when selected, allows numeric characteristics to have intervals as values. The Restrictable checkbox, when selected, allows the characteristic to have a value from a predefined set of values.

The description entered in the Basic Data tab is also automatically supplied in the Descriptions tab (in the logon language). If a description in another language is required, it can also be stored in that view. The Values tab is used to define values that the characteristics can have when creating a batch. The Addnl Data (Additional Data) tab is especially useful if the value of the characteristic is to be automatically filled, as shown in Figure 2.41. Fields that are automatically filled require no input from you, so the more characteristics you can add here, the more time you will save. Here, for example, we have made the MCH1-HSDAT field a default value for the date of manufacturing, meaning that the date on which the batch is created (MCH1-HSDAT) is also the value for the Date of Production field. (This is a reasonably good assumption generally and a very good assumption if you're creating the batch automatically.)

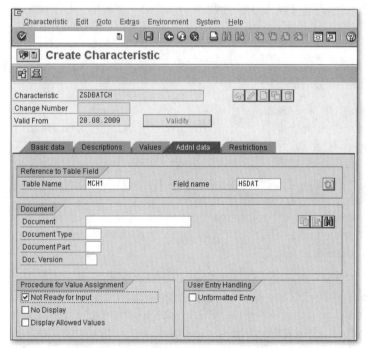

Figure 2.41 Create Characteristics (Additional Data)

> **Foreign Trade Master Data**
>
> Foreign-trade-related master data is accessed through a single point (the General Foreign Trade Processing Cockpit) but is part of four separate master records: vendor master record, purchasing info record, material master record, and customer master record. The menu path to access the General Foreign Trade Processing Cockpit is SAP EASY ACCESS • LOGISTICS • SALES AND DISTRIBUTION • FOREIGN TRADE/CUSTOMS • GENERAL FOREIGN TRADE PROCESSING • GENERAL FOREIGN TRADE PROCESSING • COCKPIT – GENERAL FOREIGN TRADE PROCESSING (Transaction EN99). All of the master data fields relevant for foreign trade processing can be accessed and maintained via this cockpit transaction. We'll discuss some of the important foreign trade master data fields in Chapter 3.

2.5 Overview of Other Master Data

In this section, we offer a brief introduction to vendor master data, employee master data, general ledger master data, and user master data. There are other types of master data as well, but these are the types that are most relevant for Sales and Distribution. We'll discuss condition records (e.g., pricing, output) in subsequent chapters. The more time you spend on master data (and on organizational structure), the better you'll understand the different processes and how master data impacts them.

2.5.1 Vendor Master Data

Vendors are individuals or organizations that sell goods and/or services to you or your organization. Carriers or transporters are the group of vendors who are most important for us to understand from a sales and distribution perspective. This is because transportation is very closely integrated to delivery, which we'll discuss later. Transporters or carriers are created as partner functions for customers and attached to their customer master record. Employees (especially sales employees) are also treated as vendors for the reimbursement of travelling expenses. If you understand the customer master data well, you can visualize the vendor master data as a mirror image of it.

Transactions XK01/2/3 are used to centrally create/change/display vendor master data. Transactions FK01/2/3 are used to create/change/display vendor master accounting data, and Transactions MK01/2/3 are used to create/change/display vendor master purchasing data. Message control, industry sector, the minority indicator (whether the vendor is a minority or owned by a minority), number range, and text IDs are all customized in Financial Accounting for the vendor master record. In SAP IMG • MATERIAL MANAGEMENT • PURCHASING • VENDOR MASTER (Transaction OLME), you can customize the terms of payment, INCO terms, vendor hierarchy, contact person, and so on. If you want customers who are also vendors to belong to particular customer account groups, you can define that here. As for customer master records, we advise creating vendor master records with reference to an existing vendor.

As with customer account groups, you create vendor account groups in the Financial Accounting module using Transaction OBD3 (menu path: SAP IMG • FINANCIAL ACCOUNTING (NEW) • ACCOUNTS RECEIVABLE AND ACCOUNTS PAYABLE • VENDOR ACCOUNTS • MASTER DATA • PREPARATIONS FOR CREATING VENDOR MASTER DATA • DEFINE ACCOUNT GROUPS WITH SCREEN LAYOUT (VENDORS)). You also decide the field statuses of different vendor master records here. As for the customer account group, you can customize field statuses to vary depending upon the company code and the transaction used.

Each vendor master record is created for a particular company code and a purchasing organization. As shown in Figure 2.42, the vendor master record has three major areas: General Data, Company Code Data, and Purchasing Organization Data. There are nine screens, as can be seen in Figure 2.42, which you access when you select the checkboxes and press [Enter]. We discuss each of these areas in the subsections below.

Figure 2.42 Vendor Master Record Screens

General Data

As for customer master records, the vendor master record General Data area consists of three screens that are used by both the accounting and purchasing departments. The *Address* screen stores address fields that are stored in Tables ADRC and ADR2/3/4/5, which are linked to the tables for vendor master data general data (e.g., Table LFA1) by the field address number (e.g., LFA1-ADRNR and ADRC-ADDRNUMBER). The Control screen is used to store various tax-related information, authorization objects that restrict users who can modify the master record, and customer numbers (if the vendor is also a customer). The Payment Transaction screen stores the vendor's bank details.

Company Code Data

The four screens of the Company Code Data area store, among other things, the reconciliation account for the vendor, payment terms, payment methods, and withholding tax details. The reconciliation account is a general ledger account for several vendors who are similar in nature; it is a balance sheet item. When employees are created as vendors in the Accounting Info screen, the personnel number field determines the employee for which this vendor master record is created.

Purchasing Organization Data

The purchasing department maintains this data. The ordering currency, terms of payment, INCO terms, schema applicable for the vendor (which is equivalent to the customer pricing procedure), minimum order value, account number for the organization in the sales department of the vendor (LFM1-EIKTO), shipping conditions, planned delivery time, and other vendors attached to the vendor master through partner functions are stored in the Purchasing Data screen. In the Partner Functions screen, different partner functions are attached to the vendor master record.

2.5.2 Employee Master Data

SAP ERP 6.0 allows you to create employee master records without implementing HR components. The tables of HR components are imported via the menu path SAP IMG • SALES AND DISTRIBUTION • MASTER DATA • BUSINESS PARTNERS • USE SALES EMPLOYEE WITHOUT HR. Employee master records are created/changed/displayed via Transactions VPE1/2/3 (menu path: SAP MENU • LOGISTICS • SALES AND

2.5 Overview of Other Master Data

DISTRIBUTION • MASTER DATA • BUSINESS PARTNERS • SALES PERSONNEL • CREATE / CHANGE / DISPLAY).

As shown in Figure 2.43, a minimum of six screens (or, as they are called in the HR components, *infotypes*) are filled for a particular employee.

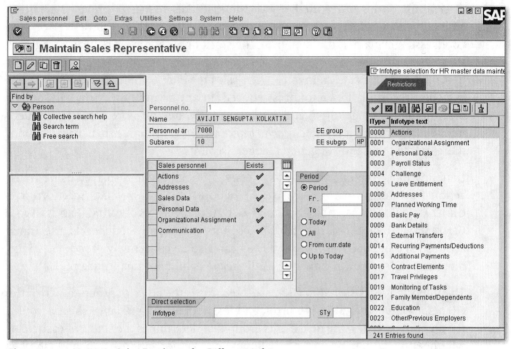

Figure 2.43 Maintain Sales Employee for Different Infotypes

The sales data maintained for sales employees includes the sales organization, sales office, sales group, and search term, as shown in Figure 2.44. The data is stored in Table PA0900.

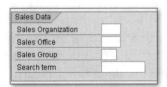

Figure 2.44 Sales Data in Employee Master Record

2.5.3 General Ledger Master Data

Much of what you do in your SAP system is eventually reflected in either a profit and loss statement or a balance sheet. For example, the creation of a standard sales order in Sales and Distribution has no direct impact on either the profit and loss statement or the balance sheet, but when you look at the complete process of creating a sales order (delivery of the materials requested, invoice creation, and payment receipt), each of the steps do. Similarly, when you deliver or post goods issue (explained in Chapter 6), the stock or inventory is reduced (a balance sheet item), and the cost of goods sold account increases (a profit and loss account item); when you create an invoice, your sales revenue account increases and your customer reconciliation account is reduced. In any accounting document, one or more accounts are credited, and, simultaneously, one or more accounts are debited. These accounts are called *general ledger accounts*. Even in a small organization, there can be thousands of general ledger accounts.

General ledger accounts are centrally created, modified, and displayed using Transaction FS00 (menu path: SAP MENU • ACCOUNTING • FINANCIAL ACCOUNTING • GENERAL LEDGER • MASTER RECORDS • G/L ACCOUNTS • INDIVIDUAL PROCESSING • CENTRALLY). To do this at the chart of accounts or company code levels, use Transactions FSP0 or FSS0, respectively. They can also be collectively processed. Maintenance of GL accounts, however, is the responsibility of finance team.

The important data stored in GL master records is the account group to which the GL belongs, whether a GL is a profit and loss statement or balance sheet account, the account currency, the field status group that determines the status of each field, whether only automatic posting is allowed, the authorization group, and whether a reconciliation account is for a customer, vendor, or asset.

2.5.4 User Master Data

Although user master data is the last thing we're discussing, it's the first thing you need to log on to an SAP system. Maintaining user master records is primarily a BASIS activity. It involves creating and maintaining user IDs via Transaction SU01. The user master record mainly stores the roles, profiles, and authorization-related data, but certain aspects can be maintained by the user, using Transaction SU3. The three things the user should maintain are contained in the *Address*, *Default*, and *Parameters* tabs, all of which we discuss below.

Address Tab

In the Address tab, the name, title, address, phone numbers, fax numbers, mobile numbers, email address, language, function, and department of the user are maintained.

Defaults Tab

In the Defaults tab, as shown in Figure 2.45, you can save your preference for the area menu with which your SAP system opens; Appendix C provides a list of area menus. Most of the area menus behave like transaction codes. You can save the logon language, decimal notation, and date format based on your own preferences. The Spool Control section indicates the name of the output device, whether output is to be issued immediately, and whether it is to be deleted after output. In the Personal Time Zone section, you can maintain a personal time zone in addition to the system time zone.

Figure 2.45 Default Tab

> **Area Menus**
>
> Area menus are alphanumeric strings (for example, VA00), just like transaction codes (for example, VA01). When executed, an area menu opens a new SAP menu and transaction list. In the Default tab (of the user master record), you can maintain area menus in the Start menu field, but not the transaction code.

Parameters Tab

In the Parameters tab, you can include several different parameter IDs with specific values in the Parameter value column. If the company code parameter ID (BUK) with a specific parameter value (e.g., 1000) is saved in a particular user profile, the Company Code field is always automatically filled with this default value (1000) for the user. You can save parameter IDs for many important organizational units and other fields in your own user master record using Transactions SU2 and SU3. This will save you a lot of time.

There are other uses for parameters as well. For example, the value of parameter ID SCL with possible values X or blank determines whether the text you type in a program will be uppercase or lowercase. Another parameter, MMPI_READ_NOTE, which takes a value in YYYYMMDD format, allows the user to use Transaction MMPI for initializing the MM period for the day mentioned in the YYYYMMDD format (for more details, refer to Appendix D). Finally, in the current version of SAP ERP, the Services for Object icon is, by default, not available in Transactions VA02 and VA03. This icon is used to attach Word, Excel, or PDF documents from your laptop or desktop to a particular SAP document. To make this icon available for Transactions VA02 and VA03, add parameter ID SD_SWU_ACTIVE with a value of X in the user master record. As you can see, parameter IDs and parameter values can be used for many diverse purposes and are very useful.

2.6 Summary

In this chapter, we discussed customer master data, customer credit master data, material master data (SD views), and batch management master data in detail. You got an overview of customer-material info records and foreign trade master data. We also offered a brief introduction to other types of master data, specifically, vendor master data, employee master data, general ledger master data, and user master data. Though we didn't discuss every field of the master data records, we'll introduce you to other fields we didn't discuss as they become relevant in subsequent chapters.

Thus far, we have dealt with static elements such as organizational structure and master data. Beginning with the next chapter, we'll discuss dynamic elements such as sales, deliveries, goods issues, billing, and more.

In this chapter, you'll learn about the different types of sales documents, including sales orders, outline agreements, and complaints. You'll discover how to optimize automatic determination of partners, free goods, material determination, and much more, and learn how to customize foreign trade processing and special business processes such as consignment sales, third-party sales, and others when necessary.

3 Sales

Sales is the process of exchanging of goods and services. In modern economies, this process is quite complex. Take, for example, the case of the last shirt you purchased from a store. It may have been manufactured in another country. The manufacturer may have used the design of an outside designer. The fabrics and threads used in it may have been from different manufacturers. The cotton used in them could have been from several growers. The cotton growers had probably purchased seeds and other inputs for their crops from different companies. The man-made fiber used for blending could be from different sources. So when you paid for your shirt, you paid for hundreds of goods and services that went into its making. Economies of scale, competitive advantage, and the division of labor have all made us produce very specific, specialized goods or services and consume a huge number of goods and services. It's also important to recognize that sales can happen between an individual and an organization, and vice versa. As an individual, you don't require an SAP ERP system to optimize your earnings and spending, but it makes sense for a large organization. For any organization, sales is the process of earning revenue that results in profit (or loss). It's important for the organization that the customers find it easy to order from them and they are able to *fulfill* the order. The *fulfillment* is matching the *specifications* of the customer requirement. When a customer makes a purchase order, he specifies his requirements. The purchase order of your customer is the sales order for you.

In this chapter, we'll primarily be discussing sales documents. We'll start with explaining the basic principle of sales document processing. From there, we'll discuss different sales order types. You'll learn how to customize item and schedule line categories and how to create a sales document with reference to another document. You'll also gain an understanding of the different tools available in SAP ERP. So, let's get started.

3.1 Principles of Processing Sales Documents

Customizing the sales process depends on the purchasing process that your customers follow. You also group your customers differently if there is significant difference in their purchasing processes. The Sales and Distribution functionality in SAP ERP is necessary if sales processes are complex, for example, if you want the system to:

- Check availability and transfer the requirement for production planning
- Evaluate and block certain orders based on credit worthiness assessment
- Pick the oldest batch for delivery
- Print the order confirmation automatically when it's complete
- Automatically post the elements of the invoice value (e.g., freight) to the correct GL

A typical sales process starts with a customer making an *inquiry* and *request of quotation* (RFQ), which are nonobligatory in nature. Your response is voluntary. If you do submit a quotation, your customer may decide to buy from you, in which case they would issue a purchase order that is either based on the quotation or an agreement or contract. So, the content of a quotation can be legally binding for you. A purchase order issued by your customer is recorded as a sales order in your system. The order is processed according the details mentioned in it. Once the goods and services are delivered to the customer, you create an invoice based on the terms and conditions detailed in the sales order. The customer, upon receiving the invoice, verifies it and makes the payment. During invoice verification, the customer may find your goods or services deficient compared to their purchase order and request a sales return or credit memo. For sales returns, you take back the material (or part of it) supplied and issue a credit memo. For a credit memo request, no physical return of material is involved, and the customer issues the credit memo. In certain cases, the invoice price may be, by mistake, less than the price agreed upon by you and your customer, and you have to issue debit note. The debit note is similar to an invoice from a financial accounting point of view.

In the SAP system, there are several types of sales documents. All sales documents have a header level and an item level, and certain types of sales documents have a schedule line if physical movement is involved. Normally, the documents that are referred to as sales documents are:

- Presales documents (e.g., inquiry and quotation)
- Sales orders (e.g., order, cash sale, and rush order)
- Outline agreements(e.g., value contract and scheduling agreement)
- Complaints (e.g., credit memo request, debit memo request, and return)

Now that you understand sales documents in general, let's move on to the different types.

3.2 Sales Document Types

Several standard sales document types come preconfigured in SAP ERP. You can create your own document types using Transaction VOV8 or by going to SAP IMG • SALES AND DISTRIBUTION • SALES • SALES DOCUMENTS • SALES DOCUMENT HEADER • DEFINE SALES DOCUMENT TYPES. This is essentially configuring the header level of the sales document. Transaction VOV8 is very important and has been divided into nine figures, Figures 3.2 to 3.4 and Figures 3.6 to 3.11 help highlight the important features of this screen.

As you can see in Figure 3.2, every sales order type must be assigned to a sales document category, listed in Table 3.1. If the Sales Document Block is selected, it will prevent the user from accidentally using the order types that are not required or are outdated. It's also possible to only allow automatic creation by choosing A: Only Automatic Creation Allowed. This field can be maintained in the initial screen of Transaction VOV8, as shown in Figure 3.1.

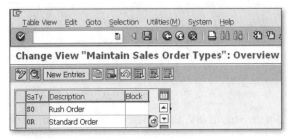

Figure 3.1 Sales Order Types

> **Note**
>
> You should block the standard SAP order types and the customized order types that aren't in use rather than deleting or modifying them for new requirements.

Table 3.1 lists the SD Document Categories that appear in the Transaction VOV8 screen and their descriptions.

Code	SD Document Category
A	Inquiry
B	Quotation
C	Order
D	Item proposal
E	Scheduling agreement
F	Scheduling agreement with external service
G	Contract
H	Returns
I	Order w/o charge
K	Credit memo request
L	Debit memo request
W	Independent reqts plan
0	Master contract

Table 3.1 List of SD Document Categories

To create a customized sales order by copying the standard order (OR), the first step is to give it a name starting with Y or Z and a description. The SD Document Category field can take a value, as listed in Table 3.2. The Sales Document Block indicator can take a value of X or A. When blank, the document type is not blocked for use. The value X indicates that the document type cannot be used for creating any new order. The value A means this type of document will only be created automatically.

The numbering object for sales documents is BV_BELEG. The number range for internal assignment is 01 (000000001 to 599999999), which means that if you save a document without an external document number, it will take the next available number in the above number range. The number range for an external assignment is 02 (6000000 to 99999999), meaning you're allowed to pick any available number from this range for a new document. The item number increment will determine how the items are numbered. If the value is 10, as shown in Figure 3.2, the items will be numbered as 10, 20, 30, and so on. The subitem increment will determine how the subitems are numbered (e.g., BoM).

Several order types can have the same number range. Often separate number ranges are required for one order type, depending on the sales office or sales group. This is not possible in the standard SAP system. You can achieve this by adding new number ranges in the RV_BELEG numbering object, creating a z-table that will determine the number range to be selected for each situation. Then you can write your code in Transaction SE38, using the form USEREXIT_NUMBER_ RANGE of the include program MV45AFZZ. We'll discuss this further in Chapter 7. For a different sales office, sales group, or customer account group, you may require different number ranges even when the order type is the same. You can have different a number range for orders belonging to different sales offices even when the sales order type is not different.

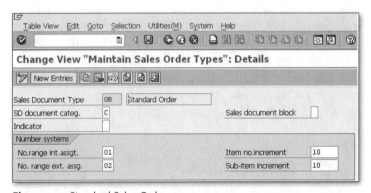

Figure 3.2 Standard Sales Order

In general, in the General Control section, as shown in Figure 3.3, the Reference Mandatory field is left blank to make the reference to other sales documents such as quotation, inquiry, or invoice optional.

> **Note**
>
> In certain types of sales document, such as the sales return or request for credit or debit memo, we recommend making reference mandatory. Often the order types that aren't mandatory for the reference are in the system at the time of go-live because the reference to legacy invoices isn't possible or recommended. Generally, these types are not blocked subsequently.

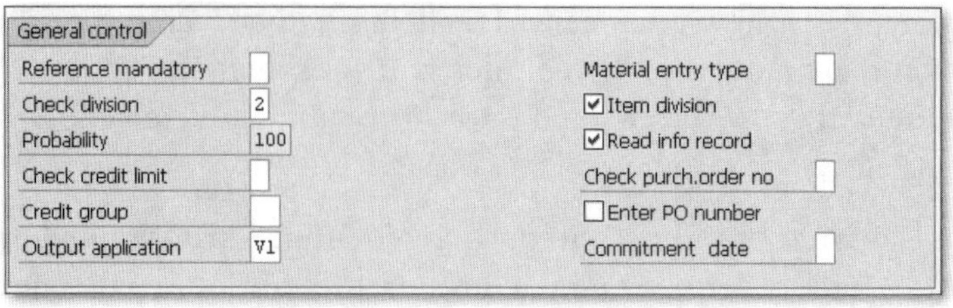

3 | Sales

General control			
Reference mandatory		Material entry type	
Check division	2	☑ Item division	
Probability	100	☑ Read info record	
Check credit limit		Check purch.order no	
Credit group		☐ Enter PO number	
Output application	V1	Commitment date	

Figure 3.3 Standard Sales Order (General Control)

When the Check Division field is left blank, the system will not check whether the division of the sales document header and the items are the same. When Item Division is selected, the division of the material recorded in the material master record is copied to the sales document. If the Check Purchase Order No checkbox is selected, the system will display an error (or information) message when there is already a sales order with same purchase order number from the same customer.

The fields in the Transaction Flow group (shown in Figure 3.4) determine how the different screens in Transactions VA01, VA02, and VA03 behave. Screen Sequence Grp. determines the screens for the document header and item that will appear while creating, changing, and displaying it and the sequence in which they appear. To modify the screens and sequence, you can create a screen and transaction variant using Transaction SHD0. The transaction variant will be applicable to the particular document type only if it is entered in the Variant field shown in Figure 3.4. The Document Pricing Procedure (Doc. Pric. Procedure) field is used to determine pricing procedure.

> **Note**
>
> The incompletion procedure assigned to document type is in disabled mode because it's not assigned here. We'll discuss this later in this chapter.

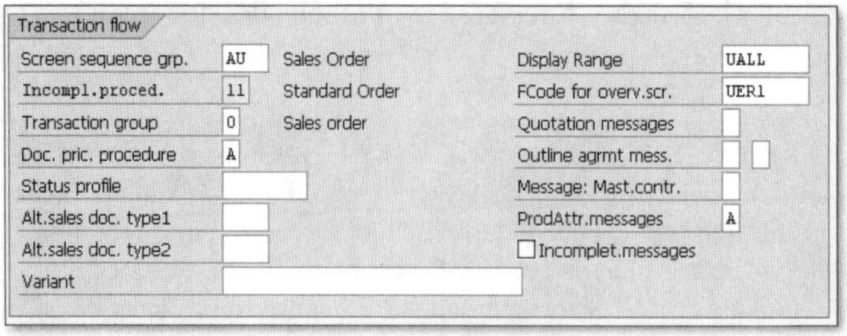

Transaction flow					
Screen sequence grp.	AU	Sales Order	Display Range	UALL	
Incompl.proced.	11	Standard Order	FCode for overv.scr.	UER1	
Transaction group	0	Sales order	Quotation messages		
Doc. pric. procedure	A		Outline agrmt mess.		
Status profile			Message: Mast.contr.		
Alt.sales doc. type1			ProdAttr.messages	A	
Alt.sales doc. type2			☐ Incomplet.messages		
Variant					

Figure 3.4 Standard Sales Order (Transaction Flow)

Alternate Sales Document types 1 and 2 are used to change the documents created using one document type to another. Suppose there are two document types, YOR and ZOR, and the document created using one document should be changed to the other type. Then you maintain both as the alternate sales document type for each other. That is, you maintain ZOR in the Alt.sales. Doc. Type1 field for YOR and maintain YOR in the Alt.sales. Doc. Type1 field in the customization of the ZOR document type (in Transaction VOV8). If alternate sales document types are maintained then, as you can see in Figure 3.5, the alternate document type will appear as a radio button in the Sales tab of the Sales Overview, allowing you to change the document type and save the document using Transaction VA02. This functionality can be used when you don't know the exact document type until the order is saved. For example, your order type depends on the plant from where you will supply the material.

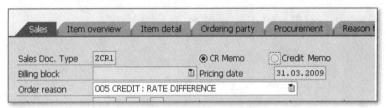

Figure 3.5 Alternate Sales Document Type in Sales Tab in Transaction VA02

The Quotation Messages field is used to check and copy the open quotation to the sales order. Outline Agreement Message is used to check open contracts and make them available for copying to the sales document. The Message: Master Contract field is used to check and copy the master contract data to the contract. Product Attribute Messages checks the product attributes of only the manually entered items. For the product attributes not acceptable to the ship-to party an error or warning message can be issued. If the Incomplete Message checkbox is selected, it will not allow a document of this type to be saved if it's incomplete.

The fields shown in Figure 3.6 are used for the document types of document category E (Scheduling Agreements). The usage indicator (Use) field is customized via Transaction OVA4 or by following the menu path SAP IMG • SALES AND DISTRIBUTION • SALES • SALES DOCUMENTS • SALES DOCUMENT HEADER • DEFINE USAGE INDICATORS. The Delivery Block set will automatically apply to the scheduling agreements created using this document type. In the Corr.delivery Type field, you specify the delivery type that will be used for this purpose. The MRP for DlvSchType field defines whether forecast delivery schedules or just-in-time (JIT) delivery schedules (of the scheduling agreement) are relevant for material requirements planning (MRP) and/or delivery. JIT is a concept where the buyer gets the material just when he requires it and doesn't have to stock it for long time.

```
Scheduling agreement
Corr.delivery type      [    ]           Delivery block      [    ]
Use                     [    ]
MRP for DlvSchType      [    ]
```

Figure 3.6 Standard Sales Order (Scheduling Agreement)

Figure 3.7 illustrates the Shipping group, which determines the delivery type that processes the sales document type. The Immediate Delivery indicator allows you to automatically create delivery as soon as the order is saved, as for cash sales (BV) or Rush Orders. The Delivery Block and Shipping Conditions values specified here become the default values for all documents of this type. The shipping condition overwrites the value that flows from the customer master record.

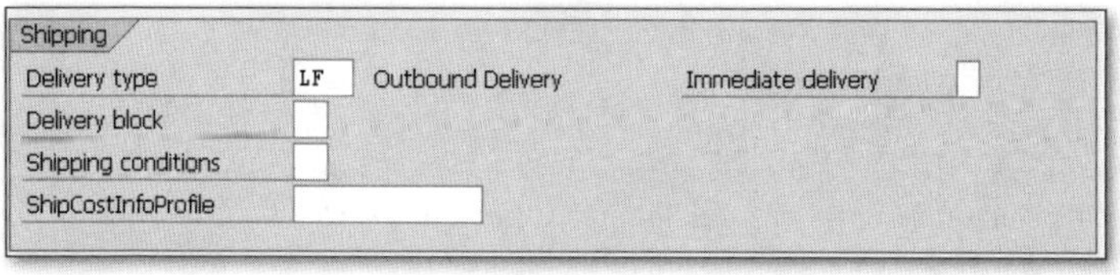

```
Shipping
Delivery type        [LF]  Outbound Delivery     Immediate delivery  [ ]
Delivery block       [  ]
Shipping conditions  [  ]
ShipCostInfoProfile  [  ]
```

Figure 3.7 Standard Sales Order (Shipping)

Figure 3.8 illustrates the billing group, which determines the billing document type that will process the sales document for delivery-related billing, order-related billing, or intercompany billing. If the Billing Block field is not blank, its content will automatically move to all orders of this type, and those orders will be blocked for billing. For example, you may want to automatically block (for billing) all credit memo requests when they're created. The block is to be removed by an approving authority before the credit memo is issued.

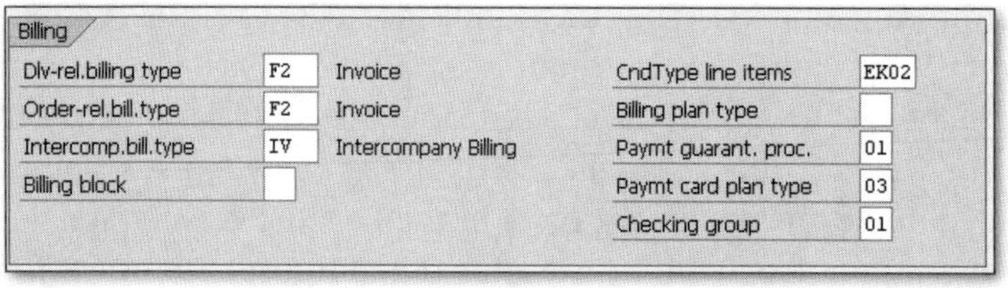

```
Billing
Dlv-rel.billing type  [F2]  Invoice              CndType line items    [EK02]
Order-rel.bill.type   [F2]  Invoice              Billing plan type     [    ]
Intercomp.bill.type   [IV]  Intercompany Billing Paymt guarant. proc.  [01]
Billing block         [  ]                       Paymt card plan type  [03]
                                                 Checking group        [01]
```

Figure 3.8 Standard Sales Order (Billing)

In the CndType Line Items field, you enter the cost condition type (e.g., EK01, EK02) that will determine the cost of the items in a make-to-order scenario. Condition type EK01 transfers the actual production cost of the controlling functionality, including different overheads, to order as price. Condition type EK02 does the same but is statistical, and the actual price is compared to it for determining the profit margin. For further details, refer to SAP Note 155212. In the Billing plan, you can specify whether the periodic or milestone type of billing plan is to be used. We'll discuss this in Chapter 7. The Paymt Guarant. Proc., Paymt Card Plan Type, and Checking Group fields will be discussed in Chapter 5.

When there's a value in the Lead Time in Days field (see Figure 3.9), the system adds that value to current date (also referred to as system date, SYDATUM field) to propose the requested delivery date. You have the option of specifying the date type (1 – day, 2 – week, 3 – month, 4 – posting period, and 5 – planning calendar period) for the schedule line that's created for a particular document type. The Proposed Pricing Date (options are blank – System date, A – requested delivery date, B – valid from date, and C – contract start date) is the modifiable default value for automatic pricing determination. The Proposed Valid-From date (options are blank – no proposal, A – system date, B – beginning of next month) becomes the default valid-from date (which can be changed) when you create a document of this document type. The Proposed Delivery Date and Proposed PO Date checkboxes, when selected, propose the current date as the delivery date and PO date, respectively.

Figure 3.9 Standard Sales Order (Dates)

We'll discuss these fields under Contract group, shown in Figure 3.10, in Section 3.8, Outline Agreements.

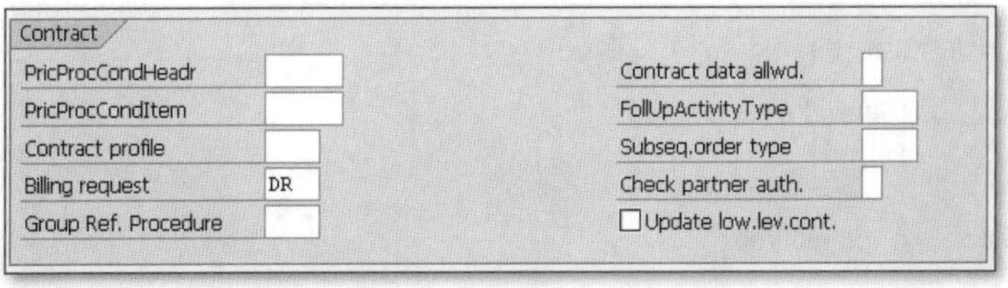

Figure 3.10 Standard Sales Order (Contract)

The Business Transaction field, shown in Figure 3.11, is selected if the SAP APO system is to be used for availability checks. Refer to the text box in Section 3.7 for more information.

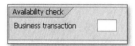

Figure 3.11 Standard Sales Order (Availability Check)

In addition to defining the sales document type, which we just discussed, you have to assign different sales areas to it. When a sales area (combination of sales organization, distribution channel, and division) is assigned to an order type, other sales areas cannot use the order. The assignment is not required for the sales document types, which are valid for all sales area. The assignment is made via Transaction OVAZ or by going to SALES AND DISTRIBUTION • SALES • SALES DOCUMENTS • SALES DOCUMENT HEADER • ASSIGN SALES AREA TO SALES DOCUMENT TYPES.

Another important step is to define the order reason. This is important for reporting and sometimes pricing purposes. It's done via Transaction OVAU (SAP IMG • SALES AND DISTRIBUTION • SALES • SALES DOCUMENTS • SALES DOCUMENT HEADER • DEFINE ORDER REASONS). Each reason is an alphanumeric key with a description.

In Table 3.2, we have listed important standard sales document types. We have also provided the subsequent standard document types used for delivery and billing. A close look at the table can reveal a lot of information. For example, an inquiry can be neither delivered nor invoiced, whereas you can create a pro forma invoice ([F5]) with reference to a quotation.

Sales Document Type		Del type	Billing Type		
			Dlv	Ord	Inter-Co
IN	Inquiry				
QT	Quotation			F5	
B1	Rebate credit memo request			B1	
B2	Rebate correction request			B2	
B3	Part rebate settlement request			B3	
B4	Rebate request for manual accruals			B4	
BV	Cash sale		BV	BV	IV

Table 3.2 Important Sales Document Types

Sales Document Type		Del type	Billing Type		
			Dlv	Ord	Inter-Co
CR	Credit memo request			G2	
GK	Master contract				
KA	Consignment pick-up	LR			
KB	Consignment fill-up	LF			
KE	Consignment issue	LF	F2	F2	IV
FD	Delivery free of charge	LF			
CQ	Quantity contract				
SD	Subsequent delivery free of charge	LF			
KR	Consignment returns	LR		RE	
DR	Debit memo request			L2	IV
PV	Item proposal				
RE	Returns	LR	RE	RE	IG
RK	Invoice correction request			G2	
RZ	Returns scheduling agreement	LR	F2	RE	
SO	Rush order	LF	F2	F2	IV
OR	Standard order	LF	F2	F2	IV

Table 3.2 Important Sales Document Types (Cont.)

3.3 Item Categories and Schedule Line Categories

A sales document is divided into two or three levels. At the header level, you specify who the sold-to-party is for the order or the sales office processing the order. The order type controls how the document will behave with respect to a credit check or the subsequent document type of delivery or invoice that can process it. In addition to the header level, all sales documents have an item level. This level determines whether the item is relevant for delivery (or billing). Item categories control the behavior at the item level. An item category, for example, may automatically generate a purchase order for that item. The schedule lines are not present in all types of order. For example, credit memo requests do not have schedule lines. Schedule line categories control the behavior of schedule lines. Typically, a schedule line shows when the item is scheduled for delivery based on an availability check. Schedule lines also transfer the stock requirement to production planning.

In the following two sections, we will discuss how to customize item categories and schedule line categories.

3.3.1 Item Categories

The steps for customizing item categories are given below.

1. The basic step is defining the item category using Transaction VOV7 or by going to SAP IMG • SALES AND DISTRIBUTION • SALES • SALES DOCUMENTS • SALES DOCUMENT ITEM • DEFINE ITEM CATEGORIES. The fields that you'll need to define for customizing an item category are shown in Figure 3.12.

2. Item category group is a key field that determines the material type (e.g., raw material, finished goods, trading goods, and so on). It determines the item category for a material at the item level. All of the materials that are to have the same item category at the item level should also have the same item category group in their material master records. Item categories groups are defined via Transaction OVAW or the menu path SALES AND DISTRIBUTION • SALES • SALES DOCUMENTS • SALES DOCUMENT ITEM • DEFINE ITEM CATEGORY GROUPS. The item category group is assigned to a material using material master record.

3. You assign item category groups to different material types using Transaction VOVA or by going to SALES AND DISTRIBUTION • SALES • SALES DOCUMENTS • SALES DOCUMENT ITEM • DEFINE DEFAULT VALUES FOR MATERIAL TYPE. All of the materials created in the particular material type will have the default item category group in their material master records, which can subsequently modified.

4. Item category usage is an additional field used to determine the default value of an item. Normally, a new entry is not required, but if it is required you can add it using Transaction OVVW or by going to SAP IMG • SALES AND DISTRIBUTION • SALES • SALES DOCUMENTS • SALES DOCUMENT ITEM • DEFINE ITEM CATEGORY USAGE. This indicator is stored in the customer material info records for a specific combination of material and customer if you want it to be used in the item category determination.

5. The item category in a sales document is determined by the sales document type, the item category group, the item category of the higher-level item, and the item category usage. The default values for all possible combinations are maintained in Transaction VOV4 (menu path: SAP IMG • SALES AND DISTRIBUTION •

3.3 Item Categories and Schedule Line Categories

SALES • SALES DOCUMENTS • SALES DOCUMENT ITEM • ASSIGN ITEM CATEGORIES). The higher-level item plays a role in determining the item category of subitems, for example, when you use a bill of materials (BoM) or free goods.

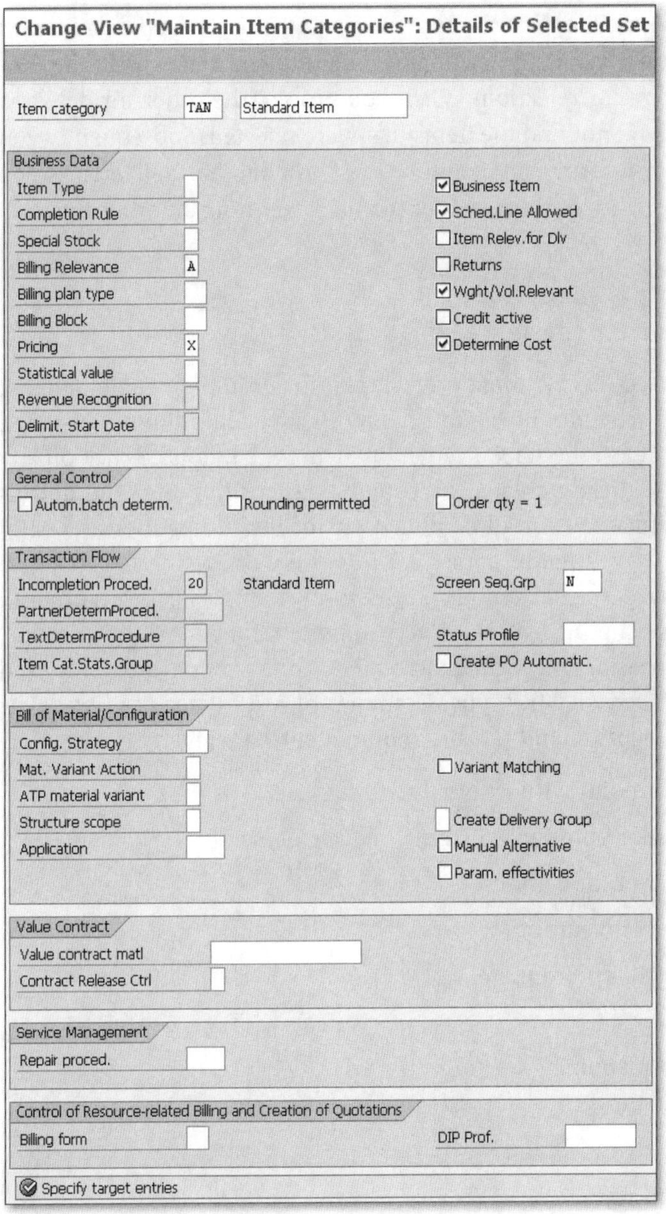

Change View "Maintain Item Categories": Details of Selected Set

Item category: TAN — Standard Item

Business Data
- Item Type:
- Completion Rule:
- Special Stock:
- Billing Relevance: A
- Billing plan type:
- Billing Block:
- Pricing: X
- Statistical value:
- Revenue Recognition:
- Delimit. Start Date:
- ☑ Business Item
- ☑ Sched.Line Allowed
- ☐ Item Relev.for Dlv
- ☐ Returns
- ☑ Wght/Vol.Relevant
- ☐ Credit active
- ☑ Determine Cost

General Control
- ☐ Autom.batch determ.
- ☐ Rounding permitted
- ☐ Order qty = 1

Transaction Flow
- Incompletion Proced.: 20 Standard Item
- PartnerDetermProced.:
- TextDetermProcedure:
- Item Cat.Stats.Group:
- Screen Seq.Grp: N
- Status Profile:
- ☐ Create PO Automatic.

Bill of Material/Configuration
- Config. Strategy:
- Mat. Variant Action:
- ATP material variant:
- Structure scope:
- Application:
- ☐ Variant Matching
- ☐ Create Delivery Group
- ☐ Manual Alternative
- ☐ Param. effectivities

Value Contract
- Value contract matl:
- Contract Release Ctrl:

Service Management
- Repair proced.:

Control of Resource-related Billing and Creation of Quotations
- Billing form:
- DIP Prof.:

☑ Specify target entries

Figure 3.12 Define Item Category

6. Reasons for rejecting an item are created using Transaction OVAG (menu path: SAP IMG • SALES AND DISTRIBUTION • SALES • SALES DOCUMENTS • SALES DOCUMENT ITEM • DEFINE REASONS FOR REJECTION). While processing a sales document, you may have to reject some items and continue to process others. For example, a customer may request to supply some immediately and delay others for a month. So those that are to be supplied later are rejected, using –the Customer Request reason for rejection. When you process the order for delivery, in the delivery you will not find the items that were rejected. Subsequently you can remove the reason for rejection and process it in another delivery. As you can see, this functionality can be used for manually splitting an order into two or more deliveries.

3.3.2 Schedule Line Categories

In addition to the item category, some order types (for example, where delivery is involved) can have schedule lines. You define the schedule line types using Transaction VOV6. To reach the screen shown in Figure 3.13, double-click on any schedule line category already created by copying an existing one. The default schedule lines are maintained for all combinations of item categories and MRP type via Transaction VOV5 (menu path: SAP IMG • SALES AND DISTRIBUTION • SALES • SALES DOCUMENTS • SCHEDULE LINES • ASSIGN SCHEDULE LINE CATEGORIES). Material requirements planning (MRP) is a very important functionality in production planning and purchasing. All of the requirements for a material are transferred to this functionality based on MRP type. Examples of MRP types used to determine schedule line categories (and transfer requirements) are given below:

- V1 – manual reorder point with external requirements
- V2 – automatic reorder point with external requirements
- VB – manual reorder point planning
- VI – vendor managed inventory
- VM – automatic reorder point planning
- VS – seasonal MRP
- VV – forecast-based planning
- ND – no planning

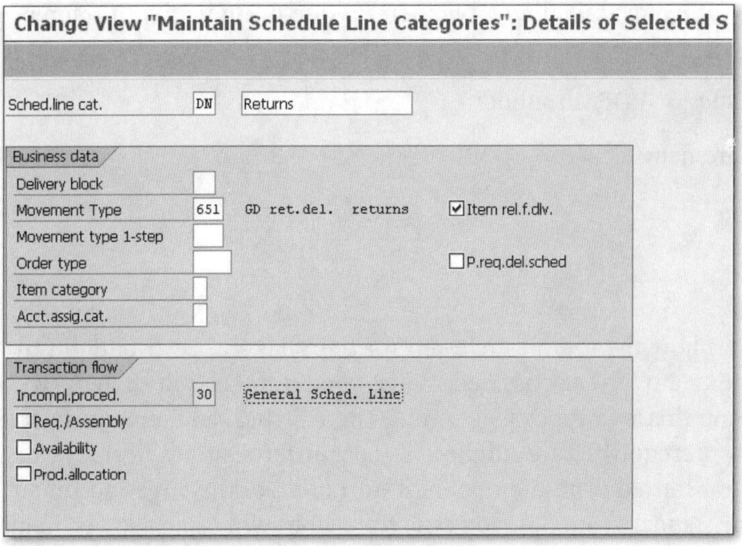

Figure 3.13 Define Schedule Line Category

> **Note**
>
> When assigning item categories and schedule line categories, you have the option of maintaining one default value. Eleven and nine other values can be maintained for item categories and schedule line categories, respectively, for possible manual entry at the time of document processing. In the Configuration overview screen only three are visible. Double-click on the particular row to define more than three manual values if required.

Now that you have a thorough understanding of item and schedule line categories, let's move on to creating a sales document with a reference.

3.4 Create with Reference

You can create a sales document with reference to another document. You put less effort and expect less error when you do this. That is optimization. Common examples are sales orders created with reference to a quotation and credit or debit memo requests created with reference to a billing document. This process reduces the redundancy of data entry and error in data entry. You can also add a validation or check, decide which data should be copied, and manipulate data. These functions are achieved through VOFM routines. SAP ERP offers several routines, which are ABAP programs called when you create one document with reference to another.

There are four types or VOFM routines:

- Copying requirements
- Data transfer
- Requirements
- Formulas

Figure 3.14 shows how the routines relevant for the Sales and Distribution functionality in SAP ERP are further classified. When you create sales documents with reference, only the first two types play a role. The copying requirement routine checks if certain prerequisites are fulfilled. Data transfer routines decide which data should be transferred from the reference document to the target document. In addition to the standard routines, you can create your own using allowed name spaces 600 to 999 for your specific requirement. You should not modify the standard routines. The standard routines are used in several situations in SAP ERP that you may not know about. Modifying them may solve your problem in one process but create trouble in another.

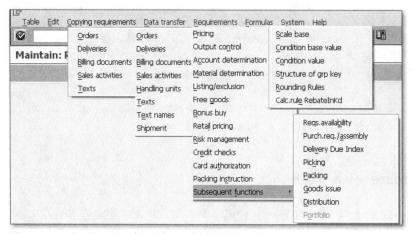

Figure 3.14 Routines Used in Sales and Distribution Processes

There are five types of copying requirements, as shown in Figure 3.14. They are:

- Orders copying requirements routines
- Deliveries copying requirements routines

3.4 Create with Reference

- Billing documents copying requirements routines
- Sales activities copying requirements routines (No standard routine is available, but you can create your own.)
- Texts copying requirements routines

The first four types of routines are executed before the creation of order, delivery, invoice, or sales activity, respectively. The texts copying requirement routine is checked to determine if text will be transferred from the reference to the target document. Table 3.3 lists the different standard order copying requirement routines and what they check for in creating the target document.

Order Copying Requirement	Checks
1 (header – same customer)	Sold-to and sales areas are same in target and reference document.
2 (header – different customer)	Sold-to can differ but sales areas are same for target and reference document.
21 (billing header)	Same sold-to, sales area, and currency. Valid header division in the reference billing document.
301 (item rejection reason)	Rejected items are not copied.
302 (do not copy item)	Item categories with this routine assigned are not copied to target document.
303 (always an item)	Item categories with this routine assigned are always copied to target document.
304 (rejection reason only)	Only the rejected items are copied.
501 (schedule qyt > 0)	Only the schedule lines with some quantity are copied.
502 (do not copy schedule line)	Schedule lines are not copied.

Table 3.3 List of Order Copying Requirement Routines

Your requirement can be the same as the order copying requirement 1 (header – same customer), the first entry in Table 3.3, but with some additional requirement. For example, in addition to sold-to party and sales area, you may want the ship-to party of both the target and source documents to be the same. You can create a new routine 601 by copying the ABAP code in routine 1 and adding your requirements to it. After activating the new program, you can assign it to the copy rules for some document types.

There are three types of delivery copy requirement routines. The first type checks the reference sales document, and includes the standard routines 1, 2, 3, 101, and 102. The second type determines if several reference documents can be combined into one delivery, and includes routines 51 and 151. The third type validates the manual addition of items into an existing delivery, and includes routines 201 and 202.

You can create a billing document with reference to an order, delivery, billing (such as invoice cancellation), or external EDI document. There are therefore four types of billing copy requirement routines. The first group (which includes 1, 2, 7, 8, 12, 20, 21, 23, 26, and 28) validates the reference order document. The second type checks the reference order document (including 3, 4, 9, 10, 11, 14, 15, 18, 19, and 24). The third type checks the reference billing document (including 5, 6, 16, 17, 27, and 29). The fourth type checks the external EDI document (13, 22, and 25).

The text copy requirement routine 1 (which references the document header) checks if the reference document header has a text entry. If it finds a text entry, this can be copied to the target document. Text copy requirement routine 50 (reference document item) does the same for items.

The copying requirements routines only check if the target document can be created from the source document. The data transfer routines do the actual data transfer. These routines can transfer data to targets from the source document or from customization with or without manipulation. The different types of these routines include orders, deliveries, billing documents, sales activities, handling units, texts, text names, and shipments.

When an order is created with reference to another sales or billing document or contract or billing plan, the order data transfer routines can be used for data transfer. For example, data transfer routines for transferring data from a bill to an order (e.g., with reference return) are 3, 4, 52, 53, 103, 104, 153, and 403.

The delivery data transfer routines transfer data from the reference document to the delivery. The routines delivered by SAP ERP are 1, 2, 3, 101, 102, 110, 201, 202, 301, 302, 303, 500, and 510.

Billing transfer routines, on the other hand, transfer data from the reference document to the billing document. The billing data transfer routines delivered by SAP ERP include 1, 2, 3, 5, 6, 7, 8, and 10. The sales activity data transfer routines transfer data from a reference sales document to a sales activity. The SAP ERP–delivered standard routines are 1 and 2. The handling unit data transfer routines play it's a role when a delivery is created with reference to a scheduling agreement. The standard routine is 1.

Text data transfer routines transfer text when you create one document with reference to another. Standard texts are automatically copied from the reference to the target document, and don't require these data transfer routines, which are only used for the user-defined routines.

Text name data transfer routines 1 to 11 are not used for data transfer. They are hard-coded in different programs and determine how the texts are stored in different tables, such as Tables STXH and STXL.

Shipment data transfer routines 1 to 12 transfer data from the delivery to the shipment.

In the post-implementation phase, the process improvement often requires the replacement of these routines, sometimes with customized routines. In the next section, we'll look at few places where these routines are assigned.

3.5 Copy Control

Copy control is one of the few tools in the Sales and Distribution functionality in SAP ERP that is revisited often in the post-implementation phase. During the implementation phase, it's very difficult to visualize the finer details of the copy control rules. Also, companies change (or improve) their business processes, which may also require changes in copy control rules, for example:

- Whether the invoice will have the same price as the order or whether it will recalculate the price
- Whether one sales return document contains items delivered from a different plant
- Whether the manual addition of a line item in a delivery is allowed

As you know, an order can be created with reference to another sales document (order, quotation, inquiry) or billing document. When one sales document is created with reference to another sales document, the copy control rules are defined via Transaction VTAA. Similarly, when a sales document is created with reference to a billing document, the copy control rules are defined via Transaction VTAF. Table 3.4 provides a complete list of the copy control transaction codes and the corresponding target and source documents.

107

Transaction	Target Document	Source Document
VTAA	Sales (A)	Sales (A)
VTAF	Sales (A)	Billing document (F)
VTLA	Delivery document (L)	Sales (A)
VTFA	Billing document (F)	Sales (A)
VTFL	Billing document (F)	Delivery document (L)
VTFF	Billing document (F)	Billing document (F)

Table 3.4 List of Copy Control Transactions

To create any order document type with reference to another order document type, you must maintain the copy control rules using Transaction VTAA. In this example, we're creating the document type OR (standard order) with reference to document type QT (quotation). Observe the data transfer (DataT) and copying requirement routines in Figures 3.15, 3.16, and 3.17. As mentioned earlier, you can have your customized routines replace these standard routines.

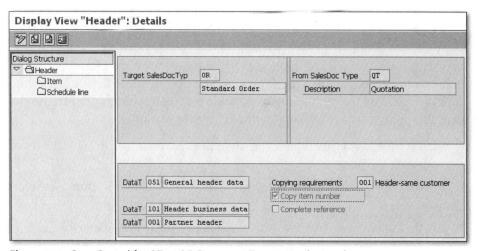

Figure 3.15 Copy Control for QT to OR Document Type at Header Level

At the header level of copy control (see Figure 3.15), the Copy Item Number checkbox copies the item number of the source document to the item number of the target document. When the Complete Reference checkbox is selected, you cannot delete items copied from the source document in the target document.

Once you've defined the copy control rules at the header level, you have to define the copy control rule for all applicable item categories. In this example, item category AGN (standard item in quotation) is shown in Figure 3.16. The FPLA field is simply a field for the copy requirement routine that checks whether certain requirements have been fulfilled when data is transferred from the Billing Plan field. Apart from the data transfer and copy requirement routines, the following fields are defined:

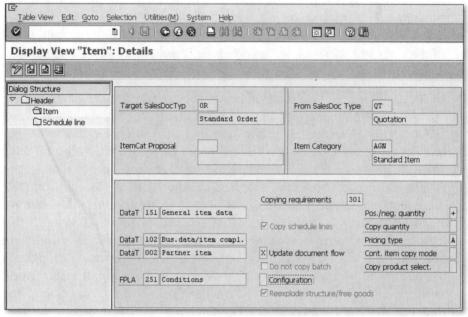

Figure 3.16 Copy Control for QT to OR Document Type and AGN Item

- The Copy Schedule Lines field is selected when the schedule lines are to be copied.
- The Pos./Neg. Quantity field is left blank (or option 0) when the quantity field in the target document will have neither a positive (option +) nor negative (option –) effect on the source document, for example a pro forma invoice created with reference to a delivery. If the target document reduces the available quantity for another source document, the effect is called positive. When the target document quantity increases the available quantity in the source document for other target documents, the effect is called negative. For example, if you have a quantity contract for 100 units, a sales order created for 20 units will

reduce the available quantity in the contract for other order to 80 units (positive effect), and a return of 10 units will increase it to 90 units from 80 unit (negative effect).

- Even when the Copy Quantity field is left blank, the system will still copy the quantity based on the routines used. So we recommend leaving it blank.

- The Pricing Type field determines the pricing in the target document. Table 3.5 lists the possible pricing types are listed. For example, pricing type G keeps the value of all of the condition types the same in the target document as it was in the source document, except for the tax. The condition types that are defined as tax are redetermined. If there is a change in condition records, then the value of the condition type automatically changes when the target document is created.

- The Update Document Flow field updates the FBVA table. Document flow is the link that connects the target and source documents. The information is stored in Table VBFA. The document flow icon, available in orders, deliveries, and invoices (application tool bar), can be used for displaying the document flow. There is a header-level document flow, and for each item, item level document flow may also exist. If the document flow is required, then select option X. If it is not required, simply leave the field blank. To create document flow records, except for delivery and goods issue and billing documents, select option 2. This option improves the system performance, and unlike the standard document flow that tracks all of the documents linked to a billing, delivery, or goods issue (GI) document, here you have to track the document flow from the target to the source document where the target is a billing, delivery, or GI document, and track the source of the sales order. The source can be a quotation or a contract. So, you avoid the redundant link between the quotation or contract and the billing or delivery document.

- If the Do Not Copy Batch checkbox is selected, the items are copied without batches.

- The Configuration field can be blank (no particular control), A (copy configuration/do not fix), B (copy/fix configuration), or C (copy configuration/automatically fixed). If the configuration is fixed, then the bill of materials for the item does not re-explode.

- The Reexplode Structure/Free Goods checkbox, when selected, reexplodes the bill of materials or free goods structure in the target document.

- The Cont. Item Copy Mode indicator is used when the source document is a value contract.
- The Copy Product Select. indicator determines if product selection should be redone in the target document or copied. Again, if you're in the target document, you can cancel the copied product selection.

Pricing Type	Description
A	Copy price components and redetermine scales
B	Carry out new pricing
C	Copy manual pricing elements and redetermine the others
D	Copy pricing elements unchanged
E	Adopt price components and fix values
F	Copy pricing elements, turn value and fix
G	Copy pricing elements unchanged and redetermine taxes
H	Redetermine freight conditions
I	Redetermine rebate conditions
J	Redetermine confirmed purch. net price / value (KNTYP=d)
K	Adopt price components and cose. Redetermine taxes
M	Copy pricing elements, turn value
N	Transfer pricing components unchanged, new cost
O	Redetermine variant conditions (KNTYP=O)
Q	Redetermine calculation conditions (KNTYP=Q)
U	Redetermine precious metal conditions (KNTYP=U)

Table 3.5 Examples of Pricing Types

Finally, as shown in Figure 3.17, you can customize copy control rules for the schedule line. In this case, we have shown the schedule line category BP. The Proposed Schedule Line Category (SchdLneCatProposal) field is left blank so that it will take a value as per the configuration setting. Copy requirement 501 means only the schedule lines with some quantity will be copied to the source document.

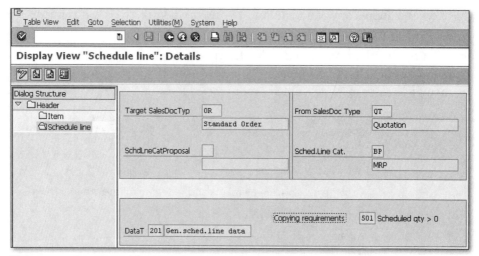

Figure 3.17 Copy Control for QT to OR Document Type and BP Schedule Line

We discussed the copy control transaction VTAA (there are five other transactions) for copy control from quotation (QT) to standard order (OR). There are usually several source documents and several target documents for item category AGN (again, several item-level categories are possible). The copy control for schedule line level is only relevant when the target document is an order (i.e., Transactions VTAA and VTAF). At all levels there are data transfer and copying requirement routines that can be standard or customized and that fine-tune the system. We also discussed the data transfer and copying requirement routines in Section 3.4, and now you know where to assign them in configuration. This is the most important activity in projects at the post-implementation stage. We are not going into details of the ABAP code of the standard routines and how you can insert your own code because that is a subject for technical developers. In the next section we'll discuss the partner determination functionality that SAP ERP offers.

3.6 Partner Determination

In Sales and Distribution documents, you can configure the system to automatically determine partners. The customers, employees, and vendors have different *partner functions*. Sometimes the one same customer can be a sold-to party (AG/SP), ship-to party (WE/SH), bill-to party (RE/BP), and payer (RG/PY). Sometimes a sold-to party can have several ship-to parties, a different payer, and a bill-to party. Normally the sold-to party issued the purchase order, the ship-to party received the delivery, the bill-to party's name appears on the invoice, and the payer issued the payment. As the business becomes more complex, the number of partner functions can increase.

The partner determination procedure can be individually assigned to the following objects:

- Customer master
- Sales document header
- Sales document item
- Delivery
- Shipment
- Billing header
- Billing item
- Sales activities (CAS)

To access these objects for partner determination, follow the menu path SAP IMG • SALES AND DISTRIBUTION • BASIC FUNCTIONS • PARTNER DETERMINATION • SET UP PARTNER DETERMINATION (Transaction VOPAN).

The steps for partner determination are as follows:

1. Partner Function Conversion: In this step the partner function keys are maintained for different languages.
2. Create Partner Functions: Several standard partner functions are available, and you can create your own partner functions if required.
3. Assign Partner Function to Customer Account Groups: Partner functions are assigned to different customer account groups.
4. Create Partner Determination Procedure: For each type of object, such as the customer master, sales document header, and others already mentioned, you can create a new partner determination procedure or modify the standard SAP-delivered procedures. In the partner determination procedure, you can list all of the allowed partner functions and indicate whether the partner function is Not Modifiable. If you select this checkbox, it means that once the Sales and Distribution document or the customer master record is created, the partner function cannot be changed. Similarly, if the Mandatory checkbox is selected, then in order to create the Sales and Distribution document or CMR, you must enter the specific partner function or functions selected.

5. Assign Partner Determination Procedure: After creation of the partner determination procedures, they are assigned to customer account groups for the customer master, to sales document types for the sales document header, and to item categories for the sales document item. Deliveries and shipments are assigned to the delivery types and shipment types, respectively, and the billing header and billing item are assigned to billing type, and the sales activities are assigned to sales activity type.

3.7 Availability Check and Transfer of Requirements (ATP)

When the customer gives you an order, he expects a confirmation that the ordered material will be delivered on time and in the quantity specified. You expect the SAP ERP system to check the availability and find out if the material is available in sufficient quantity or will be available to promise (ATP). ATP is very important not only as a customer service but also for production planning because this quantity is also transferred as a confirmed requirement. An availability check in a sales document or delivery and a transfer of requirements to material requirements planning (MRP) from Sales and Distribution are two independent processes, though they normally go together. The transfer of requirements can happen for an individual schedule line of an order (individual requirement), or all quantities in the schedule lines of all orders of a day or week can be combined (collective requirement) based on following criteria:

- Plant
- Batch
- Storage location
- Date
- Transaction
- Requirements class

The availability check and transfer of requirement are specific to a plant. When you check a material for availability you do it for one plant, regardless of whether it is available or not in other plant. So, in the case with transfer of requirements, the requirements are generated and transferred to the plant involved in the sales order or stock transfer order as the delivery plant.

> **Note**
>
> Transaction CO09 provides the availability overview for a specific material in a particular plant. You can also use Transaction MB52, MB5T, MMBE, MB5B, and other transactions used in Inventory Management for further information on availability. A material master record (Plant stock and Storage location stock tabs) gives you another way to manually check the availability (using Transaction MM03). Remember, manual checking and transfers are not what an ERP system is installed for. Regardless, this information will be useful while you test your settings for availability check and transfer of requirements.

The steps for activating the availability check and transfer of requirements (TOR) are provided as follows:

1. Activate the availability check and transfer of requirements using Transaction OVZG (menu path: SAP IMG • SALES AND DISTRIBUTION • BASIC FUNCTIONS • AVAILABILITY CHECK AND TRANSFER OF REQUIREMENTS • DEFINE REQUIREMENTS CLASSES), as shown in Figure 3.18. You can create your own requirement class if the available ones are not suitable. Selecting the first two checkboxes (Availability Check (AvC) and Transfer of Requirements (Rq)) activates the availability check and transfer of requirements functions, respectively.

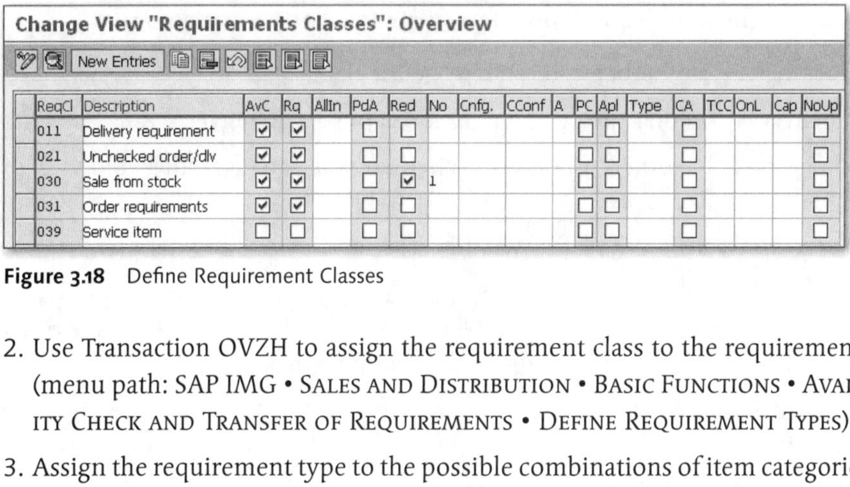

ReqCl	Description	AvC	Rq	AllIn	PdA	Red	No	Cnfg.	CConf	A	PC	Apl	Type	CA	TCC	OnL	Cap	NoUp
011	Delivery requirement	✓	✓								☐	☐		☐				☐
021	Unchecked order/dlv	✓	✓								☐	☐		☐				☐
030	Sale from stock	✓	✓			✓	1				☐	☐		☐				☐
031	Order requirements	✓	✓								☐	☐		☐				☐
039	Service item	☐	☐								☐	☐		☐				☐

Figure 3.18 Define Requirement Classes

2. Use Transaction OVZH to assign the requirement class to the requirement type (menu path: SAP IMG • SALES AND DISTRIBUTION • BASIC FUNCTIONS • AVAILABILITY CHECK AND TRANSFER OF REQUIREMENTS • DEFINE REQUIREMENT TYPES).

3. Assign the requirement type to the possible combinations of item categories and MRP types using Transaction OVZI (menu path: SAP IMG • SALES AND DISTRIBUTION • BASIC FUNCTIONS • AVAILABILITY CHECK AND TRANSFER OF REQUIREMENTS • DETERMINATION OF REQUIREMENT TYPES USING TRANSACTION). You maintain the MRP type in the material master record (MRP 1 tab) of the material.

4. The previous three steps will make the availability check and TOR active (or inactive) at a global or requirement class level. When it's active for a requirement class, you can make it inactive at the schedule line category level using Transaction OVZ8 or OVZ8X.

5. Using Transaction OVZK, you can make the availability check inactive for any delivery item category when the global setting in the preceding step ensures that the availability check is active. Please note that for this and the preceding steps, the reverse case is not valid. That is, when the global setting makes the availability check and/or TOR inactive, you cannot activate it for a specific schedule line category or delivery item category.

Now we'll discuss the specific customization requirements for availability checks and transfer of requirements in the next two subsections.

3.7.1 Availability Check

When a customer makes an order, he specifies the materials, quantity, and delivery date. The order for the customer and for the particular material is generally fulfilled from a particular delivery plant when the customer is not blocked because of a credit limit or any other reason. When an order enters the SAP system, the following information defines how the availability check is carried out.

- Date of delivery: Whether you can change the date.
- Part delivery: Whether the customer will accept partial delivery.
- Stock blocked by other processes: Whether you can use stock blocked or reserved by other processes.
- Delivery from a different plant: Whether stock available at another plant should be considered available.
- Credit and other block: Whether you'll carry out the check even when the order will not be delivered due to credit or some other reason.
- Requested Batch: Whether you'll ignore the requested batch while checking availability.
- Replenishment lead time: The average time required to make any quantity of stock available either by procurement or production. You have to decide whether to use or not use replenishment lead time during an availability check.

- Safety stock: The stock that should always be available for an emergency. Your stock level should never fall short of this level for the particular material. You have to decide whether to use it or not for the availability check.
- Stock in transit: Material that has been dispatched by a plant and is not yet received at the destination plant. You have to decide whether it is available for availability check.

Three types of availability checks are possible:

1. Available to promise (ATP): The availability check is carried out against the ATP quantity, which is calculated as per your configuration. We'll discuss this further later in this chapter.
2. Planning: The availability check is carried out for planned independent requirements, which is expected sales independent of individual orders.
3. Product allocation: The materials are allocated to different customers or customer groups (in a week or month or year). Materials will be available to the customer until the allocated quantities are used (or consumed).

The steps for customization of the first two types of availability check are given below:

1. Define checking groups: Define checking groups using Transaction OVZ2 (menu path: SAP IMG • SALES AND DISTRIBUTION • BASIC FUNCTIONS • AVAILABILITY CHECK AND TRANSFER OF REQUIREMENTS • AVAILABILITY CHECK • AVAILABILITY CHECK WITH ATP LOGIC OR AGAINST PLANNING • DEFINE CHECKING GROUPS). Using checking groups, you can club (or add up) the requirements for individual orders on a daily or weekly basis. For example, you get thousands of orders for Material A, and there are several hundred in stock. So, while doing a weekly production plan, it would be better if the production department could see the weekly requirements of last few weeks. It addition, it would also be helpful for them to know the weekly requirements during this time last year. You can use standard checking group 02 (individual requirements) when the clubbing is not required. While creating the material master record for a material, you specify the checking group applicable to it in the Sales: Sales Org.2 tab. You can define the default values for each plant and material type combination using Transaction OVZ3, which will automatically feed into the material master record when it's created. As shown in Figure 3.19, when defining the checking group you specify the following:

- The TotalSales and TotDlvReqs fields specify whether an individual record (A) or all records of a period are to be considered for sales orders and deliveries, respectively.
- The Block QtRq checkbox, when selected, blocks the material, for use by any other user, during an availability check by one user in a document. The block, whether a material can be used by two users simultaneously, can be further fine-tuned using Transaction OVZ1.
- The No Check checkbox, when selected, prevents an availability check.
- The Accumul. field defines how and whether the quantities are cumulated during order processing.
- The Response field defines whether there will be a response if the availability check results in shortfall.
- The RelChkPlan field defines whether the checking is to be done against planned quantity.

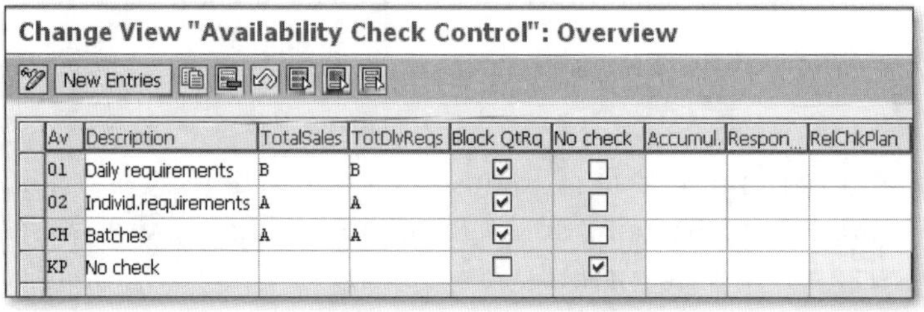

Av	Description	TotalSales	TotDlvReqs	Block QtRq	No check	Accumul.	Respon.	RelChkPlan
01	Daily requirements	B	B	☑	☐			
02	Individ.requirements	A	A	☑	☐			
CH	Batches	A	A	☑	☐			
KP	No check			☐	☑			

Figure 3.19 Checking Group for Availability Check

2. Modify checking rule: Using Transaction OVZ9 (menu path: SAP IMG • SALES AND DISTRIBUTION • BASIC FUNCTIONS • AVAILABILITY CHECK AND TRANSFER OF REQUIREMENTS • AVAILABILITY CHECK • AVAILABILITY CHECK WITH ATP LOGIC OR AGAINST PLANNING • CARRY OUT CONTROL FOR AVAILABILITY CHECK), you get the list of checking rules preconfigured and preassigned to the checking groups. When you select any entry and click on the Details icon, you go to the screen shown in Figure 3.20, where you can modify the rule (though it is not recommended).

3. Maintain requirements class: The requirement class, along with requirements type, checking group, and schedule line category, determine the availability check and transfer of requirements. You identify the standard ones that you can use or create your own using Transaction OMPO (menu path: SAP IMG •

Production • Production Planning • Demand Management • Planned Independent Requirements • Requirements Types/Requirements Classes • Maintain requirements classes). Examples of requirement classes are make-to-stock production, gross requirement planning, and so on.

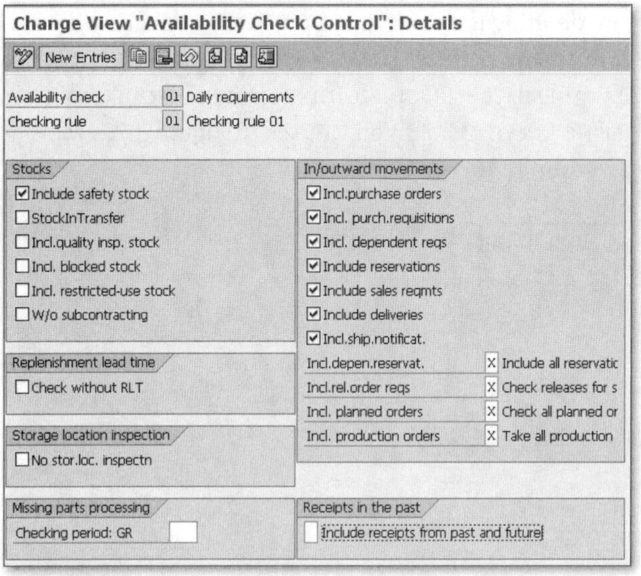

Figure 3.20 Checking Rule 01

> **Note**
>
> The combination of requirement class, requirements type, checking group, and schedule line category (or delivery item category) determine the availability check and transfer of requirements. So, you have the flexibility to keep certain materials (e.g. material that is available to you on consignment basis) out of the availability check and/or transfer of requirements. This is typically done using the checking group key for the material in the material master record.

4. Define requirements type: You create requirement types using Transaction OMP1 (menu path: SAP IMG • Production • Production Planning • Demand Management • Requirements Types/Requirements Classes • Define requirements types and allocate requirements class).

5. Create strategy group: You customize the strategy group (in the MRP 3 tab of the material master record) using Transaction OPPT (menu path: SAP IMG •

Production • Production Planning • Demand Management • Planned Independent Requirements • Planning Strategy • Define Strategy Group). A strategy group, as shown in Figure 3.21, will have one main planning strategy and seven other possible strategies. At the document level, you can change the strategy without changing the strategy group to any one of these strategies from the default strategy. Before defining the strategy group, you can define the strategy using Transaction OPPS (menu path: SAP IMG • Production • Production Planning • Demand Management • Planned Independent Requirements • Planning Strategy • Define Strategy). As you can see in Figure 3.22, the setting for standard strategy group is 40.

Figure 3.21 Strategy Group 40

6. Assign strategy group to material: There are two options for assigning a strategy group to a material.

   ▶ You can directly assign the strategy group to the material in the MRP 3 tab of the material master record.

   ▶ You can assign the strategy group to the MRP group using Transaction OPPU (menu path: SAP IMG • Production • Production Planning • Demand Management • Planned Independent Requirements • Planning Strategy • Assign MRP Group to Strategy Group). The MRP group is then assigned to the material master record MRP 1 tab.

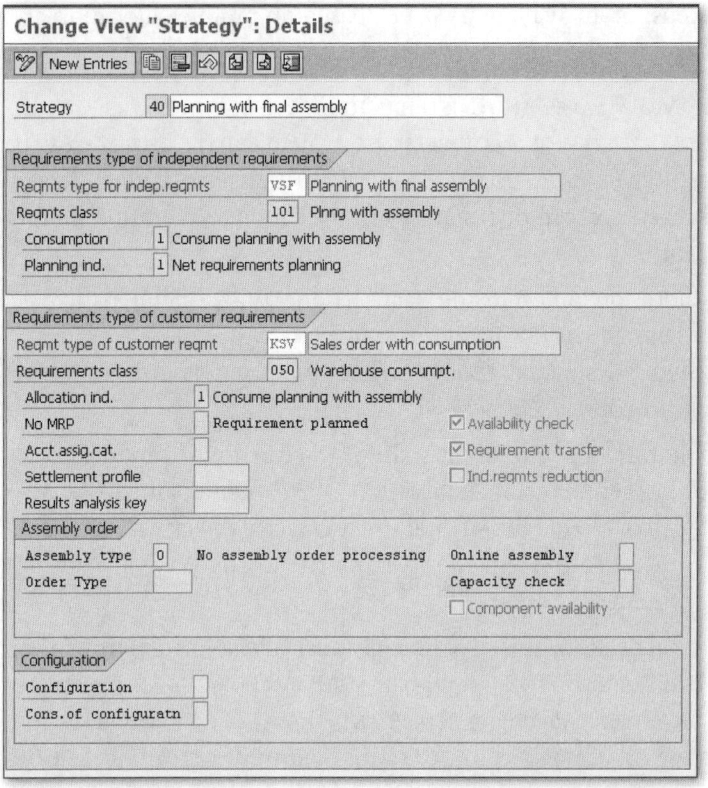

3.7 Availability Check and Transfer of Requirements (ATP)

Figure 3.22 Strategy 40

Product allocation means automatically making a material available to a group of customers. The allocated quantity to each group is subsequently allocated to each customer of that group. So, there is a fixed quantity of material available to a customer in a particular period (a day, week, or month) which is a fixed fraction of the total available quantity. In this scenario, the availability check follows a different set of rules. The central to this scenario is the standard info-structure S140, which stores the allocated quantities and is updated by the incoming orders.

> **Note**
>
> Refer to SAP notes 64636 (Procedure for statistical data setup in LIS) and 651162 (Reorganization of S140: additional information) if the sales orders are not properly updating the info-structure S140.

The customization steps for an availability check based on product allocation are:

1. Create product allocation determination procedure using Transaction OV1Z (menu path: SAP IMG • SALES AND DISTRIBUTION • BASIC FUNCTIONS • AVAILABILITY CHECK AND TRANSFER OF REQUIREMENTS • AVAILABILITY CHECK • AVAILABILITY CHECK AGAINST PRODUCT ALLOCATION • MAINTAIN PROCEDURE). Assign it to the material master record of a material in the Product Allocation field in the Basic Data 1 tab.

2. Define product allocation object using Transaction OV2Z (menu path: SAP IMG • SALES AND DISTRIBUTION • BASIC FUNCTIONS • AVAILABILITY CHECK AND TRANSFER OF REQUIREMENTS • AVAILABILITY CHECK • AVAILABILITY CHECK AGAINST PRODUCT ALLOCATION • DEFINE OBJECT).

3. Specify hierarchy. In this step you assign an info structure to the product allocation determination procedure using Transaction OV3Z (menu path: SAP IMG • SALES AND DISTRIBUTION • BASIC FUNCTIONS • AVAILABILITY CHECK AND TRANSFER OF REQUIREMENTS • AVAILABILITY CHECK • AVAILABILITY CHECK AGAINST PRODUCT ALLOCATION • SPECIFY HIERARCHY).

4. Assign product an allocation object to the product allocation determination procedure using Transaction OV4Z (menu path: SAP IMG • SALES AND DISTRIBUTION • BASIC FUNCTIONS • AVAILABILITY CHECK AND TRANSFER OF REQUIREMENTS • AVAILABILITY CHECK • AVAILABILITY CHECK AGAINST PRODUCT ALLOCATION • CONTROL PRODUCT ALLOCATION).

5. Define past and future consumption periods using Transaction OV5Z (menu path: SAP IMG • SALES AND DISTRIBUTION • BASIC FUNCTIONS • AVAILABILITY CHECK AND TRANSFER OF REQUIREMENTS • AVAILABILITY CHECK • AVAILABILITY CHECK AGAINST PRODUCT ALLOCATION • DEFINE CONSUMPTION PERIODS).

6. For collective product allocation, enter the info structure of the planning hierarchy using Transaction OV7Z (menu path: SAP IMG • SALES AND DISTRIBUTION • BASIC FUNCTIONS • AVAILABILITY CHECK AND TRANSFER OF REQUIREMENTS • AVAILABILITY CHECK • AVAILABILITY CHECK AGAINST PRODUCT ALLOCATION • PERMIT COLLECTIVE PRODUCT ALLOCATION IN INFO STRUCTURES).

7. Perform a consistency check for each combination of product allocation determination procedure and product allocation object using Transaction OV8Z (menu path: SAP IMG • SALES AND DISTRIBUTION • BASIC FUNCTIONS • AVAILABILITY CHECK AND TRANSFER OF REQUIREMENTS • AVAILABILITY CHECK • AVAIL-

ability Check Against Product Allocation • Check Settings In Product Allocation).

> **Availability Check Using SAP Advanced Planner and Optimizer (APO)**
>
> If you're using SAP APO, you can define the business transactions using the menu path SAP IMG • Sales and Distribution • Basic Functions• Availability Check and Transfer of Requirements • Availability Check • Rule-based Availability Check • Define business transaction. It should same as the business transactions defined in SAP APO using the menu path Global ATP • Settings • Rule-based ATP • Conditions • Assign rule strategy. In Transaction VOV8, for each type of order the business transaction is attached as shown in Figure 3.11.

3.7.2 Transfer of Requirements (TOR)

Besides the steps already mentioned for activating the TOR, there are no additional steps. However, you can do some fine-tuning using routines that use Transaction OVB8 and OVB5, respectively, for transfer of requirements and for preventing creation of a purchase requisition for TOR. For example, VOFM routine 102, shown below, prevents a transfer of requirements in the event of credit check.

```
*---------------------------------------------------------------*
* FORM BEDINGUNG_PRUEFEN_102 *
* User checks for subsequent functions from a sales document*
* *
* Purchase requisition *
*---------------------------------------------------------------*

FORM BEDINGUNG_PRUEFEN_102.

* if there is not in simulation mode
  IF SIMUL_MODE EQ SPACE.
* No purchase requisition if a credit block exists.
  IF VBUK-CMGST CA 'B'.
* Read the subsequent function information for the message
  PERFORM FOFUN_TEXT_READ USING GL_FOFUN
  CHANGING FOFUN_TEXT.
  DA_SY-MSGID = 'V1'.
  DA_SY-MSGNO = '849'.
  DA_SY-MSGV1 = FOFUN_TEXT.
  ERROR_EXCEPTION = TRUE.
  ENDIF.
```

```
ENDIF.
ENDFORM.
*eject
```

> **Note**
>
> The transfer of requirements is displayed at the sales or delivery document item level using the menu path ENVIRONMENT • AVAILABILITY from the overview screen. At the material level for the plant, you can use Transaction MD04.
>
> Using Transaction VA02 or VA03, press F4, select the Sales Documents – Not Fully Confirmed tab, and press Enter to get the list of unconfirmed orders.

3.8 Outline Agreements

In this section, we'll discuss customer contracts and scheduling agreements. There are four types of customer contracts: master contract, quantity contract, value contract, and service contract. Whereas the contract displays the materials and services sold during a particular period, the scheduling agreement refers to the quantities to be delivered on different dates. All outline agreements are sales document types, and the standard document types are given below. The functions related to sales document such as price determination, partner determination, incompletion log, availability check, and other functions are also applicable to outline agreements. You can create one document with reference to another based on copy control rules. Like many other sales documents, the essential parts of the outline agreements are price, quantity, sold-to party, and schedule lines. In scheduling agreements there can be different schedule lines for forecasting (and subsequent production or purchase) and for shipping.

In the next two sections, we'll discuss the customization requirements for contracts and the scheduling agreement.

3.8.1 Customer Contracts

You create contracts using Transaction VA41 (menu path: SAP EASY ACCESS • LOGISTICS • SALES AND DISTRIBUTION • SALES • CONTRACT • CREATE). The standard sales document types for scheduling agreements are:

- GK: Master contract
- KM: Quantity contract

- MV: Rental contract
- WK1: Value contract – general
- WK2: Material-related value contract
- WV: Service and maintenances contract

Contracts do not contain any schedule lines, delivery dates, or delivery quantities. Release orders, which are similar to sales orders, are created with reference to the contract. The release orders have schedule lines and are processed like standard orders. Release orders created with reference to a contract update the contract. For example, suppose the contract is for 100 units of one material. When a release order is created for 40 units, the updated quantity available for other release orders is 60 units. This is controlled by a copy control functionality. In the customizing of sales document type VOV8, you should specify for the release orders how the system will behave for the open outline agreements. The options are:

- Blank: do not check
- A: check at header level
- B: check at item level
- C: check at header level and copy if unique
- D: check at item level and copy if unique
- E: check at header level and branch directly to selection list
- F: check at item level and branch directly to selection list

When no option is selected (blank) there is no check. For options A and B, the outline agreements available for customers and materials are checked, and a dialog box appears to display the list. For options C and D, if just one outline agreement is available, it's automatically copied to the order. For options E and F, when one outline agreement is available, it behaves like options C and D. When more than one outline agreement is available, the system behaves like options A and B but goes directly to the list without the intermediate dialog box.

The sales document types used to create a contract and the document types used for release orders are controlled by the fields shown previously in Figure 3.10, in Transaction VOV8. The PricProcCondHeadr and PricProcCondItem fields are used to specify the pricing procedure of the contract at the header and item levels, respectively. In the billing request field, you specify the order type that will be used as the release order. The Contract Data Allowed indicator dictates whether the contract data is allowed for such document types and, if so, whether it's applicable to both the header (X) and item (Y) levels. The Follow Up Activity Type is maintained for service contracts. If the order type of the subsequent process is fixed, it's entered in the Subseq.order Type field. The Check Partner Authorization field checks if the user has the authorization to create a release order for the contract. The Update Lower Level Contract checkbox, when selected, updates the lower-level contract for changes in the master contract. For this, you also have to activate the workflow for master contract using Transactions SWE2 and PFTC.

The Contract profile is customized via Transaction VOVR (menu path: SAP IMG • SALES AND DISTRIBUTION • SALES • SALES DOCUMENTS • CONTRACTS • CONTRACT DATA • DEFINE CONTRACT PROFILES) and attached at the time of defining sales document type. You can select the standard contract profile (i.e., 0001) and click on the Copy As ([F6]) icon to reach the screen shown in Figure 3.23. You customize the options for the contract start and end rule and action date rule using Transaction OVBS or VOVP (menu path: SAP IMG • SALES AND DISTRIBUTION • SALES • SALES DOCUMENTS • CONTRACTS • CONTRACT DATA • DEFINE RULES FOR DETERMINING DATES). The Valid Period Category (e.g., 30 days, 3 months, or 2 years) field is customized via Transaction VOVO (menu path: SAP IMG • SALES AND DISTRIBUTION • SALES • SALES DOCUMENTS • CONTRACTS • CONTRACT DATA • DEFINE VALIDITY PERIOD CATEGORIES). The cancellation reasons, procedure, and rules are defined via Transactions VOVQ, VOVM, and VOVL, respectively. You assign the rules to the procedure using Transaction VOVN.

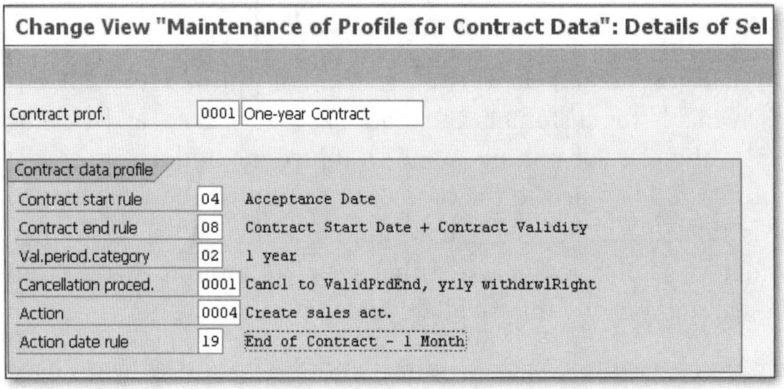

Figure 3.23 Customizing Contract Profile Using Transaction VOVR

The Group Reference Procedure field maintained in the screen shown previously in Figure 3.10 is customized via Transaction VORS (menu path: SAP IMG • SALES AND

Distribution • Sales • Sales Documents • Contracts • Master Contract • Define Referencing Procedures). By selecting the existing procedure and clicking on the Copy As icon ([F6]), you create a new procedure. Before defining the reference procedure, you must define the master and target contracts using Transaction VORB (menu path: SAP IMG • Sales and Distribution • Sales • Sales Documents • Contracts • Master Contract • Define Reference Sales Document Types). As shown in Figure 3.24, document type GK is defined as the master contract for different contacts.

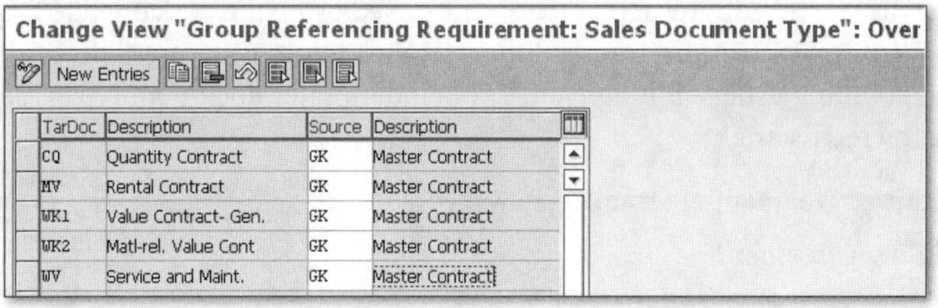

Figure 3.24 Defining Master Contract for Different Contract Types

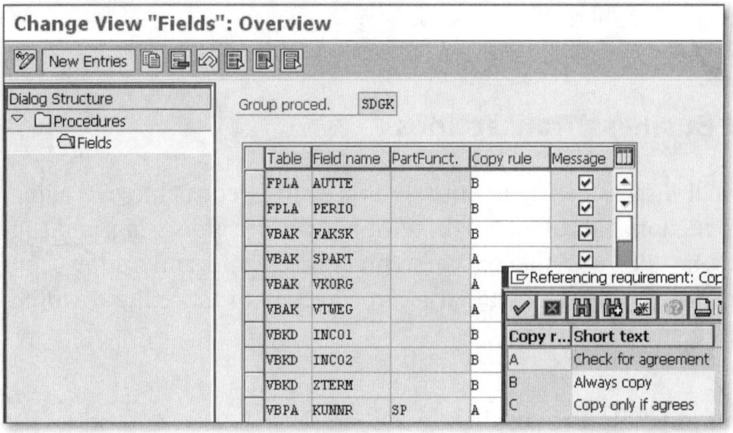

Figure 3.25 Group Reference Procedure for Contracts and Scheduling Agreements

By selecting the already created procedures and clicking on the Fields folder, you get a list of tables fields with copy rules and message checkboxes as shown in Figure 3.25. In the group reference procedure, you specify the list of table fields that must be identical (copy rule A) for referencing a target document to a master document, while referencing one contract to a master contract or copied to (copy

127

rule C) the target from the master contract or copy as default values to the target contract, which subsequently can be modified (copy rule B).

3.8.2 Scheduling Agreement

A scheduling agreement is like a quantity contract but with specific dates for the delivery of specific quantities. You create it using Transaction VA31 (menu path: SAP EASY ACCESS • LOGISTICS • SALES AND DISTRIBUTION • SALES • SCHEDULING AGREEMENTS • CREATE). There can be several schedule lines for an item in a scheduling agreement. The scheduling agreement is processed using the delivery due list (Transaction VL10 or VL10A) or Transaction VL01N to create different deliveries and subsequent billing using a billing plan. The standard sales document types for scheduling agreements are:

- LK: scheduling agreement external agency
- LP: scheduling agreement
- LZ: scheduling agreement w/rel.
- LZM: scheduling agreement w/ dly ord.
- LZS: scheduling agreement: self-bill w/inv.

3.9 Special Business Transactions

In this section, we'll discuss consignment sale processing, returnable packaging, make-to-order production, bills of materials, third-party order processing, and configurable materials in sales documents. These processes significantly differ from the normal sales process, where material is procured or produced and stored. Orders are delivered and then billed.

3.9.1 Consignment Sale Processing

Consignment sale is primarily used for industrial or trade sale, where the seller stocks the material at the buyer's premises or warehouse. Also, when the seller has only one or very few buyers, this option becomes beneficial to both buyer and seller. This is primarily done to increase sales, but there can be other reasons as well (e.g., contract). The transfer of ownership for stock does not change at the time of physical stock movement. This situation is called a *consignment process*. The seller keeps the stock at the customer's warehouse (consignment fill-up process), and the customer takes the material from the filled-up stock for his own use (consignment issue process). The consignment fill-up is subsequently delivered but not invoiced. The standard delivery type LF (outbound delivery) or NK (consignment replenishment delivery) can be used to process consignment fill-up orders. The consignment issue, on the other hand, should be invoiced either directly (order relevant) or after delivery (normal delivery document type is to be used).

For returns, you have two possible processes. You can take returns as you do in a standard return process. You can return the material, already billed, to the consignment stock, using delivery type NKR (consignment replenishment return delivery). Then that stock can be taken back to the company warehouse or used for future customer orders. Note that you can use delivery type NKR even if the material is not sold as part of a consignment sale process. The stock that's physically present with the customer either by consignment fill-up or consignment return process and not yet issued using the consignment issue process can be taken back by the seller (consignment pick-up process). The consignment pick-up is followed up by a return delivery but not a credit memo (because an ownership change did not occur). The consignment return must be followed up with an issue of credit memo with or without a delivery. If the customer wants a replacement, a subsequent free-of-charge order (SD) or free-of-charge delivery order (FD) can be used. Table 3.6 summarizes the different consignment processes.

Order type	Process	Goods Movement	Ownership Change
KB	Consignment fill-up	Company to customer	No. Company is the owner.
KE	Consignment issue	No physical movement	Company to customer
KA	Consignment pick-up	Customer to company	No. Company is the owner.
KR	Consignment return	No physical movement	Customer to company

Table 3.6 Standard Consignment Order Types

3.9.2 Returnable Packaging

In certain industries, returnable packaging material is the norm, especially when the packaging material is costly and reusable. Sometimes it can be specialized equipment supplied for installing the product sold. After installation, this equipment is expected to be returned. If the customer does not return the equipment for any reason, the customer is expected to pay for it.

The prerequisites for this process are:

1. Create the returnable package in the relevant material type. The standard material type for returnable packaging is LEIH (returnable packaging).
2. Ensure that the item category group for the packaging materials to be returned is LEIH in the material master record.

The returnable packaging material is included in the normal order-delivery-billing process and is not billed as other material. After the billing is complete, an order with document type LA (return packaging pick-up) is created that is fundamentally similar to the document type RE (return). LA documents are further processed by delivery type LR (return). A credit memo for a return is normally not issued. If the material is not returned, then you invoice the customer by the return packaging issue process. The order type is LN. The document is further processed using standard delivery document LF (outbound delivery) and invoice type F2.

3.9.3 Make-to-Order Production

The distinctive feature of the *make-to-order items* of a sales order is that when such an order is saved, they automatically create production orders. After completion of the production cycle, the stock will be available only to the original order that triggered the production process. The delivery and billing is same as that of standard order-delivery-billing cycle. The make-to-order items are those materials for which the item category group maintained in the Sales: Sales Org 2 view of the material master record is 0001 (make-to-order) or 0004 (make-to-order/assembled).

3.9.4 Bill of Materials

The bill of materials (BoM) is another tool to automatically populate the sales order with subitems. The BoM of a top-level item consists of all of the material that constitutes it. In production planning, the BoM is used extensively. In sales, it's not used as extensively but in few industry sectors it's required. In sectors such as aerospace and defense, the BoM is used in sales. A BoM is created for the top-level material using Transaction CS01 (Menu path: SAP EASY ACCESS • LOGISTICS • SALES AND DISTRIBUTION • MASTER DATA • PRODUCTS • BILLS OF MATERIAL • BILL OF MATERIAL • MATERIAL BOM • CREATE) with BoM usage 5 (sales and distribution).

The item category group maintained in the Sales: Sales Org 2 view of the material master record is ERLA or LUMF, depending on whether you want to process the pricing, inventory management at header-item level (ERLA) or at the constituent materials level (LUMF).

3.9.5 Third-Party Order Processing

When the item category group of an item in the sales order is a third party item (BANS or a customized version of it), a purchase requisition is automatically generated when the order is saved. The purchase requisition is further processed to create a purchase order for the vendor. The vendor is instructed to supply the material directly to the customer. The vendor sends the material to your customer and sends the invoice (vendor invoice) to you. The customer is invoiced by you and not your vendor. You pay your vendor, and your customer pays you. Even when the item category is not BANS, manual purchase requisitions can be created, and the process for third-party order processing can be completed. In trading companies, this process is used extensively.

3.9.6 Individual Purchase Order

In individual purchase order processing, the sales order creates the purchase order, but unlike third-party order processing, the vendor does not send it directly to the customer. The company receives the material and dispatches it against the specific sales order. It cannot be sold to other customers. The item category for such materials is BANC (individual purchase order). Even when the item category is not BANC, you can manually create a purchase order for the individual items in the sales order.

3.9.7 Configurable Material

Configurable material is a functionality that SAP ERP offers when a material can have several possible bills of materials (BoMs), especially in a make-to-order scenario. Only when the order is received is the material assembled. Typically, the price is determined by the components and operations used in assembling the final material. The configurable material is created using material type KMAT (configurable material), and the item category group maintained in material master record (Sales: Sales Org 2) should either be 0002 (configuration) or 0004 (make to order/assemble).

3.10 Incompletion Control and Its Practical Use

Incompletion control is used to define precisely what makes a specific document incomplete for specific subsequent processing. For example, a sales order may be considered complete for delivery processing but incomplete for billing. The incompletion control is used to achieve the following objectives:

1. The incompletion log is created for each document so that the user knows which fields are incomplete and still require action.
2. The incomplete documents appear in different reports to list such documents (e.g., V.00 – incomplete SD documents, V_UC – incomplete outbound deliveries).
3. It avoids further processing of documents without necessary and sufficient data.
4. The Status tab of the document shows the status of completeness based on the configuration in incompletion control.
5. During processing, a variety of fields are filled by the default values from different master records, determination procedures, or customization settings. These fields can also be defined as incompletion fields. Because usually they are filled automatically, the user rarely checks them manually.
6. If the customer-expected price is too low, the price can be determined in a sales item, and the document can be processed as incomplete until a decision is made on whether to continue with the sale, reduce the price, or stop the sale.
7. Before doing any customization in the user exit, you can check if the objective for the user exit can be achieved using the incompletion procedure. Because the incompletion control checks the value that will be present in certain table field, this allows you to define incompletion because the table field need not be present in a particular screen. It can be a field from a customized Z-table.

The following are the general steps for customizing incompletion control:

1. Define status groups to control the specific subsequent process that cannot be completed if the document is incomplete as per the incompleteness procedure assigned to it (error group).
2. Identify the incompletion group from the seven groups that the incompleteness procedure is to define.
3. Define the incompleteness procedure for different incompletion groups.

4. Assign an incompleteness procedure to the different document types that belong to different incompletion groups.

3.10.1 Define Status Groups

Status groups define precisely what subsequent activities (e.g., billing, pricing, packing, and so on) can be carried out even when a sales document is incomplete. These status groups are further used in the incompleteness procedure. A field not filled up in the sales document item may make it incomplete for bill processing, but it should not prevent the order from being delivered. As shown in the Figure 3.26, you can use several predefined status groups or Transaction OVA0 (menu path: SAP IMG • SALES AND DISTRIBUTION • BASIC FUNCTIONS • LOG OF INCOMPLETE ITEMS • DEFINE STATUS GROUPS).

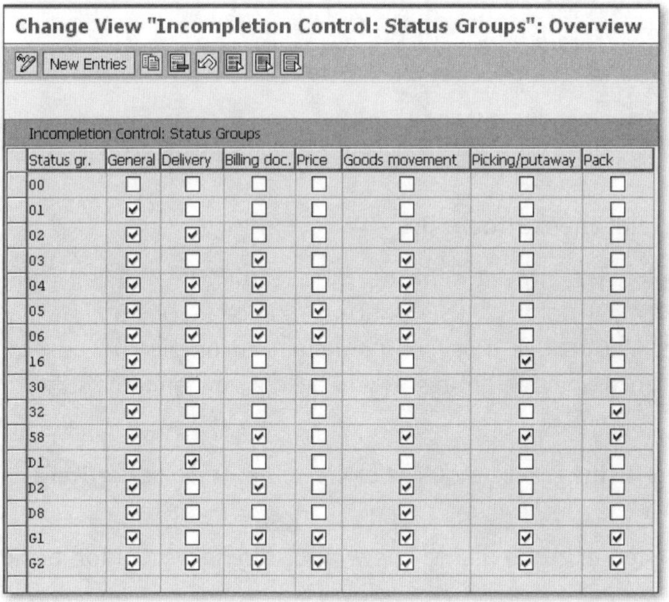

Status gr.	General	Delivery	Billing doc.	Price	Goods movement	Picking/putaway	Pack
00	☐	☐	☐	☐	☐	☐	☐
01	☑	☐	☐	☐	☐	☐	☐
02	☑	☑	☐	☐	☐	☐	☐
03	☑	☐	☑	☐	☑	☐	☐
04	☑	☑	☑	☐	☑	☐	☐
05	☑	☐	☑	☑	☑	☐	☐
06	☑	☑	☑	☑	☑	☐	☐
16	☑	☐	☐	☐	☐	☑	☐
30	☑	☐	☐	☐	☐	☐	☐
32	☑	☐	☐	☐	☐	☐	☑
58	☑	☐	☑	☐	☐	☑	☑
D1	☑	☑	☐	☐	☐	☐	☐
D2	☑	☐	☑	☐	☑	☐	☐
D8	☑	☐	☐	☐	☑	☐	☐
G1	☑	☐	☑	☑	☑	☑	☑
G2	☑	☑	☑	☑	☑	☑	☑

Figure 3.26 Status Groups for Incompletion Control – Incompletion Groups

3.10.2 Identify Incompletion Groups

There are seven standard predefined incompletion groups that you can use to define the new incompleteness procedures. The incompleteness procedure defined in a particular incompletion group can be assigned to the document types of that incompletion group. For example, the new incompleteness procedure, starting with Y or Z, created in incompletion or error group A (Sales – Header) can be assigned to the sales document type or sales header types such as OR or CR document types, but not to sales item categories such as TAN or REN. Figure 3.27 shows the seven incompletion groups (A, B, C, D, F, G, and H) and their descriptions. Adding to this list is not required or possible. You can think of the incompletion groups as the option to group the different incompletion procedures.

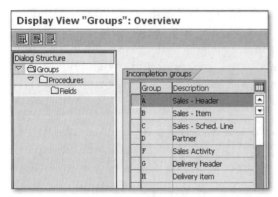

Figure 3.27 Incompletion or Error Groups – Define Incompleteness Procedure

3.10.3 Define Incompleteness Procedure

You define the incompleteness procedure using Transaction OVA2 (menu path: SAP IMG • SALES AND DISTRIBUTION • BASIC FUNCTIONS • LOG OF INCOMPLETE ITEMS • DEFINE INCOMPLETENESS PROCEDURES). Several predefined incompleteness procedures exist in different incompletion groups. If you need a new one, the steps to define it are:

1. Identify the suitable status groups required or create new ones using Transaction OVA0.

2. Identify the incompletion group that the new procedure is created for, using Transaction OVA2.

3. Select the incompletion group and double-click on the Procedure folder. In Figure 3.27, we have selected incompletion group A (Sales – Header).

4. You'll get a list of all existing incompleteness procedures in the group (in this case, we selected A). Pick the one that's closest to the one you want to create.

5. Click on the Change-Display (Pencil and Specks) icon.

6. Select the procedure you want to copy and click on the Copy As ([F6]) icon.

7. An intermediate screen will ask you if you want to copy all dependant entries. Select Copy All.

8. A dialog window will show the number of dependant entries copied to the new incompleteness procedure. Press [Enter] and proceed.

9. Select the newly created incompleteness procedure and click on the Fields folder. You'll see the screen shown in Figure 3.28.

10. The new procedure shown in Figure 3.28 is the copy of the standard incompleteness procedure 11 (standard order). You can delete the table and fields already defined as *incompletion fields* and/or add a new table-field combination to it. The incompletion field on the screen (see the Scr. column in Figure 3.28) for which the status group is defined in the Status column is the field that if not filled during processing will make the document incomplete for the subsequent processes as defined in status group applicable to it. You can have a number of incompletion fields in an incompleteness procedure. The Warning checkbox is used to issue a warning at the time of saving the document, and the Sequence column determines the sequence when multiple entries are present in the incompletion log.

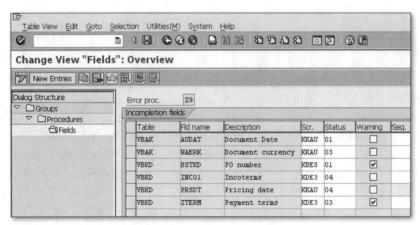

Figure 3.28 Defining Fields for Incompleteness Procedure

3.10.4 Assign Incompleteness Procedure

You assign the incompletion procedures to specific document types using Transaction VUA2 (menu path: SAP IMG • SALES AND DISTRIBUTION • BASIC FUNCTIONS •

Log of Incomplete Items • Define Incompleteness Procedures). As we already mentioned, there are seven standard incompletion groups for which incompleteness procedures are created. Based on the group for which they're created, there are seven options at the previously mentioned menu path. For example, if you have created the procedure for Group A (Sales – Header), you have to select the option Assign Procedures to Sales Document Types. You assign allowed procedure to different document types as shown in Figure 3.29.

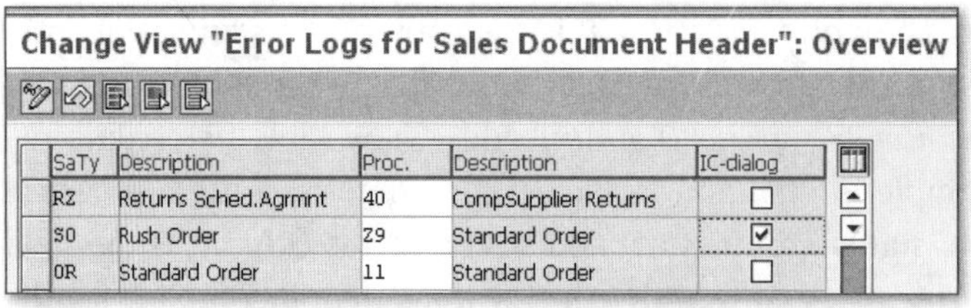
Change View "Error Logs for Sales Document Header": Overview

SaTy	Description	Proc.	Description	IC-dialog
RZ	Returns Sched.Agrmnt	40	CompSupplier Returns	☐
SO	Rush Order	Z9	Standard Order	☑
OR	Standard Order	11	Standard Order	☐

Figure 3.29 Assigning Incompleteness Procedure

Incomplete Text

Even when a text ID is not defined in the incompletion control, it can still appear on the incompletion log if it's defined as mandatory in the text determination procedure that's described in Chapter 8.

3.11 Free Goods and Free Items

Free goods are a part of a pricing strategy. As a promotional campaign, a company gives free goods when a customer purchases a specific quantity of some material. An apparel company can offer you one shirt, free of cost, when you buy three shirts or a pair of pants. If you buy three shirts, they have to further clarify whether you will get an additional shirt free or if one of the three that you bought will be free.

You configure automatic free goods determination with the following steps. It uses the condition technique, which we'll discuss in detail in Chapter 4.

1. Define a number range for Free Goods Conditions using Transaction WC07 or SNRO (numbering object KONN).
2. Maintain the field catalog (menu path: IMG • Sales and Distribution • Basic Functions • Free Goods • Condition Technique for Free Goods • Maintain

FIELD CATALOG). This is the list of all available fields that can be used for condition records. The Transaction code is OMA5.

3. Maintain the condition table via Transaction code V/N2 (menu path: IMG • SALES AND DISTRIBUTION • BASIC FUNCTIONS • FREE GOODS • CONDITION TECHNIQUE FOR FREE GOODS • MAINTAIN CONDITION TABLE). SAP ERP provides two default condition tables: 010 (Customer-Material) and 017 (Campaign ID − Material). If you want more, you can create tables with numbers between 500 and 999.

4. Maintain the access sequence via Transaction code V/N1 (menu path: IMG • SALES AND DISTRIBUTION • BASIC FUNCTIONS • FREE GOODS • CONDITION TECHNIQUE FOR FREE GOODS • MAINTAIN ACCESS SEQUENCE). When multiple condition records are stored for the same condition type in different condition tables, the access sequence determines which of these is relevant.

5. Maintain the condition type via Transaction code V/N4 (menu path: IMG • SALES AND DISTRIBUTION • BASIC FUNCTIONS • FREE GOODS • CONDITION TECHNIQUE FOR FREE GOODS • MAINTAIN CONDITION TYPE). The SAP EPR standard-delivered condition type for free goods is NA00. If you need additional condition types, you can create them by copying from it.

6. Maintain the pricing procedure via Transaction code V/N5 (menu path: IMG • SALES AND DISTRIBUTION • BASIC FUNCTIONS • FREE GOODS • CONDITION TECHNIQUE FOR FREE GOODS • MAINTAIN PRICING PROCEDURE).

7. Activate free goods determination via Transaction code V/N6 (menu path: IMG • SALES AND DISTRIBUTION • BASIC FUNCTIONS • FREE GOODS • CONDITION TECHNIQUE FOR FREE GOODS • ACTIVATE FREE GOODS DETERMINATION).

8. Assign item categories (menu path: IMG • SALES AND DISTRIBUTION • BASIC FUNCTIONS • FREE GOODS • DETERMINE ITEM CATEGORY FOR FREE GOODS). For the standard order OR and the standard item category TAN (item category group NORM), the free goods item category to assign is TANN (free of charge item).

9. Maintain Pricing Procedure. The pricing for free goods is quite different from the pricing steps, which we'll discuss in Chapter 4. Also, it depends on whether the free goods create a separate item or, as in some cases (free goods category 3), are part of the main item. For inclusive free goods without item generation, use condition type NRAB (free goods), which uses the VOFM requirement routine 59 and formula routine 29. Condition type R100 (100% discount), used in other cases, uses requirement routine 55 and formula routine 28 in the pricing procedure.

10. Maintain condition records for free goods (menu path: SAP EASY ACCESS • LOGISTICS • SALES AND DISTRIBUTION • MASTER DATA • CONDITIONS • FREE GOODS • CREATE (VBN1). Select the default free goods condition type NA00 and the required key combination, and click on the Exclusive tab. In Figure 3.30, you'll see the Exclusive view; the tab appears as Inclusive. When you're giving 1 unit free with 10 units of material A, for an order of 10 units in the case of inclusive free goods, you sell 9 units and give 1 unit as free. With exclusive free goods, you sell 10 units and give 1 unit as free, thus delivering 11 units.

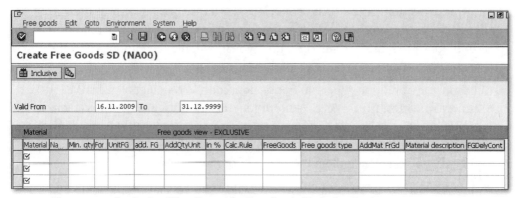

Figure 3.30 Create Condition Record for Free Goods (Exclusive Type)

To create a condition record for free goods, you have to maintain the following for a date range:

- **Material**
  Enter the material for which free goods are given.

- **Minimum quantity**
  The quantity of the material that must be ordered to get free goods.

- **For**
  The quantity for which free goods start. If for every 100 units of material A, 1 unit of material B is free, you would enter 100 here. It becomes "from" in the inclusive case.

- **Unit of measure (UnitFG)**
  The unit of measure of the material for which free goods are given.

- **Additional free goods (Add.FG)**
  The quantity of free goods to be given to the customer. It becomes "are free goods" in the inclusive case.

- **Unit of measurement (AddQtyUnit)**
  The unit of measurement of the additional quantity.

- **Calculation rule**
  In the standard SAP system, there are three rules used for calculating the free goods quantity when the order quantity is more than the minimum quantity. Select 1 (pro-rata) for a quantity that is above the minimum quantity, in which the customer gets free goods on proportional basis. So, using the pro-rata rule, if 10 units are free with a 100 unit purchase, the customer would get 12 free units with an order of 120. Select 2 (unit reference) when no additional free goods are supplied for an order more than the minimum order. Select 3 (whole unit) when no free goods are supplied for an order more than the minimum order. For example, if 100 units of material A is ordered, 10 units of material B are given as free. So, when 110 units are ordered, the customer will receive 11, 10, and 0, respectively, for calculation rules 1, 2, and 3. These rules are simply VOFM routines and can be modified. New routines can also be created using Transaction VOFM in the allowed range of 600 to 999.

- **Free goods**
  The Free Goods field can take 1, 2, or 3 as input. When the free goods rebate is exclusive, then the material that's given as additional free goods will always create a new line item in the order, and you need to select free goods category 2. But when the free goods rebate is inclusive, you have the option of generating another line item (option 1) or including the additional quantity in the main item without creating an additional line item in the order (option 3).

- **Additional material free goods (AddMat FrGd)**
  This field is not present in the inclusive type of free goods because the additional material cannot be different from the material for which free goods are given. For the exclusive type, you can maintain the same material as exclusive or you can have a different material. For example, for 10 units of material A, you can give 1 unit of material B as free goods, or you can give 1 unit of material A as free goods.

- **Free goods delivery control (FGDelyCont)**
  This controls how the free goods can be delivered with respect to the delivery of the main item.

- **Scale**
  You can use scale when you have to give a different quantity of free goods for different quantities ordered. For example, if for 100 units, 10 units are free; for 200 units, 25 units are free; for 300 units, 40 units are free; and so on, then it's maintained in scales.

3.12 Material Determination, Listing, and Exclusion

Material determination is used to replace one material with another in the sales document. The swapping can be done one-to-one or manually by selecting from a proposed list. You would use this in a situation such as nonavailability, product discontinuation, or promotional packaging during a specific period. Material listing and exclusion is the procedure to giving a customer or group of customers a predefined list of products by either listing the allowed material, listing the not allowed material (exclusion), or both. Both material determination and material listing/exclusion use the condition technique, which we'll discuss further in Chapter 4. The steps for automatic determination of a material and material listing/exclusion are as follows:

1. Add the field required in the condition table to the field catalog if not already available.

    ▶ Material determination menu path: SAP IMG • SALES AND DISTRIBUTION • BASIC FUNCTIONS • MATERIAL DETERMINATION • MAINTAIN PREREQUISITES FOR MATERIAL DETERMINATION • MAINTAIN FIELD CATALOG

    ▶ Material listing/exclusion menu path: SAP IMG • SALES AND DISTRIBUTION • BASIC FUNCTIONS • LISTING/EXCLUSION • MAINTAIN ALLOWED FIELDS FOR LISTING/EXCLUSION

2. Create condition tables using fields available in the field catalog or identify the standard SAP condition tables that are suitable for storing condition records.

    ▶ Material determination menu path: SAP IMG • SALES AND DISTRIBUTION • BASIC FUNCTIONS • MATERIAL DETERMINATION • MAINTAIN PREREQUISITES FOR MATERIAL DETERMINATION • CREATE CONDITION TABLE

    ▶ Material listing/exclusion menu path: SAP IMG • SALES AND DISTRIBUTION • BASIC FUNCTIONS • LISTING/EXCLUSION • MAINTAIN CONDITION TABLE FOR LISTING/EXCLUSION

3. Create an access sequence and assign condition tables for the system to access the condition tables in correct sequence.

    ▶ Material determination menu path: SAP IMG • SALES AND DISTRIBUTION • BASIC FUNCTIONS • MATERIAL DETERMINATION • MAINTAIN PREREQUISITES FOR MATERIAL DETERMINATION • MAINTAIN ACCESS SEQUENCES

- Material listing/exclusion menu path: SAP IMG • Sales and Distribution • Basic Functions • Listing/Exclusion • Maintain Access Sequences for Listing/Exclusion

4. Create condition types with the correct access sequence assigned to them.
   - Material determination menu path: SAP IMG • Sales and Distribution • Basic Functions • Material Determination • Maintain Prerequisites for Material Determination • Define Condition Types
   - Material listing/exclusion menu path: SAP IMG • Sales and Distribution • Basic Functions • Listing/Exclusion • Maintain Listing/Exclusion Types

5. Create a determination procedure and assign it to the condition types.
   - Material determination menu path: SAP IMG • Sales and Distribution • Basic Functions • Material Determination • Maintain Prerequisites for Material Determination • Maintain Procedure
   - Material listing/exclusion menu path: SAP IMG • Sales and Distribution • Basic Functions • Listing/Exclusion • Procedures for Maintaining Listing/Exclusion

6. Assign a determination procedure to sales document types.
   - Material determination menu path: SAP IMG • Sales and Distribution • Basic Functions • Material Determination • Assign Procedures To Sales Document Types
   - Material listing/exclusion menu path: SAP IMG • Sales and Distribution • Basic Functions • Listing/Exclusion • Activate Listing/Exclusion by Sales Document Type

7. Create condition records.
   - Material determination menu path: SAP EASY access • Logistics • Sales and Distribution • Master Data • Products • Material Determination • Create (VB11)
   - Material listing/exclusion menu path: SAP EASY access • Logistics • Sales and Distribution • Master Data • Products • Listing/Exclusion • Create (VB01)

8. In addition to the above steps for material determination, you can define substitution reasons using Transaction OVRQ (menu path: SAP IMG • Sales and Distribution • Basic Functions • Material Determination • Define Substitution Reasons).

3.13 Batch Determination in Sales

In addition to the Sales and Distribution functionality in SAP ERP, batch determination is also used in the Material Management, Production Planning, and Warehouse Management functionalities in SAP ERP. Batch determination also uses the condition technique. That is, it uses the condition tables, access sequence, condition type, and a search procedure.

3.13.1 Condition Tables

The transaction code for creating condition table in the Sales and Distribution functionality in SAP ERP for batch determination is V/C7. The menu path for condition tables is SAP IMG • LOGISTICS – GENERAL • BATCH MANAGEMENT • BATCH DETERMINATION AND BATCH CHECK • CONDITION TABLES • DEFINE SALES AND DISTRIBUTION CONDITION TABLES. There are six standard condition tables, listed in Table 3.7.

Table	Fields Used
001	Material (MATNR)
002	Customer (KUNNR) – Material (MATNR)
003	Customer (KUNNR) – Plant (WERKS) – Material (MATNR)
004	Destination Country (LAND1) – Material group (MATKL)
005	Destination Country (LAND1)
006	Material Group (MATKL)

Table 3.7 Standard Condition Tables for Batch Determination

If you want to create your own condition tables, the number should be between 501 and 999, and the fields to be used should be in the field catalog. You can use all fields in the field catalog by using the option Conditions: Allowed Fields (Sales and Distribution) at the end of the above menu path.

3.13.2 Access Sequence

Access sequences are attached to the batch strategy and control the sequence in which the condition tables are accessed. The menu path is SAP IMG • LOGISTICS – GENERAL • BATCH MANAGEMENT • BATCH DETERMINATION AND BATCH CHECK • ACCESS SEQUENCE • DEFINE SALES AND DISTRIBUTION ACCESS SEQUENCES. The access sequence determines the order in which the condition tables are accessed. SD01, SD02, and SD03 are SAP delivered access sequences. You can create your own with a code starting with Z.

3.13.3 Strategy Type

The strategy types are condition types that use the access sequence for automatic determination. Figure 3.31 displays the standard strategy type SD01. The values for class and sort sequence are entered in the production client itself after transport of the strategy type.

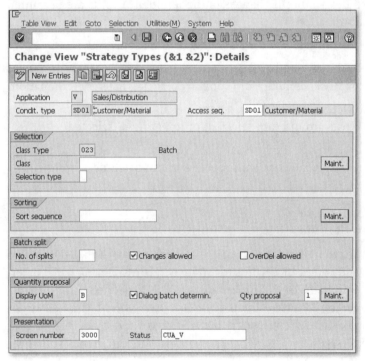

Figure 3.31 Strategy Type SD01

- The selection type determines how the batches are selected at the start of batch determination. The four available options are:
  - Blank: Batches are immediately displayed for selection that matches the selection criteria.

- N: Batches are not selected even when the selection criteria exists. The user has the option to change selection criteria.
- O: All batches are displayed for selection irrespective of selection criteria. The selection is carried out after finalization of selection criteria.
- F: Selection criteria cannot be changed for batch determination.
▶ Sort Sequence determines how the search results are sorted.
▶ No. of Splits determines how many batch splits are allowed. Because this field can take any three-digit number, the highest number (999) is the maximum batch split allowed.
▶ Changes Allowed determines if changes in the number of splits are permitted during batch determination.
▶ OverDel Allowed is not relevant for Sales and Distribution.
▶ Display UoM determines whether the unit of measurement (UoM) is document UoM (option B) or stock-keeping UoM (option A) during batch determination.
▶ The Dialog Batch Determin. checkbox determines if the batch determination is carried out in the background (not selected) or foreground (selected).
▶ Qty Proposal can be any of the four standard routines or customized routines that fine-tune the way quantities are proposed in the batch determination, as shown in Figure 3.32.

3.13.4 Batch Search Procedure

The batch search procedure lists the sequence of strategy types that the system tries to access for valid condition records (or strategy records) during batch determination. The standard batch search procedure is SD0001, defined using Transaction V/C3 or by going to SAP IMG • LOGISTICS – GENERAL • BATCH MANAGEMENT • BATCH DETERMINATION AND BATCH CHECK • BATCH SEARCH PROCEDURE DEFINITION • DEFINE SALES AND DISTRIBUTION SEARCH PROCEDURE. You can create your own search procedure beginning with Z by clicking on the New Entry tab. You can then add the strategy types you want in the appropriate sequence (steps and counter decide the sequence) by opening the Control folder and selecting New Entry.

Once the search procedure is defined, it's assigned to the combination of sales area and document type, as shown in Figure 3.33. Finally, you create the batch search strategy records using Transaction VCH1 or by going to SAP EASY ACCESS • LOGISTICS • SALES AND DISTRIBUTION • MASTER DATA • PRODUCTS • BATCH SEARCH STRATEGY • CREATE.

Batch Determination in Sales | 3.13

```
************************************************************
* FORM CHMVS_001
************************************************************
* Routine to distribute the available quantities of batches.
* The distribution is an example for a TOP-DOWN distribution
* with regard to the sort sequence.
* To set up your own distribution rules, sort the following table
* according to your requirements.
*
* Structure of internal table DISQTY (significant fields):
* ----------------------------------------------------------
*    DATA: BEGIN OF DISQTY OCCURS 0,
*          MATNR     LIKE BDBATCH-MATNR,    -> material number
*          CHARG     LIKE BDBATCH-CHARG,    -> batch number
*          WERKS     LIKE BDBATCH-WERKS,    -> plant
*          LGORT     LIKE BDBATCH-LGORT,    -> storage location
*          AVAL_QUAN LIKE V01FDK-VRFMG,     -> available quantity
*          QUANTITY  LIKE BDBATCH-MENGE,    -> target quantity
*          RES_TABIX LIKE SY-TABIX.         ->internal use
*    DATA: END OF DISQTY.
*
* Additional fields for distribution:
* -----------------------------------
* NO_OF_SPLIT -> The number of possible batch quantity splits
* QUAN_TO_DIS -> The quantity to be distributed (ordered quantity)
*
* Restrictions!
* -------------
* 1) Don't add or delete any entries from the internal table
* 2) Don't modify fields MATNR, CHARG, WERKS, LGORT, AVAL_QUAN and
*    RES_TABIX.
* 3) Don't change values of NO_OF_SPLIT and QUAN_TO_DIS
* 4) The only field that can be modified is the DISQTY-QUANTITY field
************************************************************
FORM CHMVS_001.

  DATA: lv_line TYPE kondh-chasp VALUE '1'.

  LOOP AT disqty.
    CHECK lv_line <= no_of_split.
    IF QUAN_TO_DIS > 0.
      IF DISQTY-AVAL_QUAN > QUAN_TO_DIS.
        DISQTY-QUANTITY = QUAN_TO_DIS.
      ELSEIF disqty-aval_quan > 0.
        DISQTY-QUANTITY = DISQTY-AVAL_QUAN.
      ENDIF.
      IF disqty-quantity > 0.
        quan_to_dis = quan_to_dis - disqty-quantity.
        MODIFY disqty TRANSPORTING quantity.
        ADD 1 TO lv_line.
      ENDIF.
    ENDIF.
  ENDLOOP.
```

Figure 3.32 Routine 1 of Quantity Proposal

Sales org.	Distr. Chl	Division	SalesDocTy	Search proced.	Check batch
7000	70	00	ZOR	ZD0001	☐
7000	70	00	ZSAM	ZD0001	☐
7000	71	00	DL	YD0001	☐
7000	71	00	ZSA1	YD0001	☐

Figure 3.33 Batch Search Procedure Determination

For batch determination to happen in a delivery created without reference to a sales order, you must define the default order type for the delivery type by going to SAP IMG • LOGISTICS EXECUTION • SHIPPING • DELIVERIES • DEFINE DELIVERY TYPES. From here, you must assign the default order type to a batch search procedure. Batch determination at the delivery level is also required when it's not possible to determine the batch at the order level.

3.14 Returns (Complaints) Processing

When there's a customer complaint, the company may decide to take back the material, which is handled by a returns process, issue a credit memo (without taking back the material), or send additional material without charges. These processes are called returns or complaint processing. Table 3.8 lists the sales order types that are used in complaint processing.

Order Type	Description	Physical Stock Movement	Reference
FD	Deliv.Free of Charge	Yes, outward	Not mandatory
SD	Subs.Dlv.Free of Ch.	Yes, outward	Mandatory
CR	Credit Memo Request	No	Not mandatory
DR	Debit Memo Request	No	Not mandatory
RK	Invoice Correct. Req	No	Mandatory
RE	Returns	Yes, inward	Not mandatory

Table 3.8 Standard Order Types for Complaint Processing

> **Reference to Complaint**
>
> It's always important to create the order documents with reference to the original invoice that the complaint was received in. So SD and RK are better suited. To use the types RE, CR, and DR, we recommend that you create a copy of these order types and make reference mandatory in the customized order types.

3.14.1 Free-of-Charge Delivery and Subsequent Delivery

The free-of-charge delivery (FD) type is primarily used to issue a sample free-of-charge but can also be used as part of complaint handling or a return process. This standard order type has the document pricing procedure (DoPP) C (free of charge). The pricing procedure is determined by the combination of sales area, document pricing procedure, and customer pricing procedure (CuPP), which we'll discuss in Chapter 4. The pricing procedure for any combination that contains the DoPP as C is to make the item free of charge. The free-of-charge subsequent delivery (order type SD) is the same as FD, except that reference to an existing order is mandatory for it. Order type FD can be created without reference. The free-of-charge pricing in an invoice is ensured by the copy control.

3.14.2 Invoice Correction without Return

When the company receives a complaint (or a request to take back the material), they may decide to compensate the customer by modifying the invoice without taking back the material or supplying additional material. The three standard sales document types are CR (credit memo request), DR (debit memo request), and RK (invoice correction request). They're used for complaint handling. It's important to note that for the CR and DR documents, reference to a billing document is not mandatory, whereas for RK, a reference is mandatory. While copying the billing document to the RK type order, the system creates two line items: one for credit and one for debit. For CR and DR orders, the relevant standard billing types G2 and L2 are used for issuing credit memos and debit memos, respectively. RK type orders are also processed by the G2 type invoice. The total value of an RK type order and the G2 invoice for it can be negative, so you should refer to it as a credit memo with negative value and not as a debit memo.

> **Multiple Reference**
>
> When reference is mandatory, the reference document number is entered in the first screen; only one document number can be entered here, and the complete document is then copied to the order. To add items from another reference document, use the menu path SALES DOCUMENT • CREATE WITH REFERENCE from the overview screen to enter the second referred document and copy its items. Repeat the process until all reference documents are included. There are a few standard limitations. For example, sold-to must be the same with reference to each document.

3.14.3 Returns

Companies often take back stock that has been sold to customers when there's a complaint and return the price the customer had paid for it. This is done to retain customer loyalty, improve brand image, and avoid legal costs or for social responsibility. Customers always appreciate an unambiguous and clear-cut sales return policy. The customer is allowed to return the material under specific conditions (e.g., within 15 days for any reason), and a credit memo for the return is issued to the customer. The sales document type, item category, and schedule line category used for return processing in a standard system are RE, REN, and DN, respectively. If the goods will be received as unrestricted stock, then in the schedule line category, you need to use the movement type 653 (GD returns unrestricted), whereas if the goods will be received as return, you can use the movement type 651 (GD ret.del returns). When you use movement type 653, the stock received from a customer return can be sold to another customer like any other unrestricted type stock. When you use movement type 651, the stock after receipt becomes return type stock and has to be further processed to make it available for sale (by changing it to unrestricted type using Transaction MIGO). When you use movement type 651, the stock is received in your warehouse but as blocked stock (because it has yet to be inspected after receipt from the customer for release as unrestricted, or it's to be scraped). The returns stock is not considered for valuation. This is surprising because the stock in quality inspection or restricted uses is considered for valuation.

> **Movement Type**
>
> Movement type comes into play when there's a physical or logical movement of stock. Stock moving from one plant to another is an example of physical movement, and stock getting blocked for delivery is a logical movement. Movement type also determines the GL that will be posted for the stock movement. Also note that stock or inventory is an asset and is a balance sheet item. The consumption accounts, such as cost of raw material, are expenses and are profit and loss account item. Movement types typically debit one asset/consumption account and credit another. Movement types that are configured in Material Management and used elsewhere including Sales and Distribution should be checked very closely, especially for the automatic account posting that the movement types do.

3.15 Intercompany Sales Processing

When a sales organization sells stock to the plant of another company code, the process is called intercompany sales processing. When a customer orders stock that can be supplied by a plant that belongs to another company code, you have two options:

1. Transfer the stock to a plant belonging to the same company code as that of the sales organization and complete the normal sales processing. We'll discuss the inter-company and intracompany stock transfer in Chapter 6.
2. Sell the product directly to the customer from the plant belonging to another company code. Issue a normal invoice to the customer from the company code of the sales organization and issue an intercompany invoice from the company code of the supplying plant to the company code of the sales organization.

If you choose the second option, you need to follow these steps:

1. Using Transaction OVV8 (menu path: SAP IMG • SALES AND DISTRIBUTION • BILLING • INTERCOMPANY BILLING • DEFINE THE ORDER TYPES FOR INTERCOMPANY BILLING), assign the intercompany credit memo (billing type IG) to all order types that will be issued for intercompany credit memo requests and assign intercompany billing (billing type IV) to all order types that will be issued for intercompany debit memo request or billing.

2. Using Transaction OVV9 (menu path: SAP IMG • SALES AND DISTRIBUTION • BILLING • INTERCOMPANY BILLING • ASSIGN ORGANIZATIONAL UNITS BY PLANT • ASSIGN ORGANIZATIONAL UNITS TO THE PLANTS), assign sales organizations, distribution channels, and divisions (the combination is called a sales area) to the plants for which intercompany billing is required. After the assignment of the intercompany billing from a plant to the sales areas, intercompany billing will be possible.

3. Using Transaction OVVA (menu path: SAP IMG • SALES AND DISTRIBUTION • BILLING • INTERCOMPANY BILLING • DEFINE INTERNAL CUSTOMER NUMBER BY SALES ORGANIZATION), you assign customers created for offsetting entries in the intercompany billing process to the respective sales organizations. You can do this step directly in the production server because it involves customer master records that are not transported. A typical accounting entry in the selling company will look like:

    ▶ Cr Revenue (Intercompany sales) – 100 USD
    ▶ Dr Customer (Internal customer for intercompany sale) – 100 USD

    In the purchasing company the entries will be:

    ▶ Cr Purchase (Intercompany purchase) – 100 USD
    ▶ Dr Vendor (Plant created as vendor) – 100 USD

▶ These entries are eliminated at the time of consolidation at the group level or by actual payment processing. Refer to SAP Note 308989 for more information on cross-company billing.

4. All of the steps for pricing must be maintained for intercompany billing. The steps in pricing will involve creating condition tables, access sequences, condition types, pricing procedures, and condition records. You can use the two standard condition types mentioned below for billing the dummy customer created for the sales organization in step 3.

   ▶ PI01 Intercompany: fixed amount per material unit (e.g., 10 USD/Kg)
   ▶ PI02 Intercompany: percentage of the net invoice amount (e.g., 10% of maximum retail price, 4% of PI01 condition type)

5. Create a sales order using Transaction VA01; the default value for the plant comes from either a customer-material info record, a material master record (when there's no default plant for the customer, a material combination is found in any customer material info record), or a customer master record (when the above two option do not return any default value for the plant). You can manually change this plant.

6. When the plant and the sales area (or sales organization) belong to different company codes but are permitted for intercompany billing (per step 2), necessary pricing is done either manually or automatically to complete the process of intercompany sales. (When the plants involved in stock transfer belong to same company code, it's called *intracompany stock transfer*.)

7. After the order processing, the delivery and goods issue is completed. The customer (or receiving plant) is billed and an offsetting intercompany bill is raised simultaneously or at the time of consolidation of financial statements at the holding company level. (Typically, actual payments are not involved.)

3.16 Common Integration Points with Material Management

Sales and Distribution is closely integrated with Material Management in SAP ERP. The various points of integration are:

▶ **Material master record**
The fields of material master records in the Basic Data, Sales, MRP, and Accounting tabs are important for sales and distribution processes. For example, the

sales unit maintained in the customer master record becomes the default unit of measurement for the material in an order.

- **Availability check**
  This is mostly configured in material master and production planning functionalities but used in sales and distribution processes (order and/or delivery).

- **Transfer of requirements**
  This transfers the quantity in the schedule line of an order or returns to the material requirements planning.

- **Material Requirements Planning (MRP)**
  This further processes all requirements by aggregating and processing for internal production or external procurements of different materials.

- **Sales and Operation Planning (SOP)**
  This is primarily used as a substitute or compliment to MRP in production planning. SOP data is transferred to MRP as independent requirements when both are in use. It's used for forecasting and planning. For long- and medium-term planning, SOP becomes a more practical approach. In SOP, sales targets for the future periods are entered manually, but you can use some forecasting models. If the forecasting model uses the current sales figures to forecast the future sale, then that's the integration point between SOP and the Sales and Distribution functionality in SAP ERP.

- **Intracompany and intercompany stock transfer**
  Inter- and intracompany stock transfers are integration points between the Materials Management and Sales and Distribution functionalities in SAP ERP. Some decisions, such as automatic determination of storage location, are decided in Sales and Distribution, whereas the movement type to be used and whether to use a two-step or one-step method for stock transfer are decided in Materials Management. We'll discuss this in more detail in Chapter 6.

- **Goods issue**
  The material is issued during delivery to the customer and during stock transfer. During these processes, the material document is generated in the background (can be seen in the document flow for order, delivery, or invoice). The material document generated in the background is processed in Materials Management for appropriate number range maintenance, movement type to be used, and automatic posting to accounting and creation of accounting documents.

▶ **Goods receipt**
The goods receipt during sales return and stock transfer also integrates the two logistics functionalities, similar to the goods issue just discussed.

▶ **Third-party sale and other special business processes**
We have already discussed the special business transactions such as third-party sales and individual purchase orders where the purchase requisition and/or purchase order is issued either automatically or manually for sales orders based on the item category group of the material. Purchase requisitions and purchase orders are part of the Materials Management functionality in SAP ERP.

3.17 Outputs in Sales

Output is what comes out of a system. You get the information you want in printouts, email, SMS, and several other possible forms. In sales the output of the sales order is used for various purposes such as order confirmation and material safety data sheets (MSDSs). The MSDSs are for each item or material and are required if the material is to cross the border into another country. So in what condition what type of output is to be issued to whom is determined using a condition technique in SAP ERP called the output determination process. The menu path is SAP IMG • BASIC FUNCTIONS • OUTPUT CONTROL • OUTPUT DETERMINATION – OUTPUT DETERMINATION USING CONDITION TECHNIQUE • MAINTAIN OUTPUT DETERMINATION FOR SALES DOCUMENTS. Even when you don't require the automatic determination of output, you must have an output type and output determination procedure to manually select the output. The steps for output determination in sales are as follows:

1. Add the field required in the condition table to the field catalog if it's not already available. The menu path is SAP IMG • BASIC FUNCTIONS • OUTPUT CONTROL • OUTPUT DETERMINATION – OUTPUT DETERMINATION USING CONDITION TECHNIQUE • MAINTAIN OUTPUT DETERMINATION FOR SALES DOCUMENTS • MAINTAIN CONDITION TABLES. Select Field Catalog: Messages for Sales Documents.

2. Create condition tables using fields available in the field catalog or identify the standard SAP condition tables that are suitable for storing condition records. The menu path is same as above. Select Maintain Output Condition Table for Sales Documents. Table 3.9 lists the standard available condition tables.

Condition Table	Description	Fields Used
001	Sales Organization/Customer Number	VKORG, KNDNR
005	Sales Organization/Order Type	VKORG, AUART
006	SOrg./Distrib.Ch/Division/Customer	VKORG, VTWEG, SPART, KNDNR
007	Order Type	AUART
013	Sales Org.	VKORG
015	Credit Control Area/Credit Repr. Group/Risk Category	KKBER, SBGRP, CTLPC
150	Doc.Type/Sales Org./Customer	AUART, VKORG, KUNNR
200	Overall Credit Status	CMGST

Table 3.9 Standard Condition Tables for Output Determination in Sales

3. Create an access sequence and assign condition tables for the system to access in correct sequence. You can create the assess sequence using the menu path SAP IMG • BASIC FUNCTIONS • OUTPUT CONTROL • OUTPUT DETERMINATION – OUTPUT DETERMINATION USING CONDITION TECHNIQUE • MAINTAIN OUTPUT DETERMINATION FOR SALES DOCUMENTS • MAINTAIN ACCESS SEQUENCES. The access sequence can contain several accesses or access numbers, and each access can contain one condition table. The fields of the condition table can be displayed by selecting the access number and opening the Fields folder. The key for the access sequence must start with a Z. The access sequence determines the sequence in which condition type records, output type records in this case, are searched to find the appropriate condition type record (output type record).

4. Create output types with the correct access sequence assigned to them. The condition types are called output type here. Defining output types is key in the output determination process. The list of important standard output types is as follows:
   - AF00: inquiry
   - AN00: quotation
   - BA00: order confirmation
   - BA1N: (output type for manual processing)
   - BAV0: order confirmation VMI

- ESYM: internal output
- KO00: contract
- KRML: credit processing
- LP00: scheduling agreement
- MAIL: internal output
- RD03: cash sale
- SDB: material safety data sheet (MSDS)

As an example, let's take order confirmation (BA00) to understand how you can modify the standard output type or create a Z-output type. In Transaction V/30, Output Types (Sales Document) (this is same as executing Transaction NACE and selecting the application V1 and double-clicking on the Output Type tab, as shown in Figure 3.34), when you double-click on any output type, in this case BA00, you go to the screen shown in Figure 3.35.

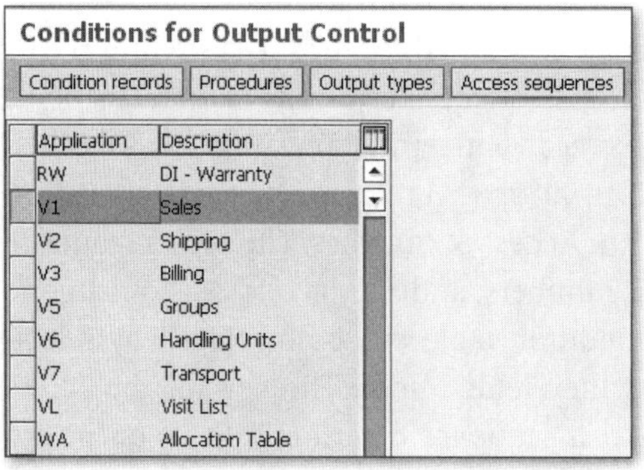

Figure 3.34 Application V1 (Sales) in Transaction NACE

The menu path for Transaction V/30 is SAP IMG • BASIC FUNCTIONS • OUTPUT CONTROL • OUTPUT DETERMINATION – OUTPUT DETERMINATION USING CONDITION TECHNIQUE • MAINTAIN OUTPUT DETERMINATION FOR SALES DOCUMENTS • MAINTAIN OUTPUT TYPES. You maintain the access sequence in the General Data tab. In the Default Values tab, you can maintain values for Dispatch Time, Transmission Medium, Partner Function, and Communication Strategy that become the default values when you create condition records.

In the processing routine, you can replace the form (RVORDER01 as shown in Figure 3.36 for output type BA00) with customized forms created using SAP Smart Form (Transaction SMARTFORMS).

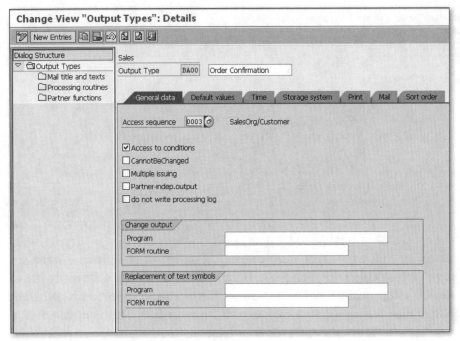

Figure 3.35 General Data of Output Type BA00

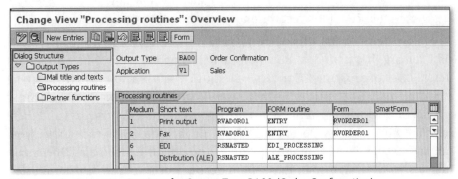

Figure 3.36 Processing Routines for Output Type BA00 (Order Confirmation)

After creating the output types, they are assigned to partner functions. The output can be issued only to the partners who are assigned to it. This basically depends on the preference (and technical feasibility) for the partner. A customer may like to get the output by courier and another by fax (if they have fax machine, which is technical feasibility). In Figure 3.37, you can see the assignment of the Output Type BA00 to the partner function sold-to party for different mediums.

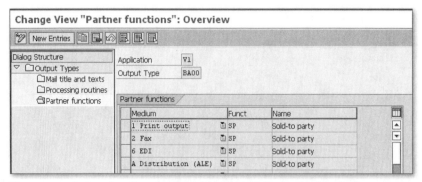

Figure 3.37 Partner Functions for Output Type BA00 (Order Confirmation)

5. Create the determination procedure and assign to it the output types. Follow the menu path SAP IMG • BASIC FUNCTIONS • OUTPUT CONTROL • OUTPUT DETERMINATION – OUTPUT DETERMINATION USING CONDITION TECHNIQUE • MAINTAIN OUTPUT DETERMINATION FOR SALES DOCUMENTS • MAINTAIN OUTPUT DETERMINATION PROCEDURE to define the output determination procedure. Different output types are assigned to each step of the procedure. The requirement routines are used for improving the performance by skipping steps that are not relevant because of the specific requirement mentioned for a step. The Exclusive checkbox is also used for improving performance by not allowing the system to search for other condition records once a condition record is found.

6. Assign a determination procedure to sales document types and item categories. You assign output determination by following the menu path SAP IMG • BASIC FUNCTIONS • OUTPUT CONTROL • OUTPUT DETERMINATION – OUTPUT DETERMINATION USING CONDITION TECHNIQUE • MAINTAIN OUTPUT DETERMINATION FOR SALES DOCUMENTS • ASSIGN OUTPUT DETERMINATION PROCEDURES and then selecting Allocate Sales Document Header. In addition to the PROCEDURE, you can specify the default output type here. The option Assign Sales Document Items is used for assigning the determination procedure, defined for a sales document item, to the item categories.

7. Create condition records using Transaction VV11 (menu path: SAP EASY ACCESS • LOGISTICS • SALES AND DISTRIBUTION • MASTER DATA • OUTPUT • SALES DOCUMENT • CREATE). Select the output type for which condition records are to be maintained and then click on Key Combination. Select the appropriate key combination. Partner Function, Partner, Transmission Medium, Time, and Language values are maintained for all condition records.

3.18 Foreign Trade

Most of the master data maintenance and document processing in foreign trade is done using area menu VX00 or cockpit Transaction VX99. Within the cockpit transaction, general processing (accessed via Transaction EN99 or by selecting the General Processing tab in Transaction VX99), master data, and documents are maintained for foreign trade. As you know, the master data is maintained in the customer master, vendor master, material master, and purchase info record accessed directly from Transaction EN99. You can also access individual documents from the general processing cockpit Transaction EN99. You can access both purchasing documents such as the purchase order, goods receipt, and invoice and sales documents such as order, delivery, and billing documents. You don't need Transaction VA02, VL02N, or VF02 for changing the foreign-trade-related data in a sales, delivery, and billing document, respectively.

In the order, the foreign trade data is entered in the Billing Document view, which you access by the following menu path from the order overview screen: GOTO • HEADER • BILLING. You enter INCO term, payment term, billing, and risk management information in this screen. At the item level in Sale A view (accessed by selecting the line and following the menu path GOTO • ITEM • SALES A), you enter the foreign trade information such as business transaction type and International Article number (EAN/UPC) if it's to be entered manually.

In the delivery document, accessed through Transaction VL02N or EN99, enter the foreign trade data at the screen accessed via the menu path GOTO • HEADER • FOREIGN TRADE/CUSTOMS from the overview screen. Similarly, you maintain the item-level data in the screen accessed from the menu path GOTO • ITEM • FOREIGN TRADE/CUSTOMS by selecting the particular line item.

In the billing document, you maintain the foreign-trade-relevant data in the screen accessed via the menu path GOTO • HEADER • FOREIGN TRADE/CUSTOMS for the header level data and GOTO • ITEM • FOREIGN TRADE ITEM after selecting an item for the item-level data.

Now, let's walk through the important customization steps for foreign trade processing for Sales and Distribution.

3.18.1 Countries

For foreign trade processing in SAP ERP, the first step is customization, sometimes referred to as a prerequisite. Most countries are available in the standard SAP system. Occasionally you may have to create one, though, because the political map of the world changes frequently. The menu path is SAP IMG • SAP NetWeaver • General Settings • Set Countries • Define Countries.

3.18.2 Currencies

The same is true for currencies. Most should be in the system, but if you need to create a new one, follow the menu path SAP IMG • SAP NetWeaver • General Settings • Currencies • Enter Exchange Rates (Transaction OB08).

> **Note**
> You can directly edit Table TCURR using Transaction SE16N and the &SAP_EDIT function. You can also develop an ABAP program and execute it in the background as a scheduled job to update the table regularly.

3.18.3 Number Ranges

Foreign trade number ranges, for example, general export/import processing (Transaction XEIP), Transaction XAUS, or documentary payment (Transaction XAKK), are accessed via the menu path SAP IMG • Sales and Distribution • Foreign Trade/Customs • Define Number Ranges. They can also be accessed from Transaction SNRO. The three transaction codes just mentioned are, respectively, EXPIMP, RV_EXPORT, and FT_AKKRED numbering objects. Table 3.10 provides a list of important transactions for maintaining number ranges for foreign trade and the numbering objects that can be used to do the same from Transaction SNRO.

Transaction Code	Number Range For	Numbering Object
XEIP	General export/import processing	EXPIMP
XAUS	Legal control	RV_EXPORT
XAKK	Documentary payment	FT_AKKRED
XAAM	Print export declaration	FT_DRU_AM
XATR	Print ATR document	FT_DRU_ATR
XAEU	Print EUR1 document	FT_DRU_EUR
XATD	Print T document	FT_DRU_T

Table 3.10 Number Range Objects Relevant for Foreign Trade

> **Note**
>
> Often, it's easier to maintain any number range using Transaction SNRO and the numbering object rather than individual transactions, but it's a matter of preference.

3.18.4 Commodity Codes and Import Code Numbers

Commodity or import codes are maintained as per the official number issued by the respective government to group materials that are similar from a customs point of view. You maintain them via the menu path SAP IMG • SALES AND DISTRIBUTION • FOREIGN TRADE/CUSTOMS • BASIC DATA FOR FOREIGN TRADE • DEFINE COMMODITY CODES/IMPORT CODE NUMBERS BY COUNTRY. These numbers are maintained in the material master, from which they are automatically copied to sales documents. A harmonized system (HS) for commodity codes developed by World Customs Organization (*www.wcoomd.org*) is accepted worldwide and is used for customs tariff rules, trade statistics, compliance, embargo, fright, and various other purposes.

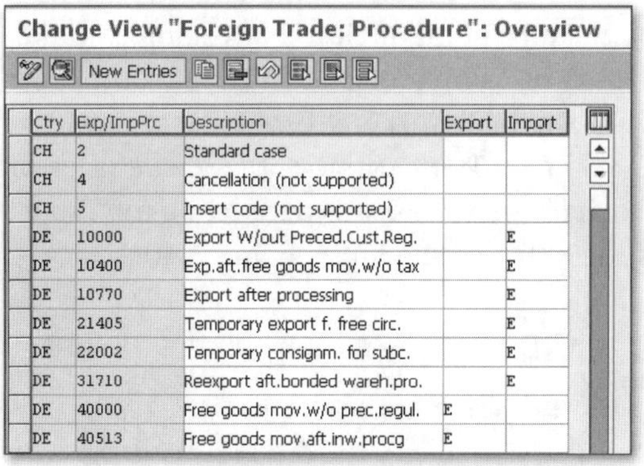
Change View "Foreign Trade: Procedure": Overview

New Entries

Ctry	Exp/ImpPrc	Description	Export	Import
CH	2	Standard case		
CH	4	Cancellation (not supported)		
CH	5	Insert code (not supported)		
DE	10000	Export W/out Preced.Cust.Reg.		E
DE	10400	Exp.aft.free goods mov.w/o tax		E
DE	10770	Export after processing		E
DE	21405	Temporary export f. free circ.		E
DE	22002	Temporary consignm. for subc.		E
DE	31710	Reexport aft.bonded wareh.pro.		E
DE	40000	Free goods mov.w/o prec.regul.	E	
DE	40513	Free goods mov.aft.inw.procg	E	

Figure 3.38 Export/Import Procedure

3.18.5 Procedure

The export/ import procedures are defined via the menu path SAP IMG • SALES AND DISTRIBUTION • FOREIGN TRADE/CUSTOMS • BASIC DATA FOR FOREIGN TRADE • DEFINE PROCEDURES AND DEFAULT VALUE • DEFINE PROCEDURE (Transaction OVE6) for different countries, as shown in Figure 3.38. Based on the country, sales organization, distribution channel, division, export/import material group, and item category, the procedure is determined automatically and maintained in the menu path SAP IMG • SALES AND DISTRIBUTION • FOREIGN TRADE/CUSTOMS • BASIC DATA FOR FOREIGN TRADE • DEFINE PROCEDURES AND DEFAULT VALUE • DEFINE PROCEDURE

Default (Transaction OVE6) (Figure 3.39). You can modify the default procedure at the document level.

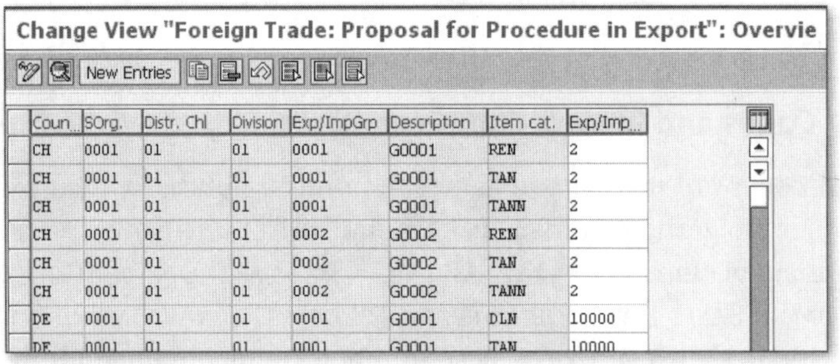
Change View "Foreign Trade: Proposal for Procedure in Export": Overvie

Coun...	SOrg.	Distr. Chl	Division	Exp/ImpGrp	Description	Item cat.	Exp/Imp...
CH	0001	01	01	0001	G0001	REN	2
CH	0001	01	01	0001	G0001	TAN	2
CH	0001	01	01	0001	G0001	TANN	2
CH	0001	01	01	0002	G0002	REN	2
CH	0001	01	01	0002	G0002	TAN	2
CH	0001	01	01	0002	G0002	TANN	2
DE	0001	01	01	0001	G0001	DLN	10000
DE	0001	01	01	0001	G0001	TAN	10000

Figure 3.39 Export/Import Procedure Determination

3.18.6 Business Transaction Type

As we touched upon earlier, the business transaction type is required for foreign trade processing in the sales order item level. The business transaction type defines the nature of the transaction from the customs point of view. For example, it indicates whether an action is a sales return or sample dispatch. The menu path is SAP IMG • Sales and Distribution • Foreign Trade/Customs • Basic Data for Foreign Trade • Define Business Transaction Types and Default Value • Define Business Types (Transaction OVE4). To define new business transaction for a country, select Copy As (F6) for any existing entry, as shown in Figure 3.40.

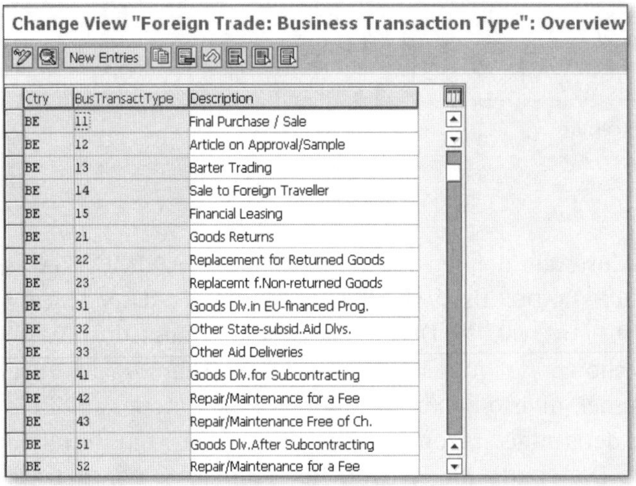
Change View "Foreign Trade: Business Transaction Type": Overview

Ctry	BusTransactType	Description
BE	11	Final Purchase / Sale
BE	12	Article on Approval/Sample
BE	13	Barter Trading
BE	14	Sale to Foreign Traveller
BE	15	Financial Leasing
BE	21	Goods Returns
BE	22	Replacement for Returned Goods
BE	23	Replacemt f.Non-returned Goods
BE	31	Goods Dlv.in EU-financed Prog.
BE	32	Other State-subsid.Aid Dlvs.
BE	33	Other Aid Deliveries
BE	41	Goods Dlv.for Subcontracting
BE	42	Repair/Maintenance for a Fee
BE	43	Repair/Maintenance Free of Ch.
BE	51	Goods Dlv.After Subcontracting
BE	52	Repair/Maintenance for a Fee

Figure 3.40 Defining Business Transaction Types for Different Countries

Based on the country, sales organization, distribution channel, and item category, the default business type is assigned to each combination via the menu path SAP IMG • SALES AND DISTRIBUTION • FOREIGN TRADE/CUSTOMS • BASIC DATA FOR FOREIGN TRADE • DEFINE PROCEDURES AND DEFAULT VALUE • DEFINE DEFAULT BUSINESS TYPE (SD) (Transaction OVE5), as shown in Figure 3.41.

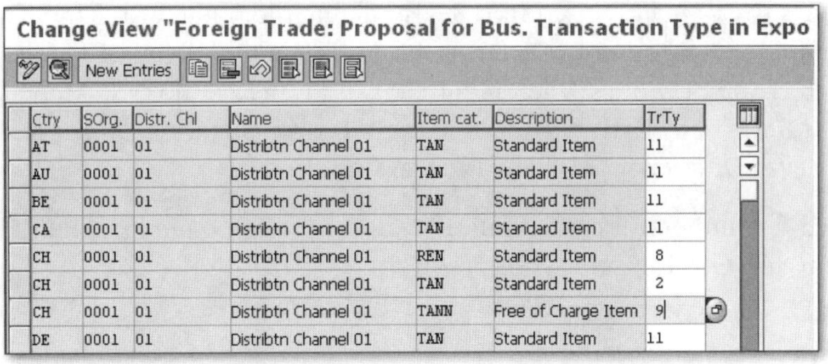
Change View "Foreign Trade: Proposal for Bus. Transaction Type in Expo

New Entries

Ctry	SOrg.	Distr. Chl	Name	Item cat.	Description	TrTy
AT	0001	01	Distribtn Channel 01	TAN	Standard Item	11
AU	0001	01	Distribtn Channel 01	TAN	Standard Item	11
BE	0001	01	Distribtn Channel 01	TAN	Standard Item	11
CA	0001	01	Distribtn Channel 01	TAN	Standard Item	11
CH	0001	01	Distribtn Channel 01	REN	Standard Item	8
CH	0001	01	Distribtn Channel 01	TAN	Standard Item	2
CH	0001	01	Distribtn Channel 01	TANN	Free of Charge Item	9
DE	0001	01	Distribtn Channel 01	TAN	Standard Item	11

Figure 3.41 Default Business Transaction Type Determination

3.18.7 Mode of Transport

You define the mode of transport for different countries via the menu path SAP IMG • SALES AND DISTRIBUTION • FOREIGN TRADE/CUSTOMS • TRANSPORTATION DATA • DEFINE MODES OF TRANSPORT (Transaction OVE2). The mode of transport defines the type of transport, including sea, rail, air, or road, used at the time of crossing the border. It can be automatically determined if the route determination is configured.

3.18.8 Customs Offices

The customs office is the point of entry to a country for foreign goods. The customs office is either selected from a proposed list or automatically determined (if route determination is configured) in the delivery. It can be manually maintained in the billing document. The menu path to define a new customs office for a country is SALES AND DISTRIBUTION • FOREIGN TRADE • TRANSPORTATION DATA • DEFINE CUSTOMS OFFICES (Transaction OVE2)

3.18.9 INCO Terms

INCO term stands for International Commercial Term and is a trademark. The International Chamber of Commerce (ICC) (*iccwbo.org/incoterm*) has published these terms. The identify different transactional costs involved in sales, for example, loading at seller premises, insurance, and unloading at port (origin). Thirteen INCO terms are used based on how the seller and buyer divide the transaction cost among, for example CIF – cost insurance and freight (second part – destination port) and FOB – free on Board (second part – port of origin). Contracts for the International Sale of Goods (CISG) promoted by United Nations and Unified Commercial Codes (UCC) mainly used in U.S. also define the trade terms. In SAP systems you can find several other INCO terms in addition to the original 13 of the ICC. You can also create new ones when required using Transaction OVSG (menu path: SAP IMG • SALES AND DISTRIBUTION • MASTER DATA • BUSINESS PARTNERS • CUSTOMERS • BILLING DOCUMENT • DEFINE INCOTERMS).

Having discussed few important configuration steps for foreign trade in SAP ERP, let's discuss what SAP GTS can offer you.

3.18.10 SAP GTS

The limitations of foreign trade in SAP ERP are addressed in SAP Global Trade Services (GTS) system. The basic configuration done in the Sales and Distribution functionality in SAP ERP is transferred to GTS and subsequent processing. GTS, which is a component of SAP NetWeaver, has three important components: Compliance Management, Customs Management, and Risk Management. GTS can be used to manage foreign trade originating both in SAP ERP and non-SAP systems. Some of the functions that SAP GTS offers you are:

- Centralized processing of all global trade related processes.
- Automated checking for embargo even for specific legs in logistics.
- Automated checking for export (or import) licenses.
- Automatic update of master data in GTS based on updates in SAP ERP.
- Automated filing of documents to government agencies. More and more governments and customs offices have now provided and prefer e-filing.
- Preferential trade agreements. For example, to export to Singapore, you may like to ship from your plant in Australia and not from India, if there is a preferential trade agreement (e.g., NAFTA, EU) between Australia and Singapore.
- Maintain customs duty rates.
- Automatic Maintenance of logbook of customs communications.

- Management of customs bonded warehouses.
- Processing of Letter of Credits.

> **Plug-in for SAP GTS**
>
> If you're using SAP ECC 5.0 or a previous release, you need to install a plug-in using Transaction SAINT. Refer SAP note 1104470 for detailed installation instructions. The plug-in is required for the SAP GTS system to communicate with the SAP ERP system.

Whether you should process the foreign trade using the foreign trade functionality of SAP ERP or via SAP GTS is a tricky question. Small and medium sized (and not an export and/or import oriented) companies, typically start with the foreign trade functionality in SAP ERP and migrate to the SAP GTS system as their global trade grows.

> **Note**
>
> Global trade (LO-GT) functionalities offered in SAP ERP are not for exclusive use in foreign trade processing. It is different from SAP GTS. This functionality offers many added features for trading (as opposed to manufacturing). This is activated by selecting the EA-GLT application available at the end of the menu path SAP IMG • ACTIVATION SWITCH FOR SAP R/3 ENTERPRISE EXTENSION SET, which lists features to manage trading contracts, trading expenses, trading execution workbench, and trading position to cover risk in this functionality.

3.19 Summary

In this chapter, we discussed how to customize the header, item, and schedule line levels of sales documents. We discussed different sales documents such as orders, outline agreements, and complaints. We discussed the use of condition techniques in automatic determination of partners, free goods, material determination, material listing and exclusion, batch, and output. We also discussed incompletion logs, foreign trade, availability checks, transfer of requirements, and special business processes.

With this knowledge, you'll be able to optimize your sales process with the customization of sales document type, item category, schedule line category, and copy control. Incompletion logs, material determination, material exclusion, and listing will further optimize your sales process. In addition to the normal sales process, you can use your knowledge for the special business processes, outline agreements, foreign trade, and return and complaint processing that your company may be using now or in the future. You should be able to use the batch management functionality that SAP offers for sales with the knowledge you got in this chapter and in the previous one. You now know the integration points between material management and sales, especially how availability checks and transfer of requirements is done. You can also use the standard outputs that SAP offers for sales.

In next chapter, we'll discuss pricing, where the condition technique is demonstrated at its best.

This chapter discusses the condition technique, routines, customization of pricing, and the improvement of system performance by the optimizing condition technique used for pricing. After reading through this, you should be able to customize rebate agreements and SAP interfaces for external tax software.

4 Pricing

Condition techniques are one of the most important functionalities in SAP ERP. In Chapter 3, you saw the use of condition techniques in automatic determination. In this chapter, we'll see its use in pricing. We'll discuss rebate agreements and tax processing, which are also part of pricing in a broader sense. The customization of pricing report discussed in this chapter will be perhaps your first step in developing your own reports.

Price is what a customer pays you for your goods and/or services. In modern economies, several factors have made it a very complex functionality. Tax is one such factor. In almost all countries goods and/or services are taxed. Keeping in mind national interest and social objectives, some goods are taxed more than others. The tax rate on cigarettes may be much higher than that for fresh fruit. You may have to pay a higher tax on an imported car than you pay for a domestically manufactured one. In addition to tax, discounts, freight, and surcharges are also considered part of your price. Discounts are given to encourage customers to buy more, pre-pone purchasing decision, or pay in advance or for a variety of other reasons. For surcharges the objective is same or similar, but the execution is different. You add a surcharge to customer's purchase for not buying a minimum quantity, delaying payment, or not buying before an agreed-upon date. Rebates are similar to discounts but are subject to certain conditions (e.g., buying a certain quantity within a time period). Only when the condition is fulfilled is the rebate paid to the customer. Unlike discounts, rebates are not paid to a customer up front. A deduction from the invoice value is also considered a payment.

In this chapter, we'll start by introducing condition techniques and then move on to condition records. We'll then discuss the application of the condition technique in pricing. The section on optimizing pricing determination will teach you how pricing is carried out and how you can optimize its performance. From there, we'll discuss the rebate agreement process and show you how to customize a pricing report. Finally, you'll be introduced to commonly available external tax software and how to integrate it with your SAP system. So, let's get started.

4.1 Introduction to Condition Techniques

In SAP ERP, condition techniques are used in automatic determination of output, batches, material listing and exclusion, text, revenue accounts, and many other places. It's not confined to the Sales and Distribution functionality in SAP ERP. They may also be used in many other SAP ERP components where automatic determination is required. We'll list the general steps for customization of condition techniques, which will give you an overview of how the elements of this type of technique are integrated. But first, let's describe these elements.

- **Field catalog**
  A field catalog is simply the collection of all fields that are or can be used in a condition table. The field catalogs for different determination functionalities (e.g., pricing, revenue GL) differ. You can add new fields to this catalog if required.

- **Condition tables**
  Condition tables store the condition records. There can be several condition tables for the determination of the same object (e.g., price). A company can have one price for a material (e.g., 100 USD), another for a particular sales organization (e.g., 90 USD for sales org 1000), and another for a customer, for example, XYZ Inc. of the sales org 1000 (e.g., 85 USD). These three prices require three kinds of condition tables to store them. The table that stores prices based on material will store the price 100 USD/unit. The table that stores prices based on material and sales organization will store the price 90 USD/unit. A third type of table is required to store the price based on material, sales organization, and customer. Some of these tables may be available in the standard system. When they're not available, you have to create them using fields available in the field catalog. A field that is not available in the field catalog (e.g., customer code) must be added to the field catalog first, to make it available for use as a key field in the condition table.

- **Access sequence**
  This is a list of condition tables that are listed in a specific sequence. Take the example that we gave for condition tables. The difficulty in the system is to

decide on the price for the customer XYZ Inc. All three prices are valid. But based on the access sequence, the price 85 USD/unit, which is valid for the material, sales org, and customer, may be accessed first. When a valid condition record is found, the system may or may not (depending on the exclusive indicator and routines used) search for records in other tables or accesses.

- **Condition type**
  For each element (e.g., price, discount) that is to be determined, you define a condition type. The condition type also specifies the access sequence to be used, among many other things. We'll discuss this further when we discuss the step for defining the pricing condition type.

- **Determination procedure**
  A determination procedure lists the condition types. It's assigned to a combination of objects (e.g., sales area, document pricing procedure, and customer pricing procedure in the case of pricing) for which determination is to be carried using the condition technique.

- **Condition records**
  Each row in a condition table represents a condition record. This is a master data element. Its value is the result of the determination process that used the condition technique. This result moves to the document (or other object) that used the condition technique.

Now let's see how these elements are used in the customization of condition techniques, which generally consists of the following seven steps:

1. Add the field required in condition table to the field catalog if it's already not available.
2. Create condition tables using the fields available in the field catalog or identify the standard SAP condition tables suitable for storing condition records.
3. Create an access sequence and assign condition tables for the system to access in the correct sequence.
4. Create condition types with the correct access sequence assigned to them. You cannot assign an access sequence if the condition type is not meant for automatic determination.
5. Create a determination procedure.
6. Assign the determination procedure.
7. Create condition records.

4.2 Condition Records

Pricing condition records, like other master records, are maintained in the production client and accessed during sales document processing. When we say "price," we're referring to the gross price, the various types of discounts that are deducted from it, surcharges that are added, freight that is included (based on INCO terms), and tax that is added. Of these price elements some are applicable to all goods and services and are difficult to allocate to individual items, such as freight or processing fees. These are *header conditions*. Others are clearly for individual items, called *item conditions,* such as tax. However, the method for calculating these conditions determines whether it's a header or item condition. For example, if you charge 10 USD for any invoice as a processing fee, then it becomes a header condition. When the processing fee is 1 USD per item, it becomes an item condition.

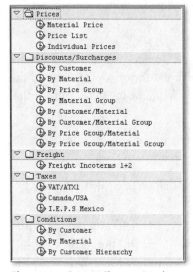

Figure 4.1 Create, Change, Display, and Create with Reference Pricing Condition Records (Transactions VK31, VK32, VK33, and VK34)

Pricing condition records are usually created for a particular sales organization and distribution channel. The transaction code for creating pricing condition record is VK31, or you can go to SAP EASY ACCESS • LOGISTICS • SALES AND DISTRIBUTION • MASTER DATA • CONDITIONS • CREATE. Then you select the folders at the left, as shown in Figure 4.1, depending on the type of condition record you want to create. The transaction codes to change, display, and create with reference are VK32, VK33, and VK34, respectively. The selection using the condition type (menu path:

SAP easy access • Logistics • Sales and Distribution • Master Data • Conditions • Selection using condition type) is also used to create (VK11), change (VK12), display, (VK13) and create with reference (VK14) condition records.

When creating a condition record using Transaction VK11, as seen in Figure 4.2, you enter the Condition Type and select the Key Combination. Depending on the key combination, the condition record is stored in different condition tables. In addition to the fields mentioned in the key combination, you also enter the sales organization and distribution channel when creating the condition record. This means the condition record is valid only for the relevant sales organization and distribution channel. In the Fast Entry mode, you can create the condition records for all materials for one customer, as shown in Figure 4.3. You can copy the list from other applications (e.g., Microsoft Excel) and paste it.

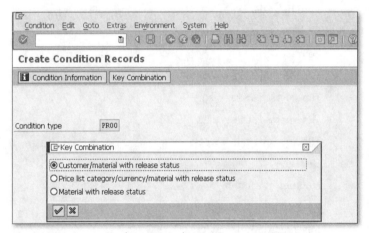

Figure 4.2 Create Condition Record Using Transaction VK11

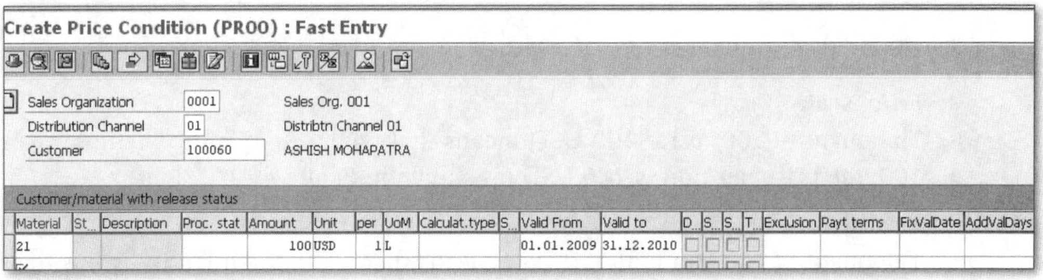

Figure 4.3 PR00 Condition Record with the Customer/Material with Release Status Key Combination

The condition record can have more than one amount stored in the condition value field. This is possible because of the *scales* functionality, which allows for different values for the condition record depending on the *scale basis*. For example, the price of a material can be 10 USD/unit when the order is for five or fewer units and 9 USD/unit when the order is for six or more units. Table 4.1 lists the different standard scale bases.

Scale Basis (Key)	Scale Basis (Text)
B	Value scale
C	Quantity scale
D	Gross weight scale
E	Net weight scale
F	Volume scale
G	Scale based on a formula
L	Point scale
M	Time period scale – month
N	Time period scale – years
O	Time period scale – days
P	Time period scale – week
R	Distance
S	Number of shipping units
T	Reserved (IS-OIL, time prices)
X	Reserved (IS-OIL, day prices)

Table 4.1 List of Scale Bases

There are three possible types of scales:

- **From scale**
  The quantity 100, price 100 USD means that when the quantity is more than 100, the price per unit is 100 USD (as shown in Figure 4.4).

- **To scale**
  The quantity 100, amount 100 USD means that when the quantity is less than 100, the price per unit is 100 USD.

- **Interval scale**
  You can't use a graduated-to interval scale for group conditions, and this can't be modified at the condition record level, which restricts its use.

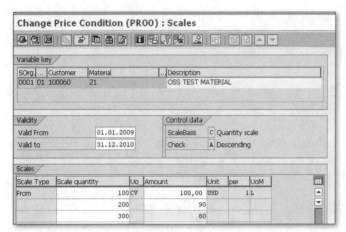

Figure 4.4 Use of Scale in Condition Type

You can modify the scale type by going to GOTO • DETAILS, as shown in Figure 4.5, except when the scale type is fixed as D (graduated-to interval) for the condition type in the customization.

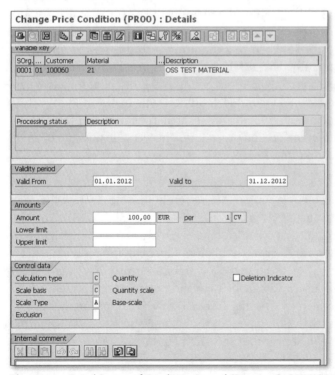

Figure 4.5 Detail Screen of Condition Record (Program SAPMV13A Screen Number 300)

When the processing status (as shown in Figure 4.5) of a condition record is blank, the condition record is active or in use. The other options are A (blocked), B (released for pricing simulation), and C (released for planning and pricing simulation).

> **Note**
>
> The important thing to note is that you can have condition records in the same condition table with the same or overlapping date ranges if the status is different. For pricing, only the records with a status of released are available for processing, but some of the customized status types can be made available for use in pricing.

Depending on customization, the value of the condition can be modified manually in the sales document. It's better to have an upper limit or lower limit (or both) for the condition type in the condition record. These fields are also filled in the Details screen. If, for example, there's is a percentage-type discount and someone manually changes it to 200% in a document, the system should throw an error or warning message.

Supplement conditions are allowed in certain condition types and can be accessed using the Supplement Condition icon or the menu path GOTO • CONDITIONS SUPPLEMENT. As shown in Figure 4.6, additional condition types with values can be added to a condition record. So when this condition record is picked up by any sales document, it automatically picks up the supplement conditions attached to it. For example, you can have a pricing policy of giving a 10% discount for customers who will bear the freight cost. So when the condition type (e.g., Z10P) for a 10% discount is selected, the condition type to add a surcharge for freight (e.g., ZFRT) is automatically picked up in the pricing procedure. This is made possible by making ZFRT a supplement condition of Z10P.

Maintaining condition records involves deleting records, changing the validity period, and changing the amount. You can delete condition records from the database with archiving functionality (Transaction SARA, object SD_COND). The system archives only those condition records that are already marked for deletion. A record marked for deletion can be reversed before the archiving program deletes it from the database. That is, you can make a condition record that's marked for deletion available for use again. To change the validity period of multiple condition records, select all of the records using Transaction VK12. Click on the Change Validity icon for changing the validity period, shown in Figure 4.7 (fifth icon from the left). A dialog screen will appear (not shown in Figure 4.7). All of the selected condition records have the new Valid From and Valid To dates in the pop-up screen.

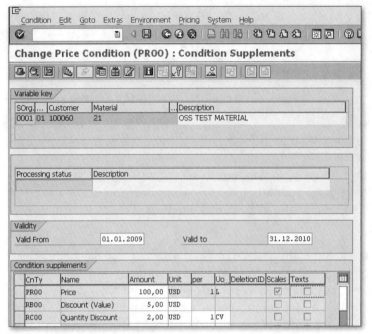

Figure 4.6 Condition Supplement

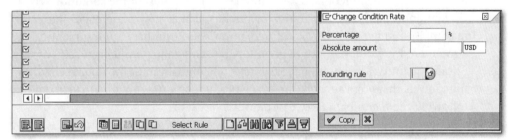

Figure 4.7 Condition Maintenance Icons

To change the amount, you click on the Change-Amount icon, shown in Figure 4.7 (the sixth icon from the left, which looks like a calculator). The pop-up gives you two options. The Percentage option allows you to enter a value (e.g., 5) in the Percentage field. When you click on the Copy button, all of the selected records will be increased by 5%. Figure 4.8 shows the intermediate screen for log display. The Absolute amount field (refer to Figure 4.7) allows you to enter a value (e.g., 10) and currency unit (e.g., USD), and all of the records will increase by that amount (e.g., 10 USD). Typically, price change rules are very complex, so you'll rarely use this functionality.

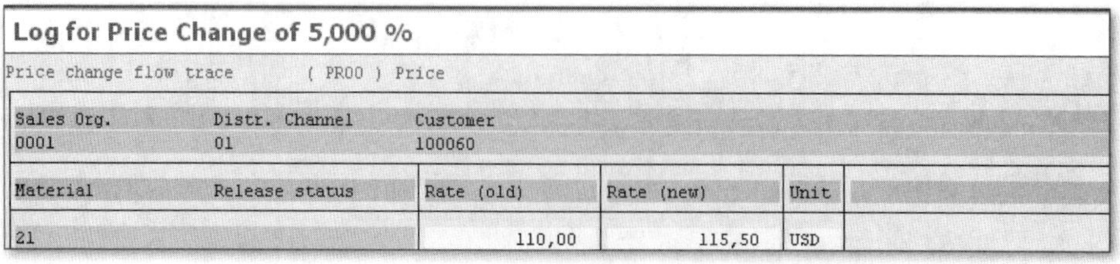

Log for Price Change of 5,000 %				
Price change flow trace	(PR00) Price			
Sales Org. 0001	Distr. Channel 01	Customer 100060		
Material	Release status	Rate (old)	Rate (new)	Unit
21		110,00	115,50	USD

Figure 4.8 Log for 5% Price Increase (PR00 Condition Type) for All Material

You can report changes to the condition records via the menu path ENVIRONMENT • CHANGES • PER CONDITION RECORD (for a single record) or CHANGE RECORD (for multiple records). The program for change record reports, RV16ACHD can be copied and modified.

The terms of payment and additional value days or fixed value days can be part of the condition record (see Figure 4.3, last three columns), and when they are, they take priority over customer master records or data from other customization settings. This information is used for processing a cash discount at the time of payment receipt, based on the terms of payment. You attach this information to the condition record using the Additional Data icon. In the same screen (shown in Figure 4.9), when the functionality for cumulating the values for the condition record, Update Condition, is active, limits for pricing such as maximum condition value, maximum number of orders, and maximum condition base value (quantity) are also entered. Cumulation can happen for the sales value, number of sales orders, or sales quantity. The additional advantage of cumulation (or the update condition function) is that you can view the usage or cumulation up to a particular time by following the menu path EXTRA • CUMULATIVE VALUE.

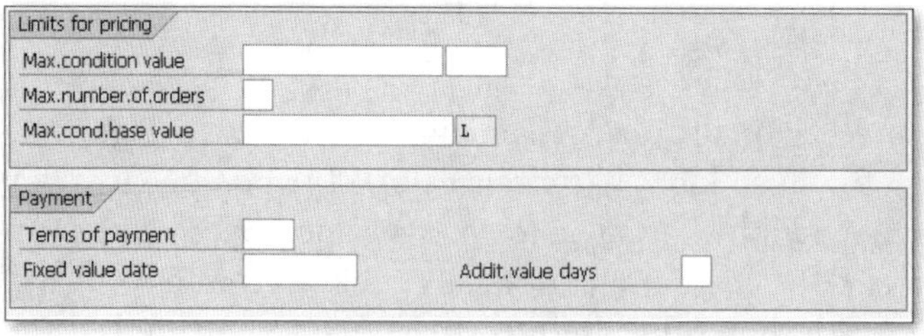

Limits for pricing		
Max.condition value		
Max.number.of.orders		
Max.cond.base value		L

Payment		
Terms of payment		
Fixed value date		Addit.value days

Figure 4.9 Additional Data for Condition Record

Condition *exclusion* is normally maintained for condition types in customization, but it can also be maintained for the condition record level (as you can see in the fourth column from the right in Figure 4.3). The important thing is that the condition supplement is given priority over exclusion. So the combination of condition supplement (at the condition record level) and exclusion (at the condition type level) can be used when normally one condition doesn't go with another unless there are exceptions.

Now that you understand condition records, let's move on to condition techniques.

4.2.1 Add Fields to Field Catalog

Add the fields required in condition table to the field catalog if they aren't already available. The menu path is SAP IMG • SALES AND DISTRIBUTION • BASIC FUNCTIONS • PRICING • PRICING CONTROL • DEFINE CONDITION TABLE • CONDITIONS: ALLOWED FIELDS.

4.2.2 Create Condition Tables

Condition tables store condition records. Several different condition tables can store the records of same condition type. For example, you can have a price for a material based on material (applicable to all sales organizations, divisions, and so on). Another price for the same material can exist for a particular sales organization. These two condition records will be stored in different condition tables. Condition tables are created using fields available in the field catalog. You can also identify and use the standard SAP condition tables that are suitable for storing condition records. The menu path for creating condition tables is SAP IMG • SALES AND DISTRIBUTION • BASIC FUNCTIONS • PRICING • PRICING CONTROL • DEFINE CONDITION TABLE • CREATE CONDITION TABLES (Transaction V/03).

4.2.3 Create Access Sequence

An access sequence is assigned to the condition types that need to be determined automatically. It consists of a sequence of condition tables. You create an access sequence and assign the condition tables for the system to access in the correct sequence. The menu path is SAP IMG • SALES AND DISTRIBUTION • BASIC FUNCTIONS • PRICING • PRICING CONTROL • DEFINE ACCESS SEQUENCE (Transaction V/07). Figure

4.10 shows the standard access sequence PR00. Note the use of requirement routine 3 in access number (AcNo) 30. This means that if the conditions specified in requirement routine 3 are not met, then the step (AcNo 30) is skipped. Also, the Exclusive checkbox is selected, which means that once a condition record is available, the system will not go to the next table in the access sequence.

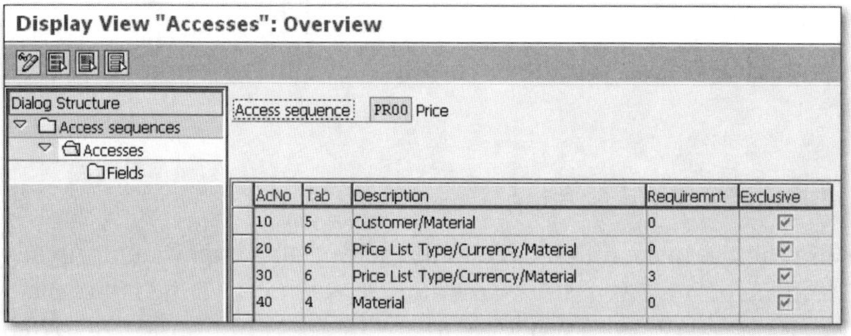

Figure 4.10 Access Sequence PR00

4.2.4 Create Condition Types

Condition types are created for each type of prices. Prices, surcharges, discounts, and taxes are general types of prices. There can be several types of discounts for a material or item, such as trade discount, off-season discount, and so on, and for each of them you need a condition type. In the condition type, you also specify how to calculate the discount (e.g., percentage or quantity based), among other things that we'll discuss. You create condition types with the correct access sequence assigned to them. You cannot assign an access sequence if the condition type is not meant for automatic determination (header conditions, for example). The menu path for defining condition types is SAP IMG • SALES AND DISTRIBUTION • BASIC FUNCTIONS • PRICING • PRICING CONTROL • DEFINE CONDITION TYPE (Transaction V/06). The screen used for defining condition type, shown in Figure 4.11, is an important screen. We'll discuss the fields that define the condition type below.

- The Condition Class determines whether the condition type is a price, discount or surcharge, or tax. The Condition Category is another way of classifying the condition type. The Calculation Type restricts the selection of the unit of measure for the Amount field of the condition record. You can also change this in the condition record level. If the value of a condition is always expected to be either positive or negative, then using the Plus/Minus field, you can change the value and prevent any error, even with manual entry. The Rounding Rule can be commercial (1.51 becomes 2 and 1.49 becomes 1), round up (both 1.51 and 1.49 become 2), or round down (both 1.49 and 1.51 become 1). The Structure Condition field determines how the condition type behaves in an order containing a bill of materials or configurable material.

- When the Group Condition checkbox is selected, the condition record of the condition type should include the material group as a field. Items belonging to same material group are grouped to get the benefit of scale, which otherwise is not available to individual items. The Group Condition Routine influences the group condition or how the values of the condition type in different items are grouped. If the Rounding Difference Comparison checkbox is selected, it will compare the difference at the header and sum of items (difference can occur due to rounding at the item level) and settle the difference by adding or subtracting it to the largest item. Please note that both item- and header-level condition types can be a group condition, so rounding the difference comparison is applicable to it.

- The option selected for Manual Entries determines whether the condition type can be added at the document processing time and whether it will take priority over the automatically determined condition record. The Header Condition is the condition type that is applicable to a document as whole and cannot be made applicable to items. Item Conditions, as opposed to header conditions, are applicable to items of a document and cannot be added manually at the header level, although the total of individual items is displayed at the header level. Please note that a condition type can be defined as a header and an item condition at the same time, and an access sequence can be assigned to such a condition type. But this does not mean the condition can be determined automatically using the access sequence, condition table, and condition record maintained for it. The header conditions are still added manually at the document level, and a condition type that is exclusively a header condition can't have an access sequence. The Delete checkbox determines if the condition record inserted manually or determined automatically can be deleted manually from a document. The Amount/Percentage, Qty Relation, Value, and Calculation type checkboxes determine if these fields of a condition record inserted in a document can be changed.

4 | Pricing

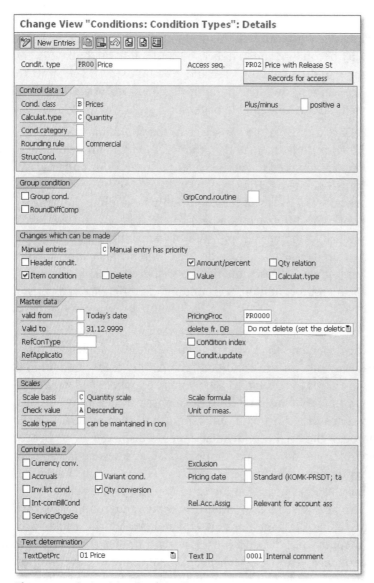

Figure 4.11 Customizing Condition Types

- The Valid From and Valid To data entered in the condition type automatically populates the condition record unless these fields are filled manually in the condition record. For the rebate and condition update function, the date range assumes more significance. The Reference Condition Type and Reference Application (Sales and Distribution is V, Purchasing is M) helps you reduce the additional master data maintenance. The Pricing Procedure field is used to store condition supplements. The Delete from Database field determines if any master data will be deleted from the database or marked for deletion. The Condition Index checkbox allows you to update some of the condition indices automatically when you create a condition record. The Condition Update checkbox makes the condition record cumulate the condition value, number of documents using the condition record, or condition base value (quantity) in the valid date range. When this checkbox is selected, you can also add a maximum condition value, maximum number of documents, and maximum condition base value (quantity) in the additional data screen of a condition record. So when you have to give a few customers a 2% discount for a year, subject to the condition that their total discount will not be more than 100 USD, you know what the setting will be.

- For maintaining scales in a condition record, you maintain Scale Basis, Check Value, Scale Type, Scale Formula, and Unit of Measure in the customization of the condition type.

- The Currency Conversion checkbox, in not selected, converts the currency of the condition record before inserting it into the condition record. If this checkbox is selected, it will convert the condition record currency to the document currency after multiplication with the quantity of the document item. The Accruals checkbox, if selected, makes the value of the condition in the sales document statistical and posted in subsequent accounting documents, if any, as accrual. The Invoice List Condition checkbox makes the condition type relevant for the invoice list. The Intercompany Billing checkbox is selected for condition types to be used for intercompany billing. When you select the Variant Condition checkbox for any condition type, only the key for the condition type appears in the conditions screen of the sales document. When the calculation type for a condition type is C (quantity), then the unit of measure of the document quantity can differ from the unit of measure for which the condition record is maintained. In such a situation the Quantity Conversion checkbox specifies if the base value for calculating the condition should be determined after converting it to the stock-keeping unit of measure. The Exclusion checkbox excludes the condition types from a document. The Pricing Date field determines the date that's relevant for deciding the condition record. The Relevant for Account Assignment field determines if the accounting indicator should be added at the time of account assignment.

4 | Pricing

> **Note**
> It's easier to maintain the upper and lower limit value for the condition type here than at the condition record level. You can use Transaction VCHECKT685A to check the customization setting for all of the pricing condition types in your system.

4.2.5 Create Pricing Procedure

The menu path to create a pricing procedure is SAP IMG • SALES AND DISTRIBUTION • BASIC FUNCTIONS • PRICING • PRICING CONTROL • DEFINE AND ASSIGN PRICING PROCEDURE • MAINTAIN PRICING PROCEDURE (Transaction V/08). A pricing procedure is a set of condition types that can be prices, discounts, surcharges, taxes, and freights. Figure 4.12 illustrates standard pricing procedure RVAA01. We will discuss the different columns (shown in Figure 4.12) and their role in pricing procedure now.

- The condition types are specified in each of the steps.
- For one step you can have different counters. This becomes relevant if you already have a pricing procedure and you want to insert new condition types between two steps that have no gaps (that is, the existing steps are already consecutive numbers). The steps and the counter determine the sequence in which the condition types are to be determined.
- The From and To columns are used to get the total value of certain condition types, as seen in step 300, where the total discount is calculated.
- The Manual (Man.) checkbox makes the condition type available to a pricing procedure only if the user adds it manually.
- When the Mandatory checkbox is selected for any condition type, it checks if the condition type is present in a document, either inserted automatically or manually, to decide if the document is complete for further processing.
- The Statistical checkbox makes the value of a condition type statistical, derived during pricing. Statistical condition types (e.g., maximum retail price [MRP]) in a pricing procedure can be used for calculating other pricing condition. (e.g., discount is 5% of MRP).
- The amount entered in the Subtotal (SubTo) column copies or carries the value to the specified table field (KOMP-CMPRE when SubTo is B or KOMP-KZWI1 to KOMP-KZWI6). These fields are important for reporting and further processes, such as credit management or costing. The values of different items in KOMP-CMPRE, for example, determine the value of a document in the credit management submodule.

4.2 Condition Records

Procedure		RVAA01	Standard									

Control data

Step	Cntr	CTyp	Description	Fro	To	Man.	Mdt	Stat	Print	SubTo	Reqt	AltCTy	AltCBV	ActKy	Accrls
8	0	EK01	Actual Costs			☑	☐	☐		B	2			ERL	
11	0	PR00	Price			☐	☑	☐			2			ERL	
13	0	PB00	Price (Gross)			☑	☐	☐			2			ERL	
20	0	VA00	Variant Price			☐	☐	☐	X		2			ERL	
100	0		Gross Value			☐	☐	☐	X	1		2			
101	0	KA00	Sales deal			☐	☐	☐	X		2			ERS	
102	0	K032	Price Group/Material			☐	☐	☐	X		2			ERS	
103	0	K005	Customer/Material			☐	☐	☐	X		2			ERS	
104	0	K007	Customer Discount			☐	☐	☐	X		2			ERS	
105	0	K004	Material			☐	☐	☐	X		2			ERS	
106	0	K020	Price Group			☐	☐	☐	X		2			ERS	
107	0	K029	Material pricing grp			☐	☐	☐	X		2			ERS	
108	0	K030	Customer/Mat.Pr.Grp			☐	☐	☐	X		2			ERS	
109	0	K031	Price Grp/Mat.Pr.Grp			☐	☐	☐	X		2			ERS	
110	1	RA01	% Disc.from Gross	100		☑	☐	☐	X		2			ERS	
110	2	RA00	% Discount from Net			☑	☐	☐	X		2			ERS	
110	3	RC00	Quantity Discount			☑	☐	☐	X		2			ERS	
110	4	RB00	Discount (Value)			☑	☐	☐	X		2			ERS	
110	5	RD00	Weight Discount			☑	☐	☐	X		2			ERS	
111	0	HI01	Hierarchy			☐	☐	☐	X		2			ERS	
112	0	HI02	Hierarchy/Material			☐	☐	☐	X		2			ERS	
120	0	VA01	Variant Price			☐	☐	☐	X		2			ERS	
300	0		Discount Amount	101	299	☐	☐	☐							
302	0	NETP	Price			☑	☐	☐			2	6	3	ERL	
310	0	PN00	Price (net)			☑	☐	☐	X		2	6		ERL	
320	0	PMIN	Minimum Price			☐	☐	☐	X		2	15		ERL	
399	0	R100	100% discount			☐	☐	☐	X		55		28	ERS	
400	0		Rebate Basis			☐	☐	☐		7					
800	0		Net Value for Item			☐	☐	☐	X	2		2			
801	0	NRAB	Free goods			☐	☐	☐	X		59		29	ERS	
805	1	KP00	Pallet Discount			☐	☐	☐	S		2		22	ERS	
805	2	KP01	Incomp.Pallet Surch.			☐	☐	☐	S		2		24	ERS	
805	3	KP02	Mixed Pallet Disc.			☐	☐	☐	S		2			ERS	
805	4	KP03	Mixed Pallet Surch.			☐	☐	☐	S		2			ERS	
810	1	HA00	Percentage Discount			☑	☐	☐	S		2			ERS	
810	2	HB00	Discount (Value)			☑	☐	☐	S		2			ERS	
810	3	HD00	Freight			☑	☐	☐	S	4	2			ERF	
815	0	KF00	Freight			☐	☐	☐	S	4	2			ERF	
820	0	HM00	Order value			☑	☐	☐	S					ERS	
895	0	PDIF	Diff.value (own)			☑	☐	☐						ERS	
900	0		Net Value 2			☐	☐	☐		3		2			
901	0	B001	Mat/Group Rebate	400		☐	☐	☐			24			ERB	ERU
902	0	B002	Material Rebate	400		☐	☐	☐			24			ERB	ERU
903	0	B003	Customer Rebate	400		☐	☐	☐			24			ERB	ERU
904	0	B004	Hierarchy Rebate	400		☐	☐	☐			24			ERB	ERU
905	0	B005	Hierarchy rebate/mat	400		☐	☐	☐			24			ERB	ERU
908	0		Net Value 3			☐	☐	☐							
909	0	PI02	Inter-company %			☐	☐	☑	B		22			ERL	
910	0	PI01	Inter-company Price			☐	☐	☑	B		22			ERL	
914	0	SKTV	Cash Discount			☐	☐	☑	D		14	2			
915	0	MWST	Output Tax			☐	☑	☐	S		10		16	MWS	
919	0	DIFF	Rounding Off			☐	☑	☐			13	16	4	ERS	
920	0		Total			☐	☐	☐	A		4				
930	0	SKT0	Cash Discount			☐	☐	☑			9		11		
932	0	RL00	Factoring Discount			☐	☐	☑			23	2		ERS	
933	0	MW15	Factoring Disc. Tax	932		☐	☑	☑			21			MWS	
935	0	GRWR	Statistical value			☐	☐	☑	C		8	2			
940	0	VPRS	Internal price			☐	☐	☑	B		4				
941	0	EK02	Calculated costs			☑	☐	☑	B						
942	0	EK03	Calculated ship.cost			☑	☐	☑							
950	0		Profit Margin			☐	☐	☐				11			
970	0	EDI1	Cust.expected price			☑	☐	☑				8			
971	0	EDI2	Cust.expected value			☑	☐	☑				8			

Figure 4.12 Control Data of Pricing Procedure RVAA01

- The Requirements (Reqt) column allows you to enter a requirements type VOFM routine that checks if specific conditions are met before processing the step against which the VOFM routine is mentioned.
- The AltCTy and AltCBV columns are used to enter the formula type VOFM routines that manipulate the condition record and/or the condition base value. The AltCTy field stores the condition formula for the alternative calculation type, and AltCBV is for the condition formula for the alternative condition base value. For example, instead of using the order quantity as a condition base value, you can use a standard available routine to use the gross weight as the base value.
- The Account Key (ActKey) is used for automatic posting of the value to a specific general ledger (GL) maintained in SAP ERP Financial Accounting. The accrual key does the same except that the posting is an accrual type.

> **Note**
> You can use Transaction VCHECKT683 to check the customization setting for all the pricing procedures in your system.

4.2.6 Assign Pricing Procedure

The menu path to assign the pricing procedure is SAP IMG • SALES AND DISTRIBUTION • BASIC FUNCTIONS • PRICING • PRICING CONTROL • DEFINE AND ASSIGN PRICING PROCEDURES • DEFINE PRICING PROCEDURE DETERMINATION (Transaction OVKK). The pricing procedure is assigned to the relevant combinations of:

- Sales area, which is the combination of following three units:
    - Sales organization
    - Distribution channel
    - Division
- Customer pricing procedure
- Document pricing procedure

4.2.7 Create Condition Records

The menu path to create the condition record is SAP EASY ACCESS • LOGISTICS • SALES AND DISTRIBUTION • MASTER DATA • CONDITIONS • CREATE (Transaction VK31). We already discussed it in a previous section.

Now let's move on to the principle of processing pricing.

4.3 Optimizing Price Determination

Before learning any tips on optimizing condition techniques for pricing, you should know how it works. The system reads the document pricing procedure (DoPP), customer pricing procedure (CuPP), and sales area (which is combination of Sales Organization, Distribution Channel, and Division) of the document to the determine pricing procedure maintained for such a combination. Once the system knows the pricing procedure applicable for a particular document, it goes step by step through the pricing procedure. In the step where the condition type is encountered, it checks if any access sequence is assigned to it. It also checks if there's an applicable VOFM routine (requirement and formula type). If there is an access sequence assigned to the condition type and the applicable requirement routine is satisfied, then the system goes to the row with the lowest access number and searches for the condition record in the condition table listed in that row. If it finds a record, it stops there and transfers the value to the document, as long as the Exclusive checkbox is selected. Otherwise it goes to the next access number and repeats the process until it finds a condition record. The value for the price then is transferred to the document. Once all of the steps in the pricing procedure are complete, the pricing is complete. All of the mandatory condition types in the pricing procedure must have some value for the pricing to be complete. The document fields that are used for searching and deciding the condition record can be from customer or material master records, from customization, or entered manually. Figure 4.13 shows the fundamentals of processing pricing.

In an optimal system:

- You can use multiple pricing procedures.
- Each of these pricing procedures should have fewer steps and fewer "automatic" condition types. The condition types that are inserted manually don't affect performance, but such condition types should not have an access sequence assigned to them.
- The access sequence should have minimal steps or access numbers with the Exclusive checkbox selected at each step (except when it's intentional).

4 | Pricing

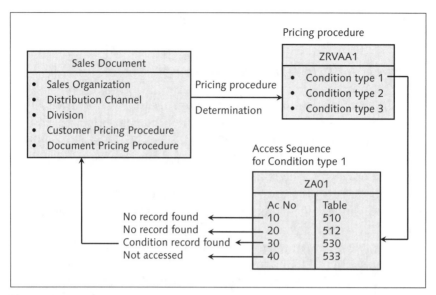

Figure 4.13 Processing Pricing

- The condition table should not contain "related" fields. If any two or more fields in the condition records are related through a customer master record or material master record, then it becomes redundant for both to be present in the condition table. A condition table with Customer, Material Group and Material as key fields is redundant because the material group is related to the material via the material master record. Therefore, the condition table should have either Customer – Material Group, or Customer – Material, as key fields.
- You don't maintain unnecessary condition records.
- You use the condition exclusion and condition supplement when possible.
- You use VOFM routines (requirement and formula type) in the pricing procedure and access sequence to avoid unnecessary table searches that reduce the performance. We'll discuss a few such routines to explain their importance in performance tuning.

You assign the requirement routines to the condition type in the Requirement column of the pricing procedure. If the conditions coded in the requirement routine is fulfilled, then only the access sequence and subsequently, condition table search is done. The Routine Item with Pricing requirement (2) checks if the item category is relevant for pricing and no previous access in the access sequence has set the condition exclusion flag. The Cost Pricing requirement (4) is met when there is a plant for the item in the document, the valuation area company code and company code of the sales organization are same, and the item is not a down payment. You should assign this requirement routine to the cost condition type (VPRS in the standard system). Pricing requirement 10 (Plant Is Set) is met when the plant in the item or departure country in the document exists. This requirement can be used for the tax condition type or condition types for which the above condition is required. The Not in Returns pricing requirement (57) is met if the item category is not a return type. We recommend that you use different though similar pricing procedures for return processing, but when the pricing procedure is the same as the one used for sales, you can use this routine to avoid certain condition types in return processing. Pricing requirement routine 24 (Only in Billing Document) is normally assigned to the rebate condition types. This requirement allows the rebate condition types that are determined or calculated in invoices, credit and debit memos, and returns but not in sales orders or pro forma invoices. Pricing requirement 25 (Only in Rebate Documents) is fulfilled only when the document is a rebate settlement document or a rebate correction document. This is normally assigned to the rebate condition types that are not based on sales volume. We've have listed just a few important requirements. You should also have a look at other standard VOFM requirement routines to see if they are relevant for a specific condition type, or you can customize your own for optimizing pricing.

In the pricing procedure, formula routines are used to manipulate or determine the scale, condition base value, and condition value. An example to help you understand these routines from a functional point of view is as follows: The scale base formula 23 (Partial Quantity) is assigned to the condition type KP03 (Mixed Pallet Surcharges), which converts the whole number (which comes before the decimal place) to zero. Thus, 10.56 becomes 0.56. The pricing procedure can include two condition types (surcharges). One of them calculates the surcharge by rounding 10.56 to 10, and the other, KP03 (or a copy of it), with formula 23 for 0.56.

Normally, the same document line item has a quantity and a sales unit. The condition records are maintained as value per sales unit. After the condition record is determined, the quantity is multiplied by the value of the condition record. If the order quantity is 10 kg and the price is 5 USD per kg, then the total value is 50 USD. But the condition record can be maintained in terms of volume or gross weight, so 10 kg can be 5 cubic meters in terms of volume or have a gross weight of 12 kg when you add the weight of packaging materials. This information is stored in material master records. To calculate the freight (condition type), you can either use condition base value formula 1 (volume) or 12 (gross weight). The condition base value formulas are also used to distribute the header condition value among the items. Another example is formula 28 (100% discount), which is assigned to condition type R100 and sets the rate of the condition to a 100% discount. The condition value formula routine 11 (profit margin) makes the value of a condition type equal to net price minus cost. It's a good idea to show the profit margin if you already have the net value calculated and are using condition type VPRS.

Now that you understand how to optimize pricing, let's move on to rebates and rebate agreements.

4.4 Rebate Agreement

A rebate is simply a discount subject to certain conditions. Until the conditions are achieved, only the accrued rebate is calculated. Accrual value is calculated based on the assumption that the customer will achieve the sales volume specified in the rebate agreement within the time specified. Once the customer achieves his targets, the accrued value is paid to the customer as a cash payment or as a credit memo. If the customer does not achieve the target, he does not receive the rebate. Instead of one target, typically there are multiple targets (some achievable, some not), and the customer gets the rebate based on the target level achieved. The following is a typical example.

If the total purchase in the date range specified in rebate agreement is:

- 100 units, you get 5% of your total invoice as rebate.
- 200 units, you get 7% of your total invoice as rebate.
- 300 units or more, you get 10% of your total invoice as rebate.

In SAP ERP the prerequisites for rebate processing are as follows:

- Sales organization is relevant for rebates.
- Payer is relevant for rebates.
- Document type is relevant for rebates.
- When material is not involved, there should be a material master record for a dummy material called the material for settlement.

All of the steps for the customization of rebate processing can be accessed through Area Menu OLS1, shown in Figure 4.14.

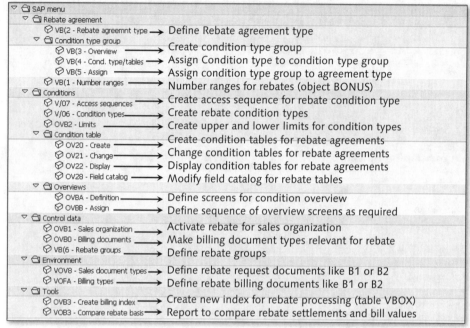

Figure 4.14 Area Menu OLS1 Listing the Customization of Rebate Processing Steps

When you try to create a rebate agreement (which is like a condition record), you need to specify the *rebate agreement type* (which is like a condition type). Figure 4.15 shows the screen where you customize rebate agreement type. The following data of a rebate agreement type are applicable for all condition records that you create within it:

- Validity period
- Status
- Rebate recipient
- Currency
- Method of payment
- Condition type group (The rebate condition types is assigned to the condition type group, which is then assigned to the rebate agreement type.)

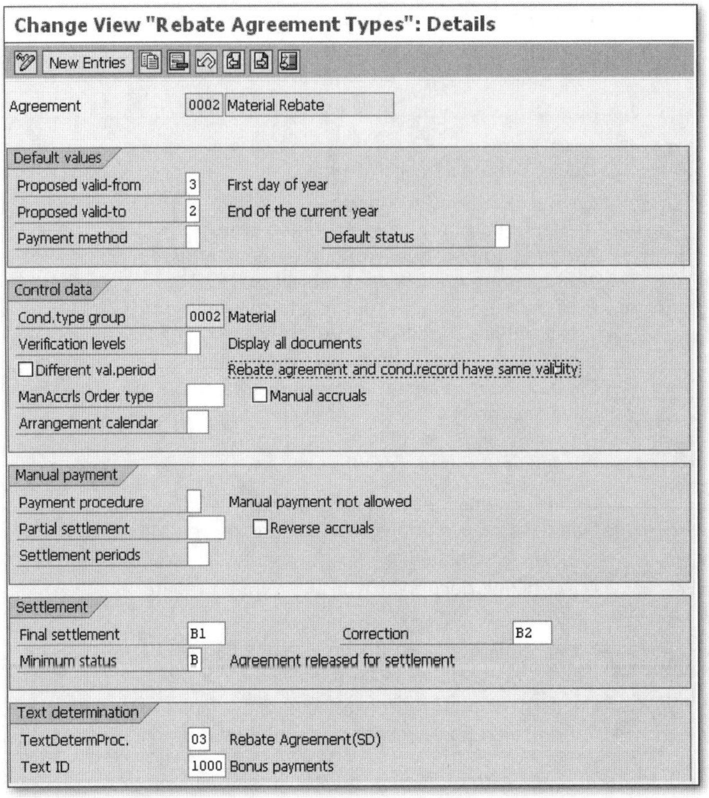

Figure 4.15 Rebate Agreement Type 0002 (Material Rebate)

The condition record for a rebate agreement, as shown in Figure 4.16, is created using Transaction VBO1 (menu path: SAP Easy Access • Logistics • Sales and Distribution • Master Data • Agreements • Rebate Agreement • Create).

- Rebate agreement type (see Table 4.2)
- Basis for the rebate (e.g., customer, customer/material)
- Validity period (same as the rebate agreement or within the validity range)
- Condition rate
- Material for settlement
- Accrual rate
- Pricing scale details

4.4 Rebate Agreement

Agreement Type	Basis of Rebate	Calculation Type	Condition Type
0001	Customer/material	Quantity based	BO01
	Customer/rebate group	Quantity based	BO01
0002	Customer/material	Quantity based	BO02
0003	Customer	Percentage	BO03
0004	Customer hierarchy	Percentage	BO04
	Customer hierarchy/material	Percentage	BO05
0005	Sales volume independent	Fixed amount	BO06

Table 4.2 Standard Rebate Agreement Types

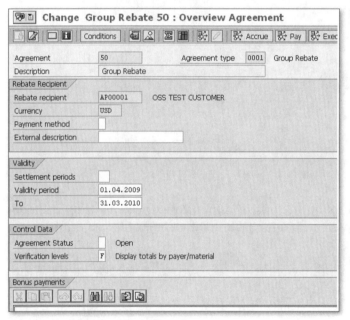

Figure 4.16 Condition Record for Rebate Agreement

Several standard rebate condition types are available for use. When required, you can create your own using Transaction V/06, which is also used to create pricing condition types. In the initial screen, you can select any standard rebate condition type (we've selected BO02) and click on the Copy As icon to go to the screen shown in Figure 4.17. The customization that you've done here controls how the condition type behaves.

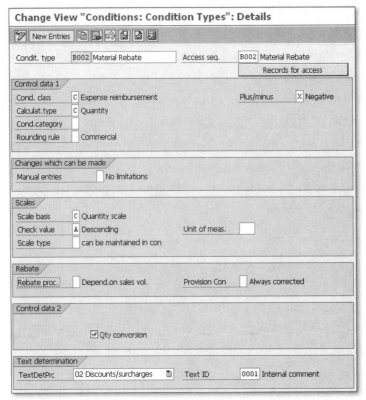

Figure 4.17 Standard Rebate Condition Type BO02 (Material Rebate)

You can customize the sequence of screens of the overview of rebate conditions using Transactions OVBA and OVBB. Table 4.3 lists some of the standard screens.

View	Description	Screen Number
0001	Condition rates	3001
0002	Administrative data	3002
0003	Sales promotion	3003
0004	Terms of payment	3004
0005	Validity periods	3005
0008	Planned values	3008

Table 4.3 Rebate Condition Overview Screens

The customization of the rebate condition type, access sequence, and condition table are similar to that of pricing.

> **Note**
>
> The tables that store the condition records for pricing are different from the tables that store the same for rebate agreements. The database table for storing pricing condition records has the same name as the pricing table with the added prefix A. So pricing table 001 becomes A001, and 501 becomes A501. For the rebate table, the prefix is KOTE. So rebate table 001 becomes KOTE001 and 501 becomes KOTE501.

Programs RV15C001 and RV15C002 are very useful for mass processing of rebate agreements as a background job. You can process rebates at night or some other time when system usage is low. This optimizes your system performance and usage. By using the Issue Verification Level option in report RV15C001, you can use the same report for listing the rebate agreements.

After the final settlement of a rebate agreement, you can modify the credit memo request for rebate (order types) using Transaction VA02 before you issue the credit memo for rebate.

Depending upon the valid-from date, a rebate agreement can be made active or valid from a date in the past. This is called a *retroactive rebate*. The usual problem with retroactive rebates is that the subtotal you need for calculating the rebate may not be available in the pricing procedure used in old documents. You can overcome this problem by executing program RV15B003 and restructuring the billing index by running program RVV05IVB. We'll discuss program RVV05IVB in the problem and solution section in Chapter 7. The billing index is simply additional tables that SAP provides (e.g., VKDFS for the billing initiator) to store information for a specific purpose, billing in this case.

> **Note**
>
> You can use Transaction VCHECKBONUS to check customization for all of the rebate agreement types in your system.

Now that you understand rebate agreements in the SAP system, let's move on to customized pricing reports and lists.

4.5 Customized Pricing Report and Price List

A customized pricing report is normally the first report that Sales and Distribution functional developers create without the help of technical developers. The report is created via Transaction V/LA, modified via Transaction V/LB, and can be displayed via Transaction V/LC. The report is executed via Transaction V/LD. Several standard pricing reports are available for you to use. Table 4.4 lists some of them.

Pricing Report	Pricing Report Name
14	Taxes
15	Material Price
16	Individual Prices
17	Discounts and Surcharges by Customer
18	Discounts and Surcharges by Material
26	Canada/USA
28	Conditions by Customer

Table 4.4 Examples of Standard Pricing Reports Available in Transaction V/LD

The first step in creating your own pricing report is to give a name and description or title to the list. In this example, we've have selected Y1, but it can be any alpha-alpha or alphanumeric code (except LE, LI, and UP). The next step is to give a suitable title to your report (e.g., State-wise Price List) and click on the Selected Field icon (or press F5). Figure 4.18 shows the outcome of these steps.

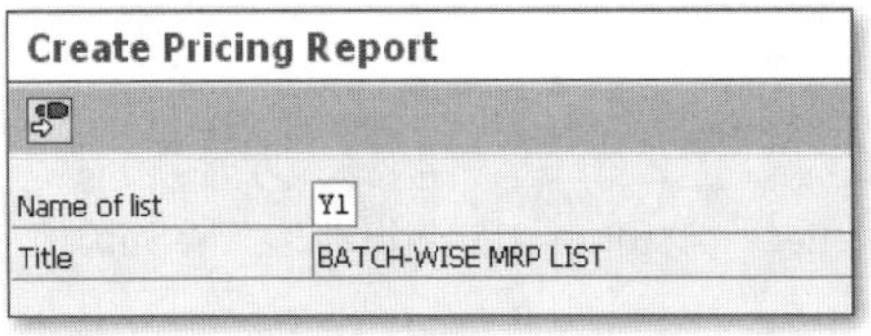

Figure 4.18 Creating Price Report Y1

Select the fields that you want to be displayed in the report. In this example, we've selected Batch (CHARG) (Figure 4.19). If you want to select more than one field, you have the option of using the OR or AND tabs on the top. OR means the selected tables contain at least one of the selected fields, whereas AND means the selected table contains all of the selected fields. Because we've selected only one field in this example, no matter which option we select, we'll get table 502 and 503. If we select Bill to Party and Batch, the AND option may not give us any table, whereas OR will give us a few tables in addition to 502 and 503. This option is also important when you're using a single field, because this decides how the tables will be joined (left-outer join or inner join). We'll discuss the difference between these joins in Chapter 9.

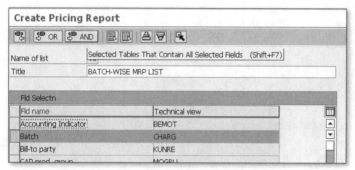

Figure 4.19 Selecting Fields for the Report

Once you get to the screen shown in Figure 4.20, you can select the tables you want and then click on Continue to List Structure ([F5]) to go to the screen shown in Figure 4.21.

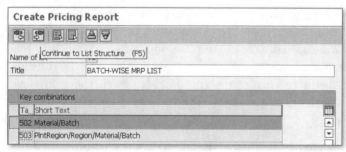

Figure 4.20 Condition Tables that Contain the Field Batch (CHARG)

All of the fields of the selected tables will appear in a list, as shown in the Field name column in Figure 4.21. In the Positioning column, you have three options:

- Position 1 (Page Header)
- Position 2 (Group Header)
- Position 3 (Item Level)

4 | Pricing

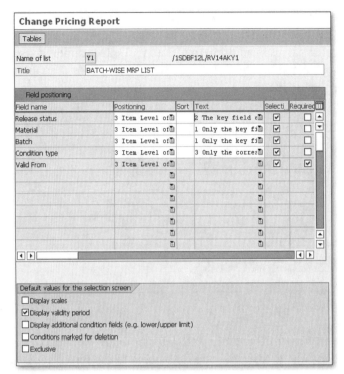

Figure 4.21 Customizing Pricing Report

You can use these positioning fields to make the report more presentable. As shown in Figure 4.24, the fields that aren't likely to change often (i.e., sales organization, distribution channel, and company code) are positioned at this level. This is to prevent these fields from appearing on all items. Fields such as material code and material group are normally assigned to the group header level. The group-level fields are the fields that group the items in the report, whereas the item-level fields appear as items it the report.

It's important for a report to be presentable. In SAP ERP, any field can have a limited number of characters and may have to start with Y or Z. The key or the code for the field may not be long enough to describe it, so in the report, you need to include the description as well. The three options available in a text column for display in the report are:

- 1 (only key field)
- 2 (key Field + its text)
- 3 (only the text of the key)

194

The selection of any field will make it available to use in the selection screen. If a field in the Required Entry column is selected, then you must enter a value for the field before executing the report.

The default values for the screen field have five checkboxes, which are also present in the selection screen of the report. So if you select any of these, they will appear in the selection screen of the report. When any of these options are selected, they will add additional columns, including Scale Type, Scale Qty, and UoM, and so on.

When you save the setting, it generates a transport request and makes the change effective for all other clients in the development server. The transport request is then transported to the product server after testing in the quality server.

To use the pricing report created using Transaction V/LA, you can use Transaction V/LD. It the first screen, select the report (Y1), and execute it to go to the reports selection screen shown in Figure 4.22.

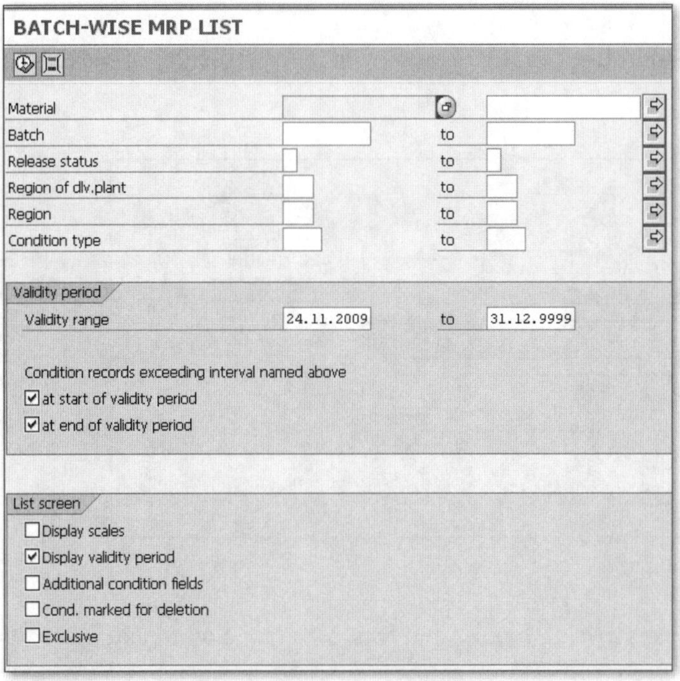

Figure 4.22 Selection Screen of Pricing Report Y1

After entering the required values in the input fields, you can execute the report to get its output, as shown in Figure 4.23. Note the Pencil (for change) and Specs (for display) icons in the output. You can keep your cursor on any particular line and use these icons to display or change the actual condition record (subject to authorization).

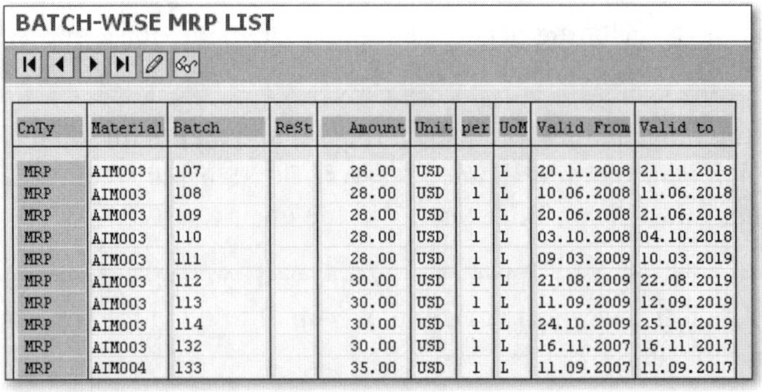

CnTy	Material	Batch	ReSt	Amount	Unit	per	UoM	Valid From	Valid to
MRP	AIM003	107		28.00	USD	1	L	20.11.2008	21.11.2018
MRP	AIM003	108		28.00	USD	1	L	10.06.2008	11.06.2018
MRP	AIM003	109		28.00	USD	1	L	20.06.2008	21.06.2018
MRP	AIM003	110		28.00	USD	1	L	03.10.2008	04.10.2018
MRP	AIM003	111		28.00	USD	1	L	09.03.2009	10.03.2019
MRP	AIM003	112		30.00	USD	1	L	21.08.2009	22.08.2019
MRP	AIM003	113		30.00	USD	1	L	11.09.2009	12.09.2019
MRP	AIM003	114		30.00	USD	1	L	24.10.2009	25.10.2019
MRP	AIM003	132		30.00	USD	1	L	16.11.2007	16.11.2017
MRP	AIM004	133		35.00	USD	1	L	11.09.2007	11.09.2017

Figure 4.23 Output of Report Y1

Figure 4.24 shows the output of another report, where the structure of the output is identifiable.

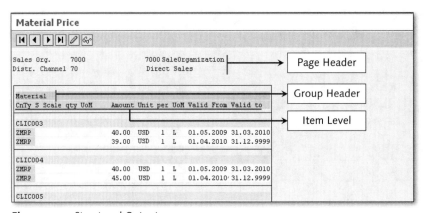

Figure 4.24 Structured Output

Now that we've discussed pricing reports and lists, let's move on to external software packages for taxes.

4.6 Common External Tax Software Packages

There are a variety of external tax software packages on the market today. Sabrix, Taxware, and Vertex are those commonly available that support the process for sales and use tax in the U.S. and Canada. Table 4.5 lists the details about the company involved, the name of the software, the SAP interface for the customized software, and the SAP release for which the tax software is applicable.

Company	Tax Software Name	SAP Interface
Sabrix, Inc. 12647 Alcosta Blvd, Suite 155 San Ramon, CA 94583	Sabrix Application Suite 5 Sabrix Managed Tax Service (MTS) 5	TAX-US-R/3 4.6 – Sales and Use Tax (US, CAN) 4.6 Available in SAP R/3 4.6 or higher releases
Taxware, LP 401 Edgewater Place, Suite 260 Wakefield, MA 01880	Sales and Use Tax 3.X Taxware Enterprise 6.X	
Vertex, Inc. 1041 Old Cassatt Road Berwyn, PA 19312	Vertex O Series 4.0 Vertex Q Series 3.3	

Table 4.5 SAP Certified External Tax Software for Sales and Use Tax (U.S. and Canada)

The suggested steps for customization are as follows.

1. Define and test the physical destination for external tax calculation.
2. Activate SAP tax interface.
3. Configure external tax document.
4. Define tax jurisdiction code.
5. Define tax category for different countries.
6. Define customer tax classifications.
7. Define material tax indicators.
8. Set tax codes.
9. Maintain tax condition records and master data records.

In the following sections, we'll discuss each of the steps listed above.

4.6.1 Defining and Testing the Physical Destination for External Tax Calculation

In this step you define the location of the server, where the external tax software is installed. The menu path for defining the physical destination is SAP IMG • FINANCIAL ACCOUNTING (NEW) • FINANCIAL ACCOUNTING BASIC SETTINGS (NEW) • TAX ON SALES/PURCHASES • BASIC SETTINGS • EXTERNAL TAX CALCULATION • DEFINE PHYSICAL DESTINATION (Transaction SM59). You can navigate to the screen shown in Figure 4.25 by clicking on the Create button in the RFC Destination screen, and provide a name for the new connection (e.g., VERTEX). From here, select Connection Type T (TCP/IP). If the tax software and SAP system are on the same server, select the Start on Application Server radio button and specify the path for the executable program name in the Program field. If the tax software is on a different server, select the Start on Explicit Host option and specify the path of the executable program and target host. Click on the Test Connection button to test the connection. If the test is successful, go on and test the four function modules using Transaction SE37 (menu path: SAP EASY ACCESS • TOOLS • ABAP WORKBENCH • DEVELOPMENT • FUNCTION BUILDER). The four function modules that should be tested one at a time, using Transaction SE37 are:

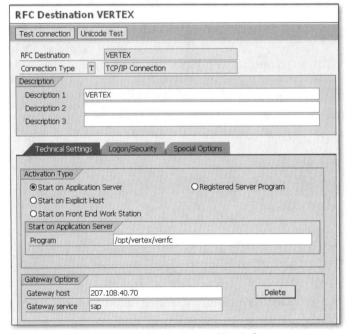

Figure 4.25 Physical Connection to External Tax Software

- RFC_DETERMINE_JURISDICTION
- RFC_CALCULATE_TAXES_DOC
- RFC_UPDATE_TAXES_DOC
- RFC_FORCE_TAXES_DOC

4.6.2 Activating the SAP Tax Interface

The SAP tax interface is activated to use the external tax software. The two steps required to activate the SAP tax interface are listed below:

1. Assign the tax calculation procedure to the country. Only one procedure can be assigned to a country, using Transaction OBBG (menu path: SAP IMG • FINANCIAL ACCOUNTING (NEW) • FINANCIAL ACCOUNTING BASIC SETTINGS (NEW) • TAX ON SALES/PURCHASES • BASIC SETTINGS • ASSIGN COUNTRY TO CALCULATION PROCEDURE). TAXUSX is used as the tax procedure in this case, because you want to use the external tax software. You can modify the tax calculation procedure by selecting it and double-clicking on the Control Data folder.

2. Activate the external tax calculation by following the menu path SAP IMG • FINANCIAL ACCOUNTING (NEW) • FINANCIAL ACCOUNTING BASIC SETTINGS (NEW) • TAX ON SALES/PURCHASES • BASIC SETTINGS • EXTERNAL TAX CALCULATION • ACTIVATE EXTERNAL TAX CALCULATION.

4.6.3 Configuring External Tax Documents

In this step you give a number range for the external tax documents that SAP ERP will receive and instruct your system to use the external tax documents only for tax purposes. The two steps for configuring the external tax documents are:

1. Define the number ranges for external tax documents using Transaction OBETX (menu path: SAP IMG • FINANCIAL ACCOUNTING (NEW) • FINANCIAL ACCOUNTING BASIC SETTINGS (NEW) • TAXES ON SALES/PURCHASES • BASIC SETTINGS • EXTERNAL TAX CALCULATION • DEFINE NUMBER RANGE FOR EXTERNAL TAX DOCUMENTS).

2. Activate the external tax document by following the menu path SAP IMG • FINANCIAL ACCOUNTING (NEW) • FINANCIAL ACCOUNTING BASIC SETTINGS (NEW) • TAXES ON SALES/PURCHASES • BASIC SETTINGS • EXTERNAL TAX CALCULATION • ACTIVATE EXTERNAL UPDATING.

4.6.4 Defining Tax Jurisdiction Codes

Use Transaction OBCO to define the structure for the tax jurisdiction code (menu path: SAP IMG • FINANCIAL ACCOUNTING (NEW) • FINANCIAL ACCOUNTING BASIC SETTINGS (NEW) • TAXES ON SALES/PURCHASES • BASIC SETTINGS • SPECIFY STRUCTURE FOR TAX JURISDICTION CODE). You can define the structure for TAXUSX as (2,2,5,5) for Sabrix, (2,5,2) for Taxware, and (2,3,4,1) for Vertex. When the TxIn checkbox is selected, the system calculates the tax based on line items. When you use the external tax software with the TxIn checkbox selected, there can be some error, so be sure to check SAP Notes 605829, 643273, 798372, 976780, and 972253 found at *service.sap.com* or via transaction SNOTE (using the menu path GOTO • DOWNLOAD SAP NOTE from the initial screen).

4.6.5 Defining the Tax Category for Different Countries

Tax determination rules determine the tax categories to be used for different countries. The tax determination rule is defined using Transaction OVK1 (menu path: SAP IMG • SALES AND DISTRIBUTION • BASIC FUNCTIONS • TAXES • DEFINE TAX DETERMINATION RULES). In the tax determination rule, you assign different tax categories to different countries. When using external tax software, you should assign only one tax category to the U.S. and Canada (UTXJ for the U.S. and CTXJ for Canada against sequence 1). No additional sequence 2 or 3 and UTX1, UTX2, CTX1, CTX2, or CTX3 tax categories should be maintained against them. You should delete all those rows that come predefined in the standard system.

4.6.6 Defining Customer Tax Classifications

A customer tax classification is a customer master record field. A customer operating in different countries can have different classifications in different countries. For example, their operations can be tax-free in one country and taxable in another. You can use Transaction OVK3 to define the tax classifications for tax categories (e.g., UTXJ, CTXJ) that will be maintained for the customer in the customer master record (menu path: SAP IMG • SALES AND DISTRIBUTION • BASIC FUNCTIONS • TAXES • DEFINE TAX RELEVANCY OF MASTER RECORDS • CHOOSE : CUSTOMER TAXES). For different tax categories, tax classifications such as 0 (tax exempt) and 1 (liable for taxes) are defined.

4.6.7 Defining Material Tax Indicators

The material tax indicator is a material master record field. A material can be taxable or tax-free. This indicator is used for storing that information. In combination with the customer tax indicator, it determines the tax status (taxable or tax-free). The possible list of tax classifications or indicators for the material for a particular tax category (e.g., UTXJ, CTXJ) are maintained in Transaction OVK4 (menu path: SAP IMG • SALES AND DISTRIBUTION • BASIC FUNCTIONS • TAXES • DEFINE TAX RELEVANCY OF MASTER RECORDS • CHOOSE: MATERIAL TAXES). Different indicators such as 0 (exempt) and 1 (taxable) are maintained as possible selections in the material master record.

4.6.8 Setting Tax Codes

In a tax code you specify the tax percentage. You also specify whether it's is to be collected from the customer (accounts receivable [A/R]) or be paid to the vendor (accounts payable [A/P]). You create the tax codes using Transaction FTXP (menu path: SAP IMG • FINANCIAL ACCOUNTING (NEW) • FINANCIAL ACCOUNTING BASIC SETTINGS (NEW) • TAXES ON SALES/PURCHASES • BASIC SETTINGS • DEFINE TAX CODES FOR SALES AND PURCHASES). Tax codes O0 (A/R sales tax, 0%) and O1 (A/R sales tax, 6% state, 1% county, 1% city) come predefined in the standard system and are copied to create new tax codes for use in the Sales and Distribution functionality in SAP ERP. To use the tax code in Sales and Distribution, the tax type must be A. For the six condition types (XR1, XR2, XR3, XR4, XR5, and XR6) of tax calculation procedure TAXUSX, all of the tax codes relevant for Sales and Distribution (e.g., O0, O2) maintain the Tax percentage as 100.

After you maintain the tax code, the following step ensures automatic posting to a specific general ledger. In the tax procedure (e.g., TAXUSX), you maintain the accounting key for a specific condition type. In Transaction OB40 (menu path: SAP IMG • FINANCIAL ACCOUNTING (NEW) • FINANCIAL ACCOUNTING BASIC SETTINGS (NEW) • TAXES ON SALES/PURCHASES • POSTING • DEFINE TAX ACCOUNTS), double-click on the Transaction for which the different account should be maintained for the different tax codes, and specify the chart of account. This takes you to the screen shown in Figure 4.26, where you maintain the different accounts for different tax codes. You can use Transaction OBCN (menu path: SAP IMG • FINANCIAL ACCOUNTING (NEW) • FINANCIAL ACCOUNTING BASIC SETTINGS (NEW) • TAXES ON SALES/PURCHASES • BASIC SETTING • CHECK AND CHANGE SETTINGS FOR TAX PROCESSING) to create a new account key or process key if required. Note that the posting indicator for processing/accounting key NVV is 3 (distribute to relevant expense/

revenue items) and all other accounting keys used in the TAXUSX procedure, the posting indicator is 2 (separate line item). The transaction keys used for determining tax accounts are the same as the accounting keys maintained in the tax procedure, which are the same as the process key when the posting indicator is 2.

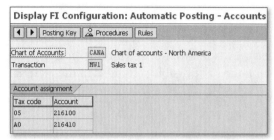

Figure 4.26 Different Accounts for Different Tax Codes for Transaction/Accounting Key MW1 Specified Using Transaction OB40

4.6.9 Maintaining Tax Condition Records and Master Data Records

Using Transaction VK11/12, you maintain the condition records for tax category UTXJ and CTXJ for the U.S. and Canada, respectively, for all possible combinations of customer tax classification (e.g., 0, 1) and material tax classification (e.g., 0, 1). There are other key combinations for export and other scenarios for which you can maintain condition records.

Using Transactions XD01 or XD02, you can maintain the customer tax classification in the Billing Document tab (Sales Area Data). A customer can have different tax classifications in different countries (e.g., 0 for U.S., 1 for Canada). Using Transactions MM01and MM02, you maintain the material tax classification in the Sales: Sales Org. 1 tab. Because a material taxable in one country can be exempted in another, you should maintain the tax classification accordingly.

> **Max Tax**
>
> SAP systems support calculating tax for a document instead of computing it for an individual line and aggregating. Instead of pricing procedure RVAXUS, you use procedure RVAXUD when you have to calculate tax per document. We recommend this because fewer remote function calls (RFCs) to external systems are made compared to when one RFC is required for each line item, and the performance is better. Formula routine 300 assigned to tax condition UTXJ in procedure RVAXUS and routine 500 assigned to tax condition UTXD in procedure RVAXUD call the SAP tax interface. While modifying the pricing procedure, you should not change the formula. Use program RFYTXDISPLAY to display an error (marked red) during tax processing (when using external tax software).

4.7 Summary

In this chapter we discussed the pricing, rebate processing, and configuration of external tax software. In pricing, we discussed the condition technique and routines and touched upon the seven steps used in condition techniques. The importance of routines, requirements and formula types for optimizing the pricing process was also highlighted in this chapter. You should now have a solid understanding of the pricing process and how it works. We discussed the steps required for creating the pricing report, and we also covered the rebate process. In the last part of the chapter, we walked through the customization steps for using external tax software in the U.S. and Canada. With this knowledge you should be able to implement and maintain customization for pricing. The system should not only determine the correct prices but also in less time. You should be able to create your own reports for prices and use the rebate agreement functionality that SAP ERP offers. You should also be able to customize your system for using the external tax software. Again, the system should determine the correct tax amount and in less time. We hardly need to emphasize that both pricing and tax are vital elements in any business.

In the next chapter, we'll will look at credit management and touch on financial accounting in SAP ERP Financials.

This chapter teaches you how to customize automatic credit control, which is the fundamental functionality of credit management in the SAP system. You'll also be able to customize your system to block customers for different sales and distribution processes. Finally, you'll learn how to define the different forms of payment guarantee and their determination procedure for automatic determination during sales document processing.

5 Credit Risk Management

Eliminating risk from business is neither possible nor desirable. Risk should be managed to minimize risk and maximize profit. Generally speaking, a business that involves more risk has the potential to provide more profit. In the Sales and Distribution functionality in SAP ERP, the risk is primarily due to credit extended to the customer. You sell material to customers and then bill them expecting payment within a certain time period. If the bills are not paid within this time, it's a loss for you. Of course, this is not a risk if you sell only after receiving the total payment. But for goods and services that you have to sell without receiving the total payment up front, you can opt for one of two options to minimize or manage your risk.

1. A payment guarantee, which ensures payment to you subject to certain conditions, such as a goods receipt in good condition.
2. Credit management where there is neither payment nor any guarantee.

We'll discuss credit management and how it reduces risk in the next section and then move on to customizing for blocking and unblocking a customer, which is not directly linked to either credit management or payment guarantee but is often used for minimizing risk. Finally, we'll discuss the steps for customizing different forms of payment guarantees and their automatic determination during document processing.

5.1 Credit Management

Credit management involves managing the credit, and associated risk of default, that a company extends to its customers. From a narrow operational point of view

5 | Credit Risk Management

it involves deciding when to stop sales. From a broader perspective, it involves the accurate credit rating of customers (and grouping them with customers with similar risk), follow-up for receiving payment, fast action in response to customer complaints, improved communication, regular internal review, and so on. Many of these are not what we'll discuss in this book. Our discussion will be confined to what SAP ERP offers for credit management.

The general steps for configuring credit management are as follows:

1. Set prerequisites for automatic credit control.
2. Maintain customer credit master records.
3. Define automatic credit control.

Now, let's walk through the first step.

5.1.1 Prerequisites for Automatic Credit Control

Most of the steps should be completed as part of customization for other processes before you do the automatic credit control customization. If a step is discussed elsewhere in the book, we'll review it here, so you can use this section as a checklist. If the step has not been discussed so far in the book, we'll discuss it here. We will also emphasize the role of each step in the final setting. The following steps are the prerequisites for activating automatic credit control. Most of these steps are already configured at the time of defining and assigning the enterprise structure or at the time of customizing the customer credit master record.

1. Define credit control areas. As discussed in Chapters 1 and 2, the important fields you need to define in the credit control area are Update Group, Currency, the rule for DSO, and accounts receivable.

2. Assign the sales area and company codes to the credit control area. As discussed in Chapter 1, use Transactions OVFL (menu path: SAP IMG • ENTERPRISE STRUCTURE • ASSIGNMENT • SALES AND DISTRIBUTION • ASSIGN SALES AREA TO CREDIT CONTROL AREA) and OB38 (menu path: SAP IMG • ENTERPRISE STRUCTURE • ASSIGNMENT • FINANCIAL ACCOUNTING • ASSIGN COMPANY CODE TO CREDIT CONTROL AREA) to assign the sales area and company code, respectively, to the credit control area.

3. If needed, assign the additional company codes to the credit control area, as discussed in Chapter 2. In addition to assigning a company code to a credit control area, you can it to other credit control areas as well, using Transaction OBZK

(menu path: SAP IMG • FINANCIAL ACCOUNTING (NEW) • ACCOUNTS RECEIVABLE AND ACCOUNTS PAYABLE • CREDIT MANAGEMENT • CREDIT CONTROL ACCOUNT • ASSIGN PERMITTED CREDIT CONTROL AREAS TO COMPANY CODE).

4. You can define the customer credit groups using Transaction OB12 (menu path: SAP IMG • FINANCIAL ACCOUNTING (NEW) • ACCOUNTS RECEIVABLE AND ACCOUNTS PAYABLE • CREDIT MANAGEMENT • CREDIT CONTROL ACCOUNT • DEFINE GROUPS). The customer credit group is used to group customers for reporting purposes and is assigned to the customer in the Status screen of the customer credit master record. The Customer Group field is also present in the Status screen. This field is different from the customer credit group but is also used for grouping and reporting purposes and is freely definable (that is, in the credit master record, you can assign any value to it). This step is optional from the credit management point of view. As shown in Figure 5.1, the credit group is created for a particular credit control area (CCAr) with a meaningful description.

Figure 5.1 Define Customer Credit Groups

5. The document credit group that is used to group documents is defined via Transaction OVA6 (menu path: SAP IMG • SALES AND DISTRIBUTION • BASIC FUNCTIONS • CREDIT MANAGEMENT/RISK MANAGEMENT • CREDIT MANAGEMENT • DEFINE CREDIT GROUPS). As shown in Figure 5.2, the three standard groups for orders, deliveries, and goods issue are sufficient for practical purposes. You can create a new one by selecting any existing group, copying it, and providing a new key or code and a description. Because different settings for different document groups are possible for automatic credit control, this field is very important.

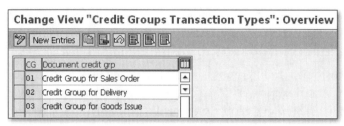

Figure 5.2 Document Credit Groups

6. Risk categories group customers with the same levels of risk. You can have, for example, one risk category for all new customers. Risk categories, as shown in Figure 5.3, are defined via Transaction OB01 (menu path: SAP IMG • FINANCIAL ACCOUNTING (NEW) • ACCOUNTS RECEIVABLE AND ACCOUNTS PAYABLE • CREDIT MANAGEMENT • CREDIT CONTROL ACCOUNT • DEFINE RISK CATEGORIES). In the Status screen of the customer credit master record, you can enter the customer's risk category. Because different settings for different risk categories are possible for automatic credit control, this field is very important.

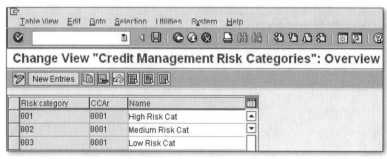

Figure 5.3 Define Risk Categories

7. Use Transaction OB02 to define credit representative groups (menu path: SAP IMG • FINANCIAL ACCOUNTING (NEW) • ACCOUNTS RECEIVABLE AND ACCOUNTS PAYABLE • CREDIT MANAGEMENT • CREDIT CONTROL ACCOUNT • DEFINE CREDIT REPRESENTATIVE GROUPS). As shown in Figure 5.4, credit representative groups are defined for particular credit control areas (CCAr), and customers are grouped using this key. You enter the credit representative group of the customer in the Status screen of the customer credit master (see Figure 5.8).

Change View "Credit Management: Credit Representative Groups"

New Entries

Credit rep.group	CCAr	Name of the credit rep.group
100	7000	Credit Representative 100
200	7000	Credit Representative 200
300	7000	Credit Representative 300

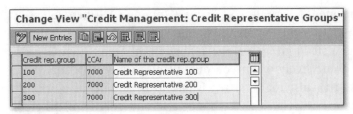

Figure 5.4 Define Credit Representative Groups

8. You define credit representatives with Transaction OB51 (menu path: SAP IMG • Financial Accounting (New) • Accounts Receivable and Accounts Payable • Credit Management • Credit Control Account • Define Credit Representatives). In this step, you can specify which employee is responsible for a credit representative group, as shown in Figure 5.5.

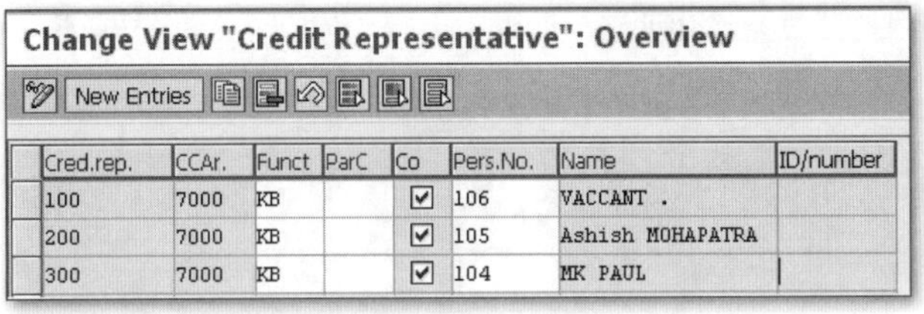

Change View "Credit Representative": Overview

New Entries

Cred.rep.	CCAr.	Funct	ParC	Co	Pers.No.	Name	ID/number
100	7000	KB		☑	106	VACCANT .	
200	7000	KB		☑	105	Ashish MOHAPATRA	
300	7000	KB		☑	104	MK PAUL	

Figure 5.5 Define Credit Representative

9. Document credit groups and credit checks are assigned to the sales and delivery document types. Using Transaction OVAK (menu path: SAP IMG • Sales and Distribution • Basic Functions • Credit Management/Risk Management • Credit Management • Assign Sales Documents And Delivery Documents • Credit limit check for order types or SAP IMG • Sales and Distribution • Basic Functions • Credit Management/Risk Management • Simple Credit Limit Check), you can assign different types of credit checks and credit groups to different order types as shown in Figure 5.6. The various types of credit checks possible are also shown in Figure 5.6. When the Check credit field in the third column is left blank, there will be no credit check for the document type. The options A, B, and C are called *simple credit limit checks* and check the customer's document pertaining to the document type when the total receivable (the update group for the credit control area further defines whether in addition to open accounting documents, open order, delivery, and billing are to be considered) is more than the credit limit. When a document fails to clear a simple check, the system can issue a warning (option A) or an error message (option

B) or block the document for creation of delivery (option C). When you select option D (Credit Management: Automatic Credit Control), you have to further specify the document credit group that we defined in the Step 5. Simple credit checks can be used effectively when you only want a single criterion (credit limit) to be checked against the total receivable to decide about blocking a document. Automatic credit check gives you the option of specifying the credit check for delivery types, which you do with Transaction OVAD (menu path: SAP IMG • SALES AND DISTRIBUTION • BASIC FUNCTIONS • CREDIT MANAGEMENT/ RISK MANAGEMENT • CREDIT MANAGEMENT • ASSIGN SALES DOCUMENTS AND DELIVERY DOCUMENTS • CREDIT LIMIT CHECK FOR DELIVERY TYPES).

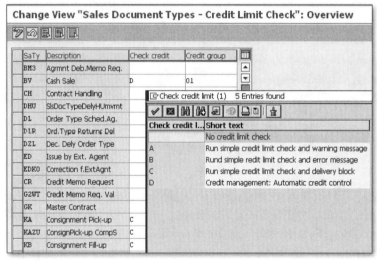

Figure 5.6 Simple Credit Check (Transaction OVAK)

10. You assign partner function KB (credit representative) and KM (credit manager) to the partner determination procedure of the customer master record, sales document header, and delivery document using Transaction VOPAN.

11. You can use Transaction OVB9 to modify requirement routine 104, which prevents a document from appearing in the delivery due list when there's a credit block (menu path: SAP IMG • SALES AND DISTRIBUTION • BASIC FUNCTIONS • CREDIT MANAGEMENT/RISK MANAGEMENT • CREDIT MANAGEMENT/RISK MANAGEMENT SETTINGS • ENTER SETTINGS • REQUIREMENT FOR CREATING DELIVERY DUE INDEX FROM ORDER).

12. You can use Transaction OVB7 to modify requirement routine 113, which doesn't allow a goods issue if a credit block exists, (menu path: SAP IMG • SALES AND DISTRIBUTION • BASIC FUNCTIONS • CREDIT MANAGEMENT/RISK MANAGEMENT • CREDIT MANAGEMENT/RISK MANAGEMENT SETTINGS • ENTER SETTINGS • REQUIREMENT FOR GOODS ISSUE FROM A DELIVERY).
13. Using Transaction OVA7 (menu path: SAP IMG • SALES AND DISTRIBUTION • BASIC FUNCTIONS • CREDIT MANAGEMENT/RISK MANAGEMENT • CREDIT MANAGEMENT/RISK MANAGEMENT SETTINGS • DETERMINE ACTIVE RECEIVABLES PER ITEM CATEGORY), you can specify all of the item categories that are relevant for credit checks and updates. The item categories, for example, the one used for stock transfer, are not specified here and are not relevant for credit management. These items don't update Tables S066 and S067, which store the open order and open delivery values
14. You define document value classes using Transaction OVBC and assign them to the credit control area and different credit values using Transaction OVBD (menu path: SAP IMG • SALES AND DISTRIBUTION • BASIC FUNCTIONS • CREDIT MANAGEMENT/RISK MANAGEMENT • CREDIT MANAGEMENT/RISK MANAGEMENT SETTINGS • MAINTAIN AUTHORIZATION • ASSIGN DOCUMENT VALUE CLASSES). These document value classes further restrict the authorization object for releasing the documents blocked by the credit check. For example, a credit representative with authorization for releasing a blocked document can be authorized only for documents of values less than 200,000 USD by assigning document value class A01 (as shown in Figure 5.7) to his profile.

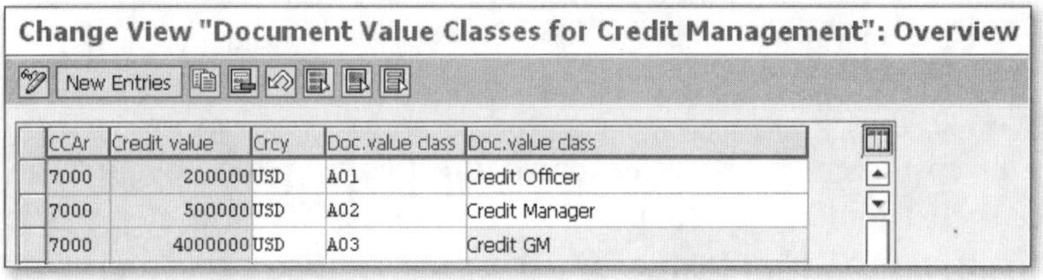
Change View "Document Value Classes for Credit Management": Overview

New Entries

CCAr	Credit value	Crcy	Doc.value class	Doc.value class
7000	200000	USD	A01	Credit Officer
7000	500000	USD	A02	Credit Manager
7000	4000000	USD	A03	Credit GM

Figure 5.7 Document Value Classes (A01, A02 and A03) Assigned to Credit Control Area (7000) and Credit Values

5.1.2 Customer Credit Master Records

As we've discussed, the credit master record can be automatically generated by specifying the default credit limit or risk category or credit representative group in the credit control area for any new customers. To get to the screen where you define the credit control area, shown in Figure 5.8, execute Transaction OB45 (menu path: SAP IMG • ENTERPRISE STRUCTURE • DEFINITION • FINANCIAL ACCOUNTING • DEFINE CREDIT CONTROL AREA) and double-clicking on the specific credit control area, which is created by copying an existing one. This way there's little chance that you'll have a customer without a customer credit master record. No customer credit master record means no credit check for that customer. For new customers, this means exposing yourself to a higher risk. So it's recommended that you create the customer credit master record automatically and then modify it using Transaction FD32 (menu path: SAP EASY ACCESS • FINANCIAL ACCOUNTING • CUSTOMERS • CREDIT MANAGEMENT • MASTER DATA • CHANGE).

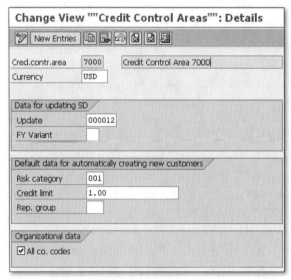

Figure 5.8 Credit Control Area

You can create the customer credit master record directly using the above transaction. You enter the customer code (obtained after creating the customer master record using Transaction XD01, FD01, or VD01) in the Customer field and credit control area (as you saw previously in Figure 2.15). Select only the Central Data and Status screen for data entry. The fields of other the views are filled automatically from the customer master records (e.g., Address screen), transactions pertaining to the customer (e.g., Payment History, shown in Figure 5.11), or other screens of the customer's credit master record (e.g., Overview screen shown in Figure 5.9).

Credit Management | 5.1

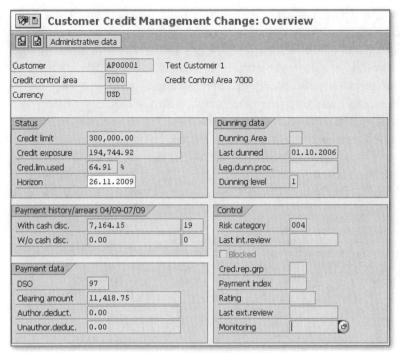

Figure 5.9 Customer Credit Master Record (Overview Screen)

In the Central Data screen, you can enter the Total Limit and Individual Limit. This is applicable when a customer is assigned to several credit control areas (via different company codes), and there is a total limit for the customer for all of the credit control areas and an individual limit for the specific credit control area. The currency becomes important because different credit control areas can have different currencies.

The Status screen (refer Figure 5.10) has the credit limit field and credit horizon date. The credit horizon date is by default the current system date. You can define in the automatic credit control setting (shown in Figure 5.12) if it is to be system date plus specific number of days (T), week (W), month (M), or year (I).

Note that in the setting shown in Figure 5.12 (automatic credit control) the unit for credit horizon is in months (M), and the value is not modifiable. In fact, it's the same as the update unit for info-structure S066. To change it to days (T) or any other period use, Transaction OMO1 (menu path: SAP IMG • LOGISTICS – GENERAL •

213

LOGISTICS INFORMATION SYSTEM (LIS) • LOGISTICS DATA WAREHOUSE • UPDATING • UPDATING CONTROL • ACTIVATE UPDATE • SALES AND DISTRIBUTION). Upon execution, you'll get a list of all info-structures of Sales and Distribution. If you double-click on S066, you'll get a dialog box where you can change the period unit (e.g., from months to days). After selecting for the radio button you want, click on the Save icon. There is no way to specify the currency, so the currency of the credit control area automatically becomes the currency for the customer's credit limit. The fields defined for the group customer (e.g., risk category, Credit rep. group, Cust.cred.group) are also specified for the customer. You can block the customer by selecting the Block checkbox. This blocking is different from blocking the customer for sales, delivery, billing, or other operations that we'll discuss in the next section.

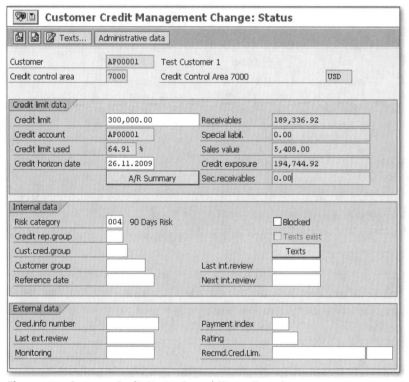

Figure 5.10 Customer Credit Master Record (Status Screen)

Information about the last internal review date, next internal review date, and customer obtained from external rating organization are also entered in this screen.

Credit Management | **5.1**

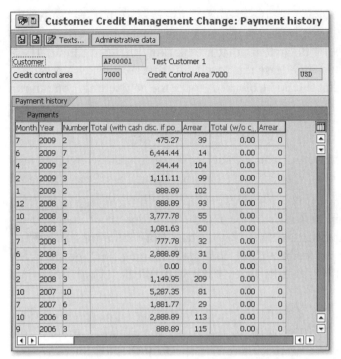

Figure 5.11 Customer Credit Master Record (Payment History Screen)

5.1.3 Automatic Credit Control

For each combination of credit control area, risk category, and credit group, you maintain different rules for automatic credit control. The update group and currency maintained for the credit control area become the default for each credit strategy. The credit control can be done during the order, delivery, or post goods issue (PGI). Once the goods issue is complete, the credit control is no longer relevant because the material is no longer physically under company control. Depending on the setting, the system may not allow the creation of order, delivery, or material documents (created at the time of PGI), or for the first two types create with credit block so that further processing is prevented. This way you are proactively reducing your credit risk. Once material is with the customer, your risk increases. Risk and cost involved in recovering the stock or payment is more.

You can release the blocked documents for further processing using Transaction VKM1 or VKM2 (menu path: SAP EASY ACCESS • LOGISTICS • SALES AND DISTRIBUTION • CREDIT MANAGEMENT • SALES AND DISTRIBUTION DOCUMENTS • BLOCKED). Instead of releasing individual documents, your company can decide to change the customer credit master records (i.e., credit limit) or credit strategy (setting for an individual combination of credit control area, risk category, and credit group) or delete some other open documents that are blocking the credit limit. These actions will not automatically release the documents that are already blocked. To release the documents that should be blocked, as per the new setting, you can run the program RVKRED08.

In automatic credit management you, decide the following:

1. Whether there will be a static check (blocking document if the credit limit is exceeded) or a static and dynamic check (blocking documents if the credit limit or some other criteria specified in customization are fulfilled).

2. The other criteria mentioned in step 1 can include the document value, change in critical fields of the document, next review date, open items (percentage and days open), oldest open item, highest permitted dunning level, or any other criteria defined in the user exits LVKMPTZZ, LVKMPFZ1, LVKMPFZZ2, and LVKMPFZZ3.

    ▶ Document value: When the sales document value exceeds a predefined value (in Figure 5.12, it is 100,000.00 in the credit control area currency), the document is blocked. The process can be specially adopted for high-value order processing.

    ▶ Critical fields: The critical fields for credit management are Order Quantity, Unit of Measurement, Pricing Condition, Terms of Payment, INCO Term, and Plant. If these fields are changed, even to the original value or to a value that makes the total document value less than the original value, the credit check process reoccurs, and the released document is blocked. We recommend that you make check for critical fields active, as shown in Figure 5.12.

    ▶ Next internal review date (NextReview date): The next internal review date is maintained in the customer credit master for internal review of the customer for credit management and changing the customer credit master. If this date is in the past, it means the review and change of the customer credit master is overdue. You can use Transaction FDK43 or S_ALR_87012218 to get a report for this purpose. In this type of situation, it may be company policy to stop sales to such customers.

    ▶ Open items: To make this active, you have to fill in the additional fields of Max.OpenItem% (X) and No Days Open Item (Y). The system checks all of the items open for more than Y days and finds its percentage of the total customer balance. If the percentage calculated is more than the X, the document is blocked.

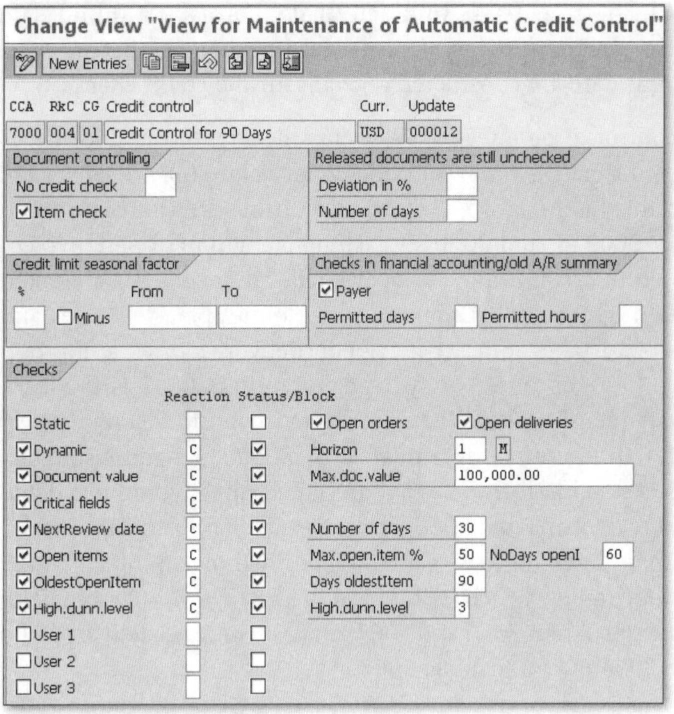

Credit Management | 5.1

Figure 5.12 Automatic Credit Control

- OldestOpenItem: This can be referred to as credit limit in days. If the oldest open invoice or debit note is over a specific age (e.g., 90 days), it may be company policy to stop sale irrespective of the fact that the total overdue outstanding is within the credit limit. So while activating this setting, you have to specify the day limit also (as you can see in Figure 5.12, it's 90 days). Note that if open invoices are not knocked off (or settled) by the payment received in the Financial Accounting component, the process won't work as intended.

- High.dunn.level: The accounting department issues dunning letters to the customers. If the dunning reaches a specific level (which is 3 in Figure 5.12), the document is blocked for the specific customer.

- User 1, 2, and 3: The prerequisite for activating users 1, 2, and 3 is to specify the details for credit checks in the user exits LVKMPTZZ, LVKMPFZ1, LVK-MPFZZ2, and LVKMPFZZ3. A user exit is the program where a user can add his own ABAP codes to influence a standard SAP business process or transaction.

> ▸ Horizon: The credit horizon refers to a date that's normally a future date maintained in the customer credit master. All of the documents that are to be delivered within this date are considered relevant for the credit check.

For automatic credit control to be effective, you must decide on the documents that are relevant for credit management and document value. *Update groups* are used to decide which documents are valid for a credit check. There are three update groups: 000012, 000015, and 000018. Each update group's open invoices (invoice yet to be posted to accounting) and open financial documents are taken into account. In addition, group 000012 takes into account open deliveries and open orders, group 000015 takes into account open deliveries only, and group 000018 takes into account open orders only. Update group 000012 is the most comprehensive and is frequently used. When it's a practice not to delete or reject very old open orders for any valid reason, update group 000015 is more suitable. Update group 000018 is suitable for items that are billed directly without delivery. Open orders are updated in Table S066, and open deliveries in Table S067. The value of the document in credit management is decided by subtotal A in the pricing procedure of a document, which is stored in the VBAP-CMPRE table field, which subsequently updates Tables S066 and S067. Once an order is delivered, the relevant entry in Table S066 moves to Table S067.

The update can fail, though this is very rare. You can schedule and run program RVKRED08 in the background so that these odd cases are also taken care of. Table 5.1 lists the other useful programs.

Program	Description
RFDKLI10	Customers with missing credit data
RFDKLI20	Reorganization of credit limit for customers
RFDKLI30	Short overview of credit limit
RFDKLI40	Overview of credit limit
RFDKLI41	Credit master sheet
RFDKLI42	Early warning list (of critical customers)
RFDKLI43	Master data list
RFDKLI50	Mass change of credit limit data
RVKRED06	Checking blocked credit documents
RVKRED08	Checking credit documents that reach the credit horizon

Table 5.1 Useful Programs for Credit Management

Program	Description
RVKRED09	Checking the credit documents from the credit view
RVKRED77	Reorganization of Sales and Distribution credit data
RFDKLI10	Customers with missing credit data
RFDKLI20	Reorganization of credit limit for customers
RFDKLI30	Short overview of credit limit
RFDKLI40	Overview of credit limit

Table 5.1 Useful Programs for Credit Management (Cont.)

5.1.4 Credit Management Operations

From the credit management point of view, various important operations include releasing and rejecting blocked documents, credit review, and mass change of customer credit master records.

Releasing Blocked Document

When a sales document is blocked when you're saving it, a warning or error message appears, like the warning message shown in Figure 5.13.

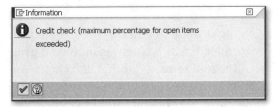

Figure 5.13 Credit Check Message

If you click on the question mark, you'll find the details of the credit checks performed for the document, the ones it cleared (OK), and the ones it failed to clear (NOK). As shown in the Figure 5.14, the document was subjected to neither a static credit limit check nor any check for user exit 1, 2, or 3. It cleared (OK) the check for dynamic credit limit, document value, critical fields, next check date, and maximum dunning level. It failed (NOK) the check for open items and oldest open item. The document can still be saved and reviewed by the credit representative using Transaction VKM1 (menu path: SAP EASY ACCESS • LOGISTICS • SALES AND DISTRIBUTION • CREDIT MANAGEMENT • EXCEPTIONS • BLOCKED SD DOCUMENTS). All of the important information required for making the decision to either release or reject the document is available here.

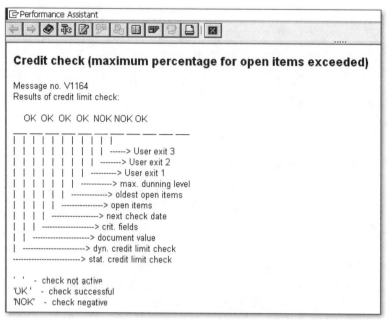

Figure 5.14 Results of the Credit Check

By selecting a document, you can access the customer master record (menu path: ENVIRONMENT • CUSTOMER MASTER) or customer credit master record (menu path: ENVIRONMENT • CUST. MASTER CREDIT) of the sold-to party for that document. You can see the other open sales (menu path: ENVIRONMENT • OPEN SALES VALUES • OPEN SALES ORDER), deliveries, or billing documents (menu path: ENVIRONMENT • OPEN SALES VALUES • OPEN DLVS/BILL DOCS). The credit master sheet (menu path: ENVIRONMENT • CREDIT MASTER SHEET) is also possible to generate via Transaction S_ALR_87012218 and is a particularly useful report to review the credit status of an individual customer. This report gives more information Transaction FDK43, but in Transaction FDK43, you can review several customers at a time. Based on all of the available information, the credit representative may decide to release the document by selecting the checkbox against the document (P.St. column, as seen in Figure 5.15) and then click on the Green Flag icon to accept or the Reject button to reject.

Credit Management | 5.1

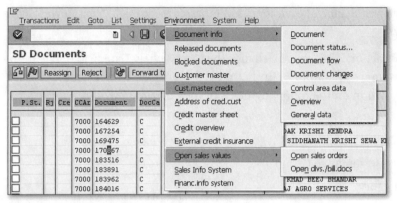

Figure 5.15 Blocked SD Document (Environment Menu)

Credit Review of Individual Customer

Individual customers are reviewed internally at regular intervals to increase or decrease their credit limits and change their risk categories in the credit master record (Transaction FD32). For a credit review, the credit master sheet report is normally sufficient for individual customers. To review a large number of customers, you can use the credit overview Transaction F.31 (menu path: SAP EASY ACCESS • LOGISTICS • SALES AND DISTRIBUTION • CREDIT MANAGEMENT • CREDIT MANAGEMENT INFO SYSTEM • OVERVIEW). The following data is re normally useful during credit reviews:

- Total sales
- Days of sales outstanding (DSO)
- Credit utilized
- Payment history
- Due days analysis

Credit Master Record Mass Change

Credit master data maintenance is the joint responsibility of accounting and sales officials responsible for credit management. In some companies, master data maintenance is a separate function. When Next Review Date is used as a reason for blocking the orders in credit management, mass maintenance becomes important. It's important to review customer credit ratings and update the customer credit master records before the expiry of next review date.

The steps for mass change of customer credit master record field Next Review Date are as follows:

1. Using Transaction F.34, you can change the Next Review Date field of any number of customers in a minute. In the initial screen, select the customers based on the restriction on the following fields of the customer credit master record:

    - Credit Account
    - Credit Control Area
    - Credit Representative Group
    - Risk Category
    - Last Internal Review
    - Next Internal Review

2. After entering the required values in the input screen, execute the process to go to the screen shown in Figure 5.16.
3. Select all of the customers by pressing [F5] or clicking on the Select All icon.
4. Click on the New Values button.
5. Enter the new date for Next Internal Review in the pop-up window shown in Figure 5.16, and click on Continue.
6. You'll get the message "New values are held and can be saved." Click on the Save icon.
7. For all successful changes, you'll get the message "Control area data <credit control area> Changed," and for failed changes the message will be "Account <customer credit account> is currently blocked by another user."

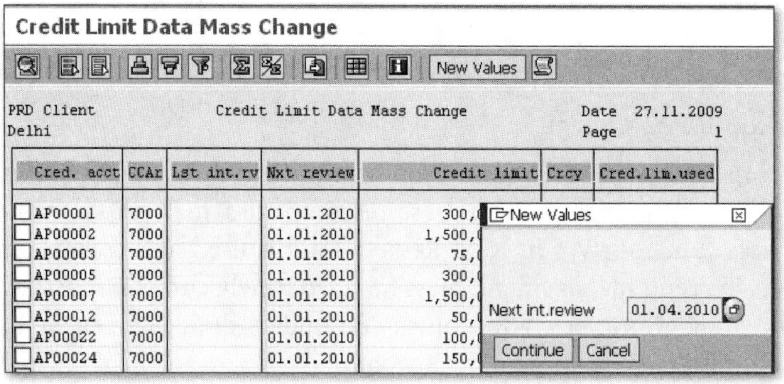

Figure 5.16 Credit Limit Data Mass Change

> **Note**
>
> For mass changes of fields such as risk category (KNKK-CTLPC), customer credit group (KNKK-GRUPP), or individual limit (KNKA-KLIME), use Transaction MASS, object KNA1, and then Table KNKK or KNKA. For mass changes of the field Credit Limit (KNKK-KLIMK), you can use Transaction SE16N with the SAP edit (&SAP_EDIT) function. For more details on these methods, see Chapter 2.

5.2 Blocking and Unblocking Customers

For an SAP ERP user, it's easier to block a customer for sales, rather than creating orders blocked for credit and then rejecting them for release or deleting them. The customer is unblocked when payment received from the customer improves his credit rating and orders are no longer expected to be blocked for credit in automatic credit checks. This is usually used as an add-on to the credit management process, rather than as substitute for it. Via reports like FDK43, customers with more than 100% credit utilization (or per the credit policy, maybe 120% credit utilization) are identified and blocked at regular intervals. The same process is followed for unblocking. Blocking and unblocking of customers is done using the following transactions:

- Transaction XD05 – for different company codes and sales areas
- Transaction VD05 – for different sales areas
- Transaction FD05 – for different company codes

Because Transaction XD05 is a more comprehensive way of blocking and/or unblocking, we'll use it for the rest of our discussion. As shown in Figure 5.17, go to Transaction XD05 and specify the company code and sales area details in the first screen.

The Posting Block is applicable to the accounting component, and no customization is involved. By selecting (or removing) the appropriate checkbox, you can block (or unblock) it for all company codes and/or the company code for which you have executed the Transaction (in this example, we've executed the transaction for Company Code 7000, refer to the company code above the highlighted area).

5 | Credit Risk Management

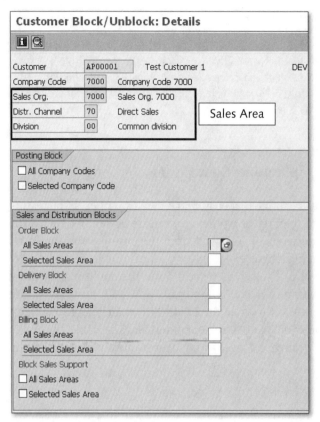

Figure 5.17 Block and Unblock Customer Using Transaction XD05

In the Sales and Distribution functionality in SAP ERP, the same thing is applicable for sales support. You can block sales support for either all sales areas or the selected sales area (we've taken 7000-70-00 as our sales area).

For order, delivery, and billing, you can block a customer for the specified sales area or all sales area. Additionally, you can specify the reason for blocking, selected from a drop-down list. There are three predefined drop-down lists as reasons for blocking the customer for order, delivery, and/or billing. You can modify these three lists using the following Transactions or menu paths.

- Order block: Transaction OVAS (menu path: SAP IMG • SALES AND DISTRIBUTION • SALES • SALES DOCUMENTS • SAP DEFINE AND ASSIGN REASON FOR BLOCKING)

- Delivery block: Transaction OVLS (menu path: SAP IMG • LOGISTICS EXECUTION • SHIPPING • DELIVERIES • DEFINE REASONS FOR BLOCKING IN SHIPPING)

- Billing block: Transaction OVV3 (menu path: SAP IMG • SALES AND DISTRIBUTION • BILLING • BILLING DOCUMENTS • DEFINE BLOCKING REASON FOR BILLING)

5.3 Payment Guarantee

Payment guarantees are documents from a bank (referred to as letters of credit), insurance company (called export credit insurance), or financing company (called payment cards) that ensure that your payment is guaranteed, subject to certain terms and conditions for the sales that you make to a specific customer. In the next two sections, we'll explain first how to define a form of payment guarantee and second, how it's automatically determined at the time of sales processing.

5.3.1 Forms of Payment Guarantee

The different forms of payment guarantees are broadly grouped into the following:

- Documentary payment (e.g., letter of credit)
- Export credit insurance
- Payment cards

While defining a form of payment guarantee using Transaction OVFD or VI52 (menu path: SAP IMG • SALES AND DISTRIBUTION • BASIC FUNCTIONS • CREDIT MANAGEMENT/RISK MANAGEMENT • RECEIVABLES RISK MANAGEMENT • DEFINE FORMS OF PAYMENT GUARANTEE), you can specify the payment guarantee category (Table 5.2), financial document category (Table 5.3), and financial document type (Table 5.3). You can also give a key and description. You go to the screen shown in Figure 5.18 by executing Transaction OVFD, selecting an existing entry (in this case, Form 01), and clicking on the Copy As (F6) icon.

Payment Guarantee Category	Description
0	Financial document
1	Export credit insurance (external link)
2	Export credit insurance with financial document (external link)
3	Payment card
4	Other payment guarantees (user exit)

Table 5.2 Examples of Payment Guarantee Categories

5 Credit Risk Management

Financial Document Category	Description
R	Revocable
U	Irrevocable unconfirmed
C	Irrevocable confirmed
O	Others

Table 5.3 Examples of Financial Document Category

Financial Document type	Description
01	Letter of credit
02	Documentary payments
04	Guarantee

Table 5.4 Examples of Financial Document Type

```
Change View "Maintain forms of payment guarantee": Details of Selected

Paymt guarantee form      01
Data for form of payment guarantee
Paymt guarantee cat.    0     Financial document
Financial doc. cat.     C     Irrevocable confirmed
Financial doc. type     01    Letter of credit
Paymt guarantee form    Confirmed irrevocable letter of credit
```

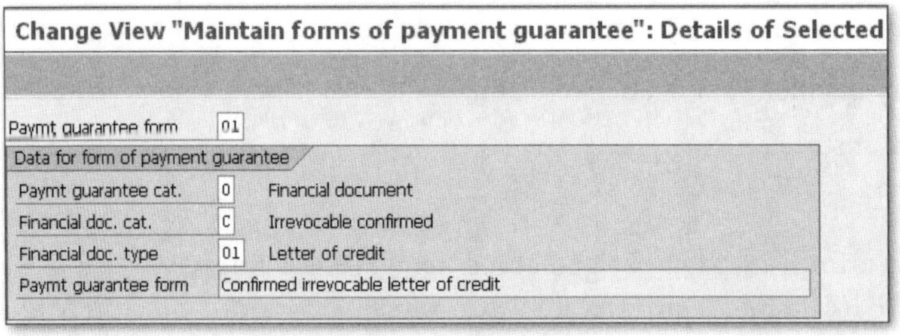

Figure 5.18 Define Forms of Payment Guarantee

Financial documents are used as payment guarantees, especially in international trade. The letter of credit (LoC) is one such financial document type. You can add to the list of financial document types by using Transaction VX50 (menu path: SAP IMG • SALES AND DISTRIBUTION • FOREIGN TRADE/CUSTOMS • DOCUMENTARY PAYMENTS • BASIC SETTINGS • DEFINE FINANCIAL DOCUMENT TYPE). You may, for example, want to differentiate letters of credit based on the bank (or country of the bank) that is issuing them.

5.3.2 Payment Guarantee Determination Procedure

After defining different forms of payment guarantee, the next step is to customize a determination procedure, which is very similar to a condition technique if you visualize the forms of payment guarantee as condition types. The six steps in the payment guarantee determination procedure are as follows:

1. Define the customer payment guarantee procedure (Cpgp).
2. Assign the customer payment guarantee procedure to the customer in the customer master record.
3. Define the document payment guarantee procedure (Dpgp).
4. Assign the document payment guarantee procedure to order types.
5. Define payment guarantee procedures.
6. Assign payment guarantee procedures to different combinations of Cpgp and Dpgp.

Now, let's discuss each of these steps in greater detail.

1. Defining the customer payment guarantee procedure (Cpgp) is similar to defining the customer pricing procedure (CuPP) and is called the *customer determination schema*. You customize it by following the menu path SAP IMG • SALES AND DISTRIBUTION • BASIC FUNCTIONS • CREDIT MANAGEMENT/RISK MANAGEMENT • RECEIVABLES RISK MANAGEMENT • DEFINE AND ASSIGN PAYMENT GUARANTEE SCHEMAS • DEFINE CUSTOMER DETERMINATION SCHEMA. You use the two standard schemas 0001 (letter of credit) or 0002 (payment cards) to create a new customer determination schema or Cpgp.

2. Assign the customer payment guarantee procedure to the customer in the customer master record via Transaction XD01/2. In the customer master record Billing Document screen (which is part of the Sales Area data), in the Payment Guarantee Procedure field (Paym.guar.proc.), you can specify the customer determination schema or Cpgp applicable to the customer.

3. Defining the document payment guarantee procedure (Dpgp) is similar to defining the document pricing procedure (DoPP) and is called the *document determination schema*. You can create new schemas by following the menu path SAP IMG • SALES AND DISTRIBUTION • BASIC FUNCTIONS • CREDIT MANAGEMENT/ RISK MANAGEMENT • RECEIVABLES RISK MANAGEMENT • DEFINE AND ASSIGN PAYMENT GUARANTEE SCHEMAS • DEFINE DOCUMENT DETERMINATION SCHEMA. To create new schemas, copy the standard schema (01) and create a new key and description.

4. To assign document payment guarantee procedures or document determination schemas to different order types, follow the menu path SAP IMG • SALES

5 | Credit Risk Management

AND DISTRIBUTION • BASIC FUNCTIONS • CREDIT MANAGEMENT/RISK MANAGEMENT • RECEIVABLES RISK MANAGEMENT • DEFINE AND ASSIGN PAYMENT GUARANTEE SCHEMAS • ASSIGN DOCUMENT SCHEMA TO ORDER TYPES.

5. YOU CREATE payment guarantee procedures or schemas by following the menu path SAP IMG • SALES AND DISTRIBUTION • BASIC FUNCTIONS • CREDIT MANAGEMENT/RISK MANAGEMENT • RECEIVABLES RISK MANAGEMENT • DEFINE AND ASSIGN PAYMENT GUARANTEE SCHEMAS • DEFINE PAYMENT GUARANTEE SCHEMA. Use standard schemas 000001 (Letters of Credit) and 000002 (Payment Cards) to copy and create a new schema, as shown in Figure 5.19. You can attach more than one payment guarantee form to a procedure with a different access sequence, as shown in Figure 5.20, which you get to by selecting a procedure and double-clicking on the Forms of Payment Guarantee folder. Double-click on any row shown in Figure 5.20 to go to the screen shown in Figure 5.21, where you can see the details of the payment guarantee form and can assign the requirement routine.

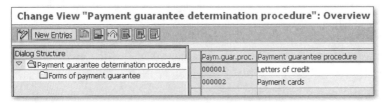

Figure 5.19 Payment Guarantee Determination Procedure

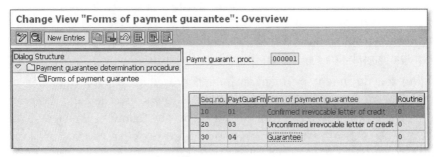

Figure 5.20 Access Sequence for Different Payment Guarantee Forms

6. Assign payment guarantee procedures to different combinations of Cpgp and Dpgp by following the menu path SAP IMG • SALES AND DISTRIBUTION • BASIC FUNCTIONS • CREDIT MANAGEMENT/RISK MANAGEMENT • RECEIVABLES RISK MAN-

agement • Define and Assign Payment Guarantee Schemas • Define Payment Guarantee Schema Determination, as shown in Figure 5.22.

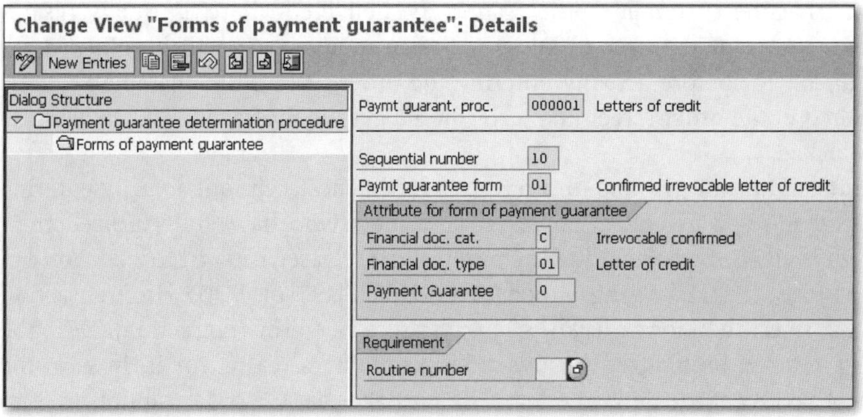

Figure 5.21 Assigning Requirements to Different Accesses

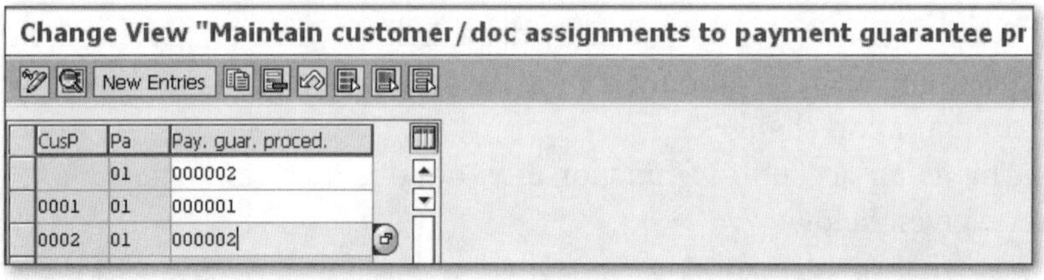

Figure 5.22 Assign Payment Guarantee Procedure

While processing a sales order, the system determines the payment guarantee procedure based on the document payment guarantee procedure (Dpgp) of the document type of the order and the customer payment guarantee procedure (Cpgp) of the customer (payer, to be specific). The payment guarantee procedure searches for any available form of payment guarantee based on the requirement routine and the specified sequence. In the access sequence, more secure forms of payment guarantees (such as payment cards) are normally given a lower sequence number so that they are accessed before less secure forms of payment guarantee (e.g., unconfirmed letter of credit). The requirements routines are used to prevent the use of payment guarantees for low-value transactions, taking into account the cost of the payment guarantee.

5.4 Common Problems and Their Solutions

- **Problem:** Our orders are too large, and when after entering the order, the user finds that the customer's order cannot be delivered, there is usually resentment. We want the user to know if the customer order will be blocked for credit or not before actually entering the order. When the customer code is entered in the order screen, the user should get the message that the customer is blocked.
  Solution: It's not possible to carry out a credit check without actually entering the credit-relevant items. However, customers who have fully utilized their credit limits and whose orders are not likely to released can be blocked. You can block the customer using either Transaction FD32 or XD05. In Transaction FD32, select the Block checkbox in the status screen. In Transaction XD05, the customer can be blocked for the order, assigning a reason for it. In both the cases, you'll get the desired effect. The message that the order cannot be completed will appear when you enter the customer code. However, this is not due to an automatic credit check.

- **Problem:** Our customers give us a security deposit at the time of appointment. They want us to include that amount during the credit check. Where should we make the configuration changes?
  Solution: This is an accounting functionality, done using Transaction OBXR. The steps are given below:
  1. Double-click on the special GL indicator for the security deposit in the first screen.
  2. Enter the credit-relevant GLs in the second screen.
  3. Click on the Properties button on the application toolbar.
  4. In the third screen that appears, select the Rel.to Credit Limit checkbox.

- **Problem:** In the customer credit master sheet (S_ALR_87012218), we find an open order value. This is blocking the customer orders in credit management. We've checked and found no open orders. When there are no open orders, how can there be an open order value for credit management?
  Solution: Open order, open delivery, and open invoice values are determined based on the entries in table fields S066-OEIKW, S067-OLIKW, and S067-OFAKW, respectively. The error in updating these fields may occur for various reasons. You can find some of those reasons in the list of SAP notes provided in Table 5.5. To update for rectifying mistakes, you can use the program RVKRED77 (in Transaction SE38).

5.4 Common Problems and Their Solutions

SAP Note	Description
626880	Credit values are not updated
748217	Changing the doc type causes incorrect statistics values
754372	Third-party: open credit value is deleted although ordered
767454	Billing plan: incorrect credit update
805704	RVKRED77: Correction program corrects incorrectly
801834	Billing plan: incorrect credit update
842927	RVKRED88: Open sales order values are not displayed
860621	Negative open delivery value with batch after billing doc
864105	Simulation credit values: incorrect results in ABAP memory
880557	RVKRED77 + sched agr w/ rel order: mult value of gds for dely
890550	RVKRED77 + sched agrmnt w/ rel: mult value of delvy goods
948824	VL02N: S073 and change docs are incorrect after credit check
950025	VL02N: S073 and change docs are incorrect after credit check
981598	Third-party: Confirmed quantity despite credit block
993714	RFDKLI20: Negative credit values
1025260	RVKRED77: Completed order receives open delivery value
1058456	EK00: Incorrect sales values for credit limit check
1067486	Incorrect credit value when you increase delivery quantity
1070715	Credit value reduced twice with "Deliver Sales Order"
1072322	Open quantity (OLFMNG) not reduced by delivery
1116400	Sales documents are not or only partially updated
1126067	BW + LIS: Incorrect open qty when credit management is active
1297946	RVKRED07: Incorrect credit values due to incorrect election

Table 5.5 SAP Notes on Failure to Update Open Order, Delivery, and Bill Values

▸ **Problem:** Is there any report where we can see the log for open credit values? We're using Tables S066 and S067 so far for this purpose, but it becomes very difficult to track the entries to the documents that created them. Also, we want information about the user who created the document and when.
Solution: There's no standard report as such. However, you can follow the steps listed in SAP Note 1042857 (Logging Credit Values) to create your own report for this purpose.

▶ **Problem:** When we release any order from a credit block, we expect the availability check to be carried out again, especially for items that were not fully confirmed at the time of the first credit check. This does not happen in our system. What modification should we make?
Solution: This happens in a standard system. The availability check is carried out again after the credit release only when the confirmed quantity (VBAP-KBMENG) is nil. You can, however, use user exit USEREXIT_AVAIL_CHECK_CREDIT in include program MV45AFZF (using Transaction SE38) to do the availability check in all (or some) scenarios.

▶ **Problem:** We use rush orders that generate delivery automatically. Even when we've activated a credit check for the rush order (SO), deliveries are still created automatically, when there is insufficient credit limit. Why is this happening?
Solution: Refer to SAP Notes 1224912 and 365271. Please note that use of rush orders and update group 15 is not compatible in SAP ERP. So you have to choose one or the other of them. Because you've ruled out the possibility of a standard setting for rush orders where a credit check is not activated, update group 15 may be the cause of the problem.

5.5 Summary

In this chapter, we discussed how to activate the automatic credit control in the Sales and Distribution functionality of SAP ERP and how credit management works. We also discussed how to block and unblock customers for accounting posting and for various sales and distribution operations such as order, delivery, billing, and sales activities. In the last part of this chapter, we discussed different forms of payment guarantees and how they are determined at the time of sales order processing. With this knowledge, you should be able customize your system as per your company's credit policy and processing procedures. You should be able to change the system when there is a change in the credit policy or process. You should be able to understand the different forms of payment guarantee that your company receives from its customers and use them in the sales processes with these customers. You should also able to block and unblock customers for different sales processes. In the next chapter, we'll discuss different logistics operations.

This chapter teaches you how to customize delivery document types. You'll review the processes for individual document and mass processing and familiarize yourself with special processes such as route determinations, stock transfer, serialization, and batch determination. You'll also learn about output determination and how to use SAP ERP to help facilitate these processes.

6   Logistics Management

The "distribution" part of sales and distribution is what we'll discuss in this chapter. This chapter deals with the physical movement of materials: how the material is picked as per the order and packed and shipped as per the route determined. These processes are getting more and more automated, with the option for manual intervention. In SAP ERP, these processes are part of the Logistics Execution functionality. We'll discuss the Shipping and Transportation components of the Logistics Execution functionality in this chapter. You'll learn how to customize the processes and functionalities available in SAP ERP for delivery of material to customers, including internal customers. The other plants or group of the company are considered as internal customers for a plant during stock transfer. Plants transfer the stock between each other so that the stock is available to the customers in a make-to stock scenario. Once the delivery with or without reference to an order is complete, the customer is billed for collecting payment. The sales return process, which is the reverse process of sales, also involves a delivery (return type). You have a substantial opportunity to reduce the total cost of shipping by optimizing the shipments and selecting the correct route and mode of transport.

In this chapter, we'll start with the various elements of the delivery document and then discuss delivery processing for both individual and multiple documents using the delivery due list. From there, we'll move on to defining routes and route determination, followed by scheduling. We'll also discuss the customization steps for both intra- and intercompany stock transfer and output control in general with a focus on shipping outputs. We'll discuss batch and serial number processing and the steps needed for customizing the SAP interface for external carrier software.

6 | Logistics Management

Finally, we'll list some common errors during post–goods issue (PGI) processing and summarize the chapter.

6.1 Delivery Types and Delivery Item Categories

The delivery primarily consists of a header (stored in Table LIKP and others) and items (stored in Table LIPS and others). It's like the sales documents discussed earlier in that it has both header- and item-level data, much of which is copied from the sales order. Of course, you can create a delivery without reference to an order. In the next sections, we'll discuss the following:

1. How to customize a delivery type, which in turn controls the delivery header.
2. How to customize delivery item categories, which control the delivery items.
3. How to customize automatic item category determination for delivery types.

6.1.1 Delivery Types

You define delivery types using Transaction OVKL (menu path: SAP IMG • LOGISTICS EXECUTION • SHIPPING • DELIVERIES • DEFINE DELIVERY TYPES). After executing the transaction, you'll get a list of existing delivery types. Select any one and click on the Copy As ([F6]) icon to go to the screen shown in the Figure 6.1. The Sales and Distribution document categories J (delivery) and T (return delivery for order) are used for delivery document types. The standard number range maintained for outbound deliveries (LF) is 17 (80000000 to 83999999) for internal assignments. When you don't provide any manual number at the time of document processing, the next available number becomes the delivery document number, 18 (85000000 to 88999999) for external assignments, which means that if you want to give a number to the delivery manually, you can choose any available number from this range. Different customized delivery types can have different number ranges. You can use the form USEREXIT_NUMBER_RANGE in include program MV50AFZ1 to give different delivery number ranges for the same document type, similar to billing documents. The item number increment is the difference between two consecutive items in a delivery. The first item number is automatically zero (0) plus the item number increment.

> **Note**
> The sales document type BV (cash sale), which has the Sales and Distribution document category C, and delivery document type BV (cash sale), which has the Sales and Distribution document category J, are two different document types that can be confusing because the delivery document is automatically created for the sales document for cash sales.

Order reference for the delivery can be mandatory or optional (the Order Required field is left blank). If mandatory, the reference can be further specified as sales order (X Sales Order Required as shown in Figure 6.1) or work order from the production planning interface (W), stock transfer order (B), or other permitted reference. The default order type and item requirement routine (which copies the requirement for deliveries routine) gives you the option of creating a delivery without order reference. You use Transaction VL01NO to create a delivery without reference. Free samples are often delivered without orders. Also, in many industry sectors, it is standard practice to send newly introduced materials to some customers with good relationships. To create your own routine, use Transaction VOFM. After executing the transaction, go to COPYING REQUIREMENTS • DELIVERIES and select any existing routine to copy and use to create a new routine. Routine 202 is especially important because it allows you to add new items to deliveries manually. The new items have references to an order. By default, the values for the default order type determine the nature of the new item. However, this functionality is not available once the goods issue (PGI) or goods receipt (post–goods receipt [PGR], as in case of return delivery) for the delivery is complete. You cannot change any field other then text fields after PGI is complete. The other possible operation after PGI is additional output (e.g., printing the delivery header).

In the Document Content area of the screen shown in Figure 6.1, some fields are not ready for input (or are disabled). The values for these fields are decided by other transactions, and the values assigned in the other transactions or customization settings are only available for display here. The following is a list of such fields and the transaction and/or menu path where you assign the values to the delivery document.

- **Storage Location Rule**

    The rule MALA uses the combination of shipping point, plant, and storage condition to automatically determine the storage location for any specific item of a delivery. Storage location is determined as per the setting in Transaction OVL3 (menu path: SAP IMG • LOGISTICS EXECUTION • SHIPPING • PICKING • DETERMINE

Picking Location • Assign Picking Locations). The rule RETA uses the combination of plant, situation, and storage condition for automatic determination of the storage location. When this rule is used, the storage location is determined by the customization in Transaction S_ALR_87006703 (menu path: SAP IMG • Logistics Execution • Shipping • Picking • Determine Picking Location • Storage Location Determination with Situation). The third standard rule, MARE, first tries to find a storage location as per the MALA rule and then tries to find one using the RETA rule. A new rule can be defined using the include program MV50AFZZ (Transaction SE38). If you have valid reasons to use MALA for some materials and RETA for others, this is where to do it.

- **Output Determination Procedure**
  Transaction V/71 (menu path: SAP IMG • Logistics Execution • Shipping • Basic Shipping Functions • Output Control • Output Determination • Maintain Output Determination for Outbound Deliveries • Assign Output Determination Procedures • Assign deliveries (header)). The output determination procedure assigned here appears in the screen shown in Figure 6.1 in display mode.

- **Text Determination Procedure**
  Transaction VOTXN (menu path: SAP IMG • Logistics Execution • Shipping • Basic Shipping Functions • Text Control • Define And Assign Text Determination Procedures). Select the Delivery Header radio button and click on Change. Double-click on the Text Assignment Procedure folder on the left of the screen. The complete list of delivery types will appear, and you can assign a text determination procedure as per requirements. The assignment done here appears in the screen shown in Figure 6.1 in Display Mode.

- **Output Type**
  You can refer the menu path for assigning output determination procedure to the delivery document type (Transaction V/71). In addition to assigning a determination procedure to the delivery document type, you can also specify a default output type, which is displayed in Figure 6.1.

- **Document Statistical Group**
  Transaction OVRK (menu path SAP IMG • Logistics – General • Logistics Information System (LIS) • Logistics Data Warehouse • Updating • Updating Control • Settings: Sales • Statistics Groups • Assign Statistics Groups for each Delivery Type). The assignment done here appears in the screen shown in Figure 6.1 in Display Mode.

- **Application**
  This is the same as the application of the default output type. It is V2 (Shipping).

- **Route Determination**
  We'll discuss this in Section 6.5.2.

- **Partner Determination Procedure**
  Transaction VOPAN (menu path: SAP IMG • SALES AND DISTRIBUTION • BASIC FUNCTIONS • PARTNER DETERMINATION • SET UP PARTNER DETERMINATION • SET UP PARTNER DETERMINATION FOR DELIVERY • PARTNER DETERMINATION PROCEDURE ASSIGNMENT (FOLDER)).

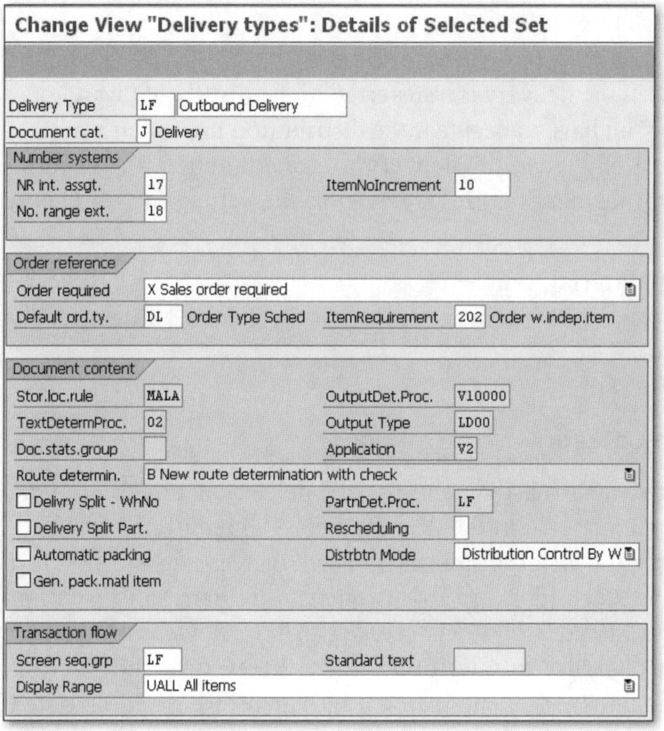

Figure 6.1 Define Delivery Types

The fields for which the values are defined in Transaction OVLK are as follows.

- **Delivery Split – Warehouse Number**
  When this checkbox is selected, the items in different warehouses will be processed by different deliveries.

6 | Logistics Management

- **Delivery Split for Additional Partner**
  When this checkbox is selected, even for the partner function other than ship-to party (e.g., forwarding agent), if partners are different for different items, the delivery will splits

- **Rescheduling**
  This indicator determines if rescheduling should take place for backlog entries (option X), when the route is redetermined (Y), or if the new deadline should be set for the delivery (option A). When it's left blank, there will be no rescheduling.

- **Automatic Packing**
  The automatic packing of all items using packing proposals happens when this checkbox is selected.

- **Distribution Mode**
  This field controls when the delivery is transferred to the distributed warehouse management system. You have to decide if the distribution to happen manually (option 1) or automatically when the delivery is created (option 2). When it's left blank, the control for distribution depends on the setting for warehouse number.

- **Generate Packaging Material Item**
  If this checkbox is selected, the delivery automatically creates an item for the packaging material.

6.1.2 Delivery Item Category

The delivery item category controls the behavior of a delivery item. For example, it determines whether the material in the delivery item will reduce the stock and increase the stock in transit (stock transfer case) or will increase the stock (return case) or only reduce the stock (delivery to customer). The item category of an order becomes the item category of a delivery, as per the copy control setting. For a delivery without reference to sales order, the delivery type and item category of the material maintained in the material master record decide the item category. You customize the delivery item category Transaction 0VLP (menu path: SAP IMG • LOGISTICS EXECUTION • SHIPPING • DELIVERIES • DEFINE ITEM CATEGORIES FOR DELIVERIES). After you execute the transaction, select any item category (e.g., REN) and click on the Copy As ([F6]) icon to go to the screen shown in Figure 6.2. Except for the text determination procedure assigned via Transaction V/73, other fields are maintained here for the delivery item category. Two other fields, Incompletion Procedure and Item Category Statistical Group, are also available in Table

6.1 Delivery Types and Delivery Item Categories

TVLP, which stores the configuration setting of the item category, but neither is available or required for display in the maintenance view, V_TVLP (screen shown in Figure 6.2). The assignment of item categories to these fields is done elsewhere. Table TVLK stores delivery type settings.

> **Note**
>
> Transaction 0VLP, used for customizing delivery item categories, is different from Transaction OVLP, which you use to make item categories relevant for picking.

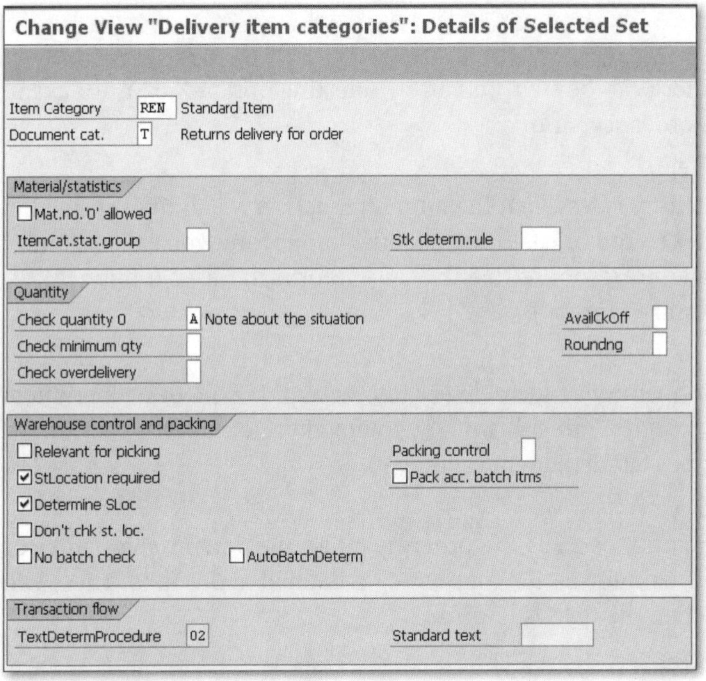

Figure 6.2 Delivery Item Category

We will now discuss the fields (and their role) for customization of the delivery item categories.

- **Mat.no.'0' Allowed**
  If this checkbox is selected, it's not mandatory for the delivery item to contain a material number (e.g., text item).

- **ItemCat.stat.group**
  You can specify the statistics group that the delivery item will use. The statistics

groups are used in updating the structures of sales information system (SIS) reports. We'll discuss this in Chapter 9.

▶ **Stk.determ.rule**
The stock determination rule, along with the stock determination group, determines the stock determination strategy.

▶ **Check Quantity 0**
In this field, you define if the system will give information (A), an error message during delivery creation (C), or an error message during delivery change as well (B). If the field is left blank, there will be no dialog box when the delivery quantity is zero.

▶ **AvailCkOff**
The availability check can be switched off by selecting option X or Y, for example, in a make-to-order scenario.

▶ **Check Minimum Qty**
If the delivery quantity is less than the minimum delivery quantity specified in the material master record or customer-material info record, you can customize the system to have no response (blank), only inform the user (option A), or issue an error message (option B).

▶ **Roundng**
You specify if the quantity of the delivery item with this type of delivery item category will have no rounding (blank), be rounded off (option X), be rounded up (option +), or be rounded down (option –).

▶ **Check overdelivery**
If the delivery quantity exceeds the order quantity, the system gives an error message (option B) or information (option A), as defined in this field. These will be no response when the field is left blank.

▶ **Relevant for Picking**
The item category can be made relevant for picking via Transaction OVLP or by selecting this checkbox.

▶ **StLocation Required**
If this checkbox is selected, the delivery item must have a storage location for the delivery to be complete.

▶ **Determine SLoc**
When this checkbox is selected, the system attempts to determine the storage location automatically.

- **Don't Chk St. Loc.**
  If this checkbox is selected, the system will check if the material is created for the storage location (determined automatically or entered manually).

- **No Batch Check**
  When this checkbox is selected, the system will not check if the material of the batch is available.

- **AutoBatchDeterm**
  If you want the automatic batch determination to take place, select this checkbox.

- **Packing Control and Pack acc. Batch Items**
  You customize these two fields using Transaction VLPP, which will be discussed later in this chapter, in Packing (Section 1.2.3).

6.1.3 Automatic Determination of Delivery Item Category

You customize the determination of item categories for delivery using Transaction 0184 (menu path: SAP IMG • LOGISTICS EXECUTION • SHIPPING • DELIVERIES • DEFINE ITEM CATEGORY DETERMINATION IN DELIVERIES). Once you've executed the transaction, you'll see the screen shown in Figure 6.3. The default item category and allowed item categories are maintained for the different combinations of delivery document type, item category group (maintained in material master records), usage indicator, and higher-level item category. During document (delivery) processing, you can change the item category from the default item category to any one of the allowed item categories. So if the choice of item category needs occasional manual intervention, you know how to do that. The usage indicator is customized via Transaction OVVW (menu path: SAP IMG • LOGISTICS EXECUTION • SHIPPING • DELIVERIES • DEFINE ITEM CATEGORY USAGE). Standard item usages such as CHSP (batch split), SEIN (delivery item relevant for billing), SENI (delivery item not relevant for billing), Text (text item), V (purchase order), FREE (free goods), and others are used as sources to create new usages by copying. The usage indicator is maintained for a combination of material and customer in the customer material info record. Because this is a factor in determining delivery item category, you can use it in various business scenarios. For example, you can make a material not relevant for billing for a particular customer (by maintaining a customer material info record). The same material may be relevant for billing to all other customers.

6 | Logistics Management

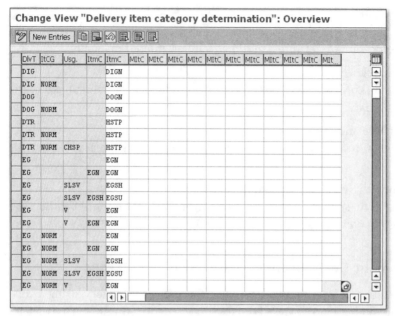

Figure 6.3 Delivery Item Category Determination

6.2 Picking, Handling Unit Management, Packing, and Goods Issue

During delivery processing, the activities carried out are either basic functions or specialized functions. We'll deal with the specialized functions, which include batch determination, serial number allocation, creating an inspection lot, stock transfer, and route determination, separately in this chapter. In this section, we'll discuss four basic functionalities: picking, handling unit management, packing, and goods issue. These are important from Inventory Management point of view, especially the goods issue (or receipt).

6.2.1 Picking

Picking is the process of identifying the materials that will be included in a delivery. The steps for customizing the picking functionality are as follows:

1. Define item categories relevant for picking using Transaction OVLP (menu path: SAP IMG • LOGISTICS EXECUTION • SHIPPING • PICKING • DEFINE RELEVANT ITEM

CATEGORIES). All of the item categories will be proposed with a checkbox. When you select a checkbox, the corresponding item category is selected for picking.

2. The result of picking comes from the Warehouse Management functionality in SAP ERP. When you do not use Warehouse Management, you can still report the result of picking back to the delivery item by using the picking confirmation requirement functionality. You define the picking confirmation requirement for each shipping point using Transaction VSTK (menu path: SAP IMG • LOGISTICS EXECUTION • SHIPPING • PICKING • DEFINE CONFIRMATION REQUIREMENTS). The system will propose all shipping points, and in the Confirmation Requirement column, you can leave the field blank if no confirmation is required or select A if confirmation is required. You can customize the confirmation requirement setting by coding the form USEREXIT_LIPS-KOQUI_DETERMINE in include program MV50AFZ3.

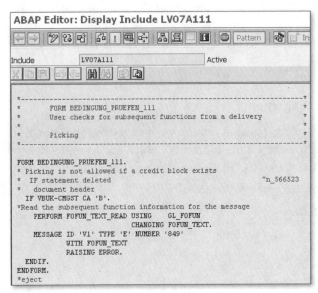

Figure 6.4 Picking Requirement Routine 111

3. Modify picking requirement routine 111 if necessary, using Transaction OVB6 (menu path: SAP IMG • LOGISTICS EXECUTION • SHIPPING • PICKING • DEFINE PICKING REQUIREMENTS). By default, this routine does not allow picking to happen if there's a credit block, but you may want the picking to be complete for a few special customers. You can modify it by clicking on the Pencil icon shown in Figure 6.4. You go to the screen shown in Figure 6.4 by using Transaction

OVB6, selecting the row for routine 111, and clicking on the Req.maintenance tab below it. In the intermediate screen, select routine number 111 and click on the Select Text icon or press [F5]. You can also use Transaction SE38 and program LV07A111 to go to this screen for inserting modifications.

4. Automatic determination of the picking location is another optimization tool SAP offers you. You can use automatic determination of the picking location via Transaction OVL3 (menu path: SAP IMG • LOGISTICS EXECUTION • SHIPPING • PICKING • DETERMINE PICKING LOCATION • ASSIGN PICKING LOCATIONS) when the storage location rule is MALA or Transaction S_ALR_87006703 (menu path: SAP IMG • LOGISTICS EXECUTION • SHIPPING • PICKING • DETERMINE PICKING LOCATION • STORAGE LOCATION DETERMINATION WITH SITUATION) when the rule is RETA. For the first option, the storage location is maintained for all combinations of shipping point, plant, and storage condition (maintained in that material master record) and is automatically proposed at the time of delivery processing. In the second case, the storage location is maintained using a combination of plant, situation, and storage condition and is proposed at the time of delivery processing.

6.2.2 Handling Unit Management

Handling units (HUs) are used for packing, which we'll cover in more detail in the next section. Handling units are tangible units, which can contain one or more materials and packaging materials. There can also be a handling unit within another handing unit as shown in Figure 6.5. A handling unit has the following:

- A unique identifying number
- A specific dimension, weight, and volume
- A status (e.g., blocked, loaded)
- Materials and their quantities
- Packaging materials (e.g., corrugated box, pallet, container)
- Packing instructions (necessary for automatic creation of HUs)
- A header level that contains information on means of transport, output determination, procedure, and so on
- An item level containing material, packaging material, and other HUs

6.2 Picking, Handling Unit Management, Packing, and Goods Issue

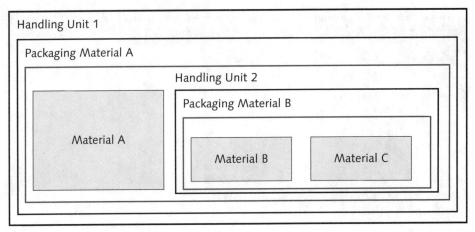

Figure 6.5 Typical Handling Unit

There are two steps for customizing an HU, which are as follows:

1. Define the number range for handling unit using Transaction SNRO (numbering object RV_VEKP) or VNKP (menu path: SAP IMG • LOGISTICS EXECUTION • SHIPPING • PACKING • DEFINE NUMBER RANGES FOR HANDLING UNITS).

2. Define the handling unit group 1 to 5 using Transaction VEG1 (menu path: SAP IMG • LOGISTICS EXECUTION • SHIPPING • PACKING • USE HANDLING UNIT SUPPLEMENTS • HANDLING UNIT GROUP 1 TO 5).

6.2.3 Packing

In customization for packing, you can decide whether the materials must be packed (option A), can be packed (left blank), or must not be packed (option B) during delivery processing. You decide for each possible delivery item category using Transaction VLPP (menu path: SAP IMG • EXECUTION • SHIPPING • PACKING • PACKING CONTROL BY ITEM CATEGORY), as shown in Figure 6.6. All delivery item categories appear by default on the screen, and in the Packing Control column, you can specify whether the material must be packed (A), can be packed (blank), or must not be packed (B) for a particular delivery item category. The pack-accumulated batch becomes relevant only when you've made the handling unit management active for the storage location. When this checkbox is selected, the accumulated quantities in the main item are considered for packing, not the batch splits.

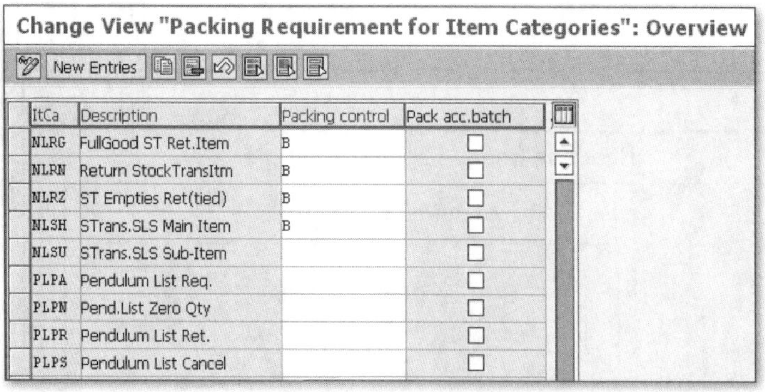
Change View "Packing Requirement for Item Categories": Overview

New Entries

ItCa	Description	Packing control	Pack acc.batch
NLRG	FullGood ST Ret.Item	B	☐
NLRN	Return StockTransItm	B	☐
NLRZ	ST Empties Ret(tied)	B	☐
NLSH	STrans.SLS Main Item	B	☐
NLSU	STrans.SLS Sub-Item		☐
PLPA	Pendulum List Req.		☐
PLPN	Pend.List Zero Qty		☐
PLPR	Pendulum List Ret.		☐
PLPS	Pendulum List Cancel		☐

Figure 6.6 Packing Requirement for Item Categories

6.2.4 Goods Issue

The goods issue is the final activity in delivery processing. Once the goods issue (or receipt) is completed, it's not possible to change the delivery (except for changes to a few text fields). The goods issue is done by clicking on the Post Goods Issue button in the task bar of the delivery overview screen (Transaction VL02N) when the delivery is complete. For return deliveries, the tab becomes Post Goods Receipt. Material and accounting documents are generated in the background when goods are issued. Material documents are the documents used in the Inventory Management functionality in SAP ERP. These documents have headers and items like sales, delivery, and billing documents. They store the information related to a particular transaction. Some of these documents are generated in functionalities other then Inventory Management. PGI is a classic example. Usually, these material documents also update the accounting posting as per customization, by generating accounting documents. Accounting documents primarily store the GL accounts that are credited and debited in both transactional currency and company code currency. Transaction VL06G is used for mass processing of goods issue. PGI or PGR can be reversed using Transaction VL09. For goods issue, receipt, or reversal of these documents, the period (both material and accounting period) that you're posting to should be open. Several accounting or fiscal periods can be open simultaneously (though not a good practice) using Transaction OB52. See Appendix C for more information on how to control a material period.

Now that you understand picking, handling units, and goods issues, let's move on to delivery processing integration with the Warehouse Management functionality in SAP ERP.

> **Note**
> Material documents store the header information in Table MKPF and item information in Table MSEG. Accounting documents store the header information in Table BKPF and item information in Table BSEG.

6.3 Delivery Processing Integration with Warehouse Management

In this section, we'll discuss how deliveries are created and how the Warehouse Management functionality in SAP ERP influences delivery processing. Delivery can be created with or without reference to the following documents:

- Sales document (e.g., order, return)
- Stock transfer order
- Subcontract order
- Project

When the delivery is created with reference to a sales document, the information is copied to the delivery document based on the copy control settings and the routines in use. If it's created without reference, the customer master record of the ship-to party, the material master record, and the customer material info records provide default values for the delivery document.

You can create individual deliveries using Transaction VL01N or by going to SALES DOCUMENT • DELIVER from the sales order overview screen. Once you've created the delivery is created, you can modify it using Transaction VL02N and display it using Transaction VL03N. A delivery consists of three screens, overview, header, and item, with several tabs. You can navigate between the screens by selecting the GoTo menu option and then selecting Overview, Header, or Item. For the header and item, you can go directly to the tab you want by selecting it in the menu, and click on the Overview or Header icon to switch between the two screens. By double-clicking on any item, you'll go to the item screen.

When the Warehouse Management functionality in SAP ERP is implemented, warehouse numbers are assigned to the combination of plant and storage locations. The picking is done by a *transfer order* created within Warehouse Management. A transfer order can be created automatically during delivery processing via delivery header output type WMTA. The other advantages that the Warehouse Management functionality in SAP ERP offers are:

- Better utilization of resources (space, employees, and equipment).
- Better compliance with first in first out (FIFO) and other accounting principles.
- Better inventory management achieved with additional functionality that warehouse number, storage type, storage bin, and the quant offer. These are available when you use the Warehouse Management functionality in SAP ERP. A warehouse number identifies the whole stock yard or warehouse complex at a location. Storage types physically or logically segregate a warehouse into separate units. Storage bin refers to the exact physical location where materials are stored or can be stored in three-dimensional space. A quant is a group material with the same features (e.g., materials with same batch number). Inventory can be managed at the storage bin level in terms of quant.
- Use of barcodes and/or radio frequency identification (RFID).
- Better management of hazardous materials by segregating them as a separate storage type. Separate storage bins can be designated exclusively to store hazardous materials such as inflammable oils or explosives.
- Compliance with employee health and safety standards.

In the future, any improvement made to the picking functionality in SAP ERP is expected via the Warehouse Management functionality. If you look at it from a management perspective, you'll find that it's not possible to improve the picking process until an efficient warehousing system is in place.

6.4 Principles of Processing Deliveries Including Delivery Due Lists

An outbound delivery can be created for a sales order when the following conditions are met, subject to availability:

1. The order is not blocked for delivery due to customization settings or credit blocks at the document or schedule line level.
2. At least one line item in the order is due for delivery.
3. The delivery quantity must not be zero for the item(s) due for delivery.

4. The product status of the material should allow delivery.

5. The order is complete (i.e., not in incompletion log).

Upon the creation of a delivery with reference to an order, the order status is automatically updated (as per copy control settings) as partially delivered or fully delivered at the header and item levels. Additional items can be added to a delivery, and items created with reference to the order can be deleted depending on customization. During delivery processing, you can perform picking, packing, shipping point determination, and goods issue. In addition, you can also perform route determination, batch determination, and serialization of materials, which we'll cover separately in this chapter.

It's possible to split and combine orders during delivery processing. An order can be split into different deliveries if the shipping point, plant, INCO term, or ship-to parties for different items are different in a standard system. You can also define a delivery split profile using Transaction OVDSP and use Transaction VLSP (subsequent delivery split) to split a delivery using the split profile. Similarly, you can process items from different orders in one delivery if the shipping point, plant, INCO term, ship-to party, and sales organization are the same. The combined orders must have value X in the Order Combination field of the Shipping tab. The value for this field is automatically proposed from the value maintained in the customer master record (Order Combination Field in the Shipping tab in the Sales Area data). During mass processing of different orders using the delivery due list, the splitting and combination happen automatically.

The delivery due list is an optimization tool available for mass processing of sales and stock transfer orders. In addition to processing, you can use it for reporting purposes as well. Table 6.1 lists the standard delivery due lists available in SAP ERP. You can customize these due lists or create your own. It's important to remember that the profiles are created and assigned to scenarios, and Table 6.1 simply lists the default profiles for the existing scenarios that have the same codes.

Transaction	Description	Profile/Scenario
VL10	User-specific delivery due list	VL10
VL10A	Sales orders due for delivery	0001
VL10C	Order items due for delivery	0101
VL10E	Order schedule lines due for delivery	0201
VL10B	Purchase orders due for delivery	0002

Table 6.1 Delivery Due Lists for Different Scenarios

Transaction	Description	Profile/Scenario
VL10F	Purchase order schedule lines due for delivery	0202
VL10G	Documents due for delivery	0003
VL10H	Items due for delivery	0103
VL10I	Schedule lines due for delivery	0203
VL10U	Cross-system deliveries	1001

Table 6.1 Delivery Due Lists for Different Scenarios (Cont.)

> **Note**
> The purchase orders relevant for outbound delivery are stock transfer orders, which we'll discuss later in this chapter.

Delivery due lists are used as work lists for creating multiple deliveries. Work lists are reports or lists that can be further processed, for example, creating deliveries as in this case. It's not possible to manually select the orders (or stock transfer orders [STOs]) that are to be delivered and that can wait. Companies usually follow very complex rules and/or use manual intervention for this. So you can incorporate all or some of this logic to include some orders for delivery processing and exclude some others. Therefore, in spite of so many standard delivery due lists, you may still want to customize your own delivery due list. The steps for customizing delivery due lists are as follows:

1. Maintain the profile for delivery creation (VL10CUC).
2. Create the profile for delivery due lists (VL10CUA or VL10CU_ALL).
3. Exclude specific function codes during list processing (VL10CUE).
4. Assign profiles to scenarios (VL10CUV).
5. Maintain requirements routines for due list processing (VOL1).
6. Modify the default layout if required (OVB9).

Now let's discuss each of these steps in further detail.

6.4.1 Profile for Delivery Creation

To define profiles for creating a delivery, use Transaction VL10CUC (menu path: SAP IMG • LOGISTICS EXECUTION • SHIPPING • WORKLISTS • MAINTAIN PARAMETERS FOR CREATING DELIVERIES), which you can see in Figure 6.7. Select any existing profile and click on the Copy As ([F6]) icon to go to Figure the screen shown in 6.8. The fields that are maintained here are:

- **Repeat Blocked**
  During processing of a delivery due list, the documents that's not blocked by any other user are processed. The system, then attempts to process the documents that it could not process in the first attempt. In the second attempt, a few documents still may not be available for processing. This process is repeated during delivery due list processing the number of times specified in this field.

- **Maximum Lines**
  Should be left as 1.

- **Package Type**
  This field refers to the grouping of items in the delivery. Option 1 groups the items of a document with same ship-to party in one package, whereas option 2 groups the items of a document together. If you want to have your own logic, you can define the package type in the FORM routine USEREXIT_PREPARE_PACKAGES_CREA in the include program LV50R_VIEWG09.

- **Maximum Number of Tasks**
  This field is for when you want to process the delivery due list as parallel multiple tasks. The system will process the delivery due list by dividing the task into groups as many times as specified here.

- **Selected Items**
  If this checkbox is selected, only the selected items are processed. Otherwise all the items of the documents are processed, even when a few of them may actually match the selection criteria.

- **Maximum Delivery Period in Future (MxDlvCrteDate)**
  In this field, a value of 30 means all of the deliveries due for delivery in next 30 days will be processed.

- **Description**
  This field describes the profile.

- **Group Parallel**
  This field specifies the server group for parallel processing of deliveries. To use this optimization functionality, which distributes the load on the servers, you'll require BASIS help.

- **No Output Determination, Rescheduling, Shipping Deadlines, SD Picking List and Country-specific Delivery Number**
  These five checkboxes, if selected, prevent output determination, rescheduling,

additional shipping deadlines, sales and distribution picking lists, and country-specific delivery numbering for the deliveries created by processing the delivery due list. For example, when the last checkbox is selected, it will not generate additional country-specific delivery numbers *only when* deliveries are created using customized delivery due lists.

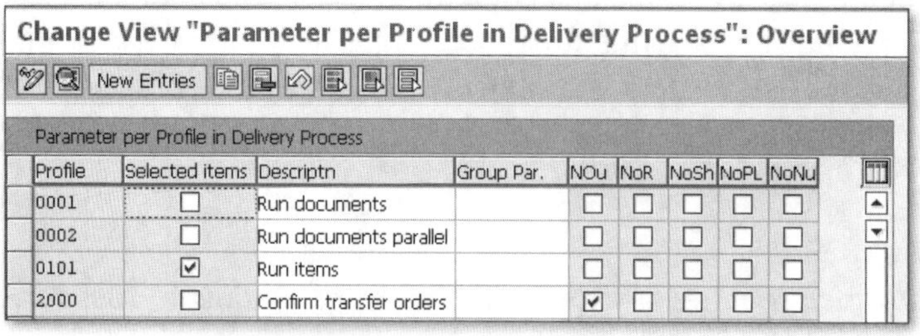

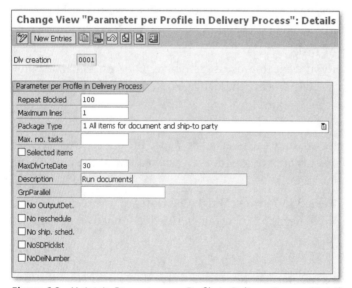

Figure 6.7 Maintain Parameters per Profile in Delivery Process (Overview)

Figure 6.8 Maintain Parameters per Profile in Delivery Process (Detail)

6.4.2 List Profile

Use Transaction VL10CUA or VL10CU_ALL to create the list profile (menu path: SAP IMG • LOGISTICS EXECUTION • SHIPPING • WORKLISTS • CONFIGURE LIST PROFILE). You can go to the screen shown in Figure 6.9 when you select any existing entry and click on the Copy As (F6) icon. As you can see, there are several fields that collectively define the profile. The fields can be grouped broadly as:

- Fields that provide default values on the selection screen
- Fields that influence the layout
- Fields that restrict the possible documents for selection
- Fields that influence delivery processing

Fields that Default Values on the Selection Screen
- The Rule DlvCrDate (Rule for the default value of the selection criteria for delivery creation date) field can take any of the following six values. It becomes the default value for the field CalcRuleDefltDlvCrDt on execution of Transaction VL10*.
  - Blank (everything up to a maximum number of days)
  - 1 (documents due for delivery today)
  - 2 (documents due for delivery today and tomorrow)
  - 3 (documents due for delivery, on or before the last day of the next week plus those due before today)
  - 4 (documents due for delivery, on or before tomorrow plus those due before today)
  - 9 (as defined in user exit)
- The Selection Criteria field can be maintained either at this customization setting or as a parameter value for the parameter LE_VL10_USER_VARIANT in the user master data record. You can create the default layout by following the menu path GOTO • VARIANTS • SAVE AS VARIANT after executing Transaction VL10*.

Fields that Influence the Layout
- **Open Deliveries**
  When this checkbox is selected, the system includes the open deliveries created manually for processing.
- **With Ship-To Party's Name**
  When this checkbox is selected, the ship-to party's name appears on the screen. However, this reduces the performance.

- **With Stock Data**
  When this checkbox is selected, the unrestricted stock of the material is displayed.

- **Display Delivery Block with Quantity 0**
  When this checkbox is selected, the blocked schedule lines with the quantity zero are displayed.

- **Use Control**
  When selected, this checkbox allows the display of output in ABAP List Viewer (ALV) format.

- **Selection Indicator at Header Level**
  When selected, this checkbox displays the list at the document level that would otherwise display the items.

- **Traffic Light**
  The Traffic Light icon that appears in output (when you execute Transaction VL10*) is red when the delivery is already due. If it is due for today or a future date, the value in the traffic light field determines when it will be green or yellow. It will be green when the delivery due date is more than the value maintained in this field.

- **Layout**
  Layout can be sequential (1) or hierarchical sequential (2) depending upon how you want it to be displayed.

- **Key Type**
  When the layout is a hierarchical sequential list, the hierarchy is defined with the key type. For example, if you select the option 1 (Ship-To Party and Source Document), the items of an order are grouped, and then all orders of a ship-to party are shown below the ship-to party. All of the ship-to parties appear one after another in the list.

- **Expand**
  When the layout is hierarchical, you can define whether it will appear as expanded (Yes) or collapsed (No) by default.

- **Stock Details**
  Here you can specify that Transaction CO06, CO09, MD04, or MMBE be used for displaying stock.

- **Log Follows**
  Here you can specify whether after processing the log will appear in the same window (Y), a new window (X), or will not appear at all (blank).

- **Log F Code**
  In this field, you can specify whether the log will appear in the same window (Y), a new window (X), or will not appear at all (blank) when the user clicks on the Display Log button or follows the menu path after processing.

- **Deletion Mode**
  You can define if during the batch input for deleting deliveries, the screens involved will be displayed (A), displayed only when there's an error (E), or not to be displayed at all (N).

- **Allowed Function Codes**
  We'll discuss the function code that will excluded from a profile in Section 6.4.3. In this field you specify the default function code for the profile.

Fields that Restrict the Possible Documents for Selection

- **Selection Criteria for Document Type Selection**
  Here you specify the list of allowed document types (e.g., sales order, purchase order, and delivery) that can be processed with the due list.

- **Do Not Select Deliveries for Preceding Documents**
  This checkbox prevents both the open delivery and its preceding document (sales order or stock transfer order) to appear in the due list simultaneously.

- **Add to Deliveries**
  This checkbox allows you to add items to a delivery already created.

- **Do Not Select Checked and Select Unchecked Deliveries**
  These two checkboxes together determines whether only the checked or unchecked deliveries are to be selected.

- **Open Deliveries**
  Select this checkbox to include open deliveries in the delivery due list even when their reference document (sale order or stock transfer order) is also present in the list.

Fields that Influence Delivery Processing

- **List Type**
  Here you define if the index list or delivery list is to be generated for processing. The delivery list, which gives more details and hence takes more time, has the added option of manually changing the delivery quantity.

- **1 Line Per Item**
  If this checkbox is selected, there will be one line per item even when multiple schedule lines exist for the item.

- **Cumulation Rule**
  This rule defines how the open schedule lines are to be added up during delivery creation.

- **Select Rules**
  In this field you define whether all or none or the schedule lines in the specified date range are to be selected by default.

- **Split Per Schedule Line**
  When there are multiple schedule lines per item, the rule specified here determines whether there will be one delivery per order or one delivery per schedule line or whether the system will combine a backlogged schedule line in one delivery item and generate one delivery item each for future schedule lines.

- **Limits at Schedule Line**
  In this field you decide if the limits that you set in the selection screen are for the delivery due date (1), route schedule (2), and/or planned goods issue date (3), or there are no constraints (blank). When there's more than one constraint, the option is coded as per the constraints included (e.g., option 23 means route schedule (2) + planned goods issue date (3)).

- **Blocked**
  You can display and process the all documents due for delivery (blank) or documents due but not blocked by a user (1).

- **Function Code Profile**
  The function code profile is a set of standard SAP function codes arranged in sequence. You can create your own profile using Transaction VL10CUF. The two standard profiles 0001 and 5000 display the delivery due list for processing and process without displaying the data, respectively.

- **Profile for Delivery Creation**
  The profile for delivery creation defined in the first step is assigned to the list profile (or user profile) here.

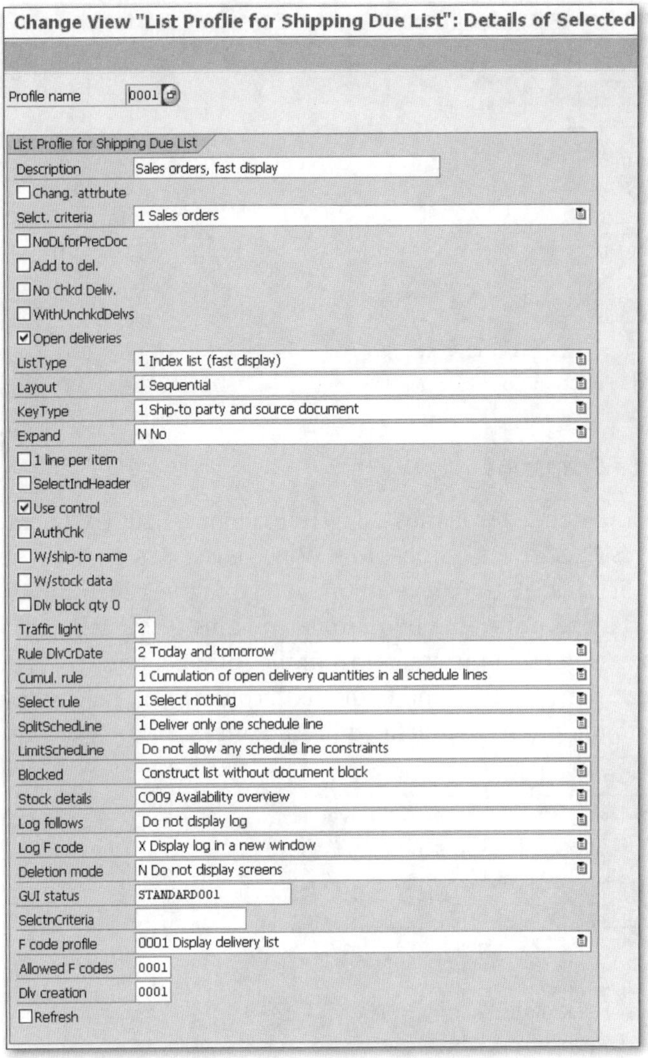

Principles of Processing Deliveries Including Delivery Due Lists | 6.4

Figure 6.9 List Profile for Delivery Due List (Detail Screen)

6.4.3 Function Codes Excluded During List Processing

You may run into the requirement to exclude function codes during list processing. This is done via Transaction VL10CUE (menu path: SAP IMG • LOGISTICS EXECUTION • SHIPPING • WORKLISTS • EXCLUDE FUNCTION CODES FROM LIST STATUS), as shown in Figure 6.10. The function code is excluded when you select the FCode Allowed checkbox. You should get the help of an ABAP developer for this step.

Change View "Include/Exclude Function Codes": Overview

New Entries

Include/Exclude Function Codes

AllwdFCode	Funct.code	FCode allowed
0001	&ABC ALV: ABC analysis	☐
0001	&XXL ALV: Spreadsheet	☐
0002	&ABC ALV: ABC analysis	☐
0002	&XXL ALV: Spreadsheet	☐
0002	VL01 Create delivery in f	☐
1001	&ABC ALV: ABC analysis	☐
1001	&XXL ALV: Spreadsheet	☐
1001	SAMD Create deliveries wi	☐
1001	VL01 Create delivery in f	☐

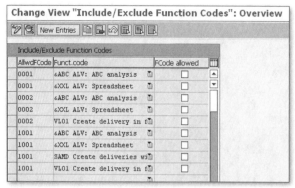

Figure 6.10 Include or Exclude Function Codes

6.4.4 Assign Profile to Scenarios

You assign profiles to the SAP-defined scenarios using Transaction VL10CUV (menu path: SAP IMG • Logistics Execution • Shipping • Worklists • Assignment of List Profile to Delivery Scenario). Upon execution, you go to the screen shown in Figure 6.11. It's important to notice the two Profile columns (third and sixth) where the profiles will be assigned to the scenarios. In the third column, you can specify the list profile created in step two, and in the sixth column you can specify the parameter according to the profile you defined in step one.

Change View "Assignment of List Profiles to Scenarios": Overview

New Entries

Assignment of List Profiles to Scenarios

Scenario	Descriptn	Profile	Sel. scrn	Allow assgnmnt	Profile
0001 Sales order:	Edit delivery list (sales orders)	0001	3 Docume	☐	
0002 Purchase orc	Edit delivery list (purch.orders)	0002	3 Docume	☐	
0003 Sales order:	Edit delivery list (sales/purch. c	0003	3 Docume	☐	
0101 Sales order	Edit delivery list (sales order ite	0101	3 Docume	☐	
0102 Purchase orc	Edit delivery list (purchase ord	0102	3 Docume	☐	
0103 Sales order	Edit delivery list (items)	0103	3 Docume	☐	
0201 Sales order	Edit delivery list (sales sched. li	0201	3 Docume	☐	
0202 Purchase orc	Edit delivery list (purch. sched	0202	3 Docume	☐	
0203 Schedule lir	Edit delivery list (schedule line:	0203	3 Docume	☐	
1001 Cross-Systen	Cross-System Deliveries	1001	3 Docume	☐	0001
2000 Confirm Trar	Confirm Transfer Orders	2000		☐	
500A	Schedule background processi		5 Schedu	☐	
500B Schedule Bac	Schedule background processi		6 Schedu	☐	
500C Schedule Bac	Schedule background processi		7 Schedu	☐	
QM01 Create Deli	Create delivery from quality nc	QM01	3 Docume	☐	
VL04 Scenario for	Upgrade VL04 to release 4.6		4 Use R	☐	
VL10 Default scer	User-specific delivery scenario	0001	3 Docume	☐	

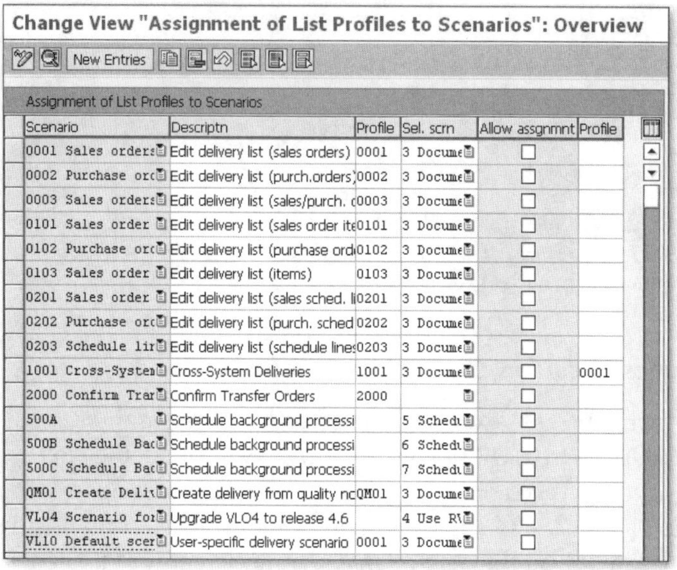

Figure 6.11 Assign Profile to Scenarios

6.4.5 Maintain Requirement Routines

The VOFM requirement routine needed for deliveries to be created using the delivery due list is maintained via Transaction VOL1 (menu path: SAP IMG • LOGISTICS EXECUTION • SHIPPING • WORKLISTS • MAINTAIN REQUIREMENTS FOR CREATING WORKLISTS), which is illustrated in Figure 6.12. You can modify Routine 104 and replace it with another routine if required.

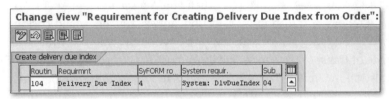

Figure 6.12 Maintain Requirement Routine

6.4.6 Modify Layout

You can define the default layout for the delivery due list using Transaction OVB9 (menu path: SAP IMG • LOGISTICS EXECUTION • SHIPPING • WORKLISTS • DEFINE LIST LAYOUT OF DELIVERY LISTS). However, this will require help from an ABAP developer.

> **Note**
> Refer to SAP Note 113411, Collective Note on VL10, and its related notes for more information on customizing delivery due lists, which are also referred to as extended delivery due lists.

Now that you understand processing deliveries, let's move on to routes and route determination.

6.5 Routes and Route Determination

You determine routes during order processing. The route determined for an item ordered is automatically copied to the delivery document header. During the data transfer, it may or may not be redetermined, as per the setting in the delivery item category and copy control. In the following three sections, we'll discuss how to define a route, how to define a route determination procedure, and then how to customize route schedule determination.

6.5.1 Define Routes

Routes consist of the mode of transport (e.g. road, rail, or sea), transportation connecting points (e.g., sea port), and shipping types (e.g., goods train, ship). The steps for defining routes are given below.

1. Define the modes of transport (e.g., road, sea, air) using Transaction 0VTB (menu path: SAP IMG • Sales and Distribution • Basic Functions • Routes • Define Routes • Define Modes of Transport), which you can see in Figure 6.13. You can create new modes of transport by selecting any existing entry and clicking on the Copy As icon. For each new entry, you have to provide a key, description, and mode of transport category. The list of possible categories for mode of transport is also shown in Figure 6.13. You access it by pressing [F4] when your cursor is on the SType field.

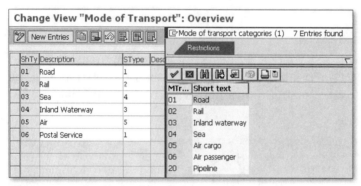

Figure 6.13 Define Mode of Transport

2. Define the Shipping Types field using Transaction 0VTA (menu path: SAP IMG • Sales and Distribution • Basic Functions • Routes • Define Routes • Define Shipping Types), as shown in Figure 6.14. You can create a new shipping type by selecting an existing entry and clicking on the Copy As icon. Then you provide a key, description, mode of transport, and shipping type procedure group. The list of shipping type procedure groups shown in Figure 6.14 is accessible by pressing the [F4] help. You create a shipping type with respect to a mode of transport. For example, the shipping type Truck is created for the mode of transport Road.

3. Define the transportation connection points using Transaction 0VTD (menu path: SAP IMG • Sales and Distribution • Basic Functions • Routes • Define Routes • Define Transportation Connection Points). Once you've entered

the transaction, the system takes you to an overview screen. You can select an existing entry and click on the Copy As icon or in this case simply click on the New Entries button to go to the screen shown in Figure 6.15. While defining the transport connection point, you have to define whether it's an airport, railway station, border crossing, or port (inland/sea). You should also specify the custom office name if applicable. The custom office is where the shipment enters the jurisdiction of another country. There are normally two customs offices, one that belongs to the country the shipment is leaving and the other belonging to the country it's entering. When you define the transportation connection, you normally specify the customs office of the receiving country. The fields in the four tabs, Scheduling, Reference Customer/Vendor, Reference Shipping Point/Plant, and Rail Data, for the transportation connection point are also specified.

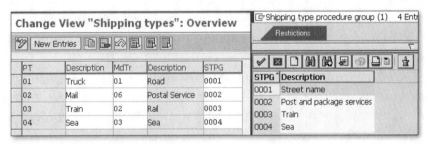

Figure 6.14 Define Shipping Types

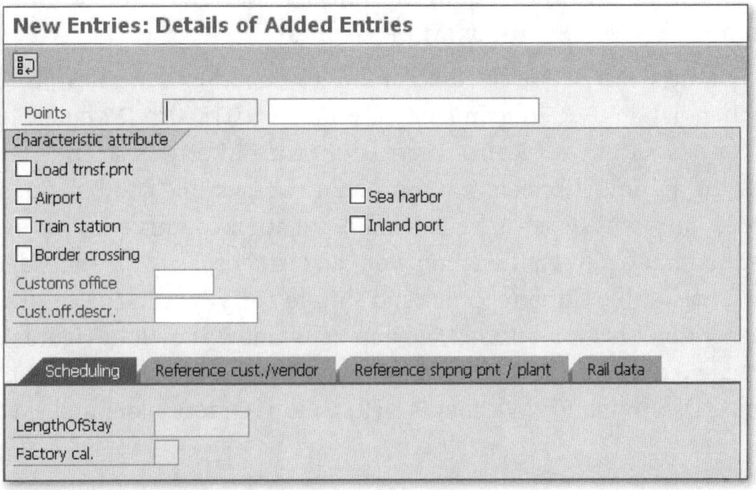

Figure 6.15 Define Transportation Connection Points

4. Define routes and route stages using Transaction 0VTC (menu path: SAP IMG • SALES AND DISTRIBUTION • BASIC FUNCTIONS • ROUTES • DEFINE ROUTES • DEFINE ROUTES AND STAGES). In the overview screen, you can select any existing entry and click on the Copy As icon to go to the screen shown in Figure 6.19. You enter the information for defining routes and for route scheduling in this screen.

6.5.2 Route Determination

Route determination is an optimization tool SAP ERP offers you. It automates the selection of routes for delivery processing. The system determines routes base on the delivery type, shipping point, and various other factors, which we'll discuss now. The customization steps for route determination are as follows:

1. Define the transportation zones for each country using Transaction OVR1 (menu path: SAP IMG • SALES AND DISTRIBUTION • BASIC FUNCTIONS • ROUTES • ROUTE DETERMINATION • DEFINE TRANSPORTATION ZONES). Transportation zones can be either departure zones for the shipping point or receiving zones for the ship-to party.

2. Assign the departure zones to the shipping points using Transaction OVL7 (menu path: SAP IMG • SALES AND DISTRIBUTION • BASIC FUNCTIONS • ROUTES • ROUTE DETERMINATION • MAINTAIN COUNTRY AND TRANSPORTATION ZONE FOR SHIPPING POINT).

3. Define transportation groups for the materials using Transaction OVSY (menu path: SAP IMG • SALES AND DISTRIBUTION • BASIC FUNCTIONS • ROUTES • ROUTE DETERMINATION • DEFINE TRANSPORTATION GROUPS).

4. Specify the routes that are selected according to the criteria in sales processing using Transaction 0VRF (menu path: SAP IMG • SALES AND DISTRIBUTION • BASIC FUNCTIONS • ROUTES • ROUTE DETERMINATION • MAINTAIN ROUTE DETERMINATION). In the initial screen, you can define all possible combinations of departure country plus departure zone and destination country plus receiving zone. While adding a new combination, you can further specify the route determination for a specific shipping point and ship-to party by clicking on the @ Enter Further Combination button. The pop-up window shown in Figure 6.16 will appear, and once you've defined a combination, you can select it and click on the Route Determination Without Weight Group (Order) folder and specify

a route for each possible combination of the shipping condition and transportation group.

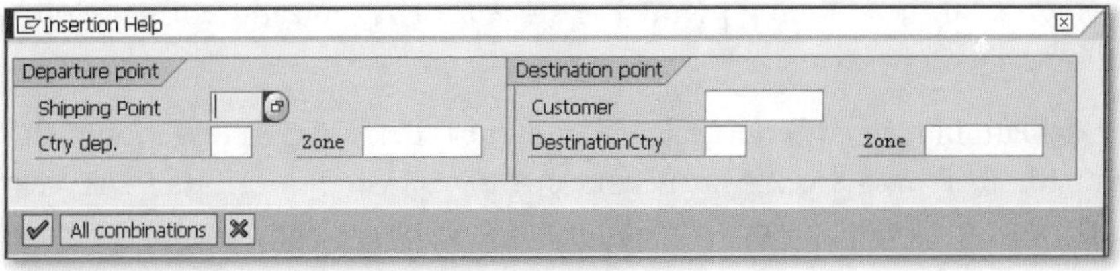

Figure 6.16 Further Criteria for Route Determination

5. Define the delivery types for repeating the route determination and set the indicator in the appropriate delivery types.
6. Define weight groups using Transaction OVS8 (menu path: SAP IMG • SALES AND DISTRIBUTION • BASIC FUNCTIONS • ROUTES • ROUTE DETERMINATION • DEFINE WEIGHT GROUPS). In addition to a key and description, the total weight with unit of measurement is specified for each weight group in the Maintain Details for Weight Groups folder. The total weight refers to the upper limit, and the total weight of delivery determines the weight group for it.
7. Specify the routes you want selected according to the criteria for delivery processing. The transaction and menu path are same as in the previous step, but this time, select the Route Determination with Weight Group (Delivery) folder. In addition to the criteria mentioned for route determination in order, you can do further fine tuning according to weight group.

6.5.3 Route Schedule Determination

A route schedule is the periodic processing of deliveries from a shipping point to the unloading points of different ship-to parties. When more than one route schedule is maintained for a combination of requirements, the system tries to find the closest one to the planned goods issue date and time. Route schedules can be active for the different shipping points for periodic processing of deliveries to the unloading point of different ship-to parties. You do this using Transaction S_ALR_87005924. When the route scheduling is active for a shipping point, it can be active or inactive for the specific sales document type (defined in Transaction S_ALR_87005922) or delivery document type (defined in Transaction S_ALR_87005932).

6.6 Scheduling

It's possible to schedule both deliveries and transportation for optimum utilization of resources at the shipping point. The steps for customization of scheduling are as follows:

8. Define scheduling for different sales document types using Transaction OVLY (menu path: SAP IMG • SALES AND DISTRIBUTION • BASIC FUNCTIONS • DELIVERY SCHEDULING AND TRANSPORTATION SCHEDULING • DEFINE SCHEDULING BY SALES DOCUMENT TYPE), which you can see in Figure 6.17. You can make delivery scheduling, transportation scheduling, or both applicable for a document type. When the Backwards checkbox is selected, it prevents forward scheduling from being carried out if the material is not available. In backward scheduling, from the requested delivery date, all of the durations such as the pick/pack time, loading time, transit time, and transportation planning time are deducted to determine the time and date the material will have to be available to promise (ATP). The first two durations (i.e., pick/pack and loading) are part of delivery scheduling, and the second two elements are part of transportation planning. If the material is not available on the date calculated on the basis of backward scheduling then forward scheduling takes place. In forward scheduling, the delivery is rescheduled by adding the durations to the earliest available date.

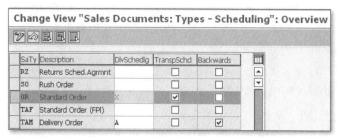

Figure 6.17 Activate Delivery and/or Transportation Scheduling

9. Define working hours and shifts using Transaction S_ALR_87006183 (menu path: SAP IMG • SALES AND DISTRIBUTION • BASIC FUNCTIONS • DELIVERY SCHEDULING AND TRANSPORTATION SCHEDULING • MAINTAIN WORKING HOURS). To maintain working hours, define the first shifts for the year (or a range of years) by the start time and finish time of each shift. Then create different shift sequences by scheduling the shifts for different working days. Finally, define the working hours for a specific calendar (e.g., US – for USA) by assigning a shift sequence to it using Transaction S_ALR_87006188 (Refer Figure 6.18).

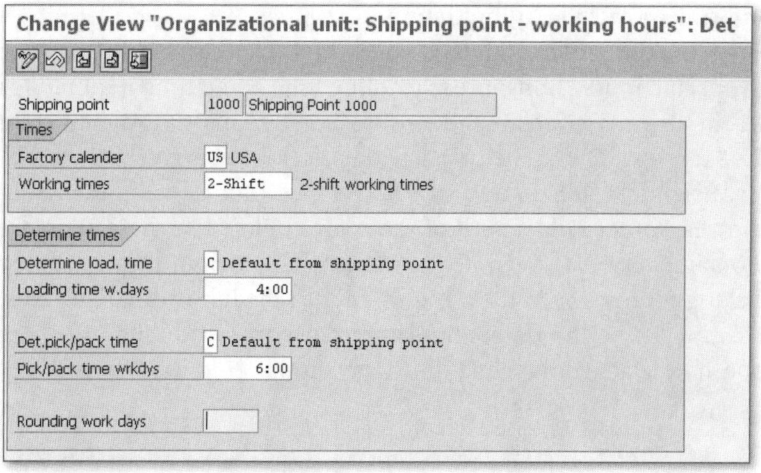

Figure 6.18 Working Hours for Shipping Point

10. Finally, define the different durations. Define the loading time and pick/pack time for each shipping point, and define the transit and transportation lead times for each route.

    ▶ **Loading time**
    Loading time is the time required to load a delivery item. It depends on the shipping point, route, and weight group of the material. You define it using Transaction OVLL (menu path: SAP IMG • SALES AND DISTRIBUTION • BASIC FUNCTIONS • DELIVERY SCHEDULING AND TRANSPORTATION SCHEDULING • MAINTAIN DURATION: and then double-click on the Loading Time Folder). The loading time in terms of both days and hours is maintained for all possible combinations of shipping point, route, and loading group. You maintain the loading group for the material in the material master record (Sales: General/Plant tab).

    ▶ **Pick/pack time**
    Pick/pack time is the time required to pick and pack a delivery item. It depends on the shipping point, route, and weight group of the material. To define it, use Transaction OVLV (menu path: SAP IMG • SALES AND DISTRIBUTION • BASIC FUNCTIONS • DELIVERY SCHEDULING AND TRANSPORTATION SCHEDULING • MAINTAIN DURATION: and then double-click on the Pick/pack Time Folder). You maintain the pick/pack time, in terms of both days and hours, for all possible combinations of shipping points, routes, and weight groups.

▶ **Transit and transport scheduling time**
Transit time is the time required for a delivery to reach a customer from your plant via a specific route. Transport scheduling time is the time required for planning a shipment. You define these using Transaction 0VTC (menu path: SAP IMG • SALES AND DISTRIBUTION • BASIC FUNCTIONS • DELIVERY SCHEDULING AND TRANSPORTATION SCHEDULING • MAINTAIN DURATION: and then double-click on the Routes Folder). All of the routes defined in the system are proposed on an overview screen. Go to the screen shown in Figure 6.19 by double-clicking on any one of these routes. In the scheduling group of fields, highlighted you define the transit time and transport scheduling time. You can also specify the actual traveling time (Trav.dur.).

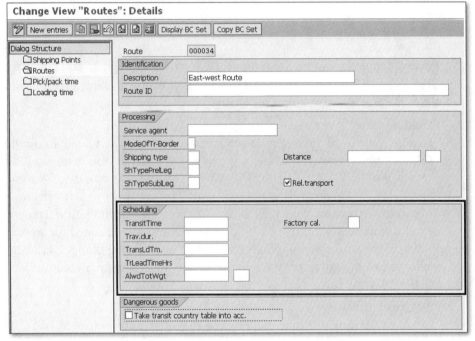

Figure 6.19 Scheduling Routes

6.7 Stock Transfer Including Intercompany Transfers

When receive a purchase order is received from a customer, it's called a *sales order*. When requirements are received from a plant within the seller's group company, they are usually fulfilled by a *stock transfer order*. A plant can be thought of as an internal customer, and a customer master record is created and assigned to the plant for this purpose. The ordering plant creates the stock transfer order for materials it requires. When the ordering plant and the supplying plant belong to the same company code, the process is called intracompany stock transfer; when they belong to different companies, the process is called intercompany stock transfer (or cross-company stock transfer). For both intra- and intercompany stock transfers, either one-step or two-step stock transfer processes can be adopted. The one-step process, also called the *transfer posting,* is normally used when no physical movement is involved. For example, stock identified for quality inspection or stock blocked for sale may not involve any physical movement. Because in these cases, physical movement is involved, a two-step process is recommended. The two-step process is a better representation or model for the actual physical process that occurs in a stock transfer. Figure 6.20 illustrates the difference between the one-step and two-step stock transfer.

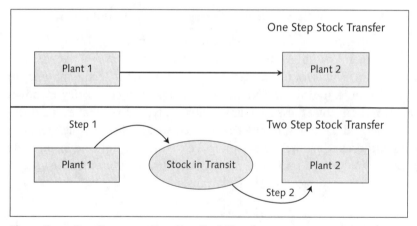

Figure 6.20 One-Step versus Two-Step Stock Transfer

The following sections describe the steps to execute customizing stock transfer processes.

6.7.1 Define the Number Range for Stock Transfer Orders

The number range for stock transfer orders specifies all of the numbers you can use to identify individual documents of a particular type of stock transfer order.

You define the number range for stock transfer orders using Transaction OMH6 or Transaction SNRO (object EINKBELEG). Please note that this is not the usual number range object (RV_BELEG), and in cannot be maintained using Transaction VN01, which is used in the Sales and Distribution functionality in SAP ERP. This number range object (EINKBELEG) is used for providing numbers to different types of purchase orders. For different types of stock transfer orders, you can assign different number ranges to distinguish between them. For example, you can use different document types (and number ranges) to differentiate between forward-moving stock transfers and returns, as illustrated in Table 6.2.

Stock Transfer Order	STO Type	Number Range
Transfer from plant 1 to plant 2	ZST1	46000000 to 46999999
Return from plant 2 to plant 1	ZST2	47000000 to 47999999

Table 6.2 Different Number Ranges Assigned to Different STO Types

6.7.2 Define the Document Type for Stock Transfer Orders

Define the document types for a stock transfer order using Transaction S_ALR_87002197 (menu path: SAP IMG • Material Management • Purchasing • Purchase Order • Define Document Types). Use the standard document type UB for intracompany stock transfer and NB for intercompany stock transfer as shown in Figure 6.21. You can copy these standard document types to create several document types as needed. Different number ranges, created in the previous step, can be assigned to different document types them. Leave the Control field blank if the document types will be used for intercompany stock transfer, or enter the value T if they'll be used for an intracompany stock transfer.

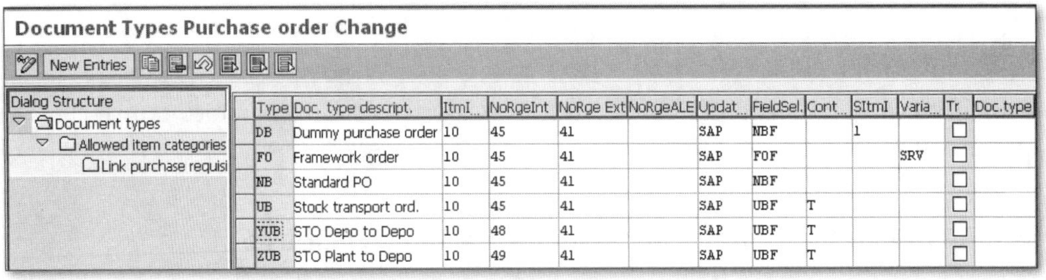

Type	Doc. type descript.	ItmI...	NoRgeInt	NoRge Ext	NoRgeALE	Updat...	FieldSel.	Cont...	SItmI	Varia...	Tr...	Doc.type
DB	Dummy purchase order	10	45	41		SAP	NBF		1		☐	
FO	Framework order	10	45	41		SAP	FOF			SRV	☐	
NB	Standard PO	10	45	41		SAP	NBF				☐	
UB	Stock transport ord.	10	45	41		SAP	UBF	T			☐	
YUB	STO Depo to Depo	10	48	41		SAP	UBF	T			☐	
ZUB	STO Plant to Depo	10	49	41		SAP	UBF	T			☐	

Figure 6.21 Define Document Types for Stock Transfer Orders

6.7.3 Create Internal Customers for Receiving Plants

You can define internal customers for the receiving plants using Transaction XD01. The customer should be created in the company code of the receiving plant. The sales area (which is a combination of sales organization, distribution channel, and division) should be the same as the shipping data for the receiving plant, which we'll explain in the next section. For these internal customers, you can define a different customer account group.

6.7.4 Define Shipping Data for Receiving Plants

Use Transaction S_ALR_87002189 to define shipping data for the ordering plant (menu path: SAP IMG • MATERIAL MANAGEMENT • PURCHASING • PURCHASE ORDER • SET UP STOCK TRANSFER ORDER • DEFINE SHIPPING DATA FOR PLANTS). As shown in Figure 6.22, simply double-click on any particular plant in the overview screen. This is where you assign the customer created in the step before the ordering/receiving plant. You should also define the sales area applicable for the plant. This should be the same as the sales area defined for the internal customer.

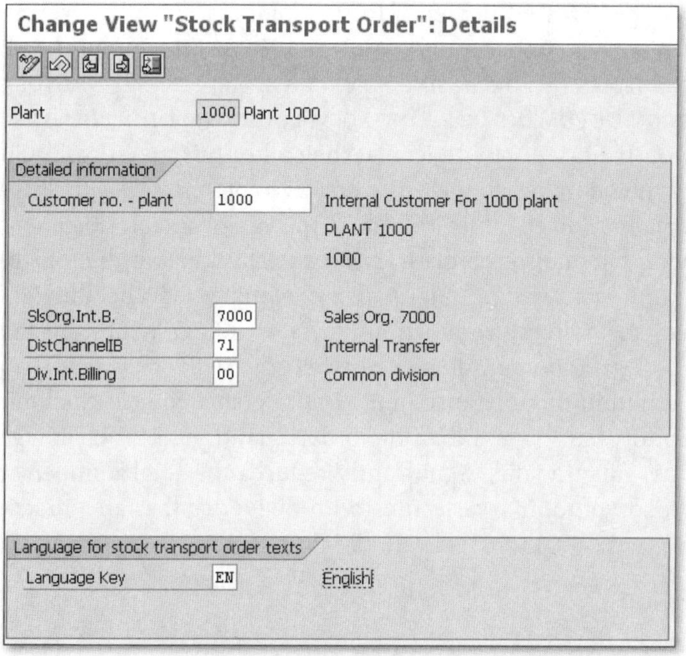

Figure 6.22 Define Shipping Data for Receiving Plants

> **Note**
>
> This step is done directly in the production server, as opposed to the normal practice of transporting changes from development via the quality server. This is because you cannot transport the customer master data from one server to another, and the customer created for the plant cannot be available in the development client. Also, it's a good practice to not create any master data in the golden client. The golden client is one of the many clients in development servers used exclusively for final customization and transport to production via the quality server. You avoid creating any master data record and thus prevent any transaction in this client. Other clients of the development server, which are used as sand-boxes for trial and testing, may contain master data. The golden client should be a mirror image of the production client of the production server, except for the master data and transactional data. Also note that the ABAP reports are not developed in the golden client because the developer will require some master and transactional data during preliminary testing while developing the report. However, because all ABAP programs are cross-client developments, they become available in the golden client immediately.

6.7.5 Assign Document Type to Plants

Assign the document types created in step 2 to the combination of delivering plant and supplying plant via Transaction S_ALR_87100966 (menu path: SAP IMG • MATERIAL MANAGEMENT • PURCHASING • PURCHASE ORDER • SET UP STOCK TRANSFER ORDER • ASSIGN DOCUMENT TYPE, ONE-STEP PROCEDURE, UNDERDELIVERY TOLERANCE). Clicking on the IMG Activity icon at the end of this menu path will take you to the screen shown in Figure 6.23. The first two columns show the supplying and receiving plants, and the third column displays the default document type. If you're following the one-step process, select the checkbox in the fourth. When the fourth column is selected, underdelivery tolerance will be allowed. If tolerance is allowed, the delivery completion indicator (EKPO-EGLKZ) in the stock transfer order gets set automatically, even when the delivery is less than the order quantity but within the tolerance limit. The tolerance limit is the limit to which delivery quantity can be less than the order quantity (as a percentage of order quantity). This functionality significantly reduces the total number of incomplete deliveries, so you don't waste time with deliveries that are "practically" complete.

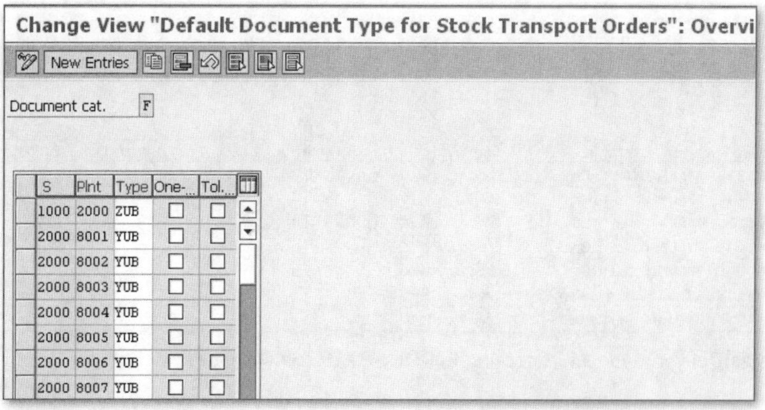

Figure 6.23 Default Document Type for STOs of Different Plants

6.7.6 Assign Delivery Type and Checking Rule to STO Document Type

You assign the delivery type and checking rules to the document types for a stock transfer order using Transaction S_ALR_87100965 (menu path: SAP IMG • MATERIAL MANAGEMENT • PURCHASING • PURCHASE ORDER • SET UP STOCK TRANSFER ORDER • ASSIGN DELIVERY TYPE AND CHECKING RULE). If you click on IMG Activity at the end of this menu path, you'll see the screen shown in Figure 6.24. For the STO document type and the supplying plant, you specify a delivery type in the Delivery Type (DlTp) column and a checking rule in the Checking Rule (CRl) column. You can also activate shipment scheduling and route scheduling functionalities by selecting the checkboxes in Ship. Sch. Route Sch. columns, respectively. If you specify a delivery type in the Delivery Type (DlTp) column and nothing in the last three columns, then the delivery type becomes relevant for intercompany stock transfers, intracompany stock transfers, and transfers to consignment stock (discussed in Chapter 3) . If for these three processes, you want to assign separate delivery types (which is normally the case), you can specify the delivery type's intracompany stock transfer in the Delivery Type 1 column, intracompany stock transfer in the Delivery Type 2 column, and transfer to consignment stock in the DTCons. column. Different users may be responsible for these processes, so the delivery type (and STO type) can be used as the basis for managing authorization. The standard delivery types for the intra- and intercompany stock transfers are NL and NLCC, respectively. If you need more than one delivery type for these processes, you can copy the standard document types to create your own.

6 | Logistics Management

Tpe	DTDesc	S	Name 1	DITp	Description	CRl	Description of	Ship.Sch.	Route Sch.	Delivery type 1	Delivery type 2	DTCons.
YUB	STO Depo to Depo	8040	Plant 8040	ZNL1	STO Dep to Dep	02	Checking rule 02	☐	☐	ZNL1		
YUB	STO Depo to Depo	8041	Plant 8041	ZNL1	STO Dep to Dep	02	Checking rule 02	☐	☐	ZNL1		
YUB	STO Depo to Depo	8042	Plant 8042	ZNL1	STO Dep to Dep	02	Checking rule 02	☐	☐	ZNL1		
YUB	STO Depo to Depo	8043	Plant 8043	ZNL1	STO Dep to Dep	02	Checking rule 02	☐	☐	ZNL1		
YUB	STO Depo to Depo	8044	Plant 8044	ZNL1	STO Dep to Dep	02	Checking rule 02	☐	☐	ZNL1		
ZUB	STO Plant to Depo	1000	Plant 1000	ZNL	STO Plant to Dep	02	Checking rule 02	☐	☐	ZNL		
ZUB	STO Plant to Depo	2000	Plant 2000	ZNL	STO Plant to Dep	02	Checking rule 02	☐	☐	ZNL		

Figure 6.24 Assign Delivery Type and Checking Rule to STO Document Types

> **Note**
>
> The customization for the checking rule, delivery document type, shipping point determination, output determination for stock transfer order, and other related customizations for stock transfer orders are not described here because we've already covered them or will be covering them shortly. You can also refer to SAP Note 498143 for FAQs on the stock transfer process. We also don't discuss the two-step stock transfer without delivery process where goods receipt is done with reference to the stock transfer order instead of delivery or the return scenario that's relevant for intercompany transfer processes.

6.7.7 Create Vendor Master Record for Receiving Plant

In an intercompany stock transfer scenario, you create a vendor master record for the receiving plant via Transaction XK01. The company code for the record is kept the same as the company code to which the supplying plant is assigned. The purchasing organization is kept the same as what is valid for the receiving and ordering plant. Note that the vendor master record we're creating is that of the supplying plant, but it's created for the receiving plant. All vendors are created for a particular plant. For purchasing, a plant (receiving plant here) can use any vendor (supplying plant here) associated with it.

> **Note**
>
> The standard schedule line categories for stock transfer are NN (intracompany) and NC (intercompany). The movement types attached for one-step and two-step processes are 645 and 643, respectively, for schedule line category NC. For schedule line NN, the movement types are 647 (one-step) and 641 (two-step). The problem you may have is how to determine these schedule line categories for the stock transfer delivery type. We know that in a sales order, the schedule line category is automatically determined.

The delivery is also determined per the delivery type mentioned in the customization of order type. So, during the goods issue of the delivery, the movement type is determined by the schedule line for the item. But in stock transfer, this is done by the default order type field and requirement routine 202 maintained in the customization of the delivery types for intra- and intercompany stock transfer.

6.8 Outputs in Shipping

In Chapter 3 we discussed the customization of sales output type using the SAP Implementation Guide (IMG) menu path. In this section, we'll discuss how to customize output using Transaction NACE. This is a general way of customizing any output in SAP ERP.

1. Execute Transaction NACE. You'll see the screen shown in Figure 6.25.
2. Select the application for which the output is to be maintained. Table 6.3 lists the applications relevant for the Sales and Distribution functionality in SAP ERP. We've selected application V2, as shown in Figure 6.25.

Figure 6.25 Conditions for Output Control

Application	Field Catalog	Condition Table	Output Type Is Assigned	
			To	Using
V1 (sales)	V/86	V/57	Header	V/43
			Item	V/69
V2 (shipping)	V/87	V/60	Delivery header	V/71
			Delivery item	V/73

Table 6.3 Applications for Output Control

Application	Field Catalog	Condition Table	Output Type Is Assigned	
			To	Using
V3 (billing)	V/88	V/63	Billing type	V/25
V5 (delivery groups)	V/89	V/G2	Group type	V/21
V6 (handling units)	V/90	V/94	Packaging material type	V/22
K1 (sales activity)	V/92	V/66	Sales activity	V/26

Table 6.3 Applications for Output Control (Cont.)

> **Note**
>
> The transactions listed for condition tables in Table 6.3 are the transactions used to change the condition tables of the respective applications. To create a new condition table, use the previous number (e.g., V/G1 for application V5) and for display, use the next number (e.g., V/67 for application K1).

3. After selecting the application, click on the Output Types button on the Application menu bar shown in Figure 6.25 to get the list of output types specific to the application.

4. Click on the Pencil icon or follow the menu path TABLE VIEW • DISPLAY CHANGE to modify or create a new condition type.

5. Click on the New Entries button to create a new output type from scratch.

6. Select any existing output type and click on the Copy As icon to copy it and create a new output type.

7. Enter the relevant data in the General Data, Default Values, Time, Storage System, Print, Mail, and Sort Order tabs. Refer to Chapter 3 for details on creating a new output type.

8. Once the output type is created, you have to customize the three folders available in the left dialog structure. These folders are Mail Title and Texts, Processing Routines, and Partner Functions. By selecting a particular output type in change mode and double-clicking on the Processing Routines folder, you can replace the form or smartform. Alternatively, you can modify the standard form attached to the output type as per your requirement.

9. To create new access sequence for the output type, click on the Access Sequences button when an application is already selected (see Figure 6.25).

10. You can create a new access sequence in the New Entries tab or by selecting an existing entry and clicking on the Copy As icon in the change mode. Please refer the discussion in Chapter 4 for condition techniques.

11. The access sequence consists of several individual *accesses* that have access numbers. The access number determines the sequence in which each access is to be executed to find out the output type, if any. Each access must contain a condition table and may contain a requirement routine and an exclusive indicator.

12. You cannot define the condition tables and insert fields of the field catalog for the condition tables using Transaction NACE. These steps, which are an important part of the condition technique we described in Chapter 4, are done using the transactions listed in Table 6.3.

13. To create a new output procedure, select the application created in the new procedure and click on the Procedures button (refer Figure 6.25).

14. The list of existing procedures will appear. Click on New Entries or select any procedure and click on the Copy As icon in change mode to create a new procedure.

15. Select any procedure already created and click on the Control folder. The steps of the procedure already created or copied will be shown. Each step must have a counter and an output type and may contain a requirement routine and indicator for manual entry. In the same step, different counters determine the sequence in which the output type will be processed. The requirements routine checks the requirements for processing the output type. For example, routine 62 in billing output checks if the invoice is posted to accounting.

16. Finally, you can create the condition records for automatic determination of the output type by selecting the application and clicking on the Condition Records tab (see Figure 6.25). Double-click on the condition type to reach the initial screen of Transaction NACR, which is used to maintain condition records for output types. The process of creating, changing, or displaying condition records is very similar to the process we discussed in Chapter 3.

> **Picking Lists**
>
> Except for customizing picking lists, which belong to the application V4, you can configure all other output types using output control Transaction NACE. For a pick list, use Transaction V/38 to maintain output, Transaction OVLT to assign picking lists to shipping points, and Transaction V/53 to assign customized forms and programs to picking lists.

6.9 Batch Determination in Deliveries

As we discussed in Chapter 3, batch determination is fairly straightforward. However, there are times in batch determination when you may not want to freeze the batch number in an order, but instead prefer that it be determined during delivery. The batch number specified in the order is assumed to be part of the information from the purchase order. It should not matter to the customer what batch number he's given. If the batch number specified in the order is not available at the time of delivery, then the order cannot be delivered. So you'll want the batch determination to happen in deliveries and not in orders. Another situation is when the delivery is created with reference to a stock transfer order (see Figure 6.26) and the batch split is to be carried out in the delivery. You can go to the screen for this by double-clicking on any delivery item and selecting the Batch Split tab.

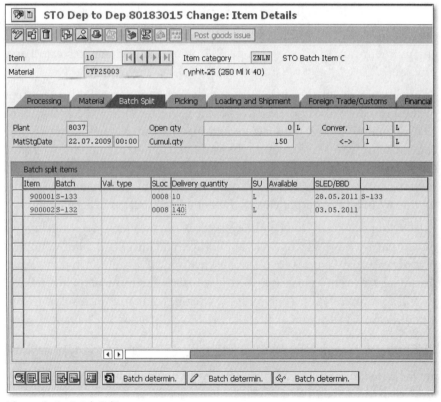

Figure 6.26 Batch Split

The batch split functionality is available in deliveries only. In an order, if you have to specify more than one batch number for a material, you can create different items for the same material. Batch splitting is basically picking more than one batch in a delivery. During the batch split, the classification system can also be used for selecting batches. There are three buttons (Refresh, Change, and Display Batch Determination) you can use to redetermine, change, or display batches selected with the quantity for the line item. From the batch determination screen, you move quantities to the delivery by clicking on the Copy tab.

6.10 Processing Serialized Materials

Serial numbers are very similar to batch management. You can think of it as a situation where each batch of the material has only one unit. The serial number and batch number can be used together, but in some industries (e.g., paint, wine, and pharmaceuticals) the batch becomes more relevant, whereas in others (e.g., automobiles, and consumer durables) the serial number is preferred. A serial number is used not only in the Sales and Distribution functionality in SAP ERP, but also in other SAP ERP functionalities, including Plant Maintenance (e.g., equipment), Quality Management (e.g., inspection lot), Production Planning (e.g., production order), and Materials Management (e.g., goods movements). In the Sales and Distribution functionality of SAP ERP, the usage is restricted to the list in Table 6.4.

Procedure	Serialized Business Process
SDAU	Assign serial number in sales order (including inquiry and quotation)
SDCC	Assign serial number during completeness check for delivery
SDCR	Assign serial number during completeness check for return delivery
SDLS	Assign serial number for deliveries
SDRE	Assign serial number for return deliveries

Table 6.4 Allowed Sales and Distribution Business Processes for Serialization

You activate the serialization by entering a valid serial number profile in the material master record of a material. The steps for creating a new serial number profile are as follows.

1. Define the serial number profile by using Transaction OIS2 (menu path: SAP IMG • Sales and Distribution • Basic Functions • Determine Serial Number Profiles), as shown in Figure 6.27.

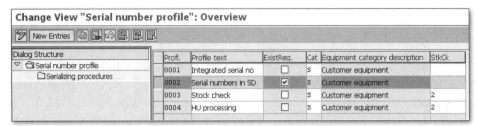

Figure 6.27 Defining Serial Number Profile

2. Copy any one of the four default serial number profiles to create a new serial number profile.

3. After creating a new serial number profile, select the new profile (profile 0002 in Figure 6.27) and click on the Serializing Procedures folder, as shown in Figure 6.28.

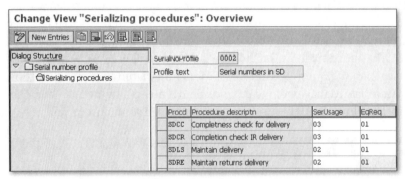

Figure 6.28 Customizing Serialization Procedure

4. As shown in Figure 6.28, you can assign a different procedure to a serial number profile. Serial number usage (SerUsage) is 01 when no serial number is to be assigned, 02 when a serial number can be assigned, 03 when serial number must be assigned, and 04 when serial number is automatically assigned to the business transaction (called a procedure). The equipment requirement (EqReq) field is 01 when it's optional and 02 when it's compulsory for the serial number master record to contain equipment details.

You create serial numbers for materials using Transaction IQ01 (menu path: SAP EASY ACCESS • LOGISTICS • SALES AND DISTRIBUTION • MASTER DATA • PRODUCTS • SERIAL NUMBERS • CREATE). To mass create serial numbers, you can use Transaction IQ04 (menu path: SAP EASY ACCESS • LOGISTICS • SALES AND DISTRIBUTION •

MASTER DATA • PRODUCTS • SERIAL NUMBERS • LIST EDITING). The mass maintenance functionality here and discussed elsewhere in the book can create problems for you if it's not well thought out, planned, and executed. A good amount of practice is required before you should use it in a production environment. You can create serial numbers for materials even when the serial number profile is not present in the material master record. However, to use the serial numbers in a business process, maintenance of a serial number profile in the material master record is required. This also gives you the option to use serialization of materials in one plant while not using this functionality in another plant.

> **Are They Numbers Only (Serial and Batch Number)?**
> Both serial numbers and batch numbers can have alphanumeric values, but only when they are created manually. When they are generated automatically, they are simply numbers, which is true for any SAP EPR internal number range.

Having discussed batch management and serialization let's discuss how to customize the SAP interface for carrier software.

6.11 Interface with Carrier Software

Shipment optimization can be done using SAP ERP, SAP SCM, or external software. Table 6.5 lists the SAP certified carrier software. The SAP interface that integrates the external software to SAP ERP is called SD TPS 4.0 (Transport Planning and Optimization Systems 4.0). The role of the interface is to transfer data from SAP ERP to the external system and, after processing in the external system, take back the output from the external system to SAP ERP for further processing.

Company	Software Name	SAP Interface
UPS Logistics Technologies 849 Fairmount Avenue, Suite 400 Baltimore, MD 21286	ROADNET TRANSPORTATION SUITE 3.20	SD-TPS 4.0 – Transport Planning and Optimization Systems 4.0
Soloplan GmbH Burgstrasse 20 Kempten 87435, Germany	CarLo® 2.0	

Table 6.5 Certified Transport Optimization Software

In the next two sections, we'll discuss how to customize the SAP ERP interface for external software and how to transfer data to and from external software.

6.11.1 Customization of the SAP Interface

The customization of the SAP ERP interface for external carrier software is given below. The first few steps, which are similar to those we discussed for external tax software, are not discussed in detail here. For these steps, in any case, you need the help of a technical (BASIS) resource person.

1. Define the external planning system using Transaction OMTX (menu path: SAP IMG • Logistics – General • Supply Chain Planning Interfaces (SCPI) • Transportation Planning Interface (TPI) • Define logical non-SAP systems).

2. Define the path and destination for RFCs using Transaction SM59 (menu path: SAP IMG • Logistics – General • Supply Chain Planning Interfaces (SCPI) • Transportation Planning Interface (TPI) • Define RFC destination).

3. Maintain the mapping of external software to SAP ERP messages using Transaction BD64 (menu path: SAP IMG • Logistics – General • Supply Chain Planning Interfaces (SCPI) • Transportation Planning Interface (TPI) • Maintain allocation of non-SAP system to ALE output). SAP ERP sends the following application link enabling (ALE) output to the external system:

   - TPSDLS (transmit delivery document)
   - TPSLOC (transmit location master data)
   - SHIPPL (declare shipment status)
   - STATUS (status notification)
   - The following ALE output is received from the external software:
   - SHIPPL (transmit shipment document)
   - STATUS (status notification)

4. Define the ALE ports for communication using Transaction WE21 (menu path: SAP IMG • Logistics – General • Supply Chain Planning Interfaces (SCPI) • Transportation Planning Interface (TPI) • Maintain ALE port definition).

5. Maintain the partner profile for the logical system maintained for the external system using Transaction WE20 (menu path: SAP IMG • Logistics – General • Supply Chain Planning Interfaces (SCPI) • Transportation Planning Interface (TPI) • Maintain ALE partner profiles).

6. Maintain the transportation planning points for external software using Transaction OVTP (menu path: SAP IMG • Logistics – General • Supply Chain Planning Interfaces (SCPI) • Transportation Planning Interface (TPI) • Maintain transportation planning points for external systems). In this step, you can define the external transport planning points by assigning an external system partner number in the TPS PartNo column, refer to Figure 6.29. The Item Type column is an LS (logical system). You must predefine the external number range using Transaction SNRO and specify it in the Ext.no.rge column. The Change Shp column is a compulsory field in which you should specify whether changes to the shipments in the external system are allowed in the SAP system (00) or not (02). You can specify in the OverallSta column the status of the shipment (e.g., 0 – planned, 1 – planning completed, and so on), which will exclude the shipment from any further modification. The Status Filtering Mode (StsFilMode) field can take the value 1 (only error message is sent to external system for failed inbound IDoc), 2 (both error and success messages are sent), or blank when no messages are to be sent. In TxId1, 2 and 3, you can specify any three delivery header texts that are to be transferred from delivery to the shipment. You can also maintain an output type (present in output procedure V10000 – shipping output) for sending information to the external system. The output used for one transport planning system (TPS) should not be in use by another.

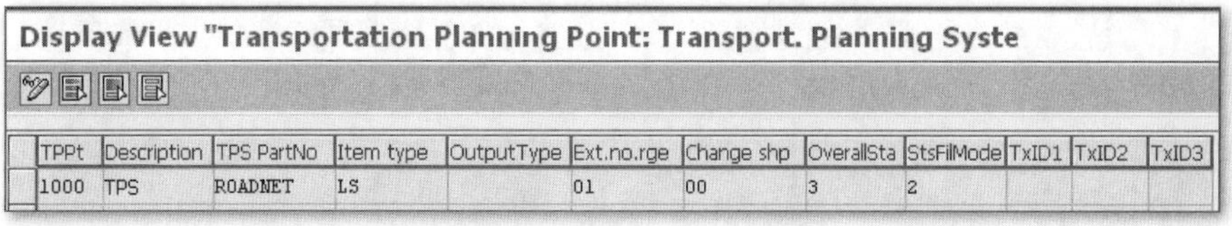

Display View "Transportation Planning Point: Transport. Planning Syste

TPPt	Description	TPS PartNo	Item type	OutputType	Ext.no.rge	Change shp	OverallSta	StsFilMode	TxID1	TxID2	TxID3
1000	TPS	ROADNET	LS		01	00	3	2			

Figure 6.29 Define Transport Planning Point

7. Maintain the material cumulation for routes using Transaction OVTG (menu path: SAP IMG • Logistics – General • Supply Chain Planning Interfaces (SCPI) • Transportation Planning Interface (TPI) • Maintain materials cumulation for routes • Cumulation of materials maintain). The materials relevant for transportation are cumulated according to their freight codes and/or as per the item's relevance for shipment. This is done by selecting the transportation planning point to be processed and entering the route for which cumulation is required or by leaving it blank if cumulation is for the entire transport planning point. If you want cumulation to be based on freight code, enter the required freight code set (which is determined by country, shipping

type, and forwarding agent) and in combination with the material freight group (maintained in the material master record Sales:General/Plant tab) determine the freight code. To activate the shipment-relevant cumulation, click on the Relevant button. If you want several routes of a transportation planning point to have the same freight code set and same setting for shipment relevance, use Transaction 0VTH, as shown in Figure 6.30. The other option for mass maintenance of transport planning points for cumulation of material is to use Transaction 0VTI, where the setting for one transport planning point and route is copied to another. In both these transactions, you have the option of overwriting all existing entries or inserting the transportation planning point (or route) only when no setting is already maintained (refer to Figure 6.31).

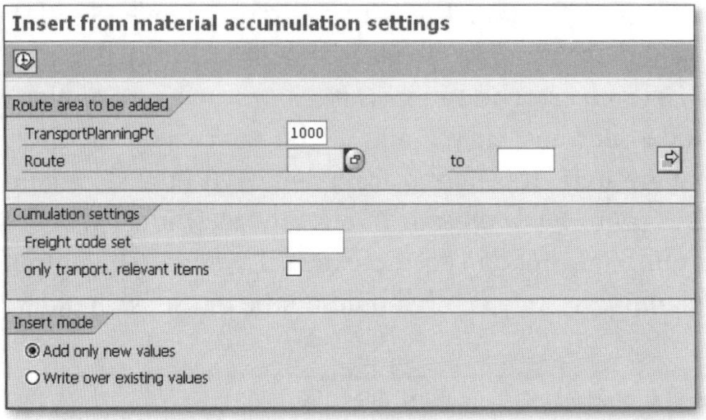

Figure 6.30 Mass Maintenance of Transport Planning Point for Cumulation

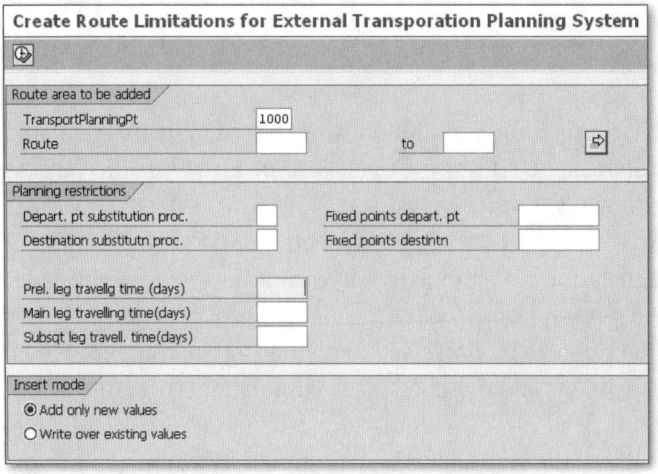

Figure 6.31 Mass Maintenance of Route Limitations

8. Maintain planning restrictions for routes via Transaction 0VTR (menu path: SAP IMG • LOGISTICS – GENERAL • SUPPLY CHAIN PLANNING INTERFACES (SCPI) • TRANSPORTATION PLANNING INTERFACE (TPI) • MAINTAIN PLANNING RESTRICTION FOR ROUTES • PLANNING RESTRICTION MAINTAIN). If goods are to be sent beyond the planning area of an external system, you can use this IMG activity to define the planning borders and replacement procedures for departure or destination locations in individual routes.

9. Maintain output types for delivery transfers using Transaction V/34 (menu path: SAP IMG • LOGISTICS – GENERAL • SUPPLY CHAIN PLANNING INTERFACES (SCPI) • TRANSPORTATION PLANNING INTERFACE (TPI) • MAINTAIN OUTPUT CONTROL FOR DELIVERY TRANSFERS • MAINTAIN OUTPUT TYPES). There should be different output types for different external systems.

10. Maintain output procedures (V10000) for external systems using Transaction NACZ (menu path: SAP IMG • LOGISTICS – GENERAL • SUPPLY CHAIN PLANNING INTERFACES (SCPI) • TRANSPORTATION PLANNING INTERFACE (TPI) • MAINTAIN OUTPUT CONTROL FOR DELIVERY TRANSFERS • NO TEXT FOUND FOR TRANSACTION).

11. Activate change control for customer and vendor master data using Transaction BD52 (menu path: SAP IMG • LOGISTICS – GENERAL • SUPPLY CHAIN PLANNING INTERFACES (SCPI) • TRANSPORTATION PLANNING INTERFACE (TPI) • ACTIVATE CHANGE MANAGEMENT FOR MASTER DATA), as shown in Figure 6.32. For the value TPSLOC, select the checkbox to activate the change management for customer and vendor master data.

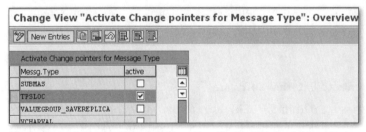

Figure 6.32 Activating Transfer of Location Master Data to External System

Note on Menu Path
For customizing the SAP ERP interface for external carrier software, you can also follow the menu path SAP IMG • LOGISTICS EXECUTION • TRANSPORTATION • INTERFACES • EXTERNAL TRANSPORTATION PLANNING SYSTEMS.

Once the external software is installed and the SAP ERP interface is customized, the next step is to know how to use it, which we'll explain below.

6.11.2 How to Use External Tax Software

Using external tax software correctly is important. The activities for interfaces can be grouped into three phases:

- Transfer of location master data to external software
- Transfer of documents to external software
- Transfer of planned shipments to SAP ERP from external software

Transfer of Location Master Data to External Software

To optimize the shipment, the master data such as addresses of customers should be identical in SAP ERP and the external software. For this, you should update the master data records maintained in SAP ERP the same as in the external software. Customer and vendor master data are transferred automatically (periodically) via Transaction BD21 (menu path: SAP EASY ACCESS • LOGISTICS • CENTRAL FUNCTIONS • SUPPLY CHAIN PLANNING INTERFACE • TRANSPORTATION PLANNING • SEND MASTER DATA CHANGES). Other relevant location master data including those for plants, nodes (transport connection points), carriers (forwarding agents), and shipping points are transferred from SAP ERP to external software manually via Transaction VT60 (menu path: SAP EASY ACCESS • LOGISTICS • CENTRAL FUNCTIONS • SUPPLY CHAIN PLANNING INTERFACE • TRANSPORTATION PLANNING • SEND LOCATION MASTER DATA) when required. As shown in Figure 6.33 which is the selection screen for Transaction VT60, you can also manually transfer data pertaining to customer and vendor.

Transfer of Documents to External Software

You transfer deliveries created in SAP ERP to external software using Transaction VT61 (menu path: SAP EASY ACCESS • LOGISTICS • CENTRAL FUNCTIONS • SUPPLY CHAIN PLANNING INTERFACE • TRANSPORTATION PLANNING • SEND DELIVERIES). You can remove a delivery from the planning schedule of the external transport planning system using Transaction VT68 (menu path: SAP EASY ACCESS • LOGISTICS • CENTRAL FUNCTIONS • SUPPLY CHAIN PLANNING INTERFACE • TRANSPORTATION PLANNING • PLAN DELIVERIES).

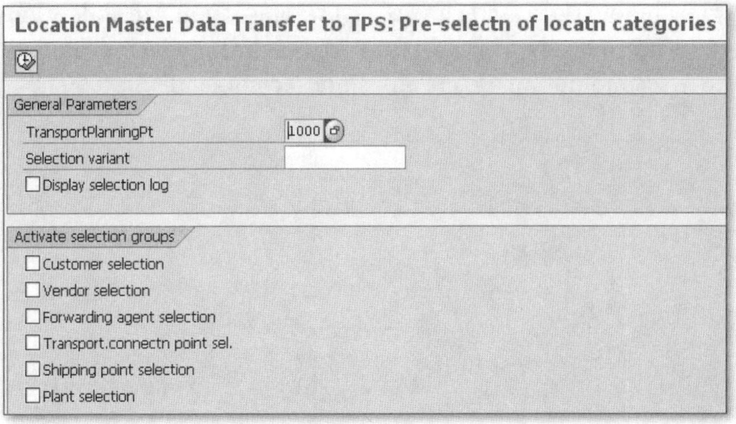

Figure 6.33 Data Transfer of Location Master Data to TPS

Transfer of Planned Shipment to SAP ERP from External Software

When the ALE outputs SHIPPL and STATUS are transferred from the external system and are received by SAP ERP, they automatically create the shipment document in SAP ERP. The status becomes planned (0) automatically. Based on the setting made for the transport planning point (see Figure 6.29, OverallSta column), you can manually modify it. The external software can modify the shipment until the status reaches a particular level.

6.12 Common Problems and Their Solutions

Listed below are a few common errors and their solutions. These errors are not necessarily part of sales and distribution or logistics execution functionality. They are listed here primarily because they occur at the time of delivery processing. In many cases, you may not even have the necessary authorization for carrying out the solution and will require help from others.

- **Problem:** You're getting the error message "This delivery 80177150 is currently being processed by another user (ABAP2). Message no. VL 046." But the user ABAP2 is not currently logged into the system. For the last three days the same error message has come for this delivery. You can't do anything, including completing the billing or reversing PGI and deleting the delivery.
  Solution: If it's verified via Transaction SM04 or Table USR41 that the user (ABAP2) is not active, then you need to delete the locked entry by following the menu path TOOLS • ADMINISTRATION • MONITOR • LOCK ENTRIES (Transaction

SM12). Then from the overview screen (see Figure 6.34), you can follow the menu path LOCK ENTRY • DELETE or LOCK ENTRY • DELETE ALL, which deletes all locked entries. The second option (delete all) is not recommended.

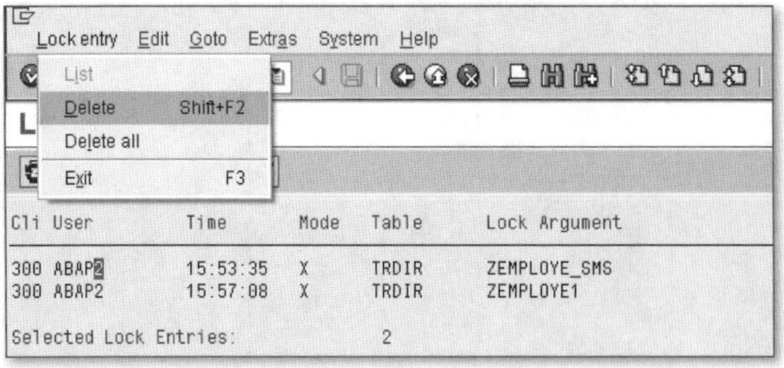

Figure 6.34 Delete Lock Entry

- **Problem:** A customer's order is getting blocked even when it shouldn't be. Upon examining the details in the customer credit master sheet (Transaction S_ALR_87012218), you find the open delivery and an open order value. But the customer has no pending/open delivery or order, which you confirmed by running Transactions VA05N, VL06, and VF04.
  Solution: Run the report RFDKLI20.

- **Problem:** While doing PGI, you get the error message "Account 23001 requires an assignment to a CO object. Message no. KI 235."
  Solution: At the time of PGI, materials documents and accounting documents are created in the background. The problem has to do with the accounting document not being generated, which prevents the PGI from being processed. Using Transaction FS00, check to see if the CO element is assigned to GL 23001. During stock transfer, if the valuations of the material are different in the receiving and supplying plants, the difference in valuation is posted to the material difference account. These material difference GL accounts are not always tested properly, because the GL, like any other master record, is not transported.

- **Problem:** While doing PGI, you get the error message "Posting only possible in periods 2010/10 and 2010/11 in company code US10. Message no. M7 053."
  Solution: The two possible periods (in the Materials Management functionality in SAP ERP) in which postings are possible include October 2010 and November 2010 if the material year is the same as calendar year. The material year can be different than the calendar year. For example, if the material year is April to March, then period 2010/10 means January 2011. 2010/01 is April 2010, 2010/02 is May 2010, and so on. The posting period is determined by the

actual GI date of the delivery document. If the actual goods issue date field is left blank, the system takes the current system date as the default value. To overcome this problem, you have to either make the Materials Management period active for the period in which your actual GI date falls or change your actual GI date to the period that's is open in the system. See Appendix C for more information on how to open a material period.

- **Problem:** While doing PGI, you get the error message "Posting period 005 2009 is not open. Message no. [F5] 201."

  Solution: Note the difference in this error message from the previous one, especially the error message number that you get only in the long message by double-clicking on the error message or clicking on the question mark icon in the error log. When the previous error is due to the material period (also called the MM period), this problem is due to the accounting period (also called the FI period). The solution is similar. Either you open the period pertaining to the actual GI date or you change the GI date to the accounting period open in the system. To open a range of accounting periods for a company code, use Transaction OB52.

- **Problem:** While doing PGI, you get the error message "Deficit of SL Unrestr. prev. 5 M.T: 1100245 2058 0001. Message no. M7 021." You have verified that sufficient stock (more that 15 MT) is available at the particular storage location of the plant.

  Solution: The problem is related to the material period (MM period). Normally, two material periods are open in a system. Of the two periods, one is called the current period, and the other is called the previous period. When posting is allowed in the previous period, you can do the PGI in the previous period. In certain cases, a PGI can cause the stock in the previous period to be negative, and the customization (negative stock not allowed in the previous period) may prevent such PGI. There are two solutions to this problem. You can change the previous period to current. The previous to present period becomes the previous period. For example, if 2010/10 (previous period) and 2010/11 (current period) are currently open, change it to 2010/09 and 2010/10 using the steps detailed in Appendix C. The second option is to do the PGI making the actual GI date fall in the current period.

- **Problem:** While doing PGI, you get the error message "Account determination for entry CAUS GBB ____ BSA 7920 not possible. Message No. M8 147."

  Solution: The problem is that the customization for automatic account posting is not complete. Using Transaction OBYC for the chart of account CAUS, transaction key GBB, assign a GL to the general modifier BSA and valuation class 7920.

6.13 Summary

In this chapter, we've discussed shipping and transportation as subsequent functions to sales. We discussed the components of a delivery document, mainly headers and items, and how the item category is determined. We discussed picking, handling unit management, packing, and goods issue processes. We discussed individual and collective delivery processing, routes, route determination, and scheduling processes. We also covered intra- and intercompany stock transfer processes and output control, batch splitting, and processing of serialized material. Finally, we described the steps for customizing the SAP interface for external carrier software and provided a list of common errors during delivery processing.

With this knowledge you should be able to optimize your delivery process in SAP ERP. You can create your own customized delivery due list and use it as a work list for creating multiple deliveries. You can automate route determination, serialization, and batch determination during shipping. You can customize your system to take care of stock transfers between different plants. You can customize the output functionality that SAP ERP offers. You also know how to integrate external carrier software with SAP ERP.

In the next chapter, we'll discuss billing as a subsequent function of delivery and sales. We'll also cover how billing in the Sales and Distribution functionality in SAP ERP is integrated with SAP ERP Financials.

Because we've already covered pricing and copy control, this chapter focuses on integration with SAP ERP Financials. You'll find useful tips and tricks throughout and a list of common errors and their solutions.

7 Billing

A bill, also called an invoice, is a legal (and commercial) document that goes to your customer for collecting the payment for goods and/or services that he received or will receive. The customer verifies the correctness of the invoice with respect to the quantity of material received, prices committed, and other commitments (e.g., commitments for quality parameters or INCO term). An accurate and unambiguous invoice is what your customer expects from you. It should be self-explanatory. Various prices, taxes, discounts, and surcharges that you've included in the invoice should not surprise your customer. In addition to price, the invoice should also spell out when the payment is expected, whether there is any cash discount if the customer pays it before due date, and what will be the rate of interest he has to pay if he does not make payment on or before due date. Your customer expects the same services for rebates, credit memos, debit memos, and returns. We'll discuss them as we move through this chapter.

Billing is the last stage in the Sales and Distribution functionality in SAP ERP. It primarily consists of the following functions:

- Creation of the invoice with reference to a sales order or delivery or with a general billing interface using external data
- Creation of documents for complaint handling (e.g., credit memo, debit memo, and return)
- Creation of a pro forma invoice
- Creating of a billing plan
- Rebate settlement
- Cancellation of billing documents
- Copy control and pricing functions

- Issuing of different types of outputs (e.g., printed, EDI, or mail)
- Transfer of data to an accounting document (SAP ERP Financials)

We'll start with the principles of processing billing and then move on to the customization of billing types. We'll discuss the customization steps for billing plans and transfer of data to accounting, with a focus on revenue account determination using condition techniques. Finally, we'll discuss some errors encountered during billing processes and their solutions before summarizing the chapter.

7.1 Principles of Bill Processing

Billing, or bill processing, is how you process individual bills. This involves how you create an invoice, what you do if the bill is found to be incorrect, and whether you process individual reference documents (delivery/order) or if multiple documents can be combined. We'll the following processes in next seven sub-sections, which will help you understand how a bill is processed in SAP ERP.

- How to create individual invoices with reference to an order or delivery
- How to combine different orders or deliveries into a single invoice
- How to split a single order or delivery into several invoices
- How to process billing due list
- How to create an invoice list
- How to cancel an invoice
- How to use a general billing interface for creating an invoice using external data

7.1.1 Creating Individual Invoices

You create invoices using Transaction VF01 or by going to SAP EASY ACCESS • LOGISTICS • SALES AND DISTRIBUTION • BILLING DOCUMENT • CREATE. The initial screen looks similar to the screen shown in Figure 7.1. In the Documents column, you can enter one or more deliveries (relevant for billing) or the orders (relevant for billing). You select the invoice type and enter the billing, pricing, and service rendered dates, and then press [Enter] for processing. This data, if not entered, is selected from the default values maintained in the document types being processed and the referenced document. The deliveries (or orders) will create one or more invoices depending on the customization settings and the difference in important data in the referenced deliveries (or orders).

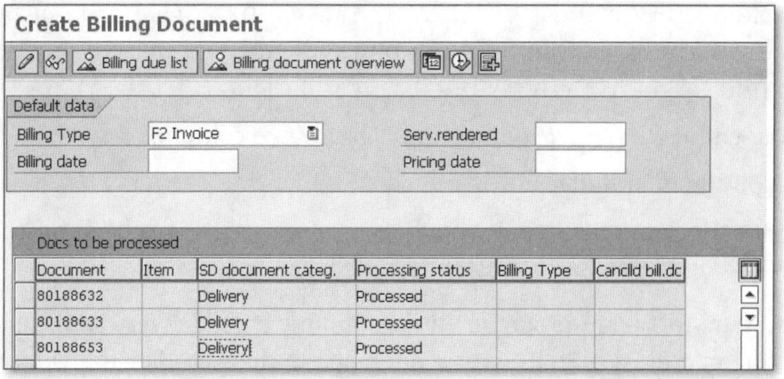

7.1 Principles of Bill Processing

Create Billing Document

Default data:
- Billing Type: F2 Invoice
- Billing date:
- Serv.rendered:
- Pricing date:

Docs to be processed:

Document	Item	SD document categ.	Processing status	Billing Type	Canclld bill.dc
80188632		Delivery	Processed		
80188633		Delivery	Processed		
80188653		Delivery	Processed		

Figure 7.1 Creating Billing Document

You maintain the customization setting in the data transfer routine, as shown in Figure 7.2. For the Data field, VBRK/VBRP has routine 007 assigned to it. You can change this to 003 (Single Invoice) if you want each reference document to only have one invoice. Data transfer routine 010 is the same as 003, with Do Not Allow Splitting even when a billing plan is involved. Routine 006 is also similar but is mainly used to restrict the maximum number of items in an invoice because of company policy or legal requirements. Note that we also used these routines in copy control settings in our discussion in Chapter 3. Other then this routine, there's no restriction on the number of line items an invoice can have. However, an accounting document cannot have more than 999 line items. So an invoice that will create more than 999 line items in its accounting document cannot be released to accounting. To avoid this error, you have no option but to delete part of the delivery and/or order and then process the invoice.

> **Note**
> One line item in an invoice can have more than one line item in an accounting document depending upon your pricing procedure. Therefore, the maximum possible number of items possible in an invoice has to be less than 999 and will vary from document to document.

Copy control for billing is an important functionality that SAP ERP offers. It reduces the effort and errors involved in creating an invoice with reference to a delivery or order. It is done using Transaction VTFL (delivery related) and VTFA (order related) to get to the screen shown in Figure 7.2, execute the following steps:

1. Enter Transaction VTFL (menu path: SAP IMG • SALES AND DISTRIBUTION • BILLING • BILLING DOCUMENTS • MAINTAIN COPYING CONTROL FOR BILLING DOCUMENTS • COPYING CONTROL: DELIVERY DOCUMENT TO BILLING DOCUMENT).
2. Select the row with F2 in target column and LF as source column.
3. Double-click on the Item folder.
4. Double click on the item category for which the customization is to be done. In Figure 7.2 we've done this for the customized item category ZTA1.

Repeat the procedure for all of the combinations of billing type, delivery type, and item category for individual billings with a reference to delivery. For individual billings with a reference to order, instead of Transaction VTFL, you should use Transaction VTFA (menu path: SAP IMG • SALES AND DISTRIBUTION • BILLING • BILLING DOCUMENTS • MAINTAIN COPYING CONTROL FOR BILLING DOCUMENTS • COPYING CONTROL: SALES DOCUMENT TO BILLING DOCUMENT).

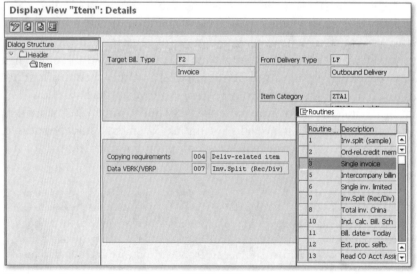

Figure 7.2 Data Transfer Routines for VBRK/VBRP

7.1.2 Collective Billing Document

By default, if the sold-to party, sales organization, and billing dates are the same, when you process several deliveries (or orders) using either Transaction VF01 or VF04 (billing due list), they combine to create a collective billing document. Certain fields, such as the net value or date of creation, should not cause any invoice split. The billing due list is a work list in which all of the documents due for billing appear that can then be processed (billed). The list of such fields can be found in the include program MV60ATOP (shown in Figure 7.3). Other then the fields listed in Table 7.1, the difference in any fields for Table VBRK (billing header) during bill processing will cause the invoice to split.

Table-Field	Description
VBRK-NETWR	Net value
VBRK-KNUMV	Document condition number
VBRK-VBELN	Billing document
VBRK-ERNAM	Created by
VBRK-ERDAT	Created on
VBRK-ERZET	Time
VBRK-AEDAT	Changed on
VBRK-BELNR	Document number
VBRK-RFBSK	Posting status
VBRK-SFAKN	Cancelled billing document
VBRK-MWSBK	Tax amount
VBRK-FKTYP	Billing category

Table 7.1 Fields That Don't Cause Invoice Splitting

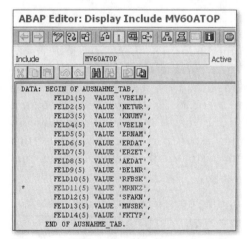

Figure 7.3 Fields Ignored During Invoice Split

The customization for copy control also determines whether invoices should be combined or split during processing. We've seen that copy control routines 003, 006, and 010 will not allow different reference documents to create a collective billing document. Routine 007 will split if the division, distribution channel, department, or receiving points differ in addition to the standard splitting rules.

To avoid unnecessary splitting during collective processing, you can use Transaction VF04 or VF06 to enter a date for the billing document. To manually enter a billing date in Transaction VF04, follow the menu path SETTINGS • DEFAULT DATA when you're at the selection screen. A dialog box appears where you can enter the billing date. You can enter the billing date in the Default Data field and then move on to create new VOFM data transfer routine for the billing document by copying any standard routine (e.g., 007) and modifying it. Then you can assign the new routine in the copy control setting in the Data VBRK/VBRP field.

In the next section, we'll discuss invoice splitting, how to avoid unnecessary splitting, and how to induce it when required.

7.1.3 Invoice Split

As we've touched on earlier, invoices are split based for the following reasons:

- The customization done for copy control
- The difference in the billing header (VBRK) fields other than those specified in Table 7.1

During invoice processing, if the invoice split happens, all of the invoices with their values will be available as a list in the billing document overview screen. You can reach this screen by pressing [F5] or clicking on the Billing Document Overview button in Figure 7.1. In the billing document overview screen, you can select any two proposed invoices at a time and click on the Split Analysis button in the application toolbar. You can see the cause of the invoice split, as shown in Figure 7.4. If you find the reason for splitting unnecessary, you can take corrective measures. You can use either a user exit or customize the routines used in copy control.

Now that you understand what invoice splitting does, let's discuss the billing due list.

Principles of Bill Processing | 7.1

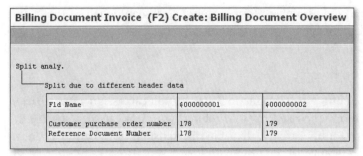

Figure 7.4 Split Analysis

7.1.4 Billing Due List

The billing due list is the functionality of generating a list of orders or deliveries or both that are due for invoicing based on certain selection criteria you specify in the selection screen. Once the list is generated, you have the option of using it as a report or doing further processing. You can generate invoices for the documents due for billing by selecting all or some of the documents and clicking on the any of the following three buttons to create the invoices:

- Individual Billing Document
- Collective Billing Document
- Collective Billing Document/Online

Before creating invoices, it's possible to simulate them. You can do mass processing of invoices in the background using Transaction VF06. You can schedule processing for a time when the server is idle to optimize system performance and prevent manual intervention.

7.1.5 Invoice List

The invoice list functionality is another optimizing tool SAP ERP offers you. You combine different invoices (and debit memos) into a single invoice list and send it to the payer for payment. Similarly, all credit memos can be grouped together. Invoice lists are created periodically (e.g., monthly) or on a fixed date (e.g., first day of every month). All of the individual billing documents become the items in an invoice list. You have the option of giving special discounts to take care of factoring services, for example. A factoring service is a service rendered by a collecting agency or organization to collect payment and involves factoring costs. For example, the service could involve reminder phone calls on behalf of the client. Standard available output types exist for invoice lists.

7.1.6 Cancellation Invoice

While defining the billing type (Transaction VOFA), you can assign a cancellation billing type that can only be used for that billing type. You can also specify the copying requirement routine, if any, that must be satisfied for creating a cancellation invoice with reference to the original invoice. You also specify the rule for the reference number and allocation number here. We'll discuss the importance of these fields later in this chapter. It's important to note that the customization done in the copy control transaction from billing document to billing document (VTFF) is not relevant when you create a cancellation invoice with reference to an invoice. You can cancel one or several invoices using Transaction VF11 or by going to SAP IMG • LOGISTICS • SALES AND DISTRIBUTION • BILLING • BILLING DOCUMENT • CANCEL.

> **Note:**
> SAP Notes 1259505 (FAQ. New Cancellation Procedure in SD) and 400000 (FAQ: Transaction VF11: Cancellation of SD Billing Documents) are quite useful for learning more about the cancellation functionality.

Having discussed the cancellation invoice, let's move to the general billing interface. Here we'll explain how to create an invoice without a reference.

7.1.7 General Billing Interface

You use the general billing interface to create invoices in SAP ERP with external data. This is like creating an invoice without a reference (to an order or delivery). Program RVAFSS00 imports the data to the interface tables of the function module GN_INVOICE_CREATE. Function module GN_INVOICE_CREATE is used for generating invoices when you use the general billing interface, instead of function module RV_INVOICE_CREATE. The fields specified in the Table 7.2 are the mandatory fields that must be present in the flat sequential file for creating an invoice (using the general billing interface). The data supplied should adhere to the length and the data type (e.g., numeric or character) requirement for the field.

Field Name	Field Length	Description
MANDT	3	Client
AUART	4	Sales document type
VKORG	4	Sales organization
VTWEG	2	Distribution channel
SPART	2	Division
FKDAT	8	Billing data
KUNAG	10	Sold-to party
MATNR and WERKS or LAND1	18 and 4 or 3	Material number and plant or country
PSTYV	4	Item category
KWMENG	8	Cumulative order quantity

Table 7.2 Mandatory Fields for Creating an Invoice with the General Billing Interface

The record type of the data in the sequential flat file determines the intended table for it. Table 7.3 lists some record types and the interface tables they populate.

Record Type	Interface Table	Purpose
A	XKOMFKGN	Item data
B	XKOMFKKO	Condition data
C	XKOMFKTX	Text data

Table 7.3 Important Interface Tables for Function Module GN_INVOICE_CREATE

When using the general billing interface you should ensure the following:

- Use standard billing type FX or a copy of it as the billing type.

- In the copy control transaction for billing (VTFA), you can maintain the Pricing Type Field in the item folder as C, D, or G. Pricing should remain unchanged. Also, use copy requirement routine 013 to ensure that the blocked customers are not billed. Items with no quantity are also removed.

- If pricing is to be transferred from an external system to SAP ERP, in the customization, the condition type should be set as modifiable. That is, the Manual Entries field should have the value A, C, or blank.

7 | Billing

- Item categories used for external billing should be relevant for pricing and billing.
- Relevant customer and material master records should exist in the system. If the material master record is not expected to exist, then the external data should also contain the information on the material short text, sales unit, currency, and material tax indicator. The NO_MARA field in the primary record of the sequential file should be marked. If the customer master record is not expected to exist, use the one-time customer master record and transfer additional information such as name, partner functions, and components of address.

Now that you understand the principles of bill processing, let's move on to billing types.

7.2 Billing Types

A bill can be an invoice, a credit memo, or a debit memo. There's significant difference in how they are treated in accounting. They are also different in respect to the reference documents they need for pricing, for output, and in various other aspects. Customizing billing types broadly includes the following steps:

- Customizing the standard billing types or creating new billing types
- Defining number ranges for billing types
- Checking customized billing types
- We'll discuss these three broad steps in the following subsections.

7.2.1 Customizing Billing Types

Use Transaction VOFA for customization of billing types or go to SAP IMG • SALES AND DISTRIBUTION • BILLING • BILLING DOCUMENTS • DEFINE BILLING TYPES • DEFINE BILLING TYPES. After pressing [Enter] or clicking on the IMG – Activity icon (clock), you get the list of all existing billing document types. To create a new one, select any existing billing type and click on the Copy As ([F6]) icon. In Figure 7.5, we've selected F2 and clicked on the Copy As icon to get to the screen shown. To create a new billing type, you have to give an alphanumeric key of a maximum of four characters starting with Y or Z. We'll cover this more in Section 7.2.2, but first, we'll discuss the following:

- General control
- Cancellation
- Account assignment/pricing
- Output/partner/texts determination

These are also the headings for different frames in the screen shown in the Figure 7.5.

General Control

- **Document Category**
  This groups different document types of the Sales and Distribution functionality in SAP ERP. A few examples of document categories for invoices are:
  - M (Invoice)
  - N (Invoice Cancellation)
  - O (Credit Memo)
  - P (Debit Memo)
  - U (Pro Forma Invoice)

- **Posting Block**
  Select this checkbox when you don't want the billing document to be posted automatically to accounts. However, you can execute a manual transfer to accounts by executing Transaction VF02 and clicking on the Release To Accounting icon (green flag). A posting block gives you the opportunity to verify the invoice before posting.

- **Transaction Group**
  Enter transaction group 7 (Billing Document) or 8 (Pro Forma Invoices) here depending on whether posting to accounts is required or not.

- **Statistics**
  When this checkbox is selected, the statistics in sales information system (which we'll discuss in Chapter 9) is updated for the billing documents of this type of billing.

- **Billing Category**
  You can use this field to group the billing document types for printing (selection criteria), creation (selection criteria), and transfer to accounting.

- **Document Type**
  In this field, you specify the accounting document type for the billing docu-

ment. The standard accounting document type for a sales invoice (e.g., F2) is RV (Billing Document Transfer).

- **Negative Posting**
  Leave this checkbox blank if you don't allow negative posting. If the company code allows negative posting, it should be allowed for the same posting period (option A) or without any restriction (option B). It's important to note that when a negative posting is not allowed, the invoice can still have a negative value. When the invoice has a negative value, the value is posted to the offsetting account as a positive value. The following example will help clarify this concept. Notice that in both cases, there is no negative figure in the accounting document. Only the GLs to be debited (Dr) or credited (Cr) are interchanged.

Example of No Negative Posting
Case 1: Invoice amount: 100 USD
Accounting document: Cr Sale Revenue Account 100 USD
Dr Customer Account 100 USD
Case 2: Invoice amount: –100 USD (negative invoice)
Accounting document: Dr Sales revenue account 100 USD
Cr Customer account 100 USD

- **Branch/Head Office**
  This field determines the partner function transferred to the accounting document. There are three possible values for this field. When the field is left blank, the payer becomes the customer and the sold-to party becomes the branch in the accounting document when the payer and sold-to party are different in invoice. This is irrespective of customization in accounting. This rule is the only option when credit management is active in the system. When credit management is not active, you can either transfer the sold-to party (option A) or payer (option B) to the accounting document as a customer, and the branch is determined as per the setting in SAP ERP Financials.

- **Credit Memo with Value Date**
  If this checkbox is not selected, the credit memo becomes due immediately. When it's selected, the fixed value date (VBRK-VALDT) field in the credit memo is filled with the baseline date of the invoice for which the memo is issued. The invoice reference field (BSEG-REBZG) of the accounting document line items is filled with the accounting document number of the referenced billing document.

- **Invoice List Type**
  You specify the invoice list type for the billing document type here. Examples of invoice list types are:
  - LG (Credit Memo List)
  - LGS (Cancel Credit Memo List)
  - LR (Invoice List)
  - LRS (Cancel Invoice List)
- **Rebate Settlement**
  Leave this field blank if this billing type is not used for rebate settlement. If it is to be used for rebate processing, depending upon its usage, it can have any of the following indicators:
  - A (Final Rebate Settlement)
  - B (Rebate Correction Document)
  - C (Partial Settlement for a Rebate Agreement)
  - D (Manual Accruals for a Rebate Agreement)
- **Relevant for Rebate**
  Select this checkbox for the billing types for rebate processing as specified above or for the billing type for which the rebate must accrue.
- **Standard Text**
  No longer used.

Cancellation

- **Cancellation Billing Type**
  In this field, you can specify the billing type used for cancelling the billing type that you're customizing. Some invoice types, for example, pro forma invoices, however, don't require a cancellation billing type and are never cancelled.
- **Copying Requirements**
  Enter the copying requirement type routine that must be fulfilled for creating a cancellation invoice with reference to the invoice in this field. The copy control setting maintained for billing document to billing document using Transaction VTFF is not applicable for copy control from invoice to cancellation invoice. This is true even though both the invoice and cancellation invoice are essentially billing documents.

- **Reference Number**
  This field defines the value of the reference key field (BKPF-XBLNR) in the accounting document that the billing document creates. You can enter any of the six figures, listed in Table 7.4, from the billing document to the accounting document (header level). This becomes important for joining Tables VBRK and BKPF.

Code	Description
A	Purchase order number
B	Sales order number
C	Delivery number
D	External delivery number
E	Current billing document number
F	External delivery number if available; otherwise delivery number

Table 7.4 Options for Reference Number and Allocation Number

- **Allocation Number**
  This field defines the value of the assignment field for the items of the accounting document (BSEG-ZUONR). You can customize the billing type to pass any of the six permitted document numbers. This along with the reference number becomes important for reporting purposes, especially cross-component reports where information from sales and distribution, and the accounting components will be extracted.

Account Assignment/Pricing

- **Account Determination Procedure**
  Assign the revenue account determination procedure for the billing document type here.

- **Document Pricing Procedure**
  In the condition technique for pricing, the pricing procedure is determined by the document pricing procedure, customer pricing procedure and sales area. You assign the document pricing procedure for the billing type here.

- **Account Determination Reconciliation Account**
  Assign the reconciliation account determination procedure for the billing document type here.

- **Account Determination Cash Settlement**
  You assign the cash account determination procedure for the billing document type here.

- **Account Determination Payment Cards**
  Assign the payment card account determination procedure for the billing document type in this field.

Output/Partner/Texts Determination

The fields in this section are customized in other sections of customization, and depending upon the customization done in those sections, the value is made available here. You do have the option of specifying the determination procedures for output, partner, and texts for a billing type in the screen shown in Figure 7.5. Normally, the customization step of assigning determination procedures to billing types is done using Transactions NACE, VOPAN, and VOTXN, respectively, for output, partner, and texts.

7.2.2 Number Ranges for Billing Types

It isn't possible to have an external number range for the billing document. You can have a different or the same number range for different document types. The document number ranges created or available by default in the RV_BELEG numbering object can be maintained in the Number Range for Internal Assignment Customizing field. You can add new number range intervals to the RV_BELEG numbering object using Transaction SNRO.

Different Number Ranges for Different Plants

You may require multiple number ranges for the same invoice type (e.g., F2) based on the delivery plant or the geographical location of the delivery plants. The standard SAP system does not provide a solution to such a requirement. There is a requirement for a user exit in such a case. The ABAP coding is done in the include program RV60AFZZ at FORM USEREXIT_NUMBER_RANGE USING US_RANGE_INTERN for this purpose.

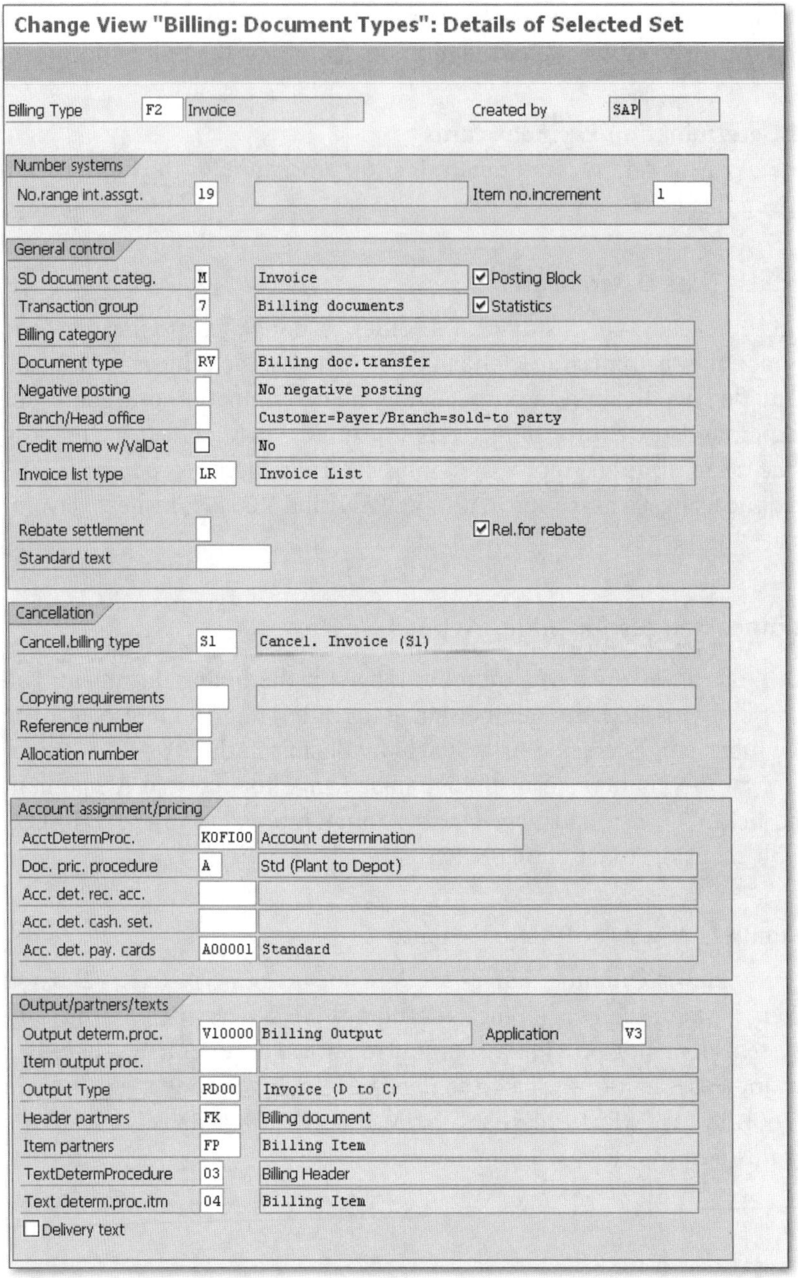

7 | Billing

| Change View "Billing: Document Types": Details of Selected Set |

Billing Type F2 Invoice **Created by** SAP

Number systems
No.range int.assgt.	19
Item no.increment	1

General control
SD document categ.	M	Invoice	☑ Posting Block
Transaction group	7	Billing documents	☑ Statistics
Billing category			
Document type	RV	Billing doc.transfer	
Negative posting		No negative posting	
Branch/Head office		Customer=Payer/Branch=sold-to party	
Credit memo w/ValDat	☐	No	
Invoice list type	LR	Invoice List	
Rebate settlement			☑ Rel.for rebate
Standard text			

Cancellation
Cancell.billing type	S1	Cancel. Invoice (S1)
Copying requirements		
Reference number		
Allocation number		

Account assignment/pricing
AcctDetermProc.	KOFI00	Account determination
Doc. pric. procedure	A	Std (Plant to Depot)
Acc. det. rec. acc.		
Acc. det. cash. set.		
Acc. det. pay. cards	A00001	Standard

Output/partners/texts
Output determ.proc.	V10000	Billing Output	Application	V3
Item output proc.				
Output Type	RD00	Invoice (D to C)		
Header partners	FK	Billing document		
Item partners	FP	Billing Item		
TextDetermProcedure	03	Billing Header		
Text determ.proc.itm	04	Billing Item		
☐ Delivery text				

Figure 7.5 Defining Billing Type

Before coding the RV60AFZZ, ensure that the following activities are complete:

1. Create a Z-table with the name ZINVNRANGE with the Client (MANDT), Document Category (VBTYP), Billing Type (FKART), Plant (WERKS), and Number Range Object for Invoice (NORANGE) fields as shown in Table 7.5.
2. For all combinations of billing type and plant combination, assign a number range object in Table ZINVNRANGE.
3. Define the number range objects used in Table ZINVNRANGE in Transaction SNRO (RV_BELEG object).

The following code in the include program RV60AFZZ will ensure that the invoice number of a delivery (or order) belonging to different plant will belong to different number ranges as defined in Table ZINVNRANGE.

```
FORM USEREXIT_NUMBER_RANGE USING US_RANGE_INTERN.
DATA: V_VBTYP type VBRK-VBTYP,
 V_FKART type VBRK-FKART,
 V_WERKS type VBRP-WERKS.
DATA: WA_ZINVNRANGE type ZINVNRANGE.
DATA: V_NUMKI type TVFK-NUMKI,
V_ANS(1).
V_VBTYP = xvbrk-vbtyp.
V_FKART = xvbrk-FKART.
V_WERKS = XVBRP-WERKS.
Select single *
from ZINVNRANGE
into wa_ZINVNRANGE
where
vbtyp eq V_VBTYP and
FKART eq V_FKART and
WERKS eq V_WERKS.
IF SY-SUBRC = '0'.
US_RANGE_INTERN = WA_ZINVNRANGE-NORANGE.
ELSE.
Message I001(ZKK) with 'ENTRY NOT FOUND IN TABLE ZINVNRANGE'.
ENDIF.
ENDFORM.
```

Different Number Ranges for Different Countries

If you want the number range to be based on geographical region (country or province), then all of the delivery plants in a region should be assigned to the same number range object in Table ZINVNRANGE. If there are five plants in three different regions, and three different number ranges are required, the entries in Table ZINVNRANGE will be similar to the entries shown in Table 7.5.

> **Note**
> SAP ERP offers the functionality of official document numbering for many countries that require special rules or norms for numbering invoices. Italy, Taiwan, Chile, Peru, Latvia, Argentina, India, and China are some such countries. Refer to the SAP notes listed below and any other SAP notes that are referenced in those notes for exploring this functionality for a specific country.
>
> 746162: Using Official Document Numbering for Italy
>
> 1259078: Official Document Numbering for Latvia
>
> 605870: Official Document Numbering for India – Program Changes
>
> 571376: Official Document Numbering – New Customizing Tables (Argentina)
>
> 385973: China: Various Problems with Official Document Numbering
>
> 408769: Peru, Chile: New Settings for Official Document Numbering

Client (MANDT)	Doc Cat. (VBTYPE)	Bill Type (FKART)	Plant (WERKS)	Number Range (NORANGE)
300	M	F2	1000	A1
300	M	F2	2000	A1
300	M	F2	3000	A2
300	M	F2	4000	A2
300	M	F2	5000	A3

Table 7.5 Table ZINVNARANGE with Sample Entries

Plants 1000 and 2000 will take same number range (A1), and so will invoices for the deliveries or orders of plant 3000 and 4000 (A2). Invoices for plant 5000 will have a different invoice range (i.e., A3). The exact number that the invoices will take will be determined by the entries made in Transaction SNRO (RV_BELEG object) for the A1, A2, and A3 number range objects.

7.2.3 Check Customized Billing Types

Use Transaction VCHECKVOFA is for checking customization of billing types (menu path: SAP IMG • SALES AND DISTRIBUTION • BILLING • BILLING DOCUMENTS •

DEFINE BILLING TYPES • CHECK CUSTOMIZING SETTINGS FOR BILLING DOCUMENT TYPES). In the initial screen, you have the option of restricting the customization check to some billing type (e.g., Z*) or executing without any restriction for checking all the billing types.

The following settings are checked in the report:

1. For the pro forma billing type, (VBTYP = U), the field account determination procedure field gets hidden in the screen shown in Figure 7.5. But if you're creating a pro forma invoice type by copying a billing type that's not a pro forma invoice and you enter a value in the account determination field first and then change the billing type, the error shown in Figure 7.6 (which shows the billing type ZF2) will occur.

2. Billing type (VBTYP) M can be cancelled by billing type N. In customization, if you enter a different cancellation billing type, you'll get an error message. However, a situation may occur in which you assigned a correct cancellation billing type to a billing type, and then the billing type field of the cancellation billing type can be changed. The change will cause an inconsistency. The billing document type ZF1 shown in Figure 7.6 has this type of error.

3. Transaction VCHECKVOFA also checks if the cancellation billing document type partner functions are empty or if those that correspond to the billing type used are empty. The billing document type ZF3 shown in Figure 7.6 has this type of error.

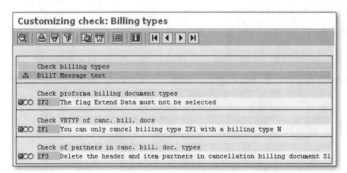

Figure 7.6 Error Messages for Transaction VCHECKVOFA

However, there will be no error for incomplete customization. For example, if any of the following fields are not maintained for a billing type, you'll have a problem in bill processing using the particular document type, but no error will be reported in Transaction VCHECKVOFA.

7 | Billing

- Cancellation invoice type
- Output determination procedure
- Number range
- Document category
- Text determination procedure at header or item level or any other field

7.3 Complaint Documents

Complaints are part of any business. When customers don't get what they want or what was promised to them, they complain. Businesses settle the valid complains by compensating the customer either after or without taking back the material. Sometimes additional material is supplied without charge or material is replaced. Certain complaints may involve charging the customer for a mistake in the invoice in terms of price, quantity, or both. Transaction CMP_PROCESSING is used for complain processing. The transaction for customizing complaint reasons, S_PLN_0600019, is not available from SAP ERP Central Component 5.0 onward. You can do the customizing either by adding entries to Table CMP_REASON, which stores the complaints reasons using Transaction SE16N with the function &SAP_EDIT, or use the BAdI BADI_CMP_PROCESSING. The steps for customizing complaints reasons using Transaction SM30 are given below.

1. Execute Transaction SM30 (you can also use Transaction SM31).
2. Enter "V_CMP_REASON" in the Table/View field.
3. Click on the Maintain button. The screen shown in Figure 7.7 will appear.
4. In the Abbreviation column, enter the four-character alphanumeric key.
5. Select the Changeable checkbox if you want to modify the bill quantity, unit of measure, and prices.

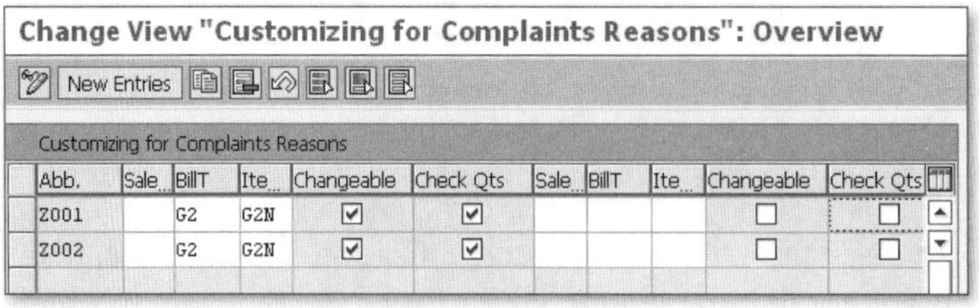

Figure 7.7 Customizing for Complaints Reasons

6. Select the Check Quantity checkbox if you want to ensure that the quantity you enter during complaint processing does not exceed the original quantity supplied.

7. If the second set of sales orders, billing types, and item categories is filled, there will be two lines for one billing item.

During complaint processing using Transaction CMP_PROCESSING (see Figure 7.8), you can enter the invoice number in the Doc. Number field. The original invoice appears on the screen. At the bottom of the screen, you can enter an item number, complaint reason, and quantity. A new item (or two, depending upon customization) with the item category specified in the customization of complaints reasons appears. After saving, the credit memo (or the billing type specified in the customization of complaints reasons) is created.

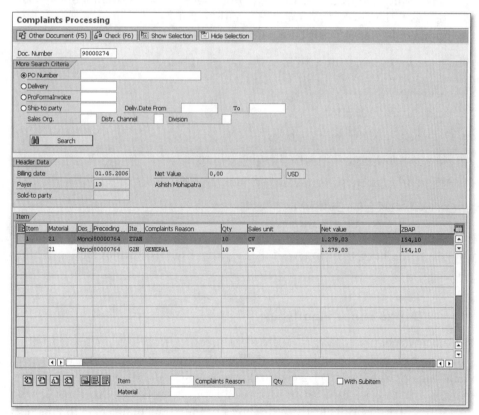

Figure 7.8 Complaints Processing

Now that we've discussed complaint processing, let's move on to billing plans.

7.4 Billing Plan

When items in a sales order should be billed on different dates as per certain rules, a billing plan becomes necessary. When a percentage of the total bill amount should be billed on different dates aggregating to cent per cent, the billing plan is called *milestone billing*. Milestones can be particular stages in a large project, for example, the different milestones in an SAP ERP implementation project using ASAP methodology (see Chapter 1). The different billing dates of this plan are called milestones. The other standard billing plan in SAP systems is called *periodic billing*. Periodic billing (e.g., rent) is done at regular intervals (e.g., monthly) for the entire amount (e.g., monthly rent as per the rent contract) for a particular period (e.g., three years as per the rent contract). During sales order processing, the items relevant for the billing plan automatically determine whether milestone billing or periodic billing is relevant for the item. In the overview screen for a billing plan, the details to be entered for the item are different depending on whether it's a milestone billing or periodic billing plan.

The steps for customizing a billing plan are given below:

1. Define billing plan types.
2. Define date descriptions.
3. Define and assign date categories.
4. Maintain date proposals for milestone billing.
5. Assign billing plan types to sales document types.
6. Assign billing plan types to item categories.
7. Define rules for determining dates.

Now that you have an overview of the steps, let's discuss each of these in further detail.

7.4.1 Define Billing Plan Types

As already mentioned, the standard system comes with two predefined billing plans: milestone billing and periodic billing. Use Transaction OVBI to change periodic billing plans (billing plan type 01) (menu path: SAP IMG • SALES AND DISTRIBUTION • BILLING • BILLING PLAN • DEFINE BILLING PLAN TYPES • MAINTAIN BILLING PLAN TYPES FOR PERIODIC BILLING). To modify a milestone billing plan (billing plan type 02), use Transaction OVBO (menu path: SAP IMG • SALES AND DISTRIBUTION • BILLING • BILLING PLAN • DEFINE BILLING PLAN TYPES • MAINTAIN BILLING PLAN

7.4 Billing Plan

TYPES FOR MILESTONE BILLING). Both the transactions, OVBI and OVBO, are for modifying the existing billing plan types. To create a new billing plan type, click on the Back icon to go to the overview screen where you can see the existing billing plan type (by default one in both periodic and milestone cases). You can select any existing billing plan type and click on the Copy As icon to go to the screen shown in Figures 7.9 and 7.10, respectively, for milestone (Transaction OVBO) and periodic (Transaction (OVBI) billing.

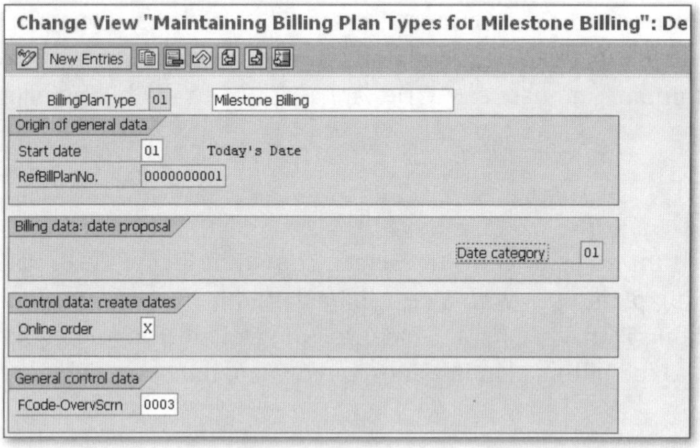

Figure 7.9 Milestone Billing

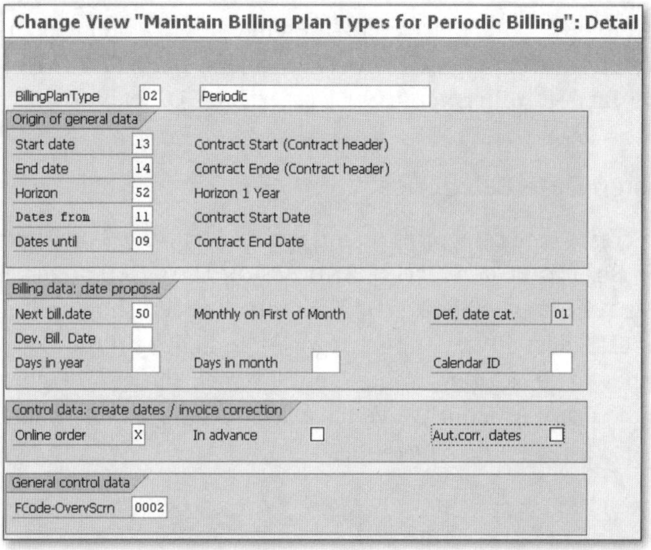

Figure 7.10 Periodic Billing

Milestone Billing

In the customization of milestone billing, in addition to the two-character key and description, you fill in three fields in the screen shown in Figure 7.9 in enable mode (white background). These fields are Start Date, Online Order, and Fcode for Overview Screen. In the Start Date field, you define the rule for the starting date of the milestone billing plan. When the Online Order field is blank, the dates of the billing plan are entered manually during order processing. Dates are automatically determined as per the date proposal, with (option X) or without (option Y) a dialog box for manual entry to overwrite the proposed dates. The Fcode for Overview Screen determines the fields that can be maintained in the overview screen. The reference billing plan number and date categories are assigned to the billing plan type in subsequent steps.

Periodic Billing

We've already described the steps to go to the screen shown in Figure 7.10. You can create periodic billing plan types with a two-character alphanumeric key and a description in the Billing Plan Type field. Except for the Default Date Category field, which you assign to the billing plan in a subsequent step, the other fields are customized in this step.

7.4.2 Define Date Descriptions

Date descriptions are used to differentiate between different dates in a billing plan. You define the date description using Transaction OVBN (menu path: SAP IMG • SALES AND DISTRIBUTION • BILLING • BILLING PLAN • DEFINE DATE DESCRIPTIONS).

7.4.3 Define and Assign Date Categories

Use Transaction OVBJ to create date categories (menu path: SAP IMG • SALES AND DISTRIBUTION • BILLING • BILLING PLAN • DEFINE AND ASSIGN DATE CATEGORIES • MAINTAIN DATE CATEGORY FOR BILLING PLAN TYPE). The initial screen shows all of the existing date categories. Select any existing categories and click on the Copy As ([F6]) icon to create a new date category. You go to the screen shown in Figure 7.11 when you click on the Copy As icon. We've have selected the standard date category 01 as the reference for creating a new one.

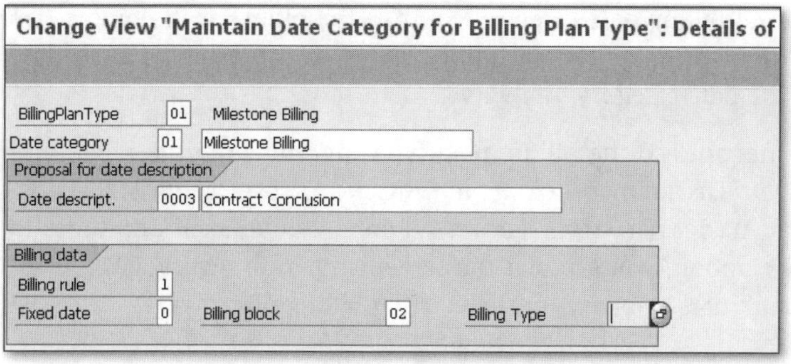

7.4 Billing Plan

```
Change View "Maintain Date Category for Billing Plan Type": Details of

BillingPlanType        01   Milestone Billing
Date category          01   Milestone Billing
Proposal for date description
Date descript.      0003  Contract Conclusion

Billing data
Billing rule        1
Fixed date          0    Billing block       02    Billing Type
```

Figure 7.11 Maintain Date Categories for Billing Plan Type

In the customization for date category, you can specify a date description for the category. The billing rule can use any of the options listed in Table 7.6.

Billing Rule	Description
1	Milestone billing on a percentage basis
2	Milestone billing on a value basis
3	Closing invoice in milestone billing
4	Down payment in milestone billing on percentage basis
5	Down payment in milestone billing on a value basis

Table 7.6 List of Billing Rules

You can also specify values for a fixed date (from any one in Table 7.7), billing block (if required), and billing type in the customization of date category.

Fixed Date	Description
Blank	Assignment to milestones not possible
0	Fixed date, date not copied from milestone
1	Planned/actual date from milestone
2	Planned/actual date from milestone if before billing date
3	Planned/actual date from milestone if after billing date

Table 7.7 Fixed Date for Date Category

The customization of billing date category controls the billing at the billing date level. The same item can have several billing dates, and the bill of each date, depending upon the date category, can vary.

You assign date categories to the billing plan types by following the menu path SAP IMG • SALES AND DISTRIBUTION • BILLING • BILLING PLAN • DEFINE AND ASSIGN DATE CATEGORIES • ALLOCATE DATE CATEGORY. When you double-click on the Allocate Date Category option, you go to at the screen shown in Figure 7.12, where you enter the default date category for the existing billing plan.

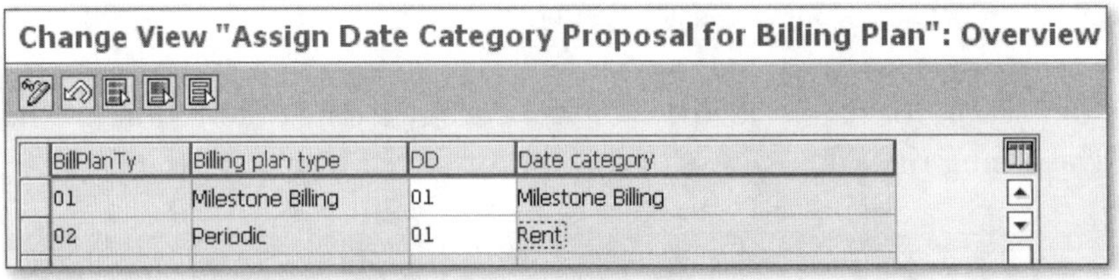

BillPlanTy	Billing plan type	DD	Date category
01	Milestone Billing	01	Milestone Billing
02	Periodic	01	Rent

Figure 7.12 Assign Default Date Category to Billing Plan Type

7.4.4 Maintain Date Proposals for Milestone Billing

The transaction code for maintaining the date proposal for milestone billing is OVBM (menu path: SAP IMG • SALES AND DISTRIBUTION • BILLING • BILLING PLAN • MAINTAIN DATE PROPOSALS FOR BILLING PLAN TYPES). The date proposal is not relevant for periodic billing. From the initial screen, you click on Maintain Date with or without entering a reference billing plan to go to the screen shown in Figure 7.13. You control the invoice to be raised on different dates with this customization. The dates in the reference billing plan are copied to the invoice and redetermined as per the rule (see the last step) specified for this purpose.

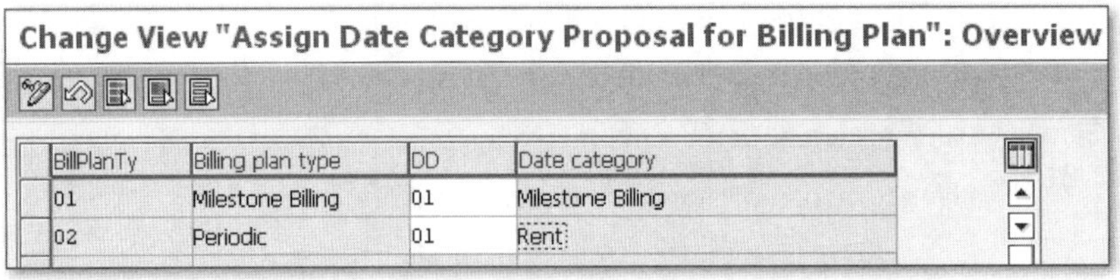

BillPlanTy	Billing plan type	DD	Date category
01	Milestone Billing	01	Milestone Billing
02	Periodic	01	Rent

Figure 7.13 Date Proposal for Milestone Billing

7.4.5 Assign Billing Plan Types to Sales Document Types

To assign billing plan types to the sales document types, use Transaction OVBP (menu path: SAP IMG • SALES AND DISTRIBUTION • BILLING • BILLING PLAN • ASSIGN BILLING PLAN TYPES TO SALES DOCUMENT TYPES). After you execute the transaction, you go to the screen shown in Figure 7.14. All of the sales document types existing in the system are proposed by the system. For those relevant for the billing plan, you specify the billing plan type in the BillPlanTy column. This step is not required if you don't use a header billing plan.

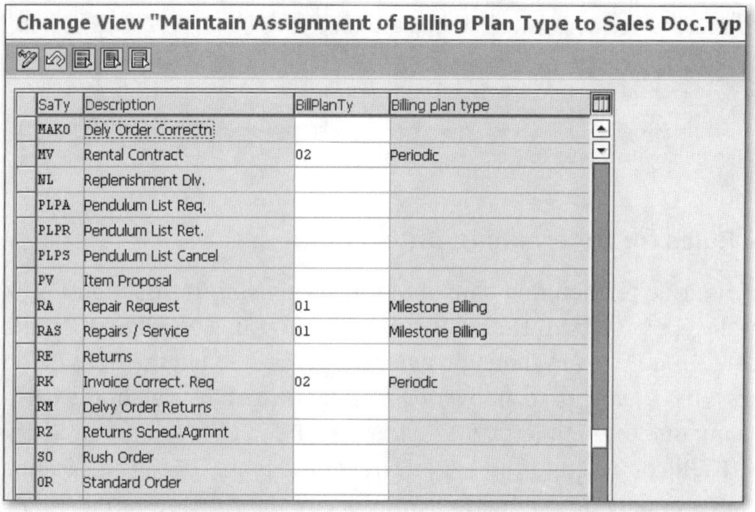
Change View "Maintain Assignment of Billing Plan Type to Sales Doc.Typ

SaTy	Description	BillPlanTy	Billing plan type
MAKO	Dely Order Correctn		
MV	Rental Contract	02	Periodic
NL	Replenishment Dlv.		
PLPA	Pendulum List Req.		
PLPR	Pendulum List Ret.		
PLPS	Pendulum List Cancel		
PV	Item Proposal		
RA	Repair Request	01	Milestone Billing
RAS	Repairs / Service	01	Milestone Billing
RE	Returns		
RK	Invoice Correct. Req	02	Periodic
RM	Delvy Order Returns		
RZ	Returns Sched.Agrmnt		
SO	Rush Order		
OR	Standard Order		

Figure 7.14 Assign Billing Plan to Sales Document Type

7.4.6 Assign Billing Plan Types to Item Categories

You define item categories as relevant for a billing plan (option I) using Transaction OVBK (menu path: SAP IMG • SALES AND DISTRIBUTION • BILLING • BILLING PLAN • ASSIGN BILLING PLAN TYPES TO ITEM CATEGORIES). On entering the transaction code in the transaction window, you go to the screen shown in Figure 7.15. You also define the billing plan type applicable for the item categories here. You cannot change the billing plan type assigned to an item category at the time of document processing.

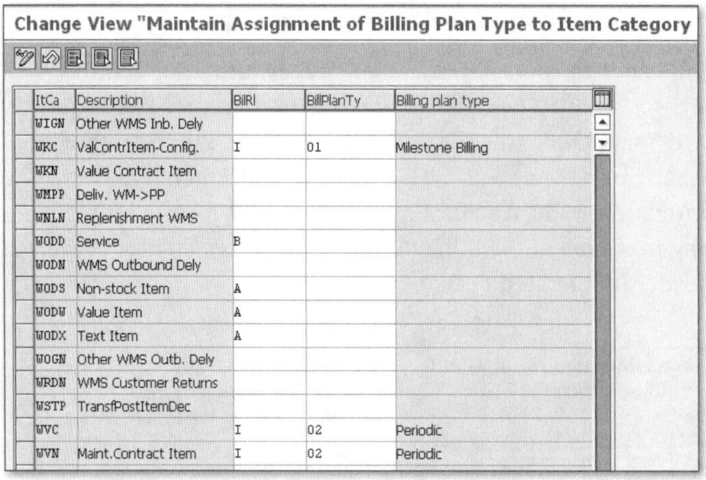

Change View "Maintain Assignment of Billing Plan Type to Item Category

ItCa	Description	BilRl	BillPlanTy	Billing plan type
WIGN	Other WMS Inb. Dely			
WKC	ValContrItem-Config.	I	01	Milestone Billing
WKN	Value Contract Item			
WMPP	Deliv. WM->PP			
WNLN	Replenishment WMS			
WODD	Service	B		
WODN	WMS Outbound Dely			
WODS	Non-stock Item	A		
WODW	Value Item	A		
WODX	Text Item	A		
WOGN	Other WMS Outb. Dely			
WRDN	WMS Customer Returns			
WSTP	TransfPostItemDec			
WVC		I	02	Periodic
WVN	Maint.Contract Item	I	02	Periodic

Figure 7.15 Assigning Billing Plan Type to Item Categories

7.4.7 Define Rules for Determining Dates

You can execute the rule for defining date determination using Transaction OVPX (menu path: SAP IMG • SALES AND DISTRIBUTION • BILLING • BILLING PLAN • DEFINE RULES FOR DETERMINING DATES). When you enter the Transaction in the transaction window and press [Enter], you go to an overview screen, which lists all of the existing rules. Select any one of them (e.g., 50 – Monthly on First of Month) and click on the Copy As ([F6]) icon to go to the screen shown in Figure 7.16. The baseline date forms the basis of date determination. You specify the rule for baseline date determination, which can be any one of the standard options listed in Table 7.8.

Baseline Date	Description
01	Today's date
02	Contract start date
04	Acceptance date
05	Installation date
06	Date contract signed
07	Billing date/invoice date
08	Contract start date plus contract duration
09	Contract end date

Table 7.8 Baseline Date Options

In the Time Period field, you can specify the number of days or month. The unit (e.g., days or months) in the Time Unit field will be added to the baseline date. The Last of Month field is used to change the date from any date to either the first or last date of the month if required. You can also specify the calendar ID for which the rule is used. Select the Contract Data checkbox if item level dates are to be ignored while calculating the baseline date.

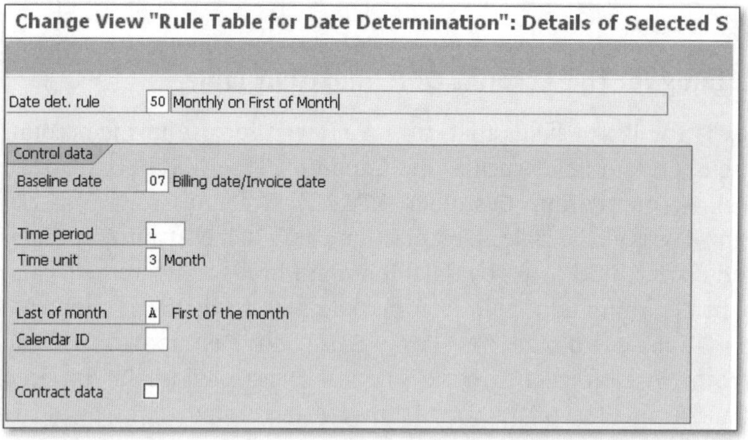

Figure 7.16 Rules for Date Determination

7.5 Revenue Account Determination

Revenue account determination also uses the condition technique, which we discussed in Chapter 4. Account determination is the basic customization for transferring the billing information to the accounting document. Until the accounting document for the bill is generated, from the accounting point of view, the revenue is not generated, profit is not made, and no tax is payable. The accounting document generated for the bill may contain several line items pertaining to several general ledgers. This is an important integration of the Sales and Distribution functionality with Financial Accounting functionality of SAP ERP. The basic steps for account determination are:

1. Include fields relevant for account determination in the field catalog for the account determination table.
2. Select the available account determination table or create customized ones.
3. Create the access sequence for the account determination table.

4. Customize the account determination type.

5. Customize the account determination procedure.

6. Customize the account key.

7. Assign GLs to account determination types.

Now that we've listed the general steps, let's discuss them in the following subsections.

7.5.1 Field Catalog for the Account Determination Table

The Field Catalog is the list of fields that can be allowed for use in the account determination table. Certain fields such as the Condition Type (KSCHA), Chart of Accounts (KTOPL), Account Group Customer (KTGRD), Account Group Material (KTGRM), Account Key (KVSL1), Sales Organization (VKORG), Distribution Channel (VTWEG), and Plant (WERKS) are by default present in the standard field catalog for the account determination table. You can add new fields to the catalogue using Transaction OV25 (menu path: SAP IMG • SALES AND DISTRIBUTION • BASIC FUNCTIONS • ACCOUNT ASSIGNMENT/COSTING • DEFINE DEPENDENCIES OF REVENUE ACCOUNT DETERMINATION • FIELD CATALOG: ALLOWED FIELDS FOR THE TABLES). The already existing entries will appear in the initial overview screen. To insert a new field, click on the New Entry button, and then press the [F4] function key. The screen shown in Figure 7.17 will appear. It's the list of all fields that you can import into the field catalog. Double-click on the field that you want to import and save it.

7.5.2 Account Determination Table

Six standard account determination tables are predefined in SAP ERP. To create an account determination table, you can use Transaction V/12 (menu path: SAP IMG • SALES AND DISTRIBUTION • BASIC FUNCTIONS • ACCOUNT ASSIGNMENT/COSTING • DEFINE DEPENDENCIES OF REVENUE ACCOUNT DETERMINATION • ACCOUNT DETERMINATION: CREATE TABLES). The customized table should have numbers between 501 and 999. You can create a condition table with or without reference to an existing condition table. If you create it without reference, then the field catalog will appear in the right side of the screen shown in Figure 7.18, and the Selected Fields are will be empty. You have to select the field in the Field Catalog and click on the Select Field button on the application toolbar to move it to the left side.

Revenue Account Determination | 7.5

New Entries: Overview of Added Entries

| Table Name | Short Text |
Field Name	Short Text
KOMCV	Maintenance
VKORG	Sales Organization
VTWEG	Distribution Channel
KTGRD	Account assignment group for this customer
WERKS	Plant
KTGRM	Account assignment group for this material
KSCHA	Condition type
KVSL1	Account key
SPART	Division
CCINS	Payment cards: Card type
LOCID	Payment cards: Point of receipt for the transaction
LIFNR	Account Number of Vendor or Creditor
MWSKZ	Sales Tax Code
BEMOT	Accounting Indicator
AUGRU	Order reason (reason for the business transaction)
KDUMMY	Dummy function in length 1
PDUMMY	Dummy function in length 1
PSTYV	Sales document item category
KOMKCV	Determination header
KTOPL	Chart of Accounts
VKORG	Sales Organization
VTWEG	Distribution Channel
KTGRD	Account assignment group for this customer
KAPPL	Application
KALSMC	Account determination procedure
RKPREL	CO account assignment exists
LIFNR	Account Number of Vendor or Creditor
LLAND	Destination country
AUGRU	Order reason (reason for the business transaction)
KDUMMY	Dummy function in length 1
IX_KOMT1_V	Index number for internal tables
IX_KOMT1_B	Index number for internal tables
CLMTY	Warranty Claim Type
RELTY	Type of Warranty Object
KATEG	Category
KOMPCV	Determination item
WERKS	Plant
KTGRM	Account assignment group for this material
KSCHA	Condition type
KVSL1	Account key
POSNR	Item number of the SD document
STUNR	Step number
KRUEK	Condition is Relevant for Accrual (e.g. Freight)
SPART	Division
CCINS	Payment cards: Card type
LOCID	Payment cards: Point of receipt for the transaction
MWSKZ	Sales Tax Code
BEMOT	Accounting Indicator
PDUMMY	Dummy function in length 1
PSTYV	Sales document item category
J_1ISTCODE	LST CST applicability code
J_1IFORMC1	Form Type
J_1IFORMC2	Form Type
POSKT	Controlling Item Type
REFKT	Reference Type
RETPA	Status for Parts that Have to Be Returned from Claimant

Figure 7.17 List of Allowed Fields for Account Determination Table

When creating with reference, the fields in the referenced table are already present in the Selected Fields part of the screen, so you may have to add only a few fields to them. To delete an already selected field, click on that field and then click on the Delete icon. Once the fields that will constitute the condition table are finalized and are in the Selected Fields part of the screen, click on the Generate icon present in the far left of the application toolbar.

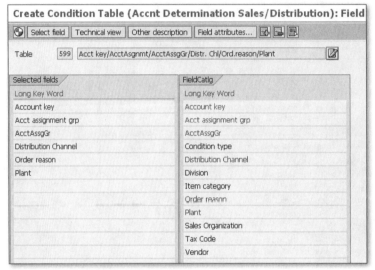

Figure 7.18 Create Condition Table

7.5.3 Access Sequence

Access sequences are assigned to the condition types that are determined automatically in a determination procedure, using a condition technique. The menu path for customizing an access sequence is SAP IMG • SALES AND DISTRIBUTION • BASIC FUNCTIONS • ACCOUNT ASSIGNMENT/COSTING • MAINTAIN ACCESS SEQUENCES FOR ACCOUNT DETERMINATION • MAINTAIN ACCESS SEQUENCES FOR ACCOUNT DETERMINATION. The existing access sequence types will appear in the right side of the initial screen. KOFI and KOFR are two standard access sequences. You can modify these sequences or create your own by selecting an existing one and clicking on the Copy As ([F6]) icon and then giving a new key and description to the access sequence. Once a sequence is created, double-click on it to go to the screen shown in Figure 7.19. You list the sequence of condition tables to be accessed for getting the desired condition record (GL account in this case). You can assign the requirement routines for account determination to optimize performance.

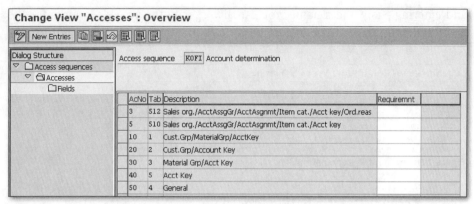

Figure 7.19 Standard Access Sequence KOFI

Another option you have to optimize performance is to use Transaction OVU1. Using this transaction, you can specify the access number for a condition type. The setting in Figure 7.20 shows that access 10 of access sequence KOFI is executed for condition type KOFI. This contradicts the customization shown in Figure 7.19. So for account determination type KOFI, access number 10 of access sequence KOFI is only executed if you expect the previous accesses 3 and 5 to be executed first. To make the customization shown in Figure 7.19 valid, you have to delete the entry shown in Figure 7.20.

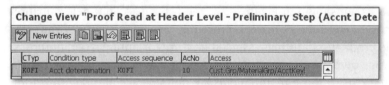

Figure 7.20 Optimize Access (Revenue Account Determination)

7.5.4 Account Determination Type

The condition type is referred to as account determination type here. You define it by following the menu path SAP IMG • SALES AND DISTRIBUTION • BASIC FUNCTIONS • ACCOUNT ASSIGNMENT/COSTING • MAINTAIN ACCESS SEQUENCES FOR ACCOUNT DETERMINATION • DEFINE ACCOUNT DETERMINATION TYPES. Double-clicking on the IMG – Activity icon at the end of the menu path takes you to the screen shown in Figure 7.21. The two standard account determination types are KOFI and KOFK. You create new account determination types by clicking on the New Entries button and entering a key and a name. You can also specify the access sequence for the account determination type, if automatic determination of GL is required.

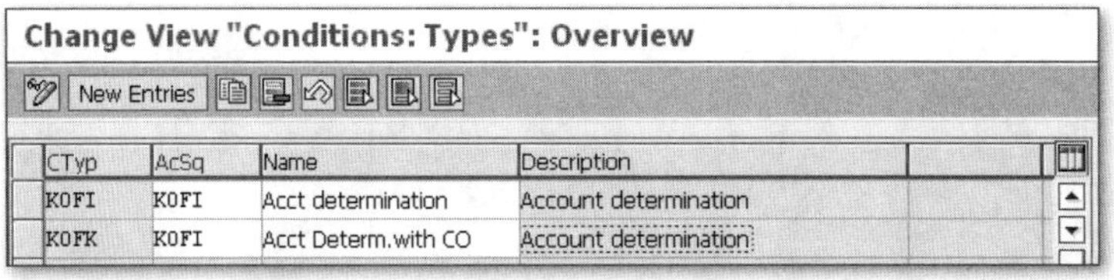
Change View "Conditions: Types": Overview
New Entries
CTyp
AcSq
Name
Description
KOFI
KOFI
Acct determination
Account determination
KOFK
KOFI
Acct Determ.with CO
Account determination

Figure 7.21 Account Determination Types

7.5.5 Account Determination Procedure

An account determination procedure must contain at least one account determination type. It is assigned to the billing types to automatically find the revenue accounts for prices, discounts, taxes, and surcharges (including freight). To define it and assign it to the billing types, use Transaction S_ALR_87007038 (menu path: SAP IMG • SALES AND DISTRIBUTION • BASIC FUNCTIONS • ACCOUNT ASSIGNMENT/COSTING • DEFINE AND ASSIGN ACCOUNT DETERMINATION PROCEDURES). After clicking on the IMG – Activity icon at the end of the menu path, you have the option of either defining or assigning the account determination procedure. Double-clicking on the Define Account Determination Procedure option takes you to the list of existing procedures. Select any procedure and click on the Control folder at the left to go to the screen shown in Figure 7.22. You list the account determination types that must be determined once the procedure becomes relevant. The standard account determination routines assigned here are for optimization purposes. You can have your own customized routines assigned here for achieving certain business requirements. If those requirements are not met, account determination stops. Assigning requirements at the procedure level is better than assigning them at the access sequence level.

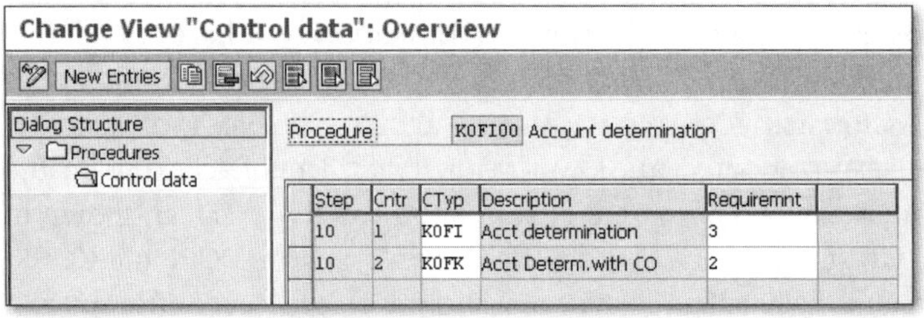
Change View "Control data": Overview
New Entries
Dialog Structure
Procedures
Control data
Procedure
KOFI00
Account determination
Step
Cntr
CTyp
Description
Requiremnt
10
1
KOFI
Acct determination
3
10
2
KOFK
Acct Determ.with CO
2

Figure 7.22 Account Determination Procedure KOFI00

After defining the account determination procedure, assigned it to the billing type by double-clicking on the option Assign Account Determination Procedure at the end of the above-mentioned menu path. You'll see the overview screen shown in Figure 7.23. For pro forma invoices, no account determination procedure is assigned, because no accounting document is to be generated for them.

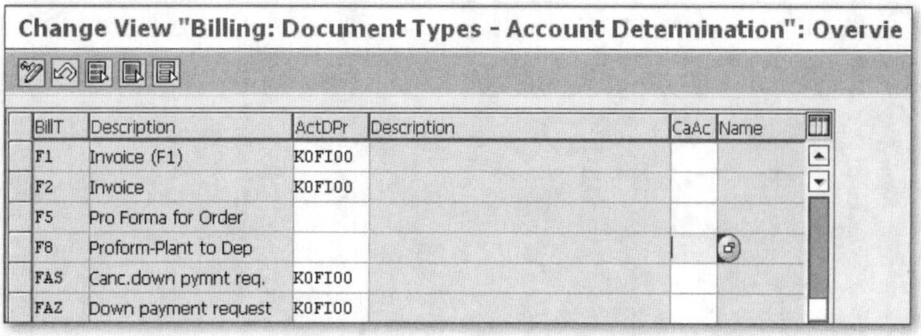
Change View "Billing: Document Types - Account Determination": Overvie

BillT	Description	ActDPr	Description	CaAc	Name
F1	Invoice (F1)	KOFI00			
F2	Invoice	KOFI00			
F5	Pro Forma for Order				
F8	Proform-Plant to Dep				
FAS	Canc.down pymnt req.	KOFI00			
FAZ	Down payment request	KOFI00			

Figure 7.23 Assign Account Determination Procedure to Billing Types

7.5.6 Account Key

Account keys are used for grouping GL accounts. These keys are also used for automatic posting of components of the pricing procedure such as sales, freight, discounts, surcharges, and taxes to relevant GL accounts. You can copy the standard account keys such as ERL (revenues), ERF (freight revenue), ERS (discounts), EVV (cash settlement), and MWS (Tax) to create new account keys. The menu path for defining and assigning account keys is SAP IMG • SALES AND DISTRIBUTION • BASIC FUNCTIONS • ACCOUNT ASSIGNMENT/COSTING • DEFINE AND ASSIGN ACCOUNT KEYS. By clicking on the IMG – Activity icon you get the option of defining and assigning. When you double-click on Define Account Key, you get a list of all existing account keys. You can select any one and click on the Copy As (F6) icon to create a new account key starting with Y or Z and a description. In the above-mentioned menu path, you can click on Assign Account Keys to assign the account keys to the condition types (not account determination type but pricing condition types) of the pricing procedure. All of the pricing procedures already defined become available in the overview screen with the assignments, if any, already made in Transaction V/08 (Define Pricing Procedure). Figure 7.24 shows the overview screen.

Proc.	Step	Cntr	CTyp	Name	ActKy	Name	Acc	Name
BVRBTI	100	0	PR00	Price	ERL	Revenue		Revenue
	300	0	B001	Mat/Group Rebate	ERB	Rebate sales deduct.	ERU	Rebate ac
	310	0	B002	Material Rebate	ERB	Rebate sales deduct.	ERU	Rebate ac
	320	0	B003	Customer Rebate	ERB	Rebate sales deduct.	ERU	Rebate ac
	330	0	B004	Hierarchy Rebate	ERB	Rebate sales deduct.	ERU	Rebate ac
	340	0	B005	Hierarchy rebate/mat	ERB	Rebate sales deduct.	ERU	Rebate ac
	350	0	B006	Sales Indpndt Rebate	ERB	Rebate sales deduct.	ERU	Rebate ac
CHCIXD	10	0	CHOD	CH Settl.Amount Deb	COD	CH Settl.amount Deb		
	20	0	CHZD	CH Interest Deb	CZD	CH Interest Deb		
	30	0	CHMD	CH Rent Debi	CMD	CH Rent Debi		
	40	0	CHGD	CH Int.Cred.Memo Deb	CZD	CH Interest Deb		
	50	0	CHND	CH Incidentals D	CND	CH Incidentals D		
	60	0	CHVD	CH Refund D	CVD	CH Refund Deb		
	70	0	CHKD	Admin.Cost Deb	CKD	Admin. cost Deb		
	80	0	CHM1	CH Rent Priv. Deb	CM1	CH Rent priv. Deb		
	90	0	CHN1	CH IEA Intern (Net)	CN1	CH IEA intern D		

Figure 7.24 Assign Account Keys to Pricing Procedure

7.5.7 Assign General Ledger to Account Determination Types

The transaction code to assign a general ledger to account determination types (e.g., KOFI) is VKOA. You can also use the general Transaction OBYF and then select application V (sales/distribution) (menu path: SAP IMG • SALES AND DISTRIBUTION • BASIC FUNCTIONS • ACCOUNT ASSIGNMENT/COSTING • ASSIGN G/L ACCOUNTS). In the initial screen, all of the account determination tables will be listed. Double-click on any table for which you want to maintain the GL accounts. You'll see the screen shown in Figure 7.25. Note that there is provision for two GL account numbers. The second GL account is to be to be specified for accruals (e.g., rebate agreements).

App	CndTy.	ChAc	SOrg.	AAG	AAG	ActKy	G/L account no.	G/L account no.
V	KOFI	7000	7000	01	01	ERB	14010	
V	KOFI	7000	7000	01	01	ERF	23010	
V	KOFI	7000	7000	01	01	ERL	14003	
V	KOFI	7000	7000	01	01	ERS	23040	
V	KOFI	7000	7000	01	01	ERU	5500	
V	KOFI	7000	7000	01	01	ZFD	23030	
V	KOFI	7000	7000	01	01	ZRF	23020	
V	KOFI	7000	7000	01	01	ZTD	23040	

Figure 7.25 Assign GL Account to Account Determination Type

In Figure 7.25, the fourth and fifth columns have the same heading AAG (Account Assignment Group). The first one is the account assignment group for customers, and the second one is for account assignment groups for materials. These groups are simply a group of customers or materials that are identical from an accounts posting point of view. For example, all customers from one country (e.g., Mexico) can be one account assignment group (for customers), and all trading materials have one account assignment group (for materials). Therefore, the sale of such a material made to such a customer will go to one specific GL account (e.g., Mexico trading account). These account assignment groups are maintained in the customer master record (Billing Document tab of Sales Area data) and material master record (Sales:Sales Org 2 tab) for individual customers or materials, respectively. You can create new account assignment groups for materials using Transaction OVK5 (menu path: SAP IMG • SALES AND DISTRIBUTION • BASIC FUNCTIONS • ACCOUNT ASSIGNMENT/COSTING • CHECK MASTER DATA RELEVANT FOR ACCOUNT ASSIGNMENT • MATERIALS: ACCOUNT ASSIGNMENT GROUPS). You can create new account assignment groups for customers using Transaction OVK8 (menu path: SAP IMG • SALES AND DISTRIBUTION • BASIC FUNCTIONS • ACCOUNT ASSIGNMENT/COSTING • CHECK MASTER DATA RELEVANT FOR ACCOUNT ASSIGNMENT • CUSTOMERS: ACCOUNT ASSIGNMENT GROUPS). Defining and assigning customer and material assignment accounts is prerequisite for account determination. We covered these customizations in Chapter 2.

Now that you understand how revenue accounts are determined, let's discuss the accounts interface for billing.

7.6 Accounts Interface

In this section, we'll discuss various topics related to the Sales and Distribution–Financial Accounting interface in SAP ERP. We'll specifically discuss revenue recognition, reconciliation account determination, cash account determination, and data that's transferred to accounting from invoices.

7.6.1 Revenue Recognition

To use the revenue recognition functionality of SAP ERP, you need explicit permission from the SAP system (see SAP Note 820417). You can get the best practice guide (in PDF format) for implementing revenue recognition functionality in SAP Note 1172799. SAP Note 1323315 is also very helpful for implementing revenue recognition. You customize revenue recognition for any sales item category using Transaction OVEP (menu path: SAP IMG • SALES AND DISTRIBUTION • BASIC FUNCTIONS • ACCOUNT ASSIGNMENT/COSTING • REVENUE RECOGNITION • SET REVENUE RECOGNITION FOR ITEM CATEGORIES). The initial overview screen lists all of the existing item categories. Double-click on any item category to view the customization. In customization, four fields — revenue recognition category, accrual period start date, revenue distribution type, and revenue event — are specified for the item category.

The revenue recognition category for an item category is specified. It can take any of the following six options:

- **Blank:** The revenue for this item category is recognized at the time of invoice creation (standard option).
- **A:** The value of this item category is recognized for the same amounts according to the accrual period.
- **B:** Revenue is recognized based on business transactions (e.g., goods receipt for delivery-relevant items, sales order creation for items not relevant to delivery).
- **D:** The value of the item is implemented in equal amounts in accordance with the accrual period for this item (billing-related).
- **E:** Billing-related, service-related revenue recognition (IS-M).
- **F:** Credit and debit memos with reference to predecessor.

The accrual period start date can take any of the following three options

- **Blank:** Not relevant.
- **A:** Proposal based on contract start date.
- **B:** Proposal based on billing plan start date. For milestone billing plans, this is the billing date of the first milestone. For periodic billing plans it's either the billing plan start date or the date of the first settlement period, whichever is earlier.

The revenue distribution type can take any of the following four options.

- **Blank:** The total value is linear, and the correction value is not distributed.
- **A:** The total value is linear, and the correction value linearly distributed.
- **B:** The total value is Bill.Plan-Reld, and the correction value is not distributed.

- **C:** The total value is Bill.Plan-Reld, and the correction value is linearly distributed.

The revenue event is the event that determines revenue recognition. The possible options it can take are:

- **Blank:** Not event-related.
- **A:** Incoming invoice.
- **B:** Acceptance date.
- **X/Y/Z:** Customer-specific event X/Y/Z, which are defined in the BADI for the specific event.

The customization done in the Sales and Distribution functionality in SAP ERP is only part of the overall customization done in SAP ERP Financials. So before doing the customization, be sure to read the SAP notes mentioned at the beginning of this section, understand the limitations of the revenue recognition functionality, and work with an SAP ERP Financials consultant.

7.6.2 Reconciliation Account Determination

The customer reconciliation account is maintained in the customer master record (Account Management tab of Company Code Data). The offsetting entry for the revenue accounts is posted to this reconciliation GL, so when you make a sale, the accounting entries look like:

- Cr Sales Revenue – 100 USD
- Cr Tax Payable – 5 USD
  - Dr Customer Reconciliation Account – 105 USD

You can use a condition technique for reconciliation account determination, similar to the revenue account determination we discussed earlier in this chapter. The steps for customizing the condition technique are available via the menu path SAP IMG • SALES AND DISTRIBUTION • BASIC FUNCTIONS • ACCOUNT ASSIGNMENT/COSTING • RECONCILIATION ACCOUNT DETERMINATION. At this node of the menu path, you have the following options for customizing the condition technique:

- Maintain Condition Tables (Transaction OV62)
- Maintain Field Catalog (Transaction OV60)
- Maintain Access Sequences (Transaction OV67)

- Maintain Condition Types (Transaction OV66)
- Maintain Account Determination Procedure (Transaction OV65)
- Assign Account Determination Procedure (Transaction OV68)
- Assign G/L Accounts (Transaction OV64)
- Define Alternative Reconciliation Accounts (Transaction S_ALR_87002480)

7.6.3 Cash Account Determination

A cash account can be involved in a sales invoice (e.g., credit memo). For example, instead of issuing credit memos that are used as payments for other purchases by the customer, you may want to issue a check for the credit memo. In such a situation, the cash account to be posted can be determined using a condition technique just like you do for revenue or reconciliation account determination. The steps for customizing cash account determination are available via the menu path SAP IMG • SALES AND DISTRIBUTION • BASIC FUNCTIONS • ACCOUNT ASSIGNMENT/COSTING • CASH ACCOUNT DETERMINATION. At this node, you can branch into any of the following IMG activities for customizing the condition technique:

- Maintain Condition Tables (Transaction OV71)
- Maintain Field Catalog (Transaction OV73)
- Maintain Access Sequences (Transaction OV74)
- Maintain Condition Types (Transaction OV75)
- Maintain Account Determination Procedure (Transaction OV76)
- Assign Account Determination Procedure (Transaction OV78)
- Assign G/L Accounts (Transaction OV77)

7.6.4 Data Forwarded to Accounting Document

Various data from billing documents of Sales and Distribution are transferred to the SAP ERP Financials accounting documents. In our discussion of the customization of billing types, we've covered how the following data is determined for accounting document based on the information available in billing document.

1. Accounting document type
2. Reference number (BKPF-XBLNR)
3. Allocation number (BSEG-ZUONR)

4. Partner function for accounting document

5. Invoice reference (BSEG-REBZG)

> **How To Make an Accounting Document Number the Same as an Invoice Number**
>
> By default, the number range assigned to accounting document types used to create accounting documents for invoices is the internal number range. There's no provision for manually entering a number for the accounting document of a bill, so the question of making it external does not arise. But if you make the number range the same as that for a billing document type and select the checkbox for external assignment, the accounting document number will be same as that of the billing document. Because several billing document types can have the same accounting document type, the number range for the accounting document type should be such that all of the number ranges for billing document types assigned to it fall within its number range. At the same time, the number range cannot overlap with the number range of any other accounting document type. Much time is wasted on tracking the billing document and corresponding accounting document and vice versa for error handling. Also, it becomes very complicated to link them in an ABAP report when they're different numbers.

7.7 Some Billing Related Problems and Their Solutions

We've included some common errors or queries that are expected of a junior- or middle-level consultant, especially in a post-implementation scenario. Most of the problems that come from super-users or junior-level consultants are of two types: mistakes in configuration or customization. We've avoided these because they would have been repetitions of what we've already covered. Errors due to customized reports, user exits, or routines are also not covered, because they're project specific. Most of these problems you can regenerate in a test environment. That was also a criterion for including any problem in this list.

- **Problem:** We have a large invoice to cancel. It should take few minutes to cancel, but each time we attempt to cancel it, we have a timeout and are unable to cancel the invoice. We can't find any options for executing the transaction for invoice cancellation, Transaction VF11, in the background.
  Solution: It isn't possible to execute Transaction VF11 in the background, so when an invoice is too large or you have included multiple invoices for cancellation, the time-out situation may arise. Your only option is to increase the time limit for the time out. You can do this by changing the time limit for the parameter rdisp/max_wprun_time using Transaction RZ11. You go to the screen

shown in Figure 7.26 when you enter the parameter rdisp/max_wprun_time in the initial screen of Transaction RZ11 and execute it. To change the existing values, click on the Change Values button, and the dialog box also shown in Figure 7.26 will appear. This is where you change the values of the parameter. Be sure to review SAP Note 25528 before attempting this.

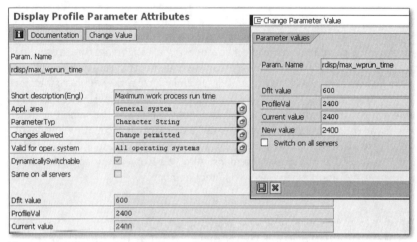

Figure 7.26 Changing Values of Parameter of rdisp/max_wprun_time

▶ **Problem:** We have few materials that are tax free, so we've made a tax code for 0% tax. This works fine until we have to create the invoice. While releasing it to accounts, we're getting the error shown below. Because there will be no value to be posted to accounts, we haven't assigned it to any GL. Even if we do, how can there be an accounting document with a zero value line item?

ERROR MESSAGE:

Error in account determination: table T030K key CANA MWS U7

Message no. FF709

Diagnosis

In the chart of accounts to be posted to, no accounts are defined for the tax code you used.

Procedure

Contact your system administrator.

Define the accounts to which a tax posting are to be made with the tax code entered in Customizing for taxes on sales/purchases.

To do this, choose Maintain entries ([F5]).

Solution: Table T030K is maintained using Transaction OB40, where you can maintain a GL for tax code U7 Transaction MWS in the chart of account CANA even when no posting is required. You can do this by executing Transaction FTXP, entering the tax code in the initial screen, and then executing and clicking on the Tax Accounts button. Selecting the chart of account (e.g., CANA) will take you to a dialog box where you have to maintain the GL accounts for different transaction keys (e.g., MWS). Note that when using Transaction FTXP, you can maintain GL accounts even when the client is not modifiable, which is not the case for Transaction OB40. Because the document value and hence the accounting document value will not be zero, there will be no error in posting to accounting. The tax GL that you've assigned to tax code U7 will, however, have no entry even after posting. If you open the accounting document using Transaction FB02/03 (or by clicking on the Accounting button from the VF02/03 overview screen) and click on the Taxes button, you'll see the screen shown in Figure 7.27.

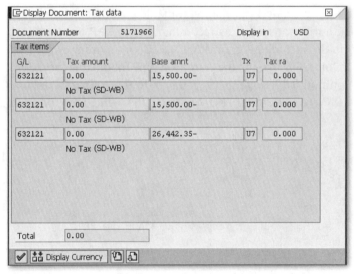

Figure 7.27 Tax Data of Accounting Document for Zero Tax Value

- **Problem:** We have a customized report using Transactions S066 and S067. Currently, we are facing serious performance issues for the report. It's taking too much time, and we noticed that these tables contain many line items with zero value (or a negligible amount, e.g., 0.01). How can we improve the performance of the report?

Solution: Run report program RVKRED77 at regular intervals. Be sure to refer to SAP Note 400311 for details.

▶ **Problem:** We've using the standard pricing condition type PR00 in both the pricing procedure for invoice (billing type F2) and pro forma invoice (billing type F8). In both cases, we've maintained condition records that are automatically determined during billing. We don't want any manual changes during billing. In the customization for the condition type PR00, we've opted for option D (Not Possible to Process Manually) in the Manual Entries field. Also, in the copy control from order to invoice (Transaction VTFA), we've opted for option G (Copy Pricing Elements Unchanged and Redetermine Taxes) for the item categories. The same condition type should be modifiable manually in a pro forma invoice without changing the customization for the invoice. Is it possible?

Solution: In the standard SAP system, there's no provision for making a condition type modifiable in certain cases and nonmodifiable in others. For this you have to use exits. For doing it in order, use the user exit USEREXIT_PRICING_PREPARE_TKOMP in the include program MV45AFZZ. If the objective is to make it modifiable for certain users and nonmodifiable for others, you can create a customized authorization object as recommended in SAP Note 105621. Then code the exit in the include program MV45AFZZ for an order or program RV60AFZZ for an invoice. For making the condition type modifiable for the F8 invoice type and nonmodifiable for others, you can do the coding in the user exit USEREXIT_PRICING_PREPARE_TKOMP of the include program RV60AFZZ.

```
FORM USEREXIT_PRICING_PREPARE_TKOMP.
DATA: i_T685A TYPE STANDARD TABLE OF T685A WITH HEADER LINE.
IF VBRK-FKART = 'F8'.
 LOOP AT XKOMV.
 IF XKOMV-KSCHL = 'PR00'.
 SELECT * FROM T685A INTO TABLE I_T685A WHERE KSCHL = 'PR00'.
 READ TABLE I_T685A WITH KEY KSCHL = XKOMV-KSCHL.
 I_T685A-KMANU = 'C'.
 MODIFY I_T685A INDEX SY-TABIX.
 MODIFY T685A FROM TABLE I_T685A.
 REFRESH I_T685A.
 ENDIF.
 ENDLOOP.
 ELSE.
 LOOP AT XKOMV.
```

```
IF XKOMV-KSCHL = 'PR00'.
SELECT * FROM T685A INTO TABLE I_T685A WHERE KSCHL = 'PR00'.
READ TABLE I_T685A WITH KEY KSCHL = XKOMV-KSCHL.
I_T685A-KMANU = 'D'.
MODIFY I_T685A INDEX SY-TABIX.
MODIFY T685A FROM TABLE I_T685A.
REFRESH I_T685A.
ENDIF.
ENDLOOP.
ENDIF.
ENDFORM.
```

▶ **Problem:** We want to send daily short message service (SMS) to customers for invoices created. We're in touch with a company that provides an HTTP API for sending bulk SMS. Can we use it to send SMS from our SAP server?

Solution: There are a lot of bulk SMS service providers who provide you with HTTP APIs. The advantage to using such services is the cost benefit, whereas the risk is data security. An example of one such provider is clickatell.com. Their API is *http://api.clickatell.com/http/sendmsg?user=xxxxx&password=xxxxx&api_id=xxxxx&to=xxxxxxxxxx&text=Hello+World*. After registration, most such providers give a few free credits to test their service. After getting the user, password, and api_id (it varies), you can insert those values in place of "xxxxx" in the API string. After "to=" you replace "xxxxxxxxxx" with the mobile number to which you want to send the message. The message in the sample API string is "Hello World." You test it by typing the whole string in the address window (where you type the website address) of any browser and press Enter. If the message reaches the intended number, then the HTTP API is ready for use. You can use the following code to enter the parameters of the API in the selection screen and execute to post the message.

```
REPORT ZSMS.
DATA: http_client TYPE REF TO if_http_client.
DATA: wf_string TYPE string,
result TYPE string,
r_str TYPE string.
DATA: result_tab TYPE TABLE OF string.

SELECTION-SCREEN: BEGIN OF BLOCK a WITH FRAME.
PARAMETERS: USER(20) LOWER CASE,
PASSWORD(20) LOWER CASE,
APIID(20) LOWER CASE,
```

```abap
    TO(50) LOWER CASE.

    TEXT(160) LOWER CASE,
    SELECTION-SCREEN: END OF BLOCK a.

    START-OF-SELECTION.
     CLEAR wf_string.
     CONCATENATE
    'http://api.clickatell.com/http/sendmsg?user='
     USER
     '&password='
     PASSWORD
    '&api_id='
     APIID
     '&to='
     TO

     '&text='
     TEXT
    INTO
     wf_string.

    CALL METHOD cl_http_client=>create_by_url
    EXPORTING url = wf_string
    IMPORTING client = http_client
    EXCEPTIONS argument_not_found = 1
    plugin_not_active = 2
    internal_error = 3
    OTHERS = 4.

    CALL METHOD http_client->send
    EXCEPTIONS
    http_communication_failure = 1
    http_invalid_state = 2.

    CALL METHOD http_client->receive
    EXCEPTIONS
    http_communication_failure = 1
    http_invalid_state = 2
    http_processing_failed = 3.
    CLEAR result.
    result = http_client->response->get_cdata( ).
```

```
REFRESH result_tab.
SPLIT result AT cl_abap_char_utilities=>cr_lf INTO TABLE result_tab.
LOOP AT result_tab INTO r_str.
WRITE:/ r_str.
ENDLOOP.
```

Note that for some service providers, the API may contain an IP address instead of a valid domain name as given below:

http://196.5.254.66/http/sendmsg?user=xxxxx&password=xxxxx&api_id=xxxxx&to =xxxxxxxxx&text=Hello+World

In such cases, you have to change it to a valid domain name because the SAP server cannot use IP addresses, though from a browser you won't have any problem. The message should not contain special characters such as ?, & or =, because they have specific uses in an API string.

Once you are able to post messages from your SAP server, the next step is to trigger the message for different events and customize the content of the message, such as invoice creation. You can also schedule the program as a background job.

▶ **Problem:** We're getting the error message "Posting period 005 2200 is not open. Message no. F5201" while trying to release a billing document to accounts. The accounting document is not getting generated.

Solution: After you release the billing document, an accounting document is generated. The posting date of the accounting document becomes the same as the billing date of the billing document. In the system, you allow the users of a particular company code to allow posting of accounting documents only for a specific time interval using Transaction OB52. If the billing date and the subsequent posting date of the accounting document don't fall in the allowed periods, then the accounting document will not be generated, and you'll get the above error message. In this case, it seems that rather than the allowed accounting period, you have to change the billing date, which as per the error message is the fifth period of the year 2200 (May if the accounting year is the same as the calendar year, August if the accounting year is April to March, as practiced in many countries). There's probably a typing error. You can rectify it by following the menu path GOTO • HEADER • HEADER from the overview screen of the invoice using Transaction VF02 and changing the billing date as shown in Figure 7.28.

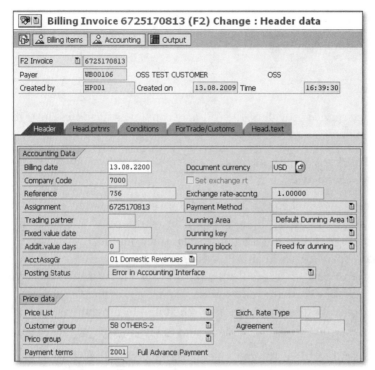

Figure 7.28 Change Billing Date

- **Problem:** While saving an invoice, we're getting the error "Foreign Trade Data is Incomplete." Why is this (especially because it's a domestic invoice)?
  Solution: There can be several reasons for it. Follow the menu path GOTO • HEADER • FOREIGN TRADE/CUSTOMS and click on the Incompleteness Analysis icon (shown in Figure 7.29) to identify the data that is not complete. Also check if in the order for this invoice, the shipping point is deleted. The possibility of this being the trouble is very high because you've mentioned that it's a domestic sale. Also read SAP Note 354222 (Foreign Trade Data Incomplete for Domestic Business) to understand the problem.

- **Problem:** We've activated number range buffering in our organization, but for our U.S. subsidiary, this feature has created trouble. There are times when the invoice numbers are not consecutive. We want to deactivate the number range buffering for U.S. invoices but not for the other countries.
  Solution: Use the following code in the FORM USEREXIT_NUMBER_RANGE USING US_RANGE_INTERN of the include program RV60AFZZ. Refer to SAP Notes 23835, 424486, and 363901 for details.

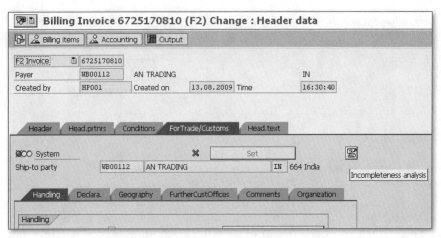

Figure 7.29 Incompleteness Analysis of Foreign Trade Data

```
DATA: LS_T001 LIKE T001.
DATA: LD_I_INTCA LIKE T005-INTCA.
CALL FUNCTION 'FI_COMPANY_CODE_DATA'
EXPORTING
I_BUKRS = XVBRK-BUKRS
IMPORTING
E_T001 = LS_T001.
CALL FUNCTION 'COUNTRY_CODE_SAP_TO_ISO'
EXPORTING
SAP_CODE = LS_T001-LAND1
IMPORTING
ISO_CODE = LD_I_INTCA.
IF LD_I_INTCA EQ 'US'.
NO_BUFFER = 'X'.
ENDIF.
```

- **Problem:** Some sales documents are shown as open documents in Transaction VA05N. They are also present in the billing due list, and their status is open in Tables VBUK and VBUP. But as per the document flow, we find that subsequent documents are created, and their status should have been complete.
  Solution: To stop these documents from appearing in the document due list, use the report program SDVBUK00. This program will update the document status. In Transaction SE38, enter the program name (SDVBUK00) and press the [F8] key. You'll go to the screen shown in Figure 7.30.

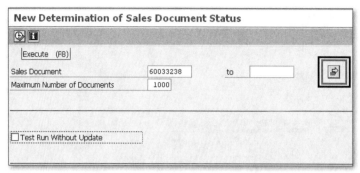

Figure 7.30 New Determination of Sales Document Status

Click on the Multiple Selection icon highlighted in the figure and enter all of the documents whose status you want to be redetermined. Unselect the Test Run Without Update checkbox. You can do a test run without unselecting it. In this case, you'll get a report, but the document status won't change. When you run the report with this criteria, the statuses of documents are rectified and updated. Refer to SAP Note 207875 for more details.

▶ **Problem:** Our accounting department has found an instance where the figures of a billing document in Sales and Distribution do not match the figures in an accounting document. We have not found the reason for this error or any other document with a similar problem. Is there any way to confirm that there is no such error in our system?
Solution: Run the report SDFI_CONSISTENCY_CHECK by doing the following steps.

1. Enter Transaction SE38.

2. In the Program field of the initial screen, enter the program name "SDFI_CONSISTENCY_CHECK."

3. Press [F8].

4. The selection screen will appear.

5. Enter the company code, fiscal year, and period (01 for January, 02 for February, and so on if the fiscal year is the same as the calendar year) for which the report is required. You can run it for few documents by specifying the document number in the selection screen.

6. Press [F8] to run a check. The screen shown in Figure 7.31 will appear.

Some Billing Related Problems and Their Solutions | **7.7**

7. Select the Difference Amnt column and click on the Summation icon. If the total in the Difference column is zero, everything is likely to be OK.

8. Select the Totals tab. Figure 7.31 shows the Differences tab. In the Totals tab, GL-related totals are available. In the Differences tab, the totals are document-related.

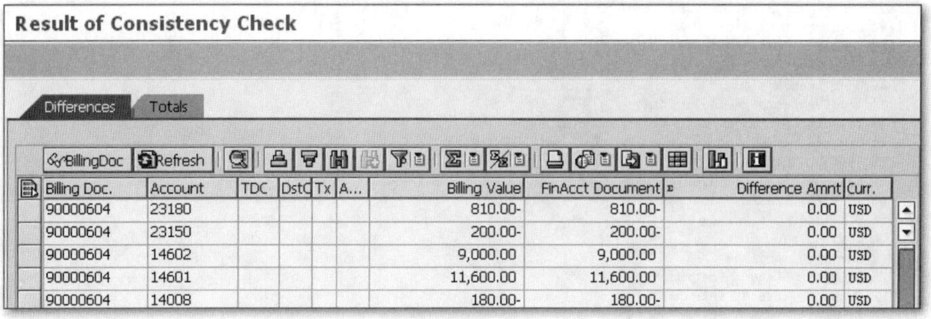

Result of Consistency Check

Billing Doc.	Account	TDC	Dstc	Tx	A...	Billing Value	FinAcct Document	≠	Difference Amnt	Curr.
90000604	23180					810.00	810.00-		0.00	USD
90000604	23150					200.00-	200.00-		0.00	USD
90000604	14602					9,000.00	9,000.00		0.00	USD
90000604	14601					11,600.00	11,600.00		0.00	USD
90000604	14008					180.00-	180.00-		0.00	USD

Figure 7.31 Result of Consistency Check for Audit

▶ **Problem:** We've been asked to provide a report on tax codes and the GL assigned to them for automatic posting. Is there any standard report for this?
Solution: You can use the standard report SAPUFKB1 for this purpose, which actually is meant for auditing. Execute the following steps:

1. Enter the program name SAPUFKB1 in the Program field in the initial screen of Transaction SE38.

2. Press [F8].

3. In the screen that appears, enter the chart of account (e.g., CANA) and company code (e.g., US01) for which report is required.

4. The screen shown in Figure 7.32 will appear. The screen lists all of the possible automatic accounting postings in the system.

5. Select the f%TX – Sales/pur. Tax checkbox. This option will give you the details about the GL assigned for automatic tax posting.

6. Press [F8].

7. The report will provide the information you need. If there's a tax code for which a GL is not assigned, you'll be able to see this and rectify it. The same thing can be done for other auto-postings scenarios (e.g., posting to revenue accounts). This is a kind of preventive maintenance.

7 | Billing

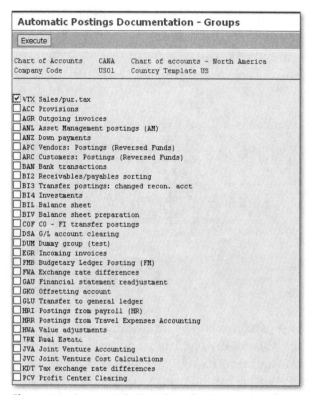

Figure 7.32 Automatic Postings (e.g., Tax Accounts) Audit

▶ **Problem:** We cancelled a credit memo, so the credit memo request for it is no longer required. When we attempt to delete it, we get an error message (see Figure 7.33). Because we cancelled the subsequent document (credit memo), why should it show such an error?

Solution: For normal sales processing of an order, delivery, and billing, if you want to cancel the order after creation of the bill, the following steps are required:

1. Cancel the invoice using Transaction VF02.
2. Reverse the PGI of the delivery using Transaction VL09.
3. Delete the delivery using Transaction VL02N.

Some Billing Related Problems and Their Solutions | 7.7

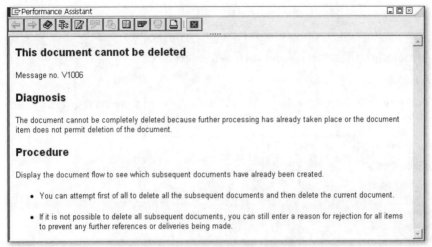

Figure 7.33 Error Message While Deleting Credit Memo Request of Cancelled Credit Memo

4. Delete the sales order using Transaction VA02.

In this situation, note that the subsequent document for the order, that is, the delivery, doesn't exist. However, the situation for a credit memo or debit memo is slightly different because there's no delivery in between. The invoices (e.g., credit memos) cannot be deleted and are only cancelled if required. In this situation, the standard practice is to do either of the following or both:

1. Reject all items of the credit memo request.
2. Change the quantity (and hence the value) to zero. Thus, everybody will ignore the zero-value open order.

If neither option suits you, you can do the following to delete the credit memo requests of the cancelled credit memos:

1. Go to Transaction SE16N.
2. Enter the table name "VBFA."
3. Activate the function &SAP_EDIT.
4. Select the lines for the credit memo request. The line linking the request to the credit memo and the document that cancelled the credit memo (S2 type invoice) will appear.
5. Delete all of the rows for this credit memo request.
6. Go to Transaction SE38.

7. Run the report program SDVBFA01.
8. In the selection screen, enter the credit memo request number.
9. Unselect the Test Run Without Update checkbox.
10. Execute.
11. In Transaction VA02, you can now delete the credit memo request.

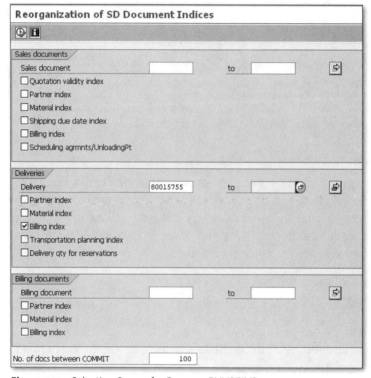

Figure 7.34 Selection Screen for Program RVV05IVB

- **Problem:** We found several deliveries in a billing due list (VF04) that should not be there. These deliveries are already billed. Is there any way rectify this error?
  Solution: Refer to SAP Note 128947. As suggested in the note, run the standard program RVV05IVB using Transaction SE38. In the selection screen, you'll find 14 checkboxes for updating indices, shown in Figure 7.34. In Table 7.9, we've listed the database tables corresponding to the checkboxes. The list in Table 7.9 is in the same sequence as the corresponding checkboxes (see Figure 7.34). So

to update the billing due list for deliveries, select the ninth checkbox. The list of deliveries that are to be updated appears in the selection list. Also select the Billing Index checkbox in the Deliveries frame, as shown in Figure 7.34. Execute the program by pressing the F8 key.

No.	Table	Table Description	Transaction
1	VAKGU	Sales Index: Quotation Validity	VA25
2	VAKPA	Sales Index: Orders by Partner Function	VA05
3	VAPMA	Sales Index: Order Items by Material	VA05
4	VEPVG	Delivery Due Index	VL04
5	VKDFS	SD Index: Billing Initiator	VF04, VF24
6	VLPKM	Scheduling Agreements by Customer Material	VA25
7	VLKPA	SD Index: Deliveries by Partner Functions	VL05, VL06
8	VLPMA	SD Index: Delivery Items by Material	VL05, VL06
9	VKDFS	SD Index: Billing Initiator	VF04, VF24
10	VTRDI	Shipment Planning Index	VT01, VT04
11	VRSLI	Receipt of Materials from Deliveries	ME2O
12	VRKPA	Sales Index: Bills by Partner Functions	VF05
13	VRPMA	SD Index: Billing Items per Material	VF05
14	VKDFS	SD Index: Billing Initiator	VF04, VF24

Table 7.9 Tables Updated by Program RVV05IVB

- **Problem:** We've have found a billing document that has not updated a sales infostructure. Is there any way to manually update an info-structure?
  Solution: Refer to SAP Note 174141. The update programs are listed below.

  1. Update SIS for orders (or old orders): RMCVNEUA
  2. Update SIS for deliveries (or old deliveries): RMCVNEUL
  3. Update SIS for invoices (or old invoices): RMCVNEUF

7.8 Summary

In this chapter, we've discussed how invoices are processed in SAP ERP. You learned about the steps involved in the customization of billing types, complaints reasons, billing plans, and revenue account determination. In the accounts interface, you also learned how to use the condition technique for reconciliation and cash account determination. We discussed how revenue reorganization can be modified, and you should now understand how the accounting document can take the billing document number. In the last part of this chapter, we listed some of the common errors for billing and their solutions. After reading this chapter, you are now well equipped to optimize billing processes. You should also be able to provide number ranges for billing documents in all possible scenarios and know how to do account determination.

In the next chapter, you'll learn about text processing, message control, Web interfaces, batch management, ABAP tools, LSMW tools, and numbering objects.

This chapter covers the topics that are useful but haven't yet been fully covered elsewhere in the book. Many of these topics are relevant not only for Sales and Distribution, but for other SAP ERP functionalities as well.

8   Cross-Functional Customization

There are several functions that are not specific to the Sales and Distribution functionality in SAP ERP. These functions can also be used in other components. For example, batch management is important not only for sales and distribution, but also for purchasing, inventory management, and production planning. We've touched on many of these topics in previous chapters, but in this chapter, we'll provide the overview, with details, that you need to understand what they are and how they impact your day to day work.

In this chapter, we'll cover topics including text processing, message control, Web interfaces, batch management, ABAP tools, and numbering objects. So, let's get started.

8.1   Text Processing

The "cockpit" transaction for text processing in Sales and Distribution is Transaction VOTXN, as shown in Figure 8.1. All of the text objects are listed with a radio button in this screen, so you can customize any one of these 16 text objects one at a time. Note that all of the text objects that you encounter in Sales and Distribution are listed here, with a few exceptions (e.g., texts used in credit management, accounting text of customer master records). The customization technique used for text processing is primarily a condition technique, which by now you should be quite comfortable with. VOFM routines also play a crucial role in text processing. Table 8.1 lists all of the text objects you can customize using Transaction VOTXN. Note that for sales, delivery, and billing documents, the text objects for header and item texts are same. It is the text group that differentiates them.

8 | Cross-Functional Customization

> **Note**
>
> To use the information stored in the text fields of a document in an ABAP report, you cannot reference it by the table field as you do for other fields. For example, sales document number is referred to as VBAK-VBELN in ABAP reports. VBAK is the table for sales document header and VBELN which store the document number is one of its many fields. The content of a text is transferred to an ABAP report using the function module READ_TEXT. To read the text of a particular document or record, you have to specify the text name, language, text ID, and text object. You'll become familiar with these terms as you go along in this chapter.

Text Object	Code	Text Group
Customer – Header	KNA1	G (Customer: Header Texts)
Customer – Contact Person	KNVK	I (Customer: Contact Person Texts)
Customer – Sales Area	KNVV	J (Customer: Sales Texts)
Customer/Material Info Record	KNMT	O (Customer/Material Info Record)
Pricing Agreements	KONA	M (Agreements)
Pricing Condition Records	KONP	N (Conditions)
Sales Document – Header	VBBK	A (Sales Document Header)
Sales Document – Item	VBBP	D (Sales Document Item)
Delivery – Header	VBBK	B (Delivery Header)
Delivery – Item	VBBP	E (Delivery Item)
Billing Document – Header	VBBK	C (Billing Header)
Billing Document – Item	VBBP	F (Billing Item)
Sales Activity – General Texts	VBKA	K (Sales Activities)
Shipment – Header	VTTK	L (Transportation Header)
Financial Doc. – General Texts	AKKP	W (Documentary Payment)
Legal Control – General Texts	EMBK	X (Legal Control)
Agency Business – Header	WBRK	P (Agency Business Header)
Agency Business – Item	WBRP	Q (Agency Business Item)
Trading Contract – Header	WBHK	Y (Trading Contract Header)
Trading Contract – Item	WBHI	Z (Trading Contract Item)

Table 8.1 Text Objects Customized Using Transaction VOTXN

> **Note**
> The text fields for a document can store any amount of text in. Only the first line of the text is visible. To view (or change or add) the complete text, double-click on it.

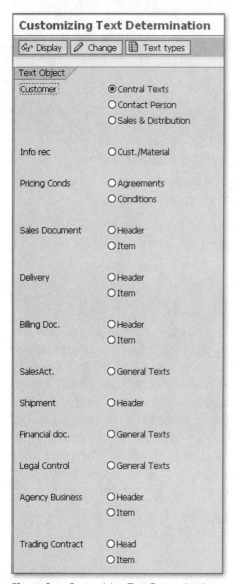

Figure 8.1 Customizing Text Determination

> **Note**
> Only the text fields can be changed when the document becomes practically nonmodifiable, such as the billing document after posting to accounting and delivery after PGI. You can use this feature of text fields to store some qualitative information (e.g., the customer has informed you that he received the material too early).

The steps for customizing text determination, which uses a condition technique, are as follows:

1. Define the text IDs for text objects.
2. Create the text determination procedure.
3. Assign text IDs to the text determination procedure.
4. Define the access sequence if automatic determination is required.
5. Assign the text determination procedure to a document type, customer account group, or as required for the specific text object and text group.

Let's discuss each of these steps in detail in the follow subsections. In Section 8.1.6, we'll discuss the text determination analysis, which analyzes whether and how the text is automatically proposed.

8.1.1 Text IDs

Text IDs, or text types, are created for specific text objects. In the screen shown in Figure 8.1, select the radio button of the text object for which you want to create the text IDs and click on the Text Types button in the application toolbar. You'll get an information message: "Caution: The table is cross-client." This means changes in any one client of a server will automatically be made to all other clients of the server. Typically, except for a production server, all others have multiple clients. When you press [Enter] or click on the Continue (checkmark) icon, you go to the screen shown in Figure 8.2. All of the existing text IDs for text objects are available here. You can change the description of any text ID to fit your purposes or create your own IDs by copying one and giving it a new key (starting with Y or Z) and description.

Note

The text IDs are specific to text objects, not text groups (third column in Table 8.1). That means a text ID created for sales document header will automatically be available for the delivery header and billing header. The text object for all three are the same: VBBK. The text groups are different.

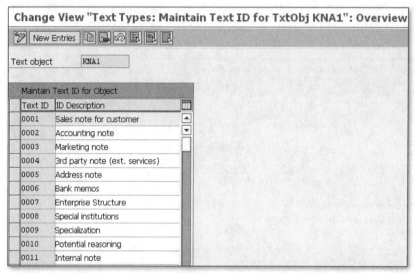

Figure 8.2 Text IDs for the Text Object KNA1 (Customer Master Header)

Note

You can save text in multiple languages for a text item. You can use this functionality while taking an output (e.g., for an invoice) in different languages. Also, you can create standard text using Transaction SO10 and use it in outputs.

8.1.2 Text Determination Procedure

The text determination procedure (or text procedure) is created for a combination of text object and text group. In Figure 8.1, select the radio button of the object (text object plus group) that the text determination procedure will be created or modified for. Click on the Change (pencil) icon in the application toolbar, and you'll go to the screen shown in Figure 8.3. All of the existing text determination procedures are available as a list on the right side of the screen. To create a new one, select any existing procedure and click on the Copy As ([F6]) icon. A new dialog box will appear as shown in Figure 8.4. Select the Copy All option, if you want to copy the text IDs already assigned to the reference procedure to the new procedure to be created. You can copy only the text determination procedure and assign text IDs as we'll explain in the next step. Also, it's important to remember that the text determination procedure is for the combination of text object and text group, so the text determination procedure for the sales document header is not relevant for either the delivery header or the billing header.

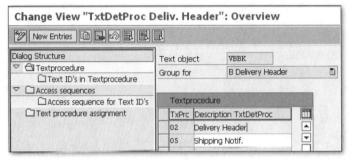

Figure 8.3 Text Determination Procedure

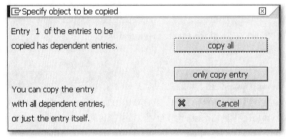

Figure 8.4 Copy Text IDs Along with Text Determination Procedure

8.1.3 Assigning Text IDs to a Text Determination Procedure

To modify the text IDs assigned to a text determination procedure or to assign new text IDs to it, you can double-click on the text IDs in the Text Procedure folder, as shown in Figure 8.5. The text IDs are listed in sequence as they'll appear in the object (e.g., customer master record). You can also specify whether the text is referenced or duplicated, if it is mandatory, and the access sequence for the text ID. As we saw in the other use of condition techniques, in Chapter 4, there's is no separate step for assigning an access sequence to a text type (equivalent of a condition type). Also note that the sequence is valid for a specific combination of text object (e.g., VBBK), text group (e.g., B delivery header), and text determination procedure (e.g., 02 delivery header).

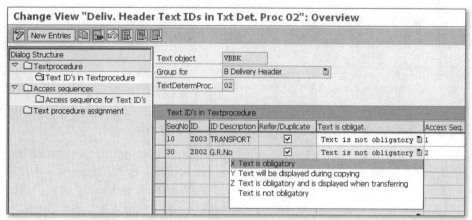

Figure 8.5 Assigning Text IDs to a Text Determination Procedure

8.1.4 Define Access Sequence

To create or change the access sequence, you can double-click on the Access Sequences folder. The list of all existing sequences appears, and you can create a new one by selecting any existing one, clicking on the Copy As (F6) icon, and providing a new key and description. By clicking on the Copy All icon, you'll copy all of the existing accesses in the reference access sequence, which are modifiable. Like the text determination procedure, and unlike the text types, the access sequence is valid for a combination of text objects and text groups. Therefore, an access sequence created for the sales document header doesn't become valid for either the delivery header or the billing header. After creating an access sequence, you can modify, add, or delete the existing accesses. For this you select any existing access sequence and select the access sequence for text ID's folder. As shown in Figure 8.6, you can maintain the text IDs along with their text object in different accesses. In the Partner Function column, you specify the partner function to be used if the text is to be copied from the customer master record to a document, and in the Language column, you specify the language of choice.

8 | Cross-Functional Customization

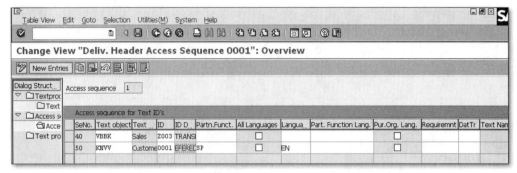

Figure 8.6 Access Sequence 0001 for Text Object VBBK (Sale Doc Header)

8.1.5 Assignment of Text Determination Procedure

You assign the text determination procedures by clicking on the Text Procedure Assignment folder. As shown in Figure 8.6, it's assigned to the delivery types in case of the text object Delivery Header (text object VBBK and text group B). The assignment for a customer master record text is not required because automatic determination for is not relevant. Text fields are to be manually maintained by going to EXTRAS • TEXTS from the General, Contact Person, or Sales Area screens for general, contact person, and sales area texts, respectively. You can assign the text determination procedure by selecting the Text Procedure Assignment folder, shown in Figure 8.7. The assignment is based on the text object and text group. For a different combination of text object and text group, the assignment of the text determination procedure is done as per the list shown in Table 8.2. Even when automatic determination is not required, this step is valid for maintaining the text manually.

Description	Text Obj. – Text Group	Text Determination Procedure Is Assigned to
Customer – Header	KNA1 – G	Customer account groups
Customer – Contact Person	KNVK – I	Customer account groups
Customer – Sales Area	KNVV – J	Customer account groups
Cust./Material Info Record	KNMT – O	Customer account groups
Pricing Agreements	KONA – M	Agreement types
Pricing Condition Records	KONP – N	Condition types
Sales Document – Header	VBBK – A	Sales document types

Table 8.2 Assignment of Different Text Objects

Description	Text Obj. – Text Group	Text Determination Procedure Is Assigned to
Sales Document – Item	VBBP – D	Sales item categories
Delivery – Header	VBBK – B	Delivery document types
Delivery – Item	VBBP – E	Delivery item categories
Billing Document – Header	VBBK – C	Billing types
Billing Document – Item	VBBP – F	Billing types
Sales Activity – General Texts	VBKA – K	Sales activity types
Shipment – Header	VTTK – L	Shipment types
Financial Doc. – General Texts	AKKP – W	Financial document indicators
Legal Control – General Texts	EMBK – X	Legal regulations plus types
Agency Business – Header	WBRK – P	Billing types (agency business)
Agency Business – Item	WBRP – Q	Billing types (agency business)
Trading Contract – Header	WBHK – Y	Contract types
Trading Contract – Item	WBHI – Z	Contract item categories

Table 8.2 Assignment of Different Text Objects (Cont.)

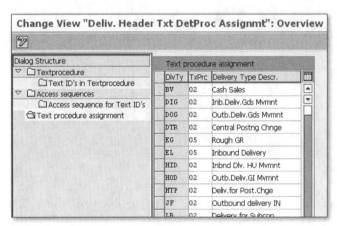

Figure 8.7 Assignment of Text Determination Procedure to Document Types

8.1.6 Text Determination Analysis

During document processing, the texts determined based on the text determination procedure and routines are populated from the following possible sources:

- Reference document (e.g., from order to delivery)
- Customer or material master record
- Condition records or info records (e.g., customer or material info record)

If you click on the Display Log icon, highlighted in Figure 8.8 in the Texts tab of the document header, you can see the details of the text determination analysis. Note that if the text IDs used in the text determination procedure are the same for document header or item in the case of an order, delivery, and billing, the content will flow automatically. The transfer of text doesn't require any determination procedure in this case. Therefore, you can customize text determination procedures for the transfer of data to an order from customer master records, material master records, or condition records, and then use the same text ID in delivery and billing to transfer the content of the text ID to the billing document.

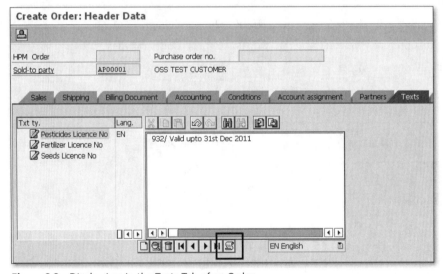

Figure 8.8 Display Log in the Texts Tab of an Order

The analysis shown in Figure 8.9 shows that the text type 0001 (of the VBBK text object and text group A) is automatically determined and populated by the text existing in the text type 0001 (or ID) of the KNA1 text object, as per access sequence 40. This means the text maintained for text type 0001 in the customer master record General Data area of the sold-to party in the order is transferred to order header text type 0001. Even though both have the same key (0001), they are completely different because they're part of different text objects — VBBK and

KNA1. The other accesses of the access sequence are not executed. For text type 0003, there's no access sequence, which means it has to be maintained manually. If any text type defined as mandatory is empty at the time of saving the document, then the document will be considered incomplete. The details will appear in the incompletion log.

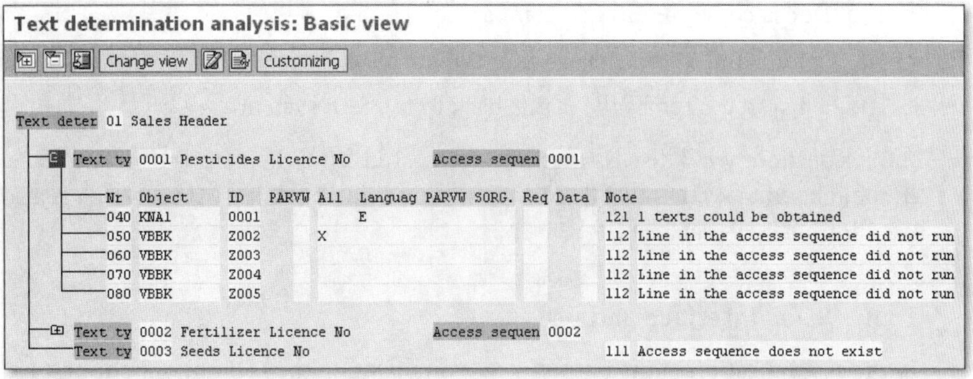

```
Text determination analysis: Basic view

Text deter 01 Sales Header
   Text ty 0001 Pesticides Licence No        Access sequen 0001
      Nr  Object  ID    PARVW All  Languag PARVW SORG. Req Data  Note
      040 KNA1    0001             E                             121 1 texts could be obtained
      050 VBBK    Z002       X                                   112 Line in the access sequence did not run
      060 VBBK    Z003                                           112 Line in the access sequence did not run
      070 VBBK    Z004                                           112 Line in the access sequence did not run
      080 VBBK    Z005                                           112 Line in the access sequence did not run
   Text ty 0002 Fertilizer Licence No        Access sequen 0002
   Text ty 0003 Seeds Licence No                                 111 Access sequence does not exist
```

Figure 8.9 Text Determination Analysis

8.2 Message Control

We've already discussed how the condition technique is used in output determination and how to use Transaction NACE for this purpose. In this section, we'll focus on data transfer using electronic data interchange (EDI) and application link enabling (ALE). EDI uses a set of standards for data exchange between two or more independent systems. Examples of such standards are UN/EDIFACT (recommended by the UN), ANSI ASC X12 (X12) (preferred in the U.S. and Canada), TTRADACOMS of ANA (Article Numbering Association), and ODETTE. In every system there should be the provision for receiving (inbound process) and sending (outbound process) the EDI document. The inbound process is for receiving information such as purchase orders from a customer. It does the following:

- Receives the EDI transmission.
- Converted the transmission into an intermediate document (IDoc), which is transferred to the SAP layer.
- Creates an SAP document (e.g., sales order).

In an outbound process, you send information such as an invoice or an advance shipment notice (ASN) to a customer. The following things happen in an outbound process:

- An IDoc is generated for the SAP document.
- The IDoc is transferred from the SAP system to the operating system.
- The IDoc is converted to EDI standards.
- The EDI document is transferred to the business partner.
- The EDI system reports the status back to the SAP system.

In next section, we'll discuss the steps for customizing the EDI or IDoc interface. In the following section, we'll cover application link enabling (ALE), which is also used for business data transfer.

8.2.1 IDoc Interface and EDI

In the customization of the output type, you maintain the EDI option (option 6) as a medium for output, as shown in Figure 8.10 (Transaction NACE). The program name for this is RSNASTED, and form routine is EDI_PROCESSING. Click on the relevant application (e.g., V3 for billing). Click on the Output Type button on the application toolbar, select the output type (e.g., RD00) that you want to assign to the EDI output, and select the Processing Routines folder (also shown in Figure 8.10). This is an overview screen that allows you to go to the detail screen by selecting an individual item. When there's only one medium as the option for an output type, the system will take you directly to the details screen.

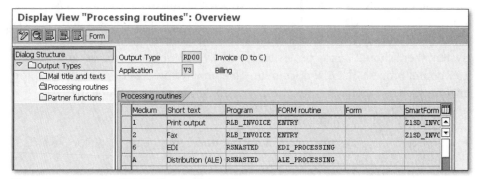

Figure 8.10 Assigning EDI Medium to Output Type

When the message control function makes the determination or you manually opt for the EDI medium for the output type for a document, the following things happen:

- The form routine EDI_PROCESSING is triggered.
- EDI_PROCESSING reads the partner profile.
- It determines the function module to be used (e.g., IDOC_OUTPUT_ INVOIC for invoices).
- The function module generates the IDoc (e.g., EXPINV02). You can use Transaction WE60 to get the documentation for an individual IDoc. In the initial screen, enter the IDoc type (e.g., EXPINV02) and select the HTML format to display the data structure of the IDoc, as shown in Figure 8.11.
- The IDoc is either sent immediately (option 4) or scheduled for dispatch (as per the option selected in the message control setting) so that it can be dispatched when the system is less busy.

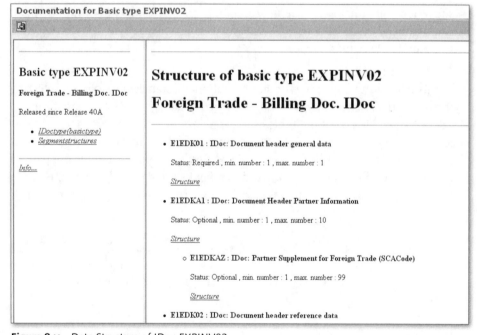

Figure 8.11 Data Structure of IDoc EXPINV02

All of the steps relevant for message control are also relevant for EDI transfer. It's important to remember that it's possible to make an EDI transfer without using message control. We'll discuss only two important activities involved in customizations of EDI transfer: defining the port and defining the partner.

Defining the Port

A port is logical/virtual connecting point for data exchange between different systems (or computers). At least one port is required for the IDoc interface to communicate with each external system. The port for EDI transfer is defined using Transaction WE21. In the initial screen, click on the folder Files and then click on the Create icon, shown in Figure 8.12. Once you provide a port name and description, you can select the radio button IDoc rec.types SAP Release 3.0/3.1 for version. Note that this has nothing to do with the SAP version you may be using. You have four tabs, described below, to use to customize the port.

- **Outbound File**
  In this tab, you can specify the directory path to use to send the IDoc to the EDI subsystem and a name for the file to be transferred in the Outbound File field. Alternatively, in the Function Module field, you can specify a function module to generate file names.

- **Outbound: Trigger**
  In this tab, you can specify whether an automatic start is possible. By selecting the Auto-Trigger checkbox, you can start the EDI subsystem by remote function call (RFC). RFC is one of the tools used for communication between an SAP system and another SAP (or non-SAP) system. You have to specify the RFC destination if Auto-Trigger is selected. In the Directory field, you can enter the path of the command file, and the Command File field should specify the name of the file that contains the commands (e.g., shell script for UNIX) to start the EDI subsystem.

> **Note**
> You can use Transaction SMGW to capture the RFCs running, Transaction ST22 to find the short dumps caused by RFCs (failed RFCs), and Transaction SM59 to maintain the RFC destination.

- **Inbound File**
  This tab has the same fields as the Outbound File tab (see Figure 8.12). You can specify the directory in which the incoming IDocs will be stored. The name for

the incoming IDocs should be specified in the Inbound File field or should be determined in the Function Module field.

- **Status File**

  This tab has the same fields as the Outbound File tab (Figure 8.12). You can specify the directory in which the status of outgoing or incoming IDocs should be stored. The name for status files should be specified in the Status File field or determined in the Function Module field.

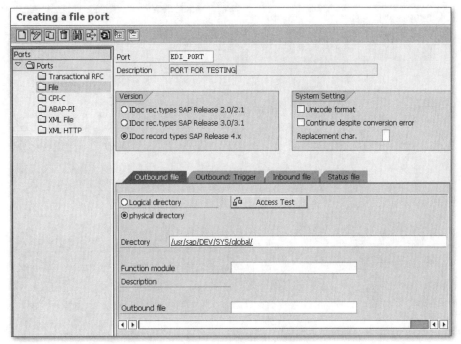

Figure 8.12 Defining Port for IDoc Communication

Defining the Partner

Customers, vendors, employees, forwarding agents, and so on are considered partners of your business in the SAP ERP system. You create master data records for them. In addition, if you communicate with them electronically using an IDoc interface, you must also define them as partners in the IDoc interface or for EDI transfer. Partners for EDI transfer are defined via Transaction WE20. This process consists of the following two broad steps: defining the partner and defining inbound and/or outbound messages for the partner. To define a partner when you

8 | Cross-Functional Customization

enter the transaction and see the screen shown in Figure 8.13, you can take the following steps:

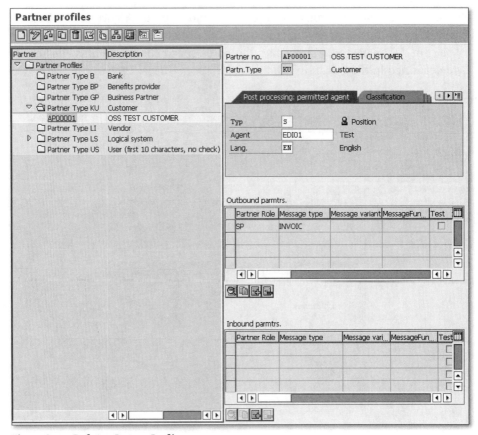

Figure 8.13 Defining Partner Profiles

1. Click on the Create icon.
2. Enter the customer code in the Partner Number field.
3. Enter the partner type (e.g., KU for customer) in the Partn. Type field.
4. In the Post Processing: Permitted Agent tab, you should specify the employees who will receive the mail (or error message) after processing of the IDoc.
5. In the Classification tab, set the partner status to A (active).
6. In the Telephony tab, you can fill the optional fields, including Telephone Number, Country Code, Name, and Company Name.

7. Once you define the partner (for IDoc communication), the icons below the Outbound Parameter and Inbound Parameter frames will be active. You can insert a new message type.
8. Double-click on any existing message type, as shown in Figure 8.14.

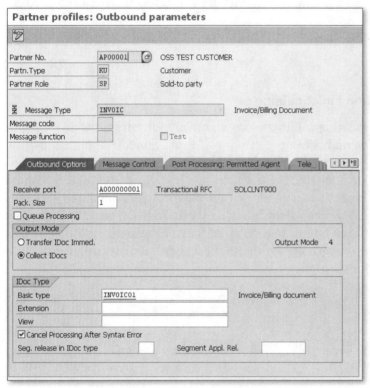

Figure 8.14 Parameter Profiles for Outbound Messages

9. In the Outbound Options tab, you can specify the port used for sending the IDoc. In the Packet Size field, you can specify the number of the IDoc that will be sent in one RFC. You can also specify whether the IDoc will be sent immediately or scheduled and the IDoc type (e.g., INVOIC01).
10. The information for the Message Control tab was covered in our discussion on output processing (Chapter 6). Also, for the Post Processing: Permitted Agent and Telephony tabs, refer the earlier steps in this list. You can leave the fields in the EDI Standard tab blank, unless required for your EDI subsys-

tem. This customization is done with a BASIS system administrator keeping in mind the system performance.

> **Note**
> The area menu transaction code for IDoc interfaces is WEDI. You can use it to get all of the transactions related to IDocs and EDI on the SAP Easy Access menu path.

Having discussed how to customize an IDoc interface for using EDI, let's move on to understand ALE.

8.2.2 Application Link Enabling

Application link enabling (ALE) is used extensively for integrating SAP components. With the *Interface Advisor*, it can link SAP and non-SAP applications. This is different from EDI, which is not used for internal data transfer. Both ALE and EDI require an IDoc interface. There is not the role of the EDI subsystem, which converts the IDoc to EDI standard. The area menu for ALE customization is SALE. When you enter SALE like a transaction in the transaction window and press [Enter], all of the customization steps relevant for ALE customization appear. This is helpful because you have a ready-to-use check-list. The basic customizing steps for ALE communication are:

1. Basic settings
2. Communication
3. Modeling and implementing business processes
4. System monitoring

As a functional expert, you're expected to contribute to the third step of customization for ALE, that is, modeling and implementing business processes.

8.3 Web Interface

Various portal-based roles are now available for the Sales and Distribution functionality of SAP ERP (e.g., sales assistant which a standard enterprise portal role). The user with these roles can carry out various sales operations such as creating a sales order, viewing the sales performance dashboard, getting an alert for a sales return, and so on. For various similar customized roles and assigning customized functionalities, you need to understand the Web interface that's used to ultimately access the SAP ERP and other systems (e.g., SAP NetWeaver BW). The Web interface is created for business server pages (BSPs). BSPs are like the web pages you see on any portal or website. You can use BSPs for reporting (e.g., displaying order lists) and for conduction operations (e.g., creating sales orders) in SAP ERP. The server-side scripting is done using JavaScript or ABAP (only JavaScript for SAP ERP Central Component 5.0).

To understand the basic concept, you should understand how the Internet works: It's a network of networks, and all systems in the Internet can be connected to each other using an IP address and domain name. An IP address is a set of four numbers separated by dots (e.g., 54.124.23.10) issued by the Internet service providers (ISP). The second important players are the domain registries, which issue domain names with extensions (e.g., .com, .net, and .us) for which they have the authorizations. Currently, there are more than a hundred such registries, at least one for each country. The registries allow the owners of the domain name to assign IP address to domain name (e.g., sap.com). You can also assign separate IP addresses to child domains (e.g., sdn.sap.com) and an mx (mail exchange) server for the domain. When a user is connected to the Internet, he can type the domain name in the web browser (e.g., Internet Explorer), press Enter, and then:

- Based on the last part of the domain name, the registry is determined.
- Based on the IP address maintained by the registry, the user reaches the server or system.

The IP address of the SAP server is registered as the A-record IP address for the domain name or any of its child names (C-name IP address). For example, sap.yourcompanyname.com may have the IP address of your SAP server.

> **Warning**
> The information provided here is meant as an overview for a functional consultant. We have not discussed many detail issues like precautions taken for data security.

Once the connectivity is established, the next issue in communication is the language. The fundamental language for the Internet is HTML (Hyper Text Markup Language). This is a very simple language with very little syntax, mainly <html> and </html>. Anything written between these two tags is read using the HTML language by any web browser. Most applications (e.g., Word) can be very easily converted to an HTML document. An HTML document is stored on a server, and when the user types the address of the web page, it's displayed on the user's browser. The address can be *http://sap.com/home.html*. When specific coding is repeated again and again on a web page, it becomes unmanageable. The solution to this is JavaScript. In JavaScript, you can put the part of the code that will be referred to again consistently. JavaScripts are stored at a specific location meant for them on the server and are referenced from the web page like any other object for executing the code written in it.

In next three sections, we'll discuss how to create a Web interface using the wizard, manually, and with other tools available in Web Interface Builder.

8.3.1 Creating A Web Interface using the Wizard

When you attempt to create a Web interface, it's best to do it using the wizard. The transaction code for creating Web interface is BPS_WB (menu path: SAP EASY ACCESS • INFORMATION SYSTEMS • BUSINESS INFORMATION WAREHOUSE • BUSINESS PLANNING AND SIMULATION • WEB INTERFACE BUILDER • CUSTOMIZING), shown in Figure 8.15. At this point, you have the option of either creating an interface using the Wizard or doing so manually. Click on the Create icon at the far left of the application toolbar for manually creating a Web interface. The Wizard icon next to it is used for creating an interface with the help of the wizard.

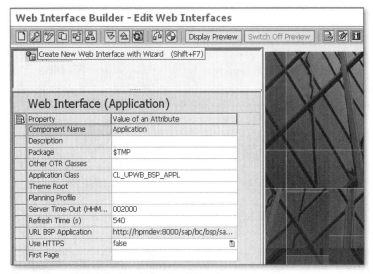

Figure 8.15 Web Interface Using the Wizard

After clicking the Wizard icon, you'll see the screen shown in Figure 8.16. The wizard option takes you through each of the steps.

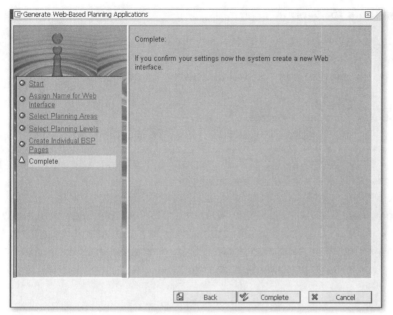

Figure 8.16 Steps of Customizing a Web Interface Using the Wizard

You'll get detailed help from the frame on the right. As with other wizards, this one is very useful for avoiding error. You cannot go to the next step until you complete the previous step, although you can return to a previous step for editing.

8.3.2 Creating a Web Interface Manually

As we've mentioned earlier, when you click on the Create icon shown in Figure 8.15, a dialog screen appears as shown in Figure 8.17. You have to specify the number of pages that the Web interface will contain. When selected, the checkboxes insert specific objects into the BSPs.

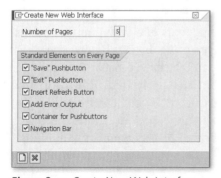

Figure 8.17 Create New Web Interface

8.3.3 Other Tools for Web Interface

Once you create the Web interface, either manually or using the wizard, you can edit it using the third icon shown in Figure 8.18. The figure shows the application toolbar available during Web interface building using Transaction BPS_WB.

Figure 8.18 Functionalities Available for Web Interface Building

The fourth icon is used to creating a new Web interface by copying an existing one. When you click on this icon, you get the dialog box shown in Figure 8.19, where you can specify if you have to generate a BSP application and copy a MIME object (e.g., picture file) by selecting the check-box.

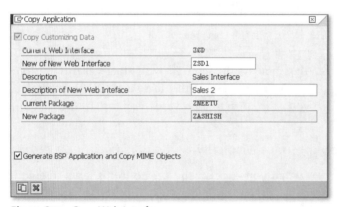

Figure 8.19 Copy Web Interface

You can use the Open Other Web Interface icon to open existing Web interfaces. The sixth icon is for the overview of an existing Web interface, and the seventh and eighth icons expand and collapse the components of a Web interface on display. The Refresh icon refreshes the BSP displayed using the Display Overview button. The tenth icon is for inconsistency checks, and the eleventh icon is to generate BSPs. The Display and Switch Off Overview buttons display and hide the BSP on the right frame of the screen. The MIME Objects icon (second icon from the right) opens a new window when clicked, shown in Figure 8.20. You can use this dialog box to import any MIME object (e.g., picture file) or CSS template (i.e., design templates) from the local system to the SAP server. The icon at the bottom of the box can be used for displaying, deleting, or changing the uploaded object.

Figure 8.20 Importing a MIME Object or CSS Template

8.4 Batch Management

We've already covered batch management in the earlier chapters, but to recap, the following are important aspects of customization:

1. How to activate batch management and define the batch level (e.g., plant, company code)
2. How to customize fields and layout of batch master records
3. How to create and assign batch number ranges
4. How to customize shelf life expiry date (SLED)
5. How to customize automatic batch determination using condition techniques
6. How to use classification techniques in batch management
7. How to modify system messages of batch management
8. How to activate document management systems for batches

> **Note**
> You activate batch management for a material by selecting the checkbox for it in the Sales: General/Plant tab of the material master record. Once selected, you cannot deactivate it until any stock in any batch is in inventory. However, occasionally, you may able to change it due to a system bug. If that happens, immediately implement SAP Note 1246638, followed by SAP Note 1266540.

In next two sections, we'll discuss the batch where-used list and the batch information cockpit. This will be the last customization detail of batch management from the Sales and Distribution functionality point of view. Please note that we've discussed the other aspects in previous chapters.

8.4.1 Batch Where-Used List

The transaction code for the customization of a batch where-used list is OMBB (menu path: SAP IMG • LOGISTICS – GENERAL • BATCH MANAGEMENT • BATCH WHERE-USED LIST • MAKE SETTINGS FOR BATCH WHERE-USED LIST), shown in Figure 8.21. The checkboxes for all existing plants in the BaWU Synchronous Posting column are selected for the plants for which you want the system to create receipts and issue records. This batch of where-used records has an impact on system performance. You can deactivate the batch where-used function for a plant by unselecting the checkbox in the BaWU deactivated column. When the batch where-used function is deactivated, the synchronous posting is irrelevant. That is, for a particular plant, both checkboxes cannot be selected.

You use the batch where-used list to track the batches (and supplier) of raw materials used in a particular batch of finished goods. So if you find a batch of finished goods to be defective, you can get all of the batches of components or ingredients that went into that batch of finished goods. The information can help you find the cause of the problem. You can discuss it with your supplier, giving reference to the exact batch number of their supply, so that they can also cross-check and rectify the mistake if it originates at their end. This is called *top-down analysis*. You can also view a batch where-used list as the different batches of finished goods that contain a particular batch of raw material. In the previous example, if you find that a particular batch of a particular raw material is defective, the next step is to identify the batches of the finished goods that used the defective raw material. These batches are likely to be defective. This is *bottom-up analysis*. The transaction for batch where-used lists is MB56 (menu path: SAP EASY ACCESS • LOGISTICS • CEN-

TRAL FUNCTIONS • BATCH MANAGEMENT • BATCH USAGE • DISPLAY). In the selection screen you have the option of selecting either top-down or bottom-up analysis.

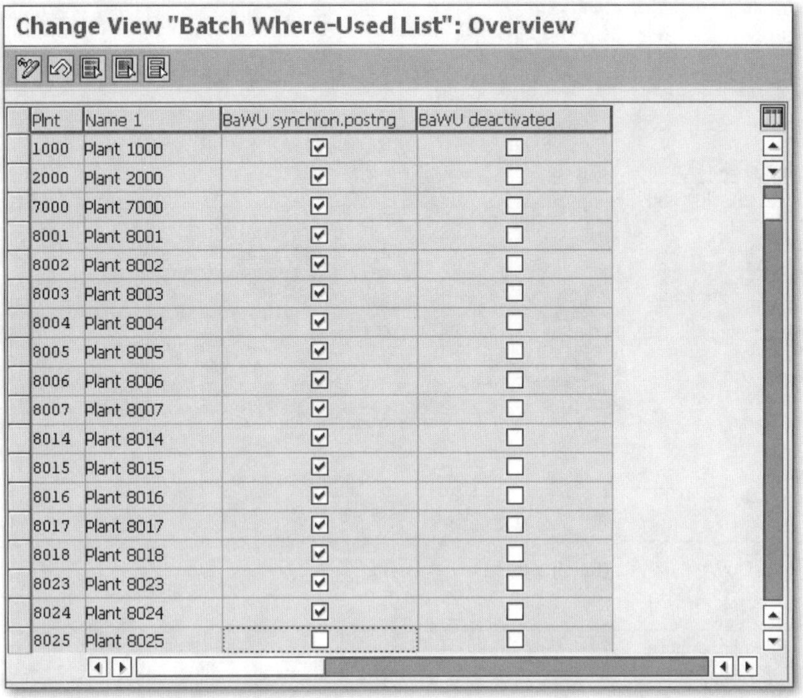
Change View "Batch Where-Used List": Overview

Plnt	Name 1	BaWU synchron.postng	BaWU deactivated
1000	Plant 1000	☑	☐
2000	Plant 2000	☑	☐
7000	Plant 7000	☑	☐
8001	Plant 8001	☑	☐
8002	Plant 8002	☑	☐
8003	Plant 8003	☑	☐
8004	Plant 8004	☑	☐
8005	Plant 8005	☑	☐
8006	Plant 8006	☑	☐
8007	Plant 8007	☑	☐
8014	Plant 8014	☑	☐
8015	Plant 8015	☑	☐
8016	Plant 8016	☑	☐
8017	Plant 8017	☑	☐
8018	Plant 8018	☑	☐
8023	Plant 8023	☑	☐
8024	Plant 8024	☑	☐
8025	Plant 8025	☐	☐

Figure 8.21 Activate Batch Where-Used List

Top-down analysis is relevant for finished goods, whereas bottom-up is relevant for raw materials. On the selection screen, if you enter a raw material and do the top-down analysis, you'll find only the purchase orders that were used to buy the particular batch of raw materials. There's no component or ingredient for a raw material, so the details that you get in top-down analysis for finished goods aren't there. For semi-finished goods, both methods are relevant. If you want the composition of the semi-finished (or finished goods), you should opt for top-down analysis. Figure 8.22 shows the result of such an analysis. If you want to know the batch numbers of the finished goods that contain a particular batch of semi-finished goods (or raw materials), you should opt for bottom-up analysis, shown in Figure 8.23.

8 | Cross-Functional Customization

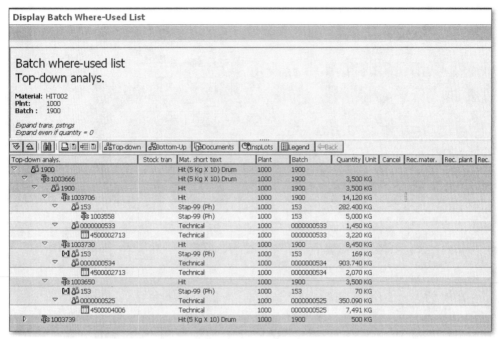

Figure 8.22 Top-Down Analysis (Batch Where-Used List)

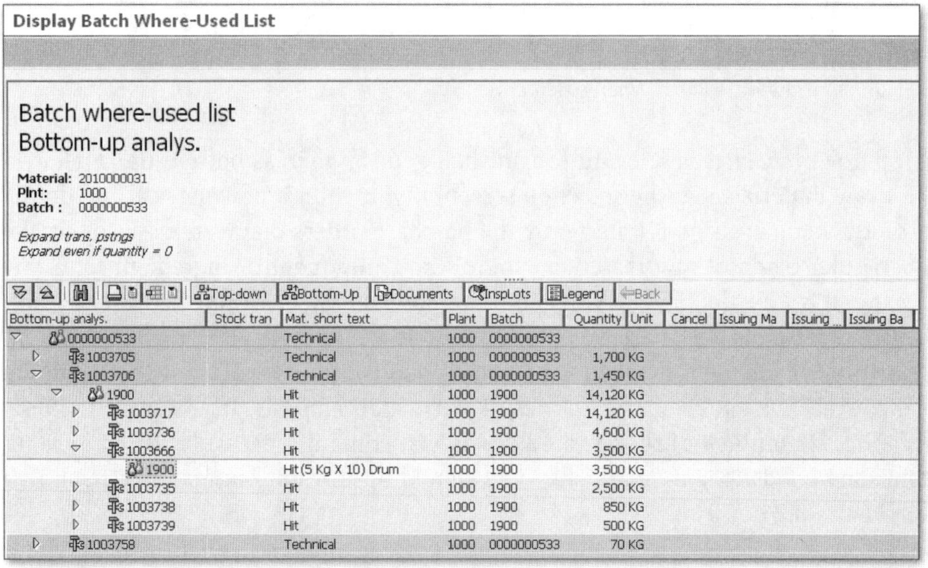

Figure 8.23 Bottom-Up Analysis (Batch Where-Used List)

When you double-click on a purchase order, shown with a document icon (e.g., 4500002713 in Figure 8.22), in the where-used list, you can see the purchase order. You use Transaction MB57 to display the records stored in Table CHVW, which stores all of the where-used records. Use Transaction MB5C to list all of the documents in the Sales and Distribution functionality (i.e., order, delivery, billing, and scheduling agreement) that contain the particular batch.

> **Note**
>
> Wherever the Batch icon (two conical flasks) (see Figure 8.22 or 8.23) is available, you can double-click on it to display the batch master record. This icon is available in the batch information cockpit from ERP Central Component 5.0 onward.

8.4.2 Batch Information Cockpit

In the Sales and Distribution functionality in SAP ERP, you won't find any reports or analyses that contain batch-level information. Sales or Logistics information systems don't provide much help either. When we discuss them in next chapter, this will become clearer to you. This shortcoming is more than compensated for by the batch information cockpit (BIC) that SAP ERP offers you. The BIC becomes a single point of access for all information and functionality that you need for batch management. You can perform the following tasks from the BIC:

- Access batch master records and modify them (subject to authorization)
- Access batch where-used lists, which we discussed in the previous section
- Get information on shelf life expiry dates (SLED)
- Get reports based on batch classification
- View batch-wise stock positions

Now that you understand how important the BIC is for batch management, let's see how we can optimize it as per our own requirements. The transaction code for the batch information cockpit is BMBC (menu path: SAP EASY ACCESS • LOGISTICS • CENTRAL FUNCTIONS • BATCH MANAGEMENT • BATCH INFORMATION COCKPIT). As the name suggests, you can do most of the frontend transactions of batch management using this transaction. Figure 8.24 shows the initial screen. If you click on the Restart button, you'll find the three standard ways of presenting the selection tabs:

8 | Cross-Functional Customization

1. SAP standard
2. SAP example 1: stock overview
3. SAP example 2: classification

It isn't possible to change the customization done for SAP standard options. You can only display it using Transaction OBIC_DIS (menu path: SAP IMG • LOGISTICS – GENERAL • BATCH MANAGEMENT • BATCH INFORMATION COCKPIT • DISPLAY SAP STANDARD SELECTION). The other two options can be modified. The transaction for changing them is OBIC (menu path: SAP IMG • LOGISTICS – GENERAL • BATCH MANAGEMENT • BATCH INFORMATION COCKPIT • DEFINE USER-GROUP-SPECIFIC SELECTION).

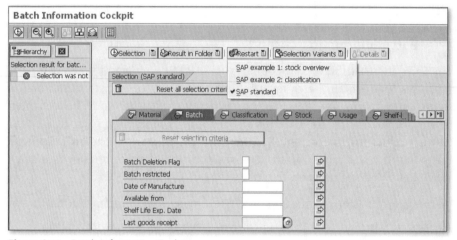

Figure 8.24 Batch Information Cockpit

After clicking on the IMG – Activity icon at the end of menu path, you'll reach the screen shown in Figure 8.25, where you'll find the two user groups provided by SAP: SAP 1 and SAP 2. You assign the users are assigned to the user group by maintaining the parameter BICUG and the value for it as the preferred user group in their respective user master records.

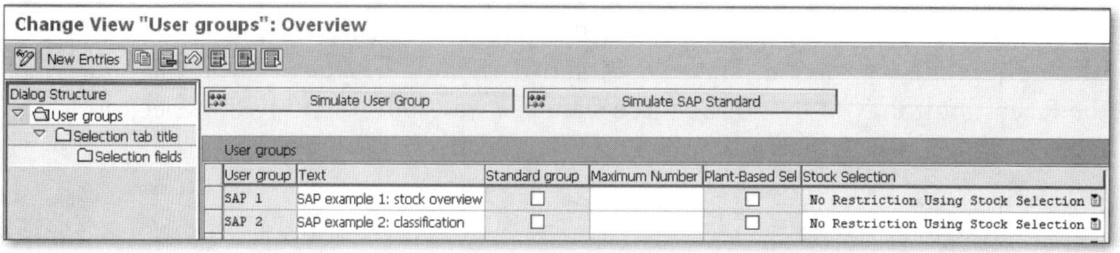

Figure 8.25 Customize User Groups for Batch Information Cockpit

8.4 Batch Management

If you want to specify a user group for all users who are not assigned any user group, select that user group as the standard group by selecting the Standard Group checkbox (see Figure 8.25) for the user group that's to become the default user group. You can add a new user group if required. The description for the SAP 1 and SAP 2 user groups can be modified to suit your purpose. If you select a user group and click on the Selection Tab Title folder (Figure 8.26), you can customize the sequence, description, and availability (active) of the tabs to be used in it. You can add and/or delete new fields to the fields already in a tab. The tabs for which selection is fixed have their Fixed Selection checkbox selected in the screen shown in Figure 8.26. Click on the Selection Fields folder to reach the screen shown in Figure 8.27.

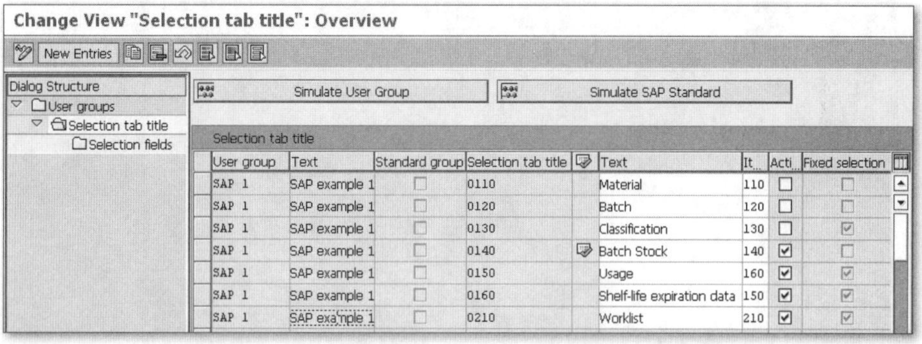

Figure 8.26 Customizing Tabs Available in the Batch Information Cockpit

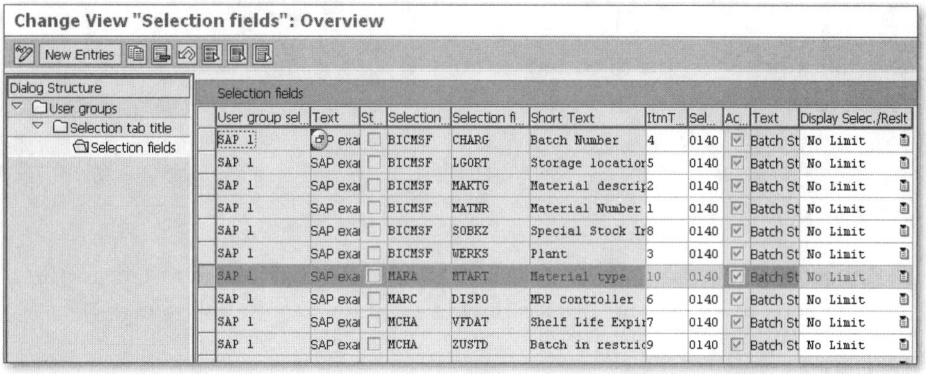

Figure 8.27 Adding the Selection Field "Material Type" to the Batch Stock Tab

After reaching the screen in Figure 8.27, you can add a new field by selecting any existing entry and clicking on the Copy As ([F6]) icon. Change the Selection Table and Selection Field fields to the table field that you want to use as a selection criteria. In this case, we've inserted field MTART of table MARA, material type, as the 10th item (10 in the ItmT column). The option No Limit in the last column means the field will be used in both the selection and result screens. After saving the settings, you can simulate the selection for the user group (SAP 1), and the screen shown in Figure 8.28 will appear. Note the bottom field in the selection screen, Material Type. This is what we've inserted.

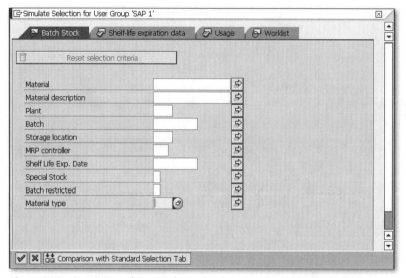

Figure 8.28 Simulation of the Batch Stock Tab to Display Added Material Type

Now that you know how to customize the BIC, let's see how some ABAP tools can be put to their best use.

8.5 ABAP Tools

In this section, we'll discuss the specific ABAP tools that are important for functional experts to know. Our discussion will be limited to the following:

1. SD user exits
2. Debugging
3. LSMW

8.5.1 SD User Exits

ABAP enhancements include user exits, field exits, and BAdIs. In this section, we'll only discuss the user exits available for the Sales and Distribution functionality in SAP ERP (e.g., user exits in the program MV45AFZZ). Technically, these are neither enhancements nor user exits. Enhancements are not affected at the time of upgrading the SAP version. User exits are created using Transaction CMOD or SMOD. What are often referred to as SD user exits are actually modifications. In the Sales and Distribution functionality, SAP ERP provides different windows in specific standard include programs. Include programs are a type of ABAP program. In these windows or forms, you can insert your own code to fine-tune the standard transactions, which we've seen in earlier chapters. Here we'll just list few such include programs.

But first, we need to see if these customer codes are inside a standard program and whether it's possible to escape the up-gradation process. Up-gradation is when you move from one version to a newer version of SAP ERP. Even while using same version (e.g., SAP ERP Central Component 6.0), SAP releases several SAP notes that are implemented collectively, and the system is upgraded. These SAP notes proactively address new tax requirements, program bugs, and similar issues. It's natural that new requirements for user exits come up. Governments in different countries tend to be innovative when it comes to taxing. Companies also make frequent changes in the Sales and Distribution functionality in SAP ERP to be on track with the market. Suppose you've made some changes in the program MV45AFZZ. There are several user exists in that program. SAP inserts another user exit and delivers it via one SAP note. So when you implement that SAP note, the new program will overwrite the program already in system, and your customized coding will be overwritten. This is not what you want. When there's a new requirement, SAP creates a new user exit where customer code can be inserted. However, instead of adding the exit to any existing include program, SAP creates a new one for it. Therefore, you'll have many include programs for sales, delivery, billing, and other functions of this functionality. These include programs listed in Table 8.3.

FV45EFZ1	MV50SFZ1	MV90VFZZ	RVCOMFZ4	V05IEXIT
FV45VFZZ	MV50SFZ2	RMCS1US1	RVCOMFZZ	V05LZZMO
FV45VTZZ	MV50SFZ3	RMCS1US2	RVKMPNNN	V05TZZMO
FV50DFZZ	MV50SFZ4	RMCS1US3	RVKMPUS2	V05WZZMO
FV50UZXX	MV55AFZ1	RMCS1US4	RVKPRFZ2	V05XZZMO

Table 8.3 Include Programs that Contain User Exits

FV50UZZZ	MV55AFZ2	RMCS1Z01	RVKPRFZ3	V51AFZZ1
FV50VTZZ	MV55AFZ3	RMCS5Z01	RVKPRFZ4	VV05HFZ1
MV45AFZ4	MV60SFZ1	RMCS6Z01	RVKREFZ1	VV05HFZ2
MV45AFZA	MV60SFZ2	RV45PFZA	RVKREFZ2	VV05LFZ1
MV45AFZB	MV60SFZ3	RV50BTOP	RVKREFZ3	VV05LFZ2
MV45AFZC	MV60SFZ4	RV53SFZ1	V05AZZEN	VV05TFZ1
MV45AFZH	MV60SFZ5	RV60AFZC	V05AZZLK	VV05TFZ2
MV45AFZU	MV61AFZA	RV60AFZD	V05AZZLP	VV05TFZ3
MV45AFZZ	MV61AFZB	RV60AFZZ	V05EA1AG	VV05WFZ1
MV45AIZZ	MV65AFZ1	RV60FUS1	V05EA1RE	VV05WFZ2
MV45AOZZ	MV65AFZ2	RV60FUS2	V05EA1RG	VV05WFZ3
MV45ATZZ	MV65BFZ1	RV60FUS3	V05EA1WE	VV05XFZ1
MV50AFZ1	MV65BFZ2	RV60FUS4	V05EZZAG	VV05XFZ2
MV50AFZ3	MV65BFZ3	RV60FUS5	V05EZZRG	VV05XFZ3
MV50AFZK	MV75AFZ1	RV60FUST	V05EZZWE	
MV50AFZZ	MV75AFZ2	RV61AFZA	V05HZZMO	
MV50BFZ1	MV75AFZ3	RV61AFZB	V05IEXI2	

Table 8.3 Include Programs that Contain User Exits (Cont.)

We've seen the use of various user exits in earlier chapters. In particular, see Chapter 3 (for MV45AFZZ), Chapter 5 (for LVKMPTZZ, LVKMPFZ1, LVKMPFZZ2, and LVKMPFZZ3), Chapter 6 (for MV50AFZ1, MV50AFZ3), and Chapter 7 (for RV60AFZZ).

8.5.2 Debugging

Debugging is how you find an error in a program. SAP ERP offers the debugging function /h. While you're still in a transaction, you can type "/h" in the transaction window. When you press [Enter], you'll get the message, "Debugging switched on." When you're in debugging mode, you move from one screen to another, step by step, examining the effects of each line of the program. The program that runs in the background to take you from one screen to the next is now visible on your screen. We turned debugging on while in the overview screen of a sales order and clicked on the Conditions tab (Figure 8.29). The red arrows on the application toolbar are used to proceed down the program code. The straight arrow on the right is used to exit debugging mode. You can click on the Fields or Table button and specify the field name or table name at the bottom of the window. Click on the arrow to go one step at a time. From there, you can see how the value of the specific field or table is populated, modified, or processed during that step in the program.

> **New Debugger**
>
> The new debugger available with SAP ERP (SAP ERP Central Component 5.0 or above) creates a new session for debugging. It has several new features that you may want to explore once you're comfortable with the basic features.

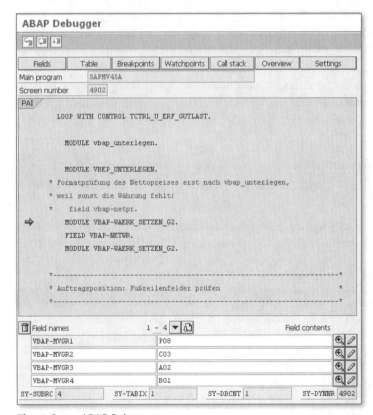

Figure 8.29 ABAP Debugger

Because all of the standard programs for standard transactions are also written with ABAP, debugging is also possible for standard transactions, which provides functional experts good insight into the logic that a particular program follows. Even if you don't know the ABAP syntax, you can get help from a technical person during the debugging process.

> **Note**
>
> If you're in a situation where the value of a particular field of a document needs to be changed manually, you can do it using debugging. To do so, you need to understand the standard program, table, and structures that store the values temporarily.

8.5.3 LSMW

LSMW stands for Legacy System Migration Workbench. The original purpose of this function is to transfer legacy data to your SAP system during an SAP project implementation before go-live. Though we've included it in the ABAP tools section, this is a cross-functional tool. With Transaction LSMW, you can record an SAP transaction and use the recording to repeat the transaction. Please go through the following post-implementation scenarios where the LSMW can come to your rescue. These five examples will help you understand how to use this tool optimally in a post-implementation scenario. We're sure everybody can find a number of occasions to use it.

1. You want to change any field of all material master records or all customer master records or a field in any other master record. There are thousands of master records.

2. Your company has introduced a new material, and today, the day the product is getting launched, 10 units of it are to be sold to all of the existing 5000 or so customers.

> **Note**
>
> LSMW is not suitable for mass creation orders if the numbers of items differ, that is, if in one order there are 5 items and in another there are 10. For that situation use the functional module BAPI_SALESDOCU_CREATEFROMDATA1, BAPI_SALESORDER_CREATEFROMDAT1, or BAPI_SALESORDER_CREATEFROMDAT2. Also note that you have to provide information on schedule lines, if relevant, because they're not created automatically while creating orders using any of the above function modules. The function module GUI_UPLOAD uploads data from your desktop to SAP ERP for mass creation of sales orders, credit memo requests, or other types of orders. An ABAP developer has to write a program using the function modules mentioned for mass creation of orders.

3. In your company, credit memos are blocked for posting by default. Once all of the credit memos are created for a month or week, they're verified. A senior manager verifies them using reports, and once they're verified, all documents are released as soon as possible. Manually doing that for thousands of documents will take hours, but with LSMW you can do it in minutes. One LSMW recording created for this purpose can be reused week after week.
4. Every day, hundreds or thousands of sales orders are verified using reports and other information for credit release, and the documents not released are to be deleted. Deleting a few thousand orders will take a few minutes using an LSMW recording.
5. Every month, the prices (condition records) of the materials change. Thousands of condition records have to be modified.

Now that you understand the importance of LSMW, not only during implementation but as a post-implementation optimizing tool, let's do an actual recording. We'll record a simple sequence of changing the field value of the Search Term 2 (KNA1-SORT2) field of a customer master record using Transaction VD02. We'll then use the recording to change this field in several customer master records. Let's walk through each step in the following subsections.

Step 1: Create Project, Subproject, and Object for LSMW Recording

In this step, you create a new project, subproject, and object for LSMW. You can use an existing project or sub-project for a new object. A LSMW recording is identified by these three elements. The combination for an LSMW must be unique. SAP provided LSMW to transfer data from legacy systems to SAP ERP during an implementation project, so the project name can be the name of the SAP implantation project. The subproject name can be Z_MASTER_DATA for master data transfer. The object can be Z_CUST_MASTER for transferring customer master data to SAP ERP. Once the data is transferred from the legacy customer master data to SAP ERP, you can use the same project, subproject, and object to create a master data record in SAP ERP by providing the input for it in an Excel file.

To start a recording, you need to create a project, subproject, and object to specify the recording. These values are important for using the recording in the future as well. By executing Transaction LSMW (you may get a welcome note), you go to the screen shown in Figure 8.30, where you can specify the project, subproject, and object. You can use any existing project and subproject to create a new object. After you enter these values in their respective fields, click on the Create icon.

You'll get a dialog box to give the description for any or all of the three elements. Press [F8] or click on the Clock icon to reach the next screen, which lists all of the steps of the LSMW. By default, the Maintain Object Attributes radio button will be selected. Press [F8] or click on the Clock icon to go to the screen shown in Figure 8.31.

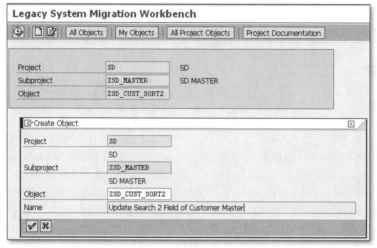

Figure 8.30 Creating an LSMW Recording

Step 2: Maintain Object Attributes

In this step you specify how the data for the LSMW is going to be provided for input into SAP ERP. For example, data can be received as IDocs (intermediate document), which we'll discuss in Chapter 9. BAPIs, direct input, and batch input sessions are three other possible forms of data entry. We'll restrict our discussion to the batch input session method.

In the screen shown in Figure 8.31 click on the Display/Change button to make the screen ready for input, and select the Batch Input Recording radio button. If you select the Overview icon to the right of it, you'll get a list of all existing recordings in the project you're in. You can create a new recording by clicking on the create icon. In the dialog box that appears, give a name and description for the recording. In the next dialog box, enter the transaction code that will be recorded (e.g., VD02 for changing the Search 2 fields of existing customers) and executed. This takes you to the initial screen of the transaction code. The initial screen will look slightly different than the initial screen of Transaction VD02, which is executed directly (not for the LSMW recording). The tabs that appear in Transaction VD02 for a customer master record will appear as the checkbox, when the same transaction is executed for the LSMW recording. Because you know that the Search Term 2 field is in the Address tab, select the Address checkbox only. Because the SORT2 field is also part of the central address management, select that check box as well. Specify the customer and the sales area (combination of sales organization, distribution channel, and division) and press [Enter]. You'll go to the Address tab of general data area, where you can enter some the new values for the customer in the Search Term 2 field, and then press [Enter].

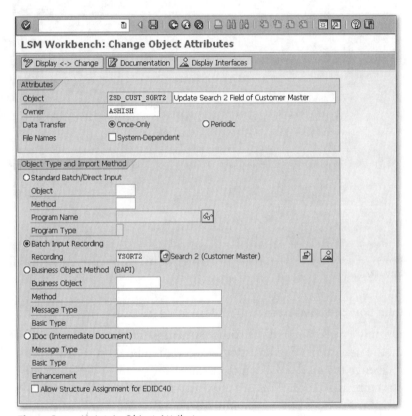

Figure 8.31 Maintain Object Attributes

You'll go to a screen similar to the one shown in Figure 8.32. If you click on the Default All button, you'll get an information dialog and field names. All of the fields in the Address tab will appear in the recording, and you should delete the fields other than SORT2 by selecting the field in the screen and clicking on the Delete Screen Field button. Make sure to save the setting, and then click on the

8 | Cross-Functional Customization

Back Arrow to return to the previous screen. The list of existing recordings along with the one you just created will be there. Be sure to Save, and then click on the Back Arrow, which will take you to the screen in Figure 8.31. You can arrow back to reach the screen where the LSMW steps are listed, which are no longer relevant for the batch input recording. The second radio button will be selected. Press [F8] or click on the Clock icon to go to the next step.

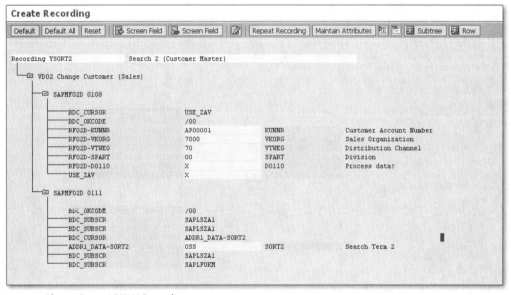

Figure 8.32 LSMW Recording

Step 3: Maintain Source Structures

In this step you only give a name to the source structure. You define the fields of the structure in the next step. After selecting the second radio button, you'll see a new screen. To change the mode, click on the Create icon, and you can specify the name of the structure and description in the pop-up screen. Save the setting and click on the Back Arrow to go back to the initial screen.

Step 4: Maintain Source Fields

In this step you define the fields for which you'll provide information. For example, while creating a customer master record, you might have to provide values for 50 fields (e.g., customer group, default delivery plant, and so on). In some fields (e.g., sales organization may be only one and all customers can have only one value) you might assign a fixed value.

After selecting the radio button, you can create and assign fields to the structure already created. In change mode, select the source structure that you want to create fields for and click on the Table Maintenance icon. In the table, you can enter the fields for the input file and whether the field will be a number or a character and the number of characters allowed for the field. Save the setting and click on the Back Arrow.

> **Note**
>
> When you're in the screen that opens by clicking on the Table Maintenance icon, you can upload a text file from your local system (e.g., desktop) to create fields. In that case, you'll get the following information dialog: "The file with the field definition must be structured as follows Field Number (optional), Name, Description, Type, and Length. The columns must be separated by tabs."

If only one field (as in our example) or multiple fields need to be modified, you can create the fields one by one by clicking on the Create icon and filling the fields in the dialog box that appears.

Step 5: Maintain Structure Relations

In this step, the relationship between the source and a target structure is established, usually automatically. An error occurs if there's a difference in their fields or if they have same name.

This step happens automatically if you've specified the name of the recording and completed the previous step correctly. Upon execution, you'll get the screen shown in Figure 8.33, but in disabled mode. Click on the Change-Display icon and save, and then click on the Back Arrow.

Figure 8.33 Assign Structure to Batch Input Recording

8 | Cross-Functional Customization

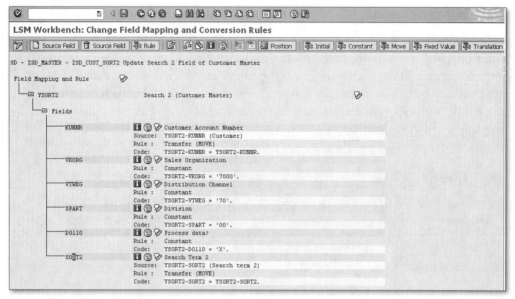

Figure 8.34 Field Mapping

Step 6: Maintain Field Mapping and Conversion Rules

In this step, you maintain how each field in the target structure will get the input value from the source structure. You also specify whether data will move with or without any conversion. Once you've clicked on the Back Arrow in the previous step, you can click on the Clock icon or press [F8] (Figure 8.34). All of the fields in the recording that aren't deleted are available in display mode. Click on the Change-Display icon and select the first field (e.g., KUNNR). The value is provided from an external data file, which in this example we defined as YSORT2. YSORT2 has two fields: KUNNR and SORT2. We've assumed that all of the customers are in same sales area. Click on the Create Source Field button so that all of the fields in the source structure will be available for selection. From here, you can click on the field that provides the data to the record. In this example, we want the KUNNR field (Customer) to provide data to the KUNNR field. You can see that one field is part of the external data file, which is the source, and the other is the target field. Both names can be different, although usually they are given the same name. In this example, we've also given the same name, YSORT2, to the batch input recording and the data structure to avoid confusion. Once you select the field, the source field name will appear next to the target field. For this example, we're simply transferring (moving) a source field to a target field without any modification. For the next three fields (sales organization, distribution channel, and division) we'll use the fixed values based on these assumptions. To fix the value, select the field, click on the Rules button, and select the Constant radio button. You'll get a dialog box to specify the constant, where you can enter the value for the constant (e.g., 7000 for sales organization). Repeat the step for all fields, and be sure to save. From there, simply Arrow back to reach the next step.

Step 7: Maintain Fixed Values, Translations, and User-Defined Routines

The next step, which is optional, is to maintain the fixed values, translations, and user-defined routines. Normally, with the two rules, move and constant, that we discussed in the previous step, you can manage data uploads. For example, in a legacy system you had stored the minimum order quantity in material master records in terms of kilograms, and in SAP ERP the same is to be maintained in terms of cartons that are equal to 10 kg. The data is to be converted suitably using these functionalities. With user-defined routines, you can achieve very complex conversions with the help of ABAP developer.

> **Note**
>
> When you specify certain values, translations, and routines for an object in this step, you can use them for any other object created in the same project.

With this or with the previous step, the LSMW object is ready for use.

Step 8: Specify Files

In this step, you specify the physical location of the file that will provide the input data. It can be on your local system or on a system that your local system can access. For example, the path to your desktop file can be *C:\Documents and Settings\Admin\Desktop\upload.txt*. The upload.txt is the actual file that provided the information to be uploaded in correct format.

The next step is to specify the files. Simply click on the Specify File button in the initial screen for the LSMW recording and specify the file you want to use. You'll reach the screen shown in Figure 8.35 in disabled mode. Click on the Change-Display icon, and execute the following steps to upload data from a text file from your PC:

1. Click on Legacy Data.
2. Click on the Create icon. The dialog box shown in Figure 8.35 appears.

8 | Cross-Functional Customization

3. In the file field, specify the path where you have stored the files that contain all of the data. In this case, we're using KUNNR and New value.
4. Name the file (e.g., ZSORT). Note: This has nothing to do the file name of the data file to be uploaded.
5. If you want the first row of the file to specify the heading (e.g., KUNNR, SORT2), select the Field Names at Start of File checkbox.
6. Save and then click on the Back Arrow to reach the initial screen.

> **Note**
>
> You may occasionally have to change the path and the files specified in this step. To do this, double-click on the file name (in enable mode). The dialog box shown in Figure 8.35 will appear.

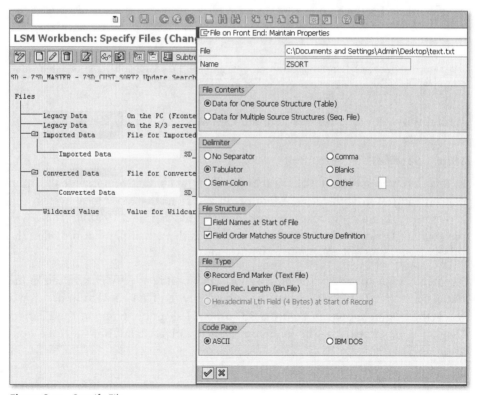

Figure 8.35 Specify File

Step 9: Assign Files

This step is typically to display or check that the file you specified in the previous step is correctly assigned. File assignment is automatic. Just execute, click on Change-Display icon, save, and click on the Back Arrow.

Step 10: Read Data

In this step, the system reads the data from the file (upload.txt file in step 8). If you change any data in the source file after this step, the change will not go to SAP ERP system.

The next step is to read the data. Select the Read Data radio button, which takes you to a screen where you can restrict the data that is read. Normally, the whole file is read, so don't put any restriction on it. Leave all of the fields blank, and unselect all of the checkboxes. The data stored in the text file on your PC will be read, and you'll get the information on the screen as shown in Figure 8.36. The screen shows that we stored new values for Search Term 2 for nine customers. If this is not true, you can verify that text file. It may contain some blank spaces if the number is just one more than the records (or rows) you've stored.

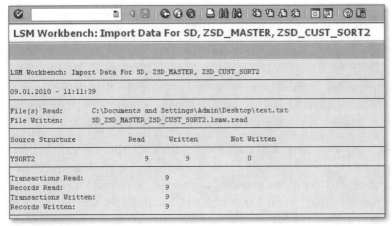

Figure 8.36 Read Data

Step 11: Display Read Data

This step allows you to manually check that everything read by SAP ERP in the previous step is correct. Errors can occur for various reasons. For example, if you're using tab-separated text files for data input and instead of one tab, there are two between two fields (e.g.,, Sales Org and Distribution Channel), this will result in the value intended for the Distribution Channel field going to the next field (which may be Division) and produce an error.

Displaying the read data is optional. On execution, all of the data read in the previous step is displayed. Click on any row to go to the screen shown in Figure 8.37. The system provides an intermediate screen where you can restrict the number of displayed rows. Simply press [Enter] to ignore that screen. Be sure to check a few records carefully, because if the source field is populated with the wrong target field, it can lead to serious problems.

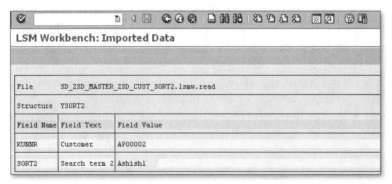

Figure 8.37 Display Read Data

Step 12: Convert Data

In this step, you execute actual data conversion, as per different routines, rules, or other objects that may have been used in the LSMW. For example, data read as 100 may become 10 after conversion, which may be what you want.

The next step is to convert the data. In addition to the data from the external file, the fields for which constant values are maintained are also read. After executing this step, you can restrict the number of transactions. Each record (or row) in the data file will run the transaction (in our case VD02) once. So the transaction here actually means the number of rows in your data file. Click on the Execution (Clock) icon, and you'll get the information on the number of rows and records processed. It should tally with your earlier number, which in this case, is nine.

Step 13: Display Converted Data

In this step, you can display the data after conversion for any possible error. Once you see that the data has been converted you can move to the next step, which is optional. It's similar to displaying the read data. Here, in addition to the data received from the external source, the fields with constant values are also displayed. Click on a few records to ensure that the data will populate the target fields correctly.

Step 14: Create Batch Input Session

The batch input session is the step when the transaction (VD02 in our case) is executed some number of times depending upon the input file. This may take few minutes or several hours, depending on the amount of data input. Various functionalities are available, such as to skip a step if an error occurs, to stop the session, and so on. In this step, you actually customize how the session will run, for example, whether it will be executed in the background. After completing this step, you will reach Figure 8.38. You can reuse the batch input file and folder by selecting the Keep Batch Input Folder(s)? checkbox. Once executed, you'll get the confirmation message, "1 batch input session with X transaction created," where X is the number of records or rows in your data file.

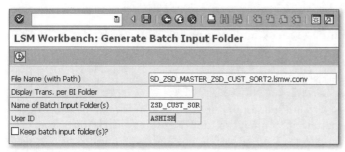

Figure 8.38 Generate Batch Input File

Step 15: Run Batch Input Session

Next, you need to run the batch input session, shown in Figure 8.39. Select the batch input session created in the previous step and click on the Process button. You'll get a dialog box asking you to specify if the processing is to be carried out in the foreground or background. We recommend the Display Error Only option for practical reasons (for performance and to display errors and escape when an error occurs).

Figure 8.39 Processing Batch Input Session

Finally, you get a confirmation message: "Processing of batch input session completed." In the session overview window, you can see the number of successful (green checkmark column) and failed (red zig-zag arrow column) transactions (or records or rows).

8.6 Numbering Objects

Before we discuss number ranges and numbering objects, let's start with a warning.

> **Do Not Transport Numbering Objects**
>
> It's a standard practice to develop and test the customization in development and quality servers before transporting it to production for use. This general principle is not applicable to numbering objects. The SAP system does give you the option of creating a transport request for numbering objects. In the production environment, use of a number range will be different from that in development. Suppose you created a numbering object and number range in development for a sales order and transported it to production. In the next month, you may have 100 orders created in production and only 10 in development. Suppose you made some changes in the object and again transported it after one month. The last number used for the number range will be 10 in production. The actual use, which is 100, in production will be overwritten by the usage level (10) in development. This will happen for all of the number ranges in the numbering object. So, when you try to create an order after transportation, it will show an error, and the order will not be saved. If the numbering object also contains number ranges for delivery or billing documents, you might also have a similar problem while creating those documents.

The cockpit transaction for number objects is SNRO (menu path: SAP EASY ACCESS • TOOLS • ABAP WORKBENCH • DEVELOPMENT • NUMBER RANGES), as shown in Figure

8.40. You get more than a thousand standard numbering objects, which are used for different purposes. The most important number range object of the Sales and Distribution functionality in SAP ERP is RV_BELEG (number ranges for sales and distribution documents). Each number range object contains several number ranges identified by a string of two characters. Each number range is customized by specifying a first (from number) and a last number. Also, you specify whether it's assigned externally. The system automatically updates usage information for number ranges that are not external. The current last number is displayed (in modifiable mode), and a number range to be used for the documents in the Sales and Distribution functionality in SAP ERP (e.g., sales, delivery, and billing documents) must be present in the RV_BELEG numbering object (or number range object). Similarly, all of the standard numbering objects have a specific purpose. You can add, delete, and modify number ranges in numbering objects. The number ranges of a numbering object should not overlap, so you don't have same number for order, delivery, and billing. You can have the same number for a billing document and accounting document. The number range object for accounting document is RF_BELEG.

> **Note**
>
> In several places, we have specified the numbering object in addition to the transaction for maintaining the specific number range. Therefore, it's easier for you to maintain them from the single cockpit transaction, SNRO. For example, the transactions for maintaining RV_BELEG (sales document number ranges) and RF_BELEG (accounting document number ranges) are VN01 and FBN1, respectively. Both can be maintained using Transaction SNRO.

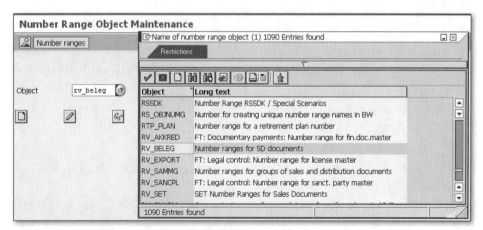

Figure 8.40 Number Range Object Maintenance

When you're in the screen displayed in Figure 8.40, you can:

1. Maintain number ranges by clicking on the Number Ranges button in the application toolbar.
2. Display all of the existing number range objects by clicking on the Overview icon in the application toolbar.
3. Create a new number range object by clicking on the Create icon.
4. Change an existing number range object by clicking on the Change icon.
5. Display an existing number range object by clicking on the Display icon.

In the next two sections, we'll discuss how to maintain number ranges and how to create new number range objects.

8.6.1 Maintain Number Ranges

When you're in the number range object maintenance screen (Figure 8.40), enter the numbering object (e.g., RV_BELEG) in the Object field and click on the Number Ranges button to go to the tools for number ranges (Figure 8.41).

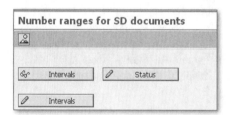

Figure 8.41 Tools for Number Ranges

Here you have the following options:

1. Get an overview of the existing number ranges by clicking on the Overview icon in the application toolbar.
2. Display the existing number ranges by clicking on the Display Intervals button. You'll go to a screen similar to the one shown in Figure 8.42. All of the columns in that screen will be in display-only mode.
3. Change the number ranges by clicking on the Change Intervals button. You'll go to the screen shown in Figure 8.42.

4. Change the status of the current number by clicking on the Change Status button. You'll go to a screen similar to the one shown in Figure 8.42. Everything but the Current Number column will be in the display-only mode.

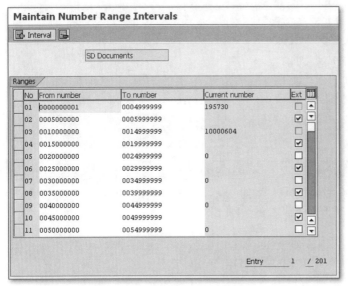

Figure 8.42 Maintain Number Range Intervals

When you reach the screen shown in Figure 8.42, you can do the following:

1. Change the From Number if the number range is not yet used.
2. Change the To Number if the new interval does not overlap any other range. You get an error message if it overlaps any other range.
3. Select or unselect the Ext checkbox if the number range is not yet used. Selecting the checkbox will make an existing internal number range external. Unselecting it will convert an existing external number range to an internal number range.
4. Add a new number range by clicking on the Add Interval icon in the application toolbar. You should give a new two-character key for the number range and specify the start and end number of the range. You'll get an error message if the new interval overlaps any existing one. You also specify whether it's to be an external number range.
5. Delete an existing number range by selecting the number range and then clicking on the Delete icon in the application toolbar if the current number is zero.

> **Note**
>
> You can also use the following function modules for maintaining number range objects using an ABAP program.
>
> - NUMBER_RANGE_OBJECT_MAINTAIN
> - NUMBER_RANGE_OBJECT_CLOSE
> - NUMBER_RANGE_OBJECT_DELETE
> - NUMBER_RANGE_OBJECT_INIT
> - NUMBER_RANGE_OBJECT_LIST
> - NUMBER_RANGE_OBJECT_READ
> - NUMBER_RANGE_OBJECT_UPDATE

> **Note**
>
> Even when a number range has been used, you can change the current number to zero and then delete it. There will be no error message.

8.6.2 Create Number Range Objects

You can create number ranges objects to provide number ranges to customized country-specific official documents types or when there are too many number ranges in the number range objects for the Sales and Distribution RV_BELEG numbering object. There can be a maximum of 1296 number ranges. To create number range object, follow these steps:

1. Enter a proposed new name for the numbering object in the Object field.
2. Click on the Create icon in the screen shown in Figure 8.40, which takes you to the Number Range Object screen (Figure 8.44).
3. Provide a short and a long description.
4. Customize the Interval Characteristics, Customizing Specifications, and Group Specification fields. If the group specifications are maintained, you can also maintain the text specifications.

We'll discuss the importance of each field to be customized in the fourth step in the following four sections.

8.6 Numbering Objects

Interval Characteristics

In this step, you can customize the behavior of the number ranges that will be created within this numbering object.

- The Subobject Data Element field is used to provide a subobject for the object (numbering object). For example, you can use VKORG (sales organization) as a subobject. In that case, the same number range (e.g., 01) can be used for several sales organizations. The initial screen for maintaining number ranges looks like Figure 8.43, instead of Figure 8.41, when VKORG is used as a subobject. A number range created in this numbering object is only valid for the subobject for which it is created.

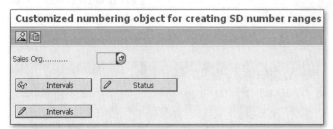

Figure 8.43 Initial Screen for Maintenance of a Numbering Object with the Subobject Sales Organization

- The To-Year Flag checkbox determines if the number range repeats itself every (fiscal) year. This checkbox needs to be selected for the number range object to be created for an accounting document. For the numbering object to be used in the Sales and Distribution functionality in SAP ERP, do not selected this checkbox. During the number range maintenance, in addition what we've specified in previous sections, there is another To Year column. This column appears between the Number Range Code/Key and the From Number columns.
- The Number Length Domain field determines the maximum number of digits or characters that the number range object can have (e.g., NUM10 for numeric 10-digit numbers, CHAR10 for alphanumeric 10-character keys).
- Select the No Interval Rolling checkbox to prevent the number range of this numbering object from repeating itself once it reaches the upper limit.

Customizing Specifications

In this step, you can specify whether a customized transaction will be used for maintaining this object, the usage level the warning is issued at, and whether (and how much) buffering is required.

- The Number Range Transaction field contains the name of the customized transaction for the new numbering object. You can also use Transaction SNRO for maintenance.

- The Warning % field determines the percentage of unused numbers to the total number in a number range (of this object) at which users start receiving warning messages.

- Select the Main Memory Buffering checkbox if buffering is required. To deactivate it, review SAP Note 23835.

- The No. of Numbers in Buffer field determines the number of numbers blocked in buffering. Sometimes you'll find an invoice number or delivery number skipping a fixed amount of numbers (e.g., 5 or 10). The error is rectified if you temporarily delete the number specified in this field. To remove buffering, use the menu path EDIT • SET-UP BUFFERING • NO BUFFERING.

> **Note**
>
> By default, SAP delivers the RV_BELEG and RF_BELEG numbering objects with buffering, but you can deactivate buffering using the procedure explained in SAP Notes 23835 and 424486. This becomes a necessity if you observe invoice numbers or any other document numbers that are not continuous. There might be some unused numbers. In some cases, you're legally required to have the documents numbered continuously. For example, you might find that the invoice numbers getting generated are 1001, 1005, 1010, and so on, instead of, 1001, 1002, 1003, and so on. This is usually due to buffering.

Group Specification

The fields in the Group Specification area are optional. You can create a number range object without specifying them. The customized Z-tables created for storing the number ranges are specified here.

- The group table must be a table with Fld NoRangeElement as a key element (e.g., Customized Z-table). The table with the KTOKD field of Table T077D can be specified for a numbering object that is to contain number ranges for customer master records.

- The Subobject field in group table specifies any other key field.

- In the Fld NoRangeElement field, you specify the key field for the number range object. For example, in the customer master record, the customer account group determines the number range object relevant for it. If the number range you're creating is used for numbering customers in customer master records, fill it with KTOKD (customer account group).

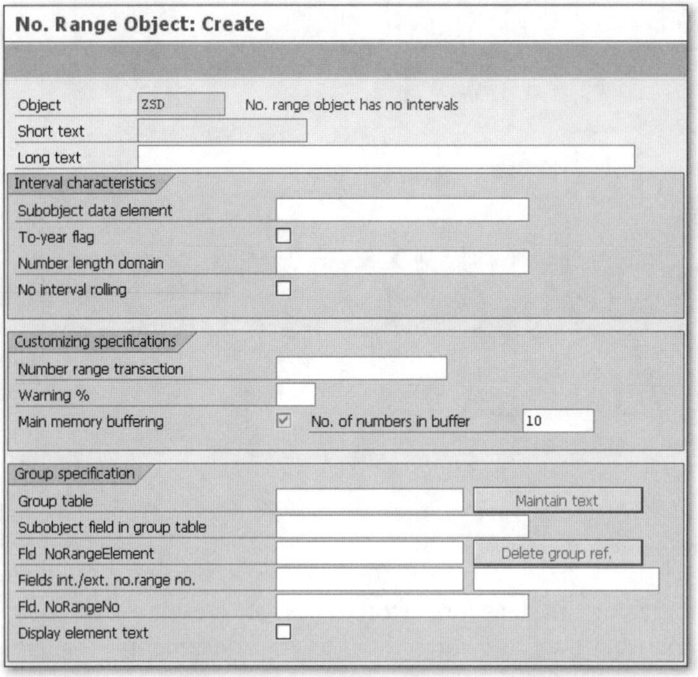

Figure 8.44 Creating Number Range Objects

- The Fields Int./Ext. No.range No. fields contain a number range for internal and external number ranges. (For example, in the customized table you can specify the NUMKI and NUMKE fields of Table T134 as internal and external number range numbers.)
- The Fld. NoRangeNo (Field for Number Range Number) field is the field in the group table (see the first item of this list) that stores the number range numbers.
- The Display Element Text checkbox, when selected, displays the preceding five fields with text during number range maintenance.

Text Specifications

You can maintain text specifications by clicking on the Maintain Text button or going to EDIT • MAINTAIN TEXT from the screen shown in Figure 8.44. The dialog box shown in Figure 8.45 appears where you can specify the following fields of the customized table that's to store the text elements.

- Element text table
- Language field
- Element field
- Text field

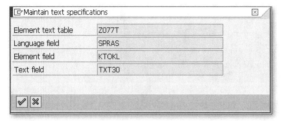

Figure 8.45 Maintain Text Specifications

8.7 Summary

We started the chapter taking the steps for customization of condition techniques for text processing. You can now bring correct text to your documents automatically. For message control, we discussed how to customize IDoc interfaces and the use of EDI and ALE for communication. For batch management, you learned about the final two topics, the customization steps for batch where-used lists and the batch information cock-pit. This knowledge will help you extract any information with respect to batches from your system. In the section on ABAP tools, we discussed Sales and Distribution user exits and debugging and listed the steps for LSMW. With this knowledge, you should be able to identify the appropriate user exit for using customized coding by ABAP developers, use LSMW optimally, and debug ABAP programs for errors.

Finally, in the numbering objects section, you learned how to maintain different number ranges and how to customize numbering objects so you can create and maintain any number range objects and number ranges in SAP ERP. Now, let's move on to the next chapter, where we'll discuss reports and analysis.

This chapter will cover the reporting and analysis tools available for Sales and Distribution and how to use them optimally.

9 Reporting and Analysis

Reporting and analysis help users extract information they need and present it in a way that's easy to understand and use. In this chapter, we'll start off with a section on standard reports. Only after you familiarize yourself standard reports and analysis can you be ready to develop your own. The following three sections will teach you the three approaches to creating your own report. You'll learn how to create an ABAP query, how to use the SIS (Sales Information System) for reporting, and how to create ABAP reports. We've provided very simple examples, so you'll be able to follow along and ultimately be able to create reports by yourself. You can start with simple cases and gradually attempt tougher ones. After learning this information, you'll be better prepared to team up with technical resources to create better report development. We'll also discuss SAP NetWeaver BW reporting, to familiarize you with the business information warehousing offered by SAP. So let's get started.

9.1 Useful Standard Reports

SAP standard reports are broadly divided into four categories: lists, work lists, analyses, and display documents. The standard reports and analyses offer you a variety of features and tools to help you meet your individual requirements.

You should have two basic objectives for studying standard reports:

1. The more you know about the standard reports and their features, the more reporting requirements you'll be able to fulfill with the standard reports. Therefore, there will be less of a need for developing customized reports.

2. While designing the customized report, this information will help you design better reports.

In the next two sections, we'll discuss different categories of standard reports.

9.1.1 Classification of Standard Reports

There are four different groups of reports, as mentioned early. It's important to be able to identify the differences between these types to help you choose which is best for you. The following subsections discuss the four types of reports.

Lists

A list is typically considered a report. There is a selection screen where you can specify your requirements. For example, you may be interested in listing the OR-type orders (first restriction) created between 01.01.2010 and 01.31.2010 (second restriction). To create this, use Transaction SDO1, as shown in Figure 9.1, and take the following steps:

1. Enter the OR value in the Document Type field.
2. Enter "01.01.2010" in the first window in the Created On field.
3. Enter "01.31.2010" in the second window in the Created On field.
4. Leave other fields (Created By and Organizational Data) blank. By doing so, you allow the list to contain sales orders matching the above selection or restriction criteria from any sales area (combination of sales organization, distribution channel, and division). Documents created by any user will be listed.

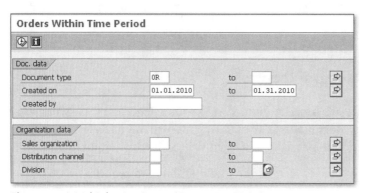

Figure 9.1 Initial Selection Screen (Transaction SDO1)

By clicking on the Execute icon (far left in the application toolbar) or pressing the [F8] key, you'll get your list, shown in Figure 9.2.

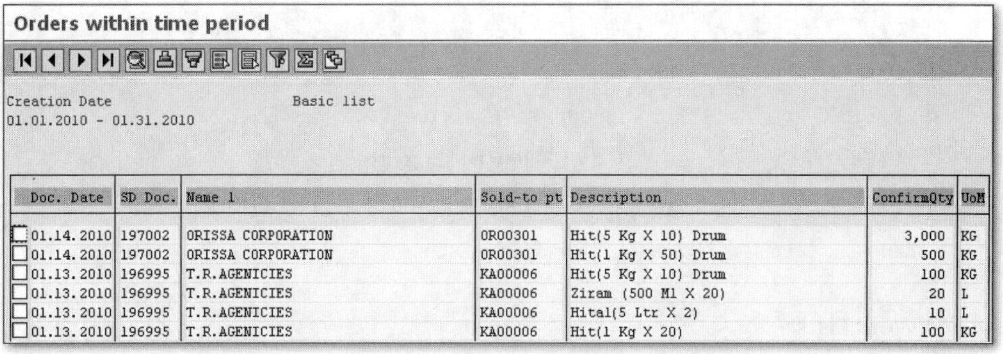

9.1 Useful Standard Reports

Orders within time period						
Creation Date 01.01.2010 - 01.31.2010		Basic list				
Doc. Date	SD Doc.	Name 1	Sold-to pt	Description	ConfirmQty	UoM
01.14.2010	197002	ORISSA CORPORATION	OR00301	Hit(5 Kg X 10) Drum	3,000	KG
01.14.2010	197002	ORISSA CORPORATION	OR00301	Hit(1 Kg X 50) Drum	500	KG
01.13.2010	196995	T.R.AGENICIES	KA00006	Hit(5 Kg X 10) Drum	100	KG
01.13.2010	196995	T.R.AGENICIES	KA00006	Ziram (500 Ml X 20)	20	L
01.13.2010	196995	T.R.AGENICIES	KA00006	Hital(5 Ltr X 2)	10	L
01.13.2010	196995	T.R.AGENICIES	KA00006	Hit(1 Kg X 20)	100	KG

Figure 9.2 List of Orders within Time Period (Transaction SDO1)

There are several standard reports in the Sales and Distribution functionality of SAP ERP. Table 9.1 lists the most common ones, with a brief description.

Transaction	Description
VA55N	Item Proposal – List by Material
VD59	List Customer-Material-Info
VA45N	List of Contracts
VB(8	List Rebate Agreements
VB35	Promotion List
VB25	List of Sales Deals
VA15N	Inquiries List
V.03	Incomplete Inquiries
VA25N	Quotations List
V.04	Incomplete Quotations
VA05N	List of Sales Orders
SDO1	Orders Within Time Period
V.02	Incomplete Orders
VA35	List of Scheduling Agreements
V.05	Incomplete Scheduling Agreements
VA45N	List of Contracts
V.06	Incomplete Contracts

Table 9.1 Examples of Standard List Transactions

Transaction	Description
V.00	Incomplete SD Documents
V_UC	Incomplete Outbound Deliveries
VF05	List of Billing Documents
VF25	List of Invoice Lists

Table 9.1 Examples of Standard List Transactions (Cont.)

Work Lists

The purpose of lists is simply to illustrate or display information. Work lists, on the other hand, allow you to process the information.

The initial step for work lists is the same as for the list transaction. You can specify the selection criteria and execute it by pressing [F8]. The list of orders, deliveries, billing documents, or any other document of the Sales and Distribution functionality that matches your selection criteria appears in the list. Once the list appears, you can select the documents you want and process further (i.e., post goods issue or release credit blocks per the specific work list transaction). Some work list transactions can be restricted to being lists by authorization management. Delivery due lists and billing due lists, for example, are used to create multiple deliveries and billings, respectively. Someone who has to create hundreds of deliveries and/or billings daily will find them very useful. You can try a few examples of work lists in Table 9.2.

Transaction	Description
VL10A	Sales Orders Due for Delivery
VL10B	Stock Transfer Orders Due for Delivery
VL10G	Documents Due for Delivery
VL06G	List of Outbound Deliveries for Goods Issue
VKM1	Blocked SD Documents (Credit Management)
VF04	Process Billing Due List
VF24	Edit Work List for Invoice Lists
VFX3	List Blocked Billing Documents
VF31	Output from Billing Documents

Table 9.2 Examples of Work Lists

Analyses

Analyses or functional analyses are available in various transaction screens for specific analyses. The following are some of the important types of analyses available in the Sales and Distribution functionality in SAP ERP.

- A pricing analysis can be called from sales and billing documents. In pricing analysis, the pricing procedure, along with the condition types it contains, used in the particular item is displayed on the left side of the window, as shown in Figure 9.3. For each condition type, the accesses made are shown in the folder with same name as the condition type. There are subfolders with the same name as the different accesses. The analysis displays whether the condition record was found for particular access. The access details are displayed on the right side, including details of the access made for the particular document. You go to Figure 9.3 by clicking on the Analysis button at the bottom of the Item Condition screen. When a user complains about a wrong price getting determined in a document item, you can use pricing analysis to find the cause of the error. The error can be due to wrong a condition record, a wrong access sequence, or an error in a pricing procedure. It can also be due to an error in the customer master record of the sold-to party and/or material master records of the material used in the item. This can result in the wrong pricing procedure getting selected. The rectification will also prevent error reoccurring in a similar situation.

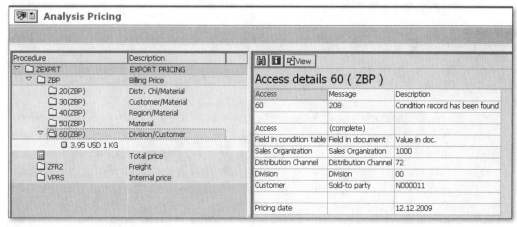

Figure 9.3 Pricing Analysis

- Account determination analysis can be done for orders and billing documents. As shown in Figure 9.4, you can access the screen for account determination analysis by going to ENVIRONMENT • ANALYSIS • ACCOUNT DETERMINATION from the sales order overview screen. For a billing document, the menu path is ENVIRONMENT • ACCOUNT DETERMINATION ANALYSIS • REVENUE ACCOUNT from the initial or overview screen. In both cases, the GL that the postings are made to are shown. The screen also shows the details about the other elements of the condition technique, including the determination procedure, condition type, access sequence, and access details used for account determination for a particular item of the document. This is often used during error analysis. If the user tells you that proper GLs are not getting posted, in a particular document, you can find the cause of the error. The error may be due to the wrong account determination procedure not getting determined, wrong sequencing in the access sequence, or an error in some other step. Once you find the error, you can rectify it, so the error does not occur in the future for similar documents.

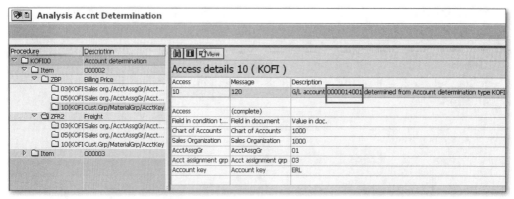

Figure 9.4 Account Determination Analysis

- Output determination analysis and output processing analysis are available for all of the output objects (e.g., order – header, order – item, delivery – header, delivery – item, etc.) that the output type is available for. In output determination analysis, you get the information about how the particular output is determined (or failed to get determined). In output processing analysis, the sequence shows how the output is processed. You can use output determination analysis following the menu paths for the output objects listed below:

  - **Sales order – header**
    EXTRAS • OUTPUT • HEADER • EDIT from the order overview screen

- **Sales order – item**

  EXTRAS • OUTPUT • ITEM • EDIT from the order overview screen selecting the particular item

- **Delivery – header**

  EXTRAS • DELIVERY OUTPUT • HEADER from the delivery overview screen

- **Delivery – item**

  EXTRAS • DELIVERY OUTPUT • ITEM from the delivery overview screen selecting the particular item

- **Billing – header**

  GOTO • HEADER • OUTPUT from the billing overview screen

Following these menu paths, you'll get to a screen similar to the background of Figure 9.6. From that screen, you can follow the menu path GOTO • DETERMIN. ANALYSIS to go to the screen shown in Figure 9.5.

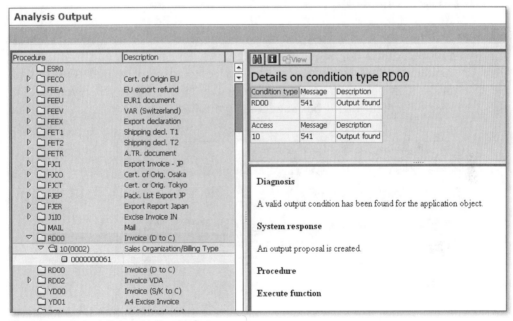

Figure 9.5 Output Determination Analysis

- Output processing analysis shows the sequence of events that happened during output processing. It shows the error (or warning) if any occurred during processing. You can follow the same menu path as for output determination analysis, but you should select Processing Log rather than Determin.analysis in the final step.

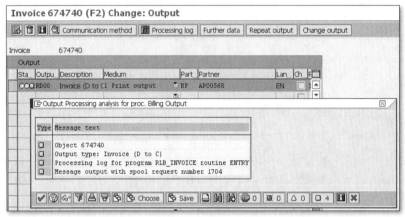

Figure 9.6 Output Processing Analysis

- Incompleteness analysis is also called incompletion log. It's available for several functions, including sales orders, deliveries, foreign trade, and so on. We've highlighted the Incompleteness Analysis icon in the Foreign Trade/Customs tab of the Item Details screen for a delivery item in Figure 9.7. When you click on this, you get the dialog box shown in Figure 9.7.

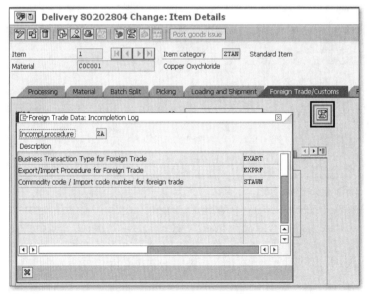

Figure 9.7 Incompleteness Analysis (Foreign Trade)

> **Note**
>
> Several other analyses are available in standard systems, such as material determination analysis, listing/exclusion analysis, invoice split analysis, text determination analysis, and so on. They're very helpful for error handling. You can get the basic understanding of the condition techniques and/or customization while using some of these analyses.

Display Documents

Most documents can be opened in display mode. A separate transaction code and authorization management for the display option make it very useful, especially in the production environment. In production servers as consultant, you normally get the restrictive authorization for display only. Changing any document in the production client, by a person other than the actual user, is not advisable. All of the analyses discussed so far can be called from the display mode of the document. Many of the lists and work lists discussed so far are also available from the transaction to create, change or display a document, such as how the list of billing documents (Transaction VF05) can be executed by going to ENVIRONMENT • LIST BILLING DOCUMENTS from the overview screen of any billing document using Transaction VF03. The following functionalities are frequently used for individual documents.

- **Status overview**

  The status of a document that is stored in Tables VBUK (header) and VBUP (item) can be displayed for an individual document.

- **Changes**

  You can display changes to a particular document or master data record by going to ENVIRONMENT • CHANGES.

- **Document flow**

  The Document Flow icon is present in most SAP documents such as orders, deliveries, and invoices. It's available on the application toolbar in the overview screen. It's possible to display the document flow at both the header and item level. To display document flow at the item level, select the item first and then click on the Document Flow icon or follow the menu path ENVIRONMENT • DISPLAY DOCUMENT FLOW ORDERS AND INVOICES. For deliveries, go to ENVIRONMENT • DOCUMENT FLOW. In all of these cases, the menu path is accessed from the overview screen.

- **Accounting document overview (for billing document)**

  To display the accounting document in the invoice's initial or overview screen,

you can click on the Accounting button in the application toolbar, which will get you the dialog box shown in Figure 9.8. You can also follow the menu path GOTO • ACCOUNTING OVERVIEW from the overview screen. The dialog box contains a list of documents from the following components.

- Accounting
- Profit Center Accounting
- Controlling
- Profitability Analysis
- Fund Management and other components if applicable

If you double-click on any accounting document, the document is displayed.

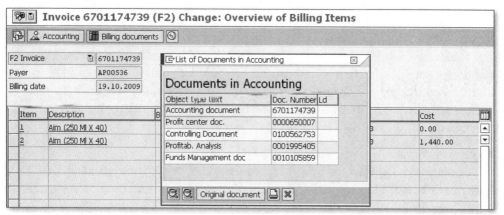

Figure 9.8 List of Documents in Accounting for Billing Document

- **Stock overview**
  You can call a stock overview (Transaction MMBE) from a delivery for an individual item by going to ENVIRONMENT • STOCK.

- **Master record display**
  You can display the customer master records and material master records from the individual document. For individual items, you can use the following menu paths for material master records.
    - Order: ENVIRONMENT • DISPLAY MATERIAL
    - Delivery: ENVIRONMENT • MATERIAL MASTER DATA

To display customer master records, you can use the following menu paths:

- Order: ENVIRONMENT • PARTNER • DISPLAY SOLD-TO PARTY / SHIP-TO PARTY / PAYER / BILL-TO PARTY / CREDIT ACCOUNT
- Delivery: ENVIRONMENT • SHIP-TO PARTY

9.1.2 Features Available in Standard Reports

Several features are available in different standard reports. We'll discuss few of them.

- **Drill-down**
  In most standard reports, if you click on any document number in a list, you'll go to the individual document. This feature is called drill-down. There can be several levels in a drill-down report. These reports are very useful to auditors of accounts, who often need to check the details of individual figures (e.g., sales revenue) that go into balance sheets or profit and loss accounts.

- **Changing layout**
  We'll discuss this in Section 9.2.6. By changing the layout, you customize your output for the report to display only the fields that you're interested in.

- **Search**
  The Search icon allows you to search in a list. In a large list, if you want to find out where a particular word or figure (e.g., 7803) occurs, doing it manually will take a lot time.

- **Sort**
  You can select a column in a list and click on the Ascending or Descending Sort icon to sort the list.

- **Filter**
  You can use the Filter icon to reduce the list as per the filter condition. For example, you have a list of documents from several sales organizations. In a filtering condition, you can define, sales organization = 1000. The list will now display only the documents of sales organization 1000.

- **Total and subtotal**
  Any numeric field can be summed up by selecting the column and clicking on the Total icon. When at least one column is summed up, you can use the Subtotal icon by selecting any field and clicking the Subtotal icon. The fields that are already summed up will now show the subtotals. Each unique entry in the column that is subtotaled will have a subtotal value in the column.

9 | Reporting and Analysis

- **Print**
  Use the Print icon to print the list.

- **Report in Excel/Lotus**
  Many standard reports can be displayed and modified directly using Lotus Notes or Microsoft Excel.

- **Exporting to other applications**
  You can send the report to other applications, such as Excel, Word, or HTML documents. You can save it on the local system or send it by mail.

- **Graphical presentation**
  You can present the report graphically using standard 2D and 3D diagrams such as pie charts or bar diagrams.

9.2 Developing Reports Using Query

The transaction code to create a simple query (also called an SAP and ABAP query) is SQVI, which is shown in Figure 9.9. You can also access it by executing Transaction SQ01 and then clicking on the Quick Viewer button. As an example, we'll use a simple case of creating a query and attaching it to a Z-transaction. Suppose one of your accounts auditors wants to see a list of customers in your SAP system but not in the Sales and Distribution functionality. For example, customers created for sales of assets fall under this category. There can be few such customers in your system. The report might be required to find customers with incomplete master data records. Customers created with Transaction FD01 won't have the sales area view and won't be available to the Sales and Distribution functionality. These customers are used by the accounting department. All customers created in SAP systems create an entry in Table KNA1, and those created for the Sales and Distribution functionality create an entry in Table KNVV, in addition to Table KNA1. Therefore, you can download the two lists and compare them using the Customer Code (KUNNR) field, which is present in both tables. But what if the report is required on a monthly or even daily basis? The best way is to create an ABAP report. However, in this case, we'll show you a second, viable option of doing the same using a query. The general steps for creating query are:

1. Create the query.
2. Decide on a data source.
3. Insert the tables you want in basis mode.

4. Join tables.
5. Select the list and selection fields.
6. Modify the look of the list in layout mode.
7. Create a Z-transaction for the query.
8. Now let's look at each of these steps in great details.

9.2.1 Create Query

When you're in the screen shown in Figure 9.9, enter a name in the QuickView field (in this case, ZOSS) and click on the Create button. You'll get a dialog box similar to the one shown in Figure 9.10.

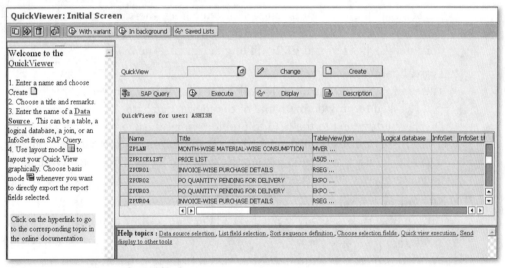

Figure 9.9 Initial Screen for SAP Query

9.2.2 Data Source

When you reach the dialog box shown in Figure 9.10, you can decide on the data source you want to use in the query. The data source can be any of the following four options:

9 | Reporting and Analysis

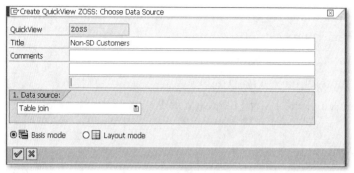

Figure 9.10 Selecting Data Source (Table Join)

- **Table or Table View**
  Because the table or table view can be displayed using Transaction SE16 or SE16N, this option is not practical. But remember, there are some useful standard table views, such as VBRK-VBRP, which is a table join of VBRK (billing documents – header) and VBRP (billing document – items).

- **Logical database**
  There are over 200 standard logical databases. When you select this option, you're asked to provide the name of the logical database. You can click on the Display button next to the field to provide a logical database, which takes you to Figure 9.11. The logical database DDF in this example stores all of the master data and transaction-related accounting data (Tables BKPF and BSEG). Logical database queries tend to perform very fast.

- **SAP Query Infoset**
  Any Query infoset already created via a table join, can be re-used.

- **Table Join**
  We've opted for this option. We'll discuss it in more detail now.

9.2.3 Insert Tables

When you're in the screen shown in Figure 9.10, you can provide a comment, which will be useful for those reviewing your query in the future. Select the Table Join option as the data source and select the Basis Mode radio button, which will take you to Figure 9.12. You can also use the menu path EDIT • INSERT TABLE to insert a table. A dialog box appears when you follow the menu path or click on the Insert Table icon (second from the left in the application toolbar). In the dialog window, as shown in Figure 9.12, enter the name of the table you want to use

412

Developing Reports Using Query | **9.2**

and press Enter, and the table will be inserted. You can repeat the steps to insert more than one table.

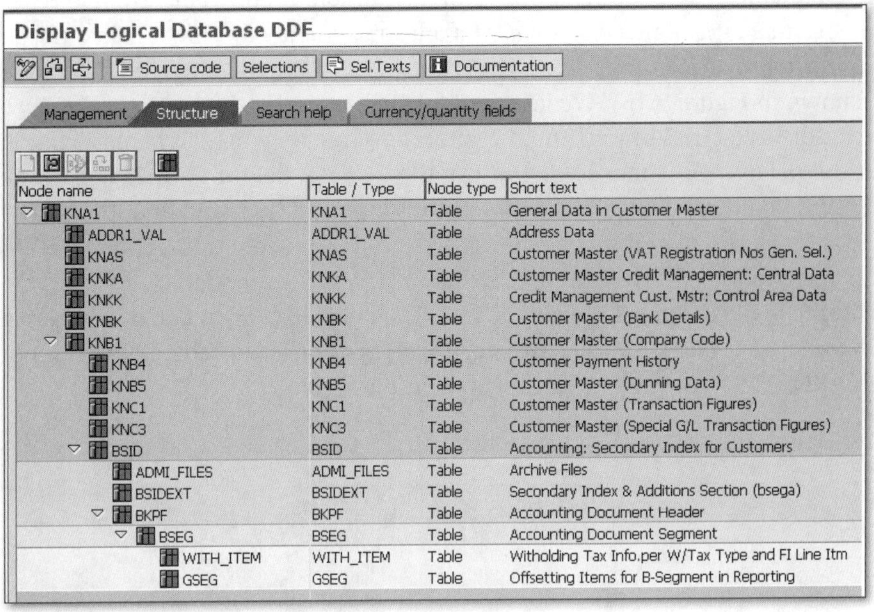

Figure 9.11 Logical Database DDF (Customer Database)

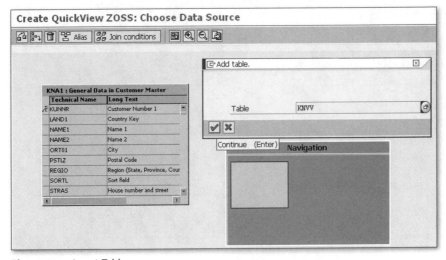

Figure 9.12 Insert Table

9.2.4 Join Tables

Once the tables are inserted, the default joins appear. It's important to understand what tables you're going to join and how to join them. There are two types of joins: *left-outer join* and *inner join*. Default joins are always inner joins. If you select and right-click on any join, you'll get the option to change or delete the join (shown in Figure 9.13). We've opted for this example to stress the difference between the two types of join and the important role they play in a query. If you select the default, the inner join, and use the KUNNR field to join Tables KNA1 and KNVV, you'll get the list of customers present in Tables KNA1 and KNVV. The inner join will result in those customers present in both Tables KNA1 and KNVV. This is not the list of customer that we want. If you use the left-outer join, the list will show all customers in Table KNA1. The fields to be populated from Table KNVV will be left blank for the customers that have entries in Table KNA1 but not in table KNVV. So you have to opt for the left-outer join.

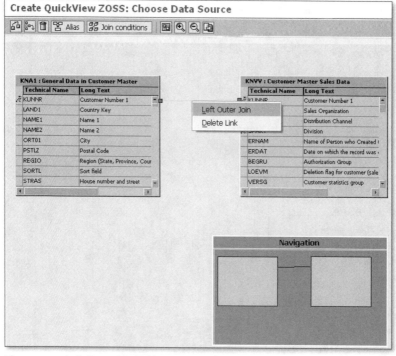

Figure 9.13 Left-Outer Join Tables KNA1 and KNVV

You can have more than one inner join between two tables. As shown in Figure 9.14, the Authorization Group field is also used to join Tables KNA1 and KNVV. To create a join, identify the fields that are to be joined, which must satisfy certain conditions such as the same length and same type (e.g., a character field cannot be joined with a numeric field). The fields to be used as joining conditions should be present in both tables. In simple terms, an inner join is like an AND condition. That is, all of the records in the first table *and* second table with a common value for the joining field will be selected. So in our example, when the system found that some customers, which are used as joining field (KUNNR), are not present in Table KNVV, they are not selected.

Similarly, a left-outer join can be called an OR condition. That is, all of the records present in the first *or* second table will be selected subject to other restrictions in selection criteria. So when we used customers as the joining fields, all of the customers in the system (present in Table KNA1) were selected, even when some of them were not present in the second table (KNVV) for the left-outer join.

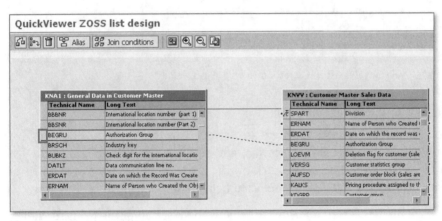

Figure 9.14 Two Inner Joins

Click on the column next to the field name and drag the cursor to the field in the next table, as shown in Figure 9.14. Two inner joins means two AND conditions. In this case, if the customer code and authorization group field value in a record in one table is same as in other table, it will be listed. Press [Ctrl] + [F] to search a field in an inserted table. Once all of the required tables are inserted and joined, click on the Back Arrow to reach the screen shown in Figure 9.15.

9.2.5 Selection and List Fields

When you reach the screen shown in Figure 9.15, you can decide on the fields you want to use in the selection or initial screen of the report (query). You also decide on the fields for the list here. There are two ways of doing this, which we'll detail in the following subsections.

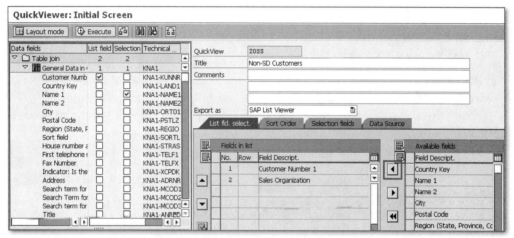

Figure 9.15 Selecting the List and Selection Fields in Basis Mode

Using Tabs in the Panel on the Right

As you can see in Figure 9.15, there are various tabs to use for selection and list fields. Click on the List Fld. Select. tab, and select the fields required in the list from the Available Fields. Next, click on the arrow pointing left (highlighted in Figure 9.15), which will shift the selected fields into the fields in list category.

Next, click on the Selection Fields tab, where you'll see all of the fields for Tables KNA1 and KNVV in the Available Fields list again. Select the fields you want and click on the Left Arrow. The fields will shift to the Selection Fields list.

Using the Table Join Folder

As you select fields for the selection and list screens, you'll notice the checkmarks appearing in the selected fields in the Table Join folder. In the Table Join folder, all of the inserted tables appear. Click on the small triangle next to the table name to display or hide fields, and select the checkbox next to the field and in the List Fields column to make the field appear in the list. Clicking on the checkbox below the Selection fields allows the field to appear in the selection screen.

Once the tables are inserted and the fields are selected for the selection and list fields, you still may be required to add another table. To change the data source, click on the Data Source tab shown in Figure 9.16. If you're interested in the table join, clicking on the Change Join button will take you to the screen shown in Figure 9.13.

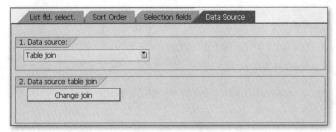

Figure 9.16 Data Source Tab to Change Join

9.2.6 List Screen Layout

We've already discussed, the two important aspects of layout are sequence and sorting. There are several options for designing the layout of the list screen. In this section, we'll discuss a few of the important ones. When you're in the screen, shown in Figure 9.15, click on the Layout Mode button in the application toolbar to go to the screen shown in Figure 9.17. We'll discuss the following basic elements of designing:

1. Decide the sequence of fields
2. Sorting
3. Description of list fields
4. Default width of columns

Sequence of Fields

You can decide the order in which fields appear by taking the following steps when you're in basis mode (Figure 9.15).

- Select a field (row) and click on the Up or Down Arrow to change its location.
- The selection fields appear in the same order as they're presented in the Selection Fields tab.

- For the List fields, they're transposed, meaning the field on the top (number 1) appears in first column and the field below it (number 2) appear to the right of the first one, and so on.

Sorting

If the list (or output) is to appear presorted, you can take the following steps:

- Select the Sort Order tab shown in Figure 9.16.
- Select the field (or fields) on which the list is to be sorted.
- Click on the Left Arrow.
- Click on the Ascending or Descending Order option for sorting.

Description of List Fields

In layout mode (Figure 9.17), the list fields' descriptions appear at the top of the screen. You can click on any field and modify the description to make it more meaningful, but any description longer than the field length is not possible. Therefore, you may need to increase the field length or column width first, which we'll explain next.

Column Width

You can modify the default column width (or field length of the list field or output length) can be modified, as shown in the bottom-left of the screen in Figure 9.17. In this case, the output length of the Sales Organization field (KNVV-VKORS) is increased from 4 (which is the standard length) to 29. This is to replace the standard description (SOrg) with a longer description (Sales Organization Code). This is important because the list's user may not understand what SOrg is, and sometimes the more information you can provide, the better.

Now you can save the setting. A warning message may appear, and after saving the query, click on the Execute button in application toolbar (Figure 9.15). This will take you to the selection screen of the query, as shown in Figure 9.18. We've selected the Customer Code (KUNNR) field of Table KNA1 and the Sales Organization (VKORG) field of Table KNVV. As you know, we had opted for left-outer join to list customers present in Table KNA1 and not present in Table KNVV. The inclusion of the KNVV-VKORG field in the selection screen will create a special situation. We're only interested in a list that doesn't have any entries in the Table KNVV, and left-outer join will make the KNVV-VKORG field blank.

9.2 Developing Reports Using Query

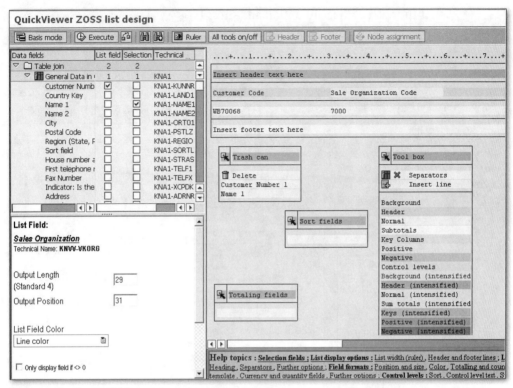

Figure 9.17 Modify List Screen Layout

So, if we fix the value of the KNVV-VKORG field (Sales Organization) to blank and then execute the report, we'll get the list we want. Note that we've left the first field, which means it can have any value. We've fixed the value of the second field to blank. Because the Sales Organization field is a key field (mandatory) in Table KNVV, it isn't possible to have an entry in Table KNVV without a value for this field. To select a single value for a selection field, you can take the following steps:

- Click on the Multiple Selection icon, which looks like an arrow pointed to the right, on the far right, against the selection field.

- A dialog box, shown in Figure 9.18, with the heading Multiple Selection for XXX will appear, where XXX is the field for which you're making the selection.

- Click on the Selection Options icon, which is highlighted in Figure 9.18, which presents you with the Select by Initial Value dialog box.

9 Reporting and Analysis

- Select the Select: Equal To option and press [Enter].
- Click on the Copy icon in the bottom-left part of the Multiple Selection dialog box.

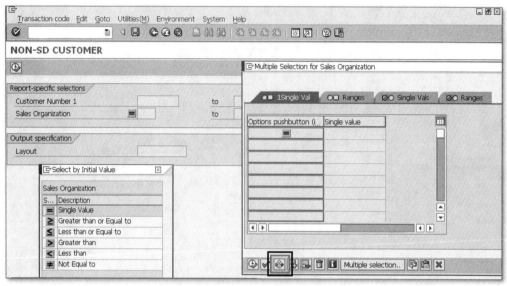

Figure 9.18 Selection Screen of the Query

Save the input setting by clicking on the Save as Variant icon. This will take you to the screen shown in Figure 9.19, where you can create a variant. In this first screen, you can provide a name starting with Y or Z for the variant. In the second field, include a description. By selecting the Protected Variant checkbox, you're preventing others from tampering with the variant while using it. When selected, the Only for Background Processing checkbox makes the variant unavailable in the list of variant icons that appears next to the Execute icon in the application toolbar. The Fields Of field can be disabled for entry and hidden, as we've done for Sales Organization. We've also neglected to select the Save field Without Values checkbox for Sales Organization to preserve the settings we made in the steps for the single value selection. Therefore, nobody using this variant will be required to do those steps again. We opted for background processing because we'll be using it in a Z-transaction. Finally, save and click on Back, which take you out of execution mode, and save the query.

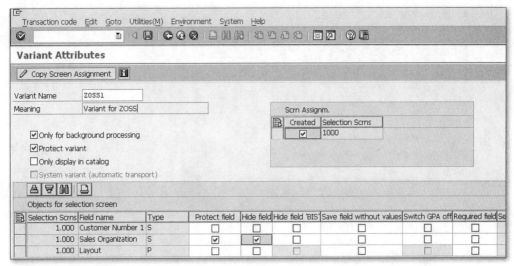

Figure 9.19 Create Protected Variant for Selection Screen

9.2.7 Create a Z-Transaction for the Query

Customer transactions are created for users so that they use the query because a query created by one user is not available for use by other users of the system automatically. Also, you can manage authorization. That is, some users are allowed to use the transaction for the query and others are not. You create customer transactions using Transaction SE93. In the initial screen, enter a code (e.g., ZOSS) and click on the Create icon, which will take you to the dialog box shown in Figure 9.20. Here you can enter a meaningful description and select the Program and Selection Screen (Report Transaction) radio button. Press Enter and you'll go to the screen shown in Figure 9.21. In this screen, the proposed transaction code and description will appear by default. For the program name, execute the query in Transaction SQVI. Follow the menu path SYSTEM • STATUS when you're in the selection screen, as shown in Figure 9.18. Copy the entry that you find in the program field to the program field in the screen shown in Figure 9.21. If the program name starts with an exclamation mark, such as !QFKSYSTQV000014ZOSS==========, replace the ! with an A. In the variant field, enter the name of the variant with which you saved the variant in Figure 9.19

9 | Reporting and Analysis

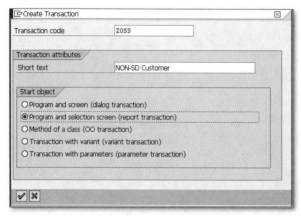

Figure 9.20 Create Transaction (ZOSS) for Query

Save the setting for creating a transaction, and you'll get a transport request. If you're creating the query in the production client and the transaction is in development, you have to transport the request with a dummy program name. In production, replace that with the program name of the query. Now when you execute the transaction (e.g., ZOSS), the query developed for it will run. You'll go to the selection screen of the query.

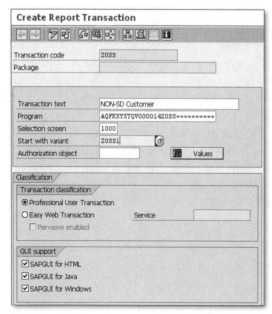

Figure 9.21 Create Report Transaction with Variant

422

9.3 Sales Information System

The Sales Information System (SIS) is part of the more general Logistics Information System (LIS). SIS consists of different standard and variable analyses, planning information, the early warning system, and the info library. It also consists of customization and archiving tools that pertains to the Sales and Distribution functionality in SAP ERP. SIS uses the data that originates during the transactions in Sales and Distribution. In addition to transactional data, various master data (e.g., customer, material, employee and so on) is used in SIS reports and analyses. There is a warning, however. The information generated in SIS is not considered perfect for statutory or legal reporting because it may not be perfect. You need to continuously monitor for any possible error in updating of SIS info-structures, which we'll discuss in Section 9.3.3 while discussing the checks for info-structures. The SIS reports and analyses use the resources of the SAP ERP server, so they affect the overall performance of the SAP ERP system. Many undesirable or unused info-structures are like parasites on your system, so you should, in general, delete the info-structures that are active in production server but in use for extracting reports or analyses.

In this section, we'll discuss four general topics concerning the Sales Information System. We'll start with the standard analyses and then move on to flexible analyses and tools available for customizing these analyses. Finally, we'll discuss how to check the consistency of info-structures.

9.3.1 Standard Analyses

There are several standard analyses in the Sales and Distribution functionality in SAP ERP. These analyses are based on individual info-structures. The info-structures are updated in real time and provide reliable, real-time analysis. The same info-structure may be in use in several analyses. We'll discuss these analyses in the next few sections.

Customer Analyses (S001)

Customer analyses use the info-structure S001. It's used for analyzing orders, invoices, credit memos, and returns for one or several customers. The other selection criteria are the sales area (sales organization, distribution channel, and division), material, and date range. Whether the date range is weekly or monthly depends on the update group. The result or list of the analysis can be drilled down like the list in Figure 9.22. You display the list by clicking on the Display Drill-

9 | Reporting and Analysis

down button in the selection screen of the analysis. Table 9.3 lists some customer analyses with their transaction codes. The drill-down structure is different for different analyses. The default fields of the output list are also different. Figure 9.23 shows the output list of MCTA (customer analysis). Press [F8] when you complete the selection criteria to get the list or result. The operations that can be done when you're in the list are drill-down, change layout to insert hidden columns, and change column width. You can also opt for Customer Code + Customer Name by following the menu path SETTINGS • CHARACTERISTIC DISPLAY • KEY AND DESCRIPTION. Other features of standard reports, such as graphical display, export to other applications, and so on, are also possible.

Transaction	Description
MC+I	SIS: Customer Credit Memos – Selection
MC+A	SIS: Customer Returns, Selection
MC+E	SIS: Customer, Sales – Selection
MC(A	SIS: Customer, Incoming Orders – Selection
MCTA	SIS: Customer Analysis – Selection

Table 9.3 Customer Analyses

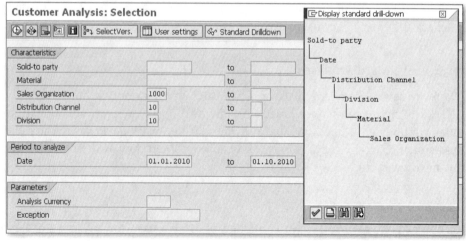

Figure 9.22 Customer Analysis Selection Screen and Drill-Down List

9.3 Sales Information System

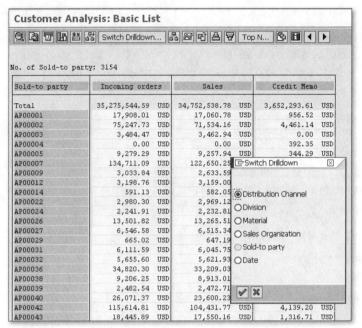

Figure 9.23 List for MCTA (Customer Analysis) with Switch Drilldown Dialog

Sales Office Analyses (S002)

The sales office analyses are stored in info-structure S002. These analyses are useful for information at the sales group and sales office levels. Note that material is not a part of this structure, so it isn't available in the selection, list, or drill-down. Table 9.4 lists some sales office analyses.

Transaction	Description
MC-E	SIS: Sales Office – Sales Selection
MC-I	SIS: Sales Office Credit Memos Selection
MC-A	SIS: Sales Office Returns, Selection
MC(M	SIS: Sales Office, Incoming Orders Selection
MCTG	SIS: Sales Office Analysis Selection

Table 9.4 Sales Office Analyses

Sales Organization Analyses (S003)

The sales organization is part of all of the standard analyses. This group of analyses would be better named Sales district analyses. These analyses are based on info-structure S003, and the sales district, customer, and material are key fields in addition to the sales area elements. Table 9.5 lists some of these analyses.

Transaction	Description
MC+Y	SIS: Sales Org. Returns, Selection
MC(I	SIS: Sales Org. Incoming Orders Selection
MC+6	SIS: Sales Org. Credit Memos Selection
MC+2	SIS: Sales Org. Invoiced Sales, Selection
MCTE	SIS: Sales Org. Analysis – Selection

Table 9.5 Sales Organization Analyses

Material Analyses (S004)

Material analyses, listed in Table 9.6, use info-structure S004. Note that the division is not part of this info-structure.

Transaction	Description
MC+U	SIS: Material Credit Memos, Selection
MC+M	SIS: Material Returns, Selection
MC+Q	SIS: Material, Sales – Selection
MC(E	SIS: Material, Incoming Orders – Selection
MCTC	SIS: Material Analysis – Selection

Table 9.6 Material Analyses

Shipping Point Analyses (S005)

The shipping point analyses, listed in Table 9.7, use info-structure S005. Shipping Point/Receiving Point, Route, Forwarding Agent and Destination Country are the key fields in the info-structure. The list contains the net and gross weights and labor requirements for outbound and/or return deliveries.

Transaction	Description
MC(U	SIS: Shipping Point Deliveries Selection
MC-O	SIS: Shipping Point Returns, Selection
MCTK	SIS: Shipping Point Analysis Selection

Table 9.7 Shipping Point Analyses

Sales Employee Analyses (S006)

Sales employee analyses, listed in Table 9.8, use info-structure S006. In addition to sales area elements, sold-to party, and material, the sales employee is a key field in this info-structure.

Transaction	Description
MC-U	SIS: Employee – Credit Memos, Selection
MC-M	SIS: Employee – Returns, Selection
MC-Q	SIS: Employee – Sales, Selection
MC(Q	SIS: Employee, Incoming Orders Selection
MCTI	SIS: Sales Employee Analysis Selection

Table 9.8 Sales Employee Analyses

> **Note**
> Shipment, sales support, and customer potential analyses are not considered part of the Sales Information System. They are part of the broader grouping of the Logistics Information System (LIS). Nevertheless, you can use them as and when required.

9.3.2 Flexible Analyses

In addition to the standard analyses, you may need customized analyses to meet your requirements. These customized analyses are called flexible analyses. The following are the broad steps of creating flexible analyses.

- Create customized info-structure (or evaluation structure).
- Create customized analysis (or evaluation).

Create Customized Info-Structure

When the available standard info-structures cannot provide the information you or your user wants, you may want to create your own info-structures. The steps involved in creating customized info-structure are given below.

1. Decide on characteristics and key figures. In an info-structure or evaluation structure, the characteristics and key fields are selected via Transaction MSC7. Examples of characteristics fields include the sales organization, sold-to party, material, billing type, or sales group. You can include the credit memo quantity, credit memo for returns value, and quantity, debit memo value, and so on as key figures.

2. Decide on a reference info-structure or table. In Transaction MSC7, you need to decide on the reference info-structure (e.g., S001) or standard tables (e.g., VBRP). The menu path for Transaction MSC7 is SAP EASY ACCESS • LOGISTICS • SALES AND DISTRIBUTION • SALES INFORMATION SYSTEM • FLEXIBLE ANALYSES • EVALUATION STRUCTURE • CREATE. In the initial screen, shown in Figure 9.24, the database table or the info-structure should contain all of the fields you've identified for characteristics and key figures.

3. Press [Enter] after entering the name, description, and reference info-structure or table.

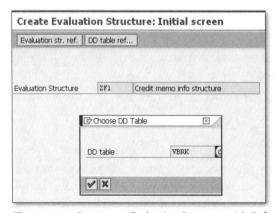

Figure 9.24 Creating an Evaluation Structure with Reference to a Database Table

4. You'll see a screen similar to the one shown in Figure 9.25. Click on the Characteristics button in the application toolbar. Two dialog boxes, as shown in Figure 9.25, will appear. The Selection list provides you with the entire list of fields available for selection as characteristics. Click on the Copy + Close icon after selecting all of the fields you want. If there are more fields you want to select, click on the Copy button at the bottom of this dialog box.

5. When all of the fields are copied to the Chosen Characteristics: Sequence dialog box, click on the Copy button.

6. All of the fields will be copied to the main screen and will appear in the Characteristics box on the left side.

7. Repeat this process to insert key fields. That is, click on the Key Figures button on the application toolbar and select and copy available fields.

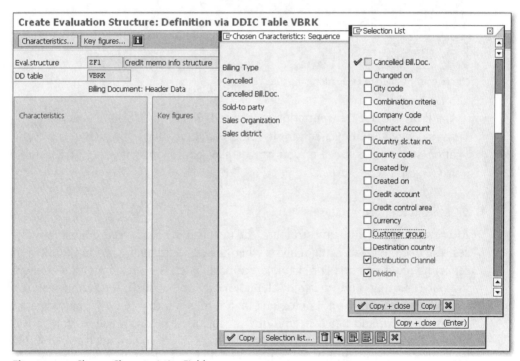

Figure 9.25 Choose Characteristics Fields

8. Once you have all of the fields you want selected, as shown in Figure 9.26, follow the menu path EVALUATION STRUCTURE • GENERATE to generate the evaluation structure.

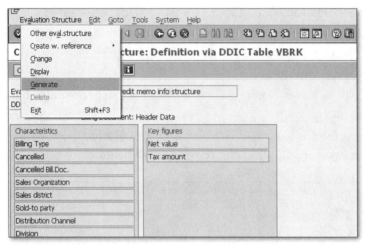

Figure 9.26 Generate Evaluation Structure

9. You'll be asked if transportation is required. Select Yes if you're generating the list in a development client, for use in production after testing. Once the evaluation structure is created, you can display and change it using Transactions MCS9 and MCS8, respectively.

Create Customized Analyses

After creating an evaluation structure, the next activity is to create a flexible analyses. You need to create your analysis when the standard analyses don't fulfill your reporting requirements. For example, suppose batch is a very important element in your reporting, and no standard analyses give you this information. You can use flexible analysis for it. Having said that, remember that there are performance issues involved, and batch is typically not included in such analyses for performance reasons. But when a typical user looks at any standard analyses, he often says, "We also want XXX next to the last column in this." XXX can be material group description, employee name, or country code. For that, you'll end up creating a customized analysis (and a customized info-structure). The transaction code to create a customized analysis is MCSA (menu path: SAP EASY ACCESS • LOGISTICS • SALES AND DISTRIBUTION • SALES INFORMATION SYSTEM • FLEXIBLE ANALYSES • EVALUATION • CREATE). The steps to create a customized analyses are as follows:

1. In the initial screen, specify the evaluation structure to be used for the evaluation.
2. Enter a key and description for the valuation.
3. Press [Enter]. You'll go to a screen similar to the one shown in Figure 9.27.
4. Click on Characteristics button in the application tool bar. All of the characteristics fields of the info-structure will be available for selection.

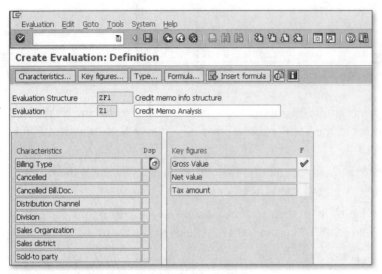

Figure 9.27 Define Evaluation for Flexible Analysis

5. Select all or some of the fields in the Selection List dialog box.
6. Click on the Copy + Close button of that dialog box.
7. Click on the Copy button of the Chosen Characteristics: Sequence dialog box.
8. Repeat the same steps for inserting key figures.
9. Once all of the fields are available in the main screen, as shown in Figure 9.27, you can move on to layout modification.
10. To decide how the characteristics that should appear in the selection screen of the analyses, select a Characteristics field.
11. Click on the Type button in the application toolbar.
12. A dialog box, shown in Figure 9.28, will appear. Customize the appearance as per your requirements.

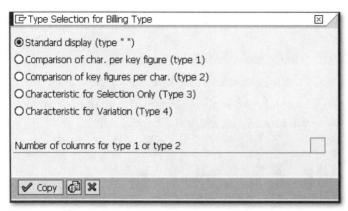

Figure 9.28 Type Selection for Characteristics Field (e.g., Billing Type)

13. You can do some simple operations with the key fields by clicking on the Add Formula button in the application toolbar. The dialog box shown in Figure 9.29 will appear.
14. Give a name to the field (or column) that will display the result of the formula. In this example, we have used Gross Value.
15. All of the key figures with their technical names will appear on the top part of the screen (Figure 9.29). You can use these fields in the formula.

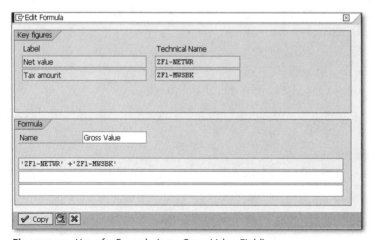

Figure 9.29 Use of a Formula (e.g., Gross Value Field)

16. Click on Copy after the field's formula is complete.
17. The field will appear along with the F field selected, as shown in Figure 9.27.

18. Save, and a dialog box will appear. You can create a transport request if required by clicking on the Yes button.

19. You can display and modify the evaluation using Transactions MCSC and MCSB, respectively.

Execute Flexible Analyses

To use the evaluation, execute Transaction MCSG (menu path: SAP Easy Access • Logistics • Sales and Distribution • Sales Information System • Flexible Analyses • Evaluation • Execute).

1. Enter the name of the structure and the evaluation in the initial screen.

2. Press [F8], and the initial screen of the analyses will appear, which will display the fields for selection/restriction as per customization. Enter the values for which a result list is required.

3. Press [F8], which will take you to the result list shown in Figure 9.30.

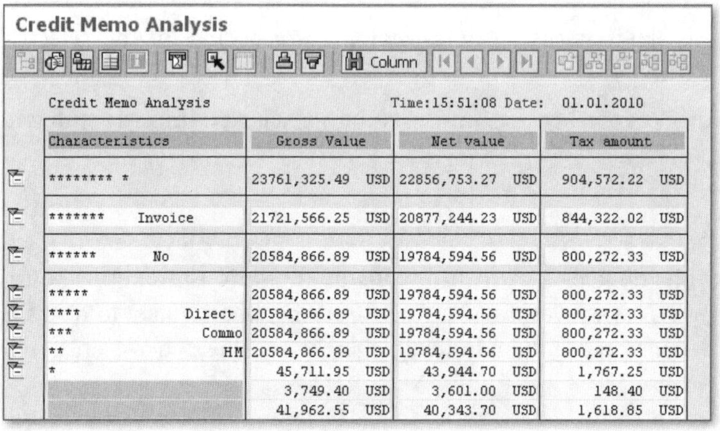

Credit Memo Analysis			
Credit Memo Analysis		Time:15:51:08 Date:	01.01.2010
Characteristics	Gross Value	Net value	Tax amount
******** *	23761,325.49 USD	22856,753.27 USD	904,572.22 USD
******* Invoice	21721,566.25 USD	20877,244.23 USD	844,322.02 USD
****** No	20584,866.89 USD	19784,594.56 USD	800,272.33 USD
*****	20584,866.89 USD	19784,594.56 USD	800,272.33 USD
**** Direct	20584,866.89 USD	19784,594.56 USD	800,272.33 USD
*** Commo	20584,866.89 USD	19784,594.56 USD	800,272.33 USD
** HM	20584,866.89 USD	19784,594.56 USD	800,272.33 USD
*	45,711.95 USD	43,944.70 USD	1,767.25 USD
	3,749.40 USD	3,601.00 USD	148.40 USD
	41,962.55 USD	40,343.70 USD	1,618.85 USD

Figure 9.30 Execution of Flexible Analysis

9.3.3 General Checks for Info-Structure

The transaction used to check a user-created info-structure user is MCSCHECK. You can use it to check the standard info-structures, which obviously will have no errors most of the time. However, in one of the checks, the Field Catalog check, a standard info-structure may even show an error. This is primarily due to the changes at the customer end during the creation of a customized info-structure.

The initial screen for Transaction MCSCHECK has several frames. On the top is the Selection frame, where you can specify the info-structure that needs to be checked. You also specify the application, which is 01 for Sales and Distribution, and the client.

There are five groups of checks that you can use with this tool. They also happen to be the frame headings for the checks they group. Each check has its own checkbox, so you can select any number checks at a time. The different kinds of checks are described in the subsections below.

LIS Control Tables

The checkboxes in this frame, when selected, check the info-structure for any error in the LIS control tables it uses. These checks are given below:

- The Control Tables field checks the assignments and interdependencies of the control tables for the selected information structures. For example, an info-structure without any LIS control table associated with it will show an error if this checkbox is selected.
- The Field Catalogs field checks all field catalogs, irrespective of the selected information structure.
- The Units field checks whether the units used in the selected info-structure are consistent.

Info-Structure

The checkboxes in this frame check the info-structure for various properties. Info-structures that show errors or warnings during these checks are likely to result is erroneous reports when you use them in flexible analyses. These checks are given below:

- Status LIS/Dictionary checks that the statuses in the information structure and the database table are the same.
- Fields LIS/Dictionary checks the fields in the information structure and the database table. If this checkbox is selected, the properties of the fields (e.g., numeric or character, length, etc.) in info-structure and database tables should match.
- Select the Assignments to Info Structures checkbox to check the assignment to information structures with different types.
- The Stock Values checkbox checks stock values.

Updating

The checkboxes in this frame check whether there is or can be any problem in updating the info-structure. If an info-structure is not correctly updated, it cannot generate a correct report. These checks are given below:

- The Update Program checkbox, when selected, gets you information on update programs.
- The Update Indicators (e.g., V1, V2, V3) are selected when this checkbox is selected.
- The Update Group/Event checkbox checks the consistency of table entries.
- Select the Characteristics/Key Figures checkbox to check if the update program can fill the info-structure with data for characteristics and key figures.
- The Formulas/Requirements checkbox checks if the formula and/or requirement routines assigned to update rule exist in active state.

Standard Analysis

These checkboxes are more for information purposes then to check info-structures for errors. For example, you can find the list of standard and flexible analyses that may be using a particular standard info-structure (first check). These checks are given below:

- The Existing Standard Analyses checkbox, when selected, gets you the list of all existing standard analyses of the selected info-structure. For example, the five standard analyses for info-structure S001 are Customer Analysis (0001), Customer Analysis: Incoming Orders (2001), Customer Analysis: Returns (2002), Customer Analysis: Invoiced Sales (2003), and Customer Analysis: Credit Memos (2004).
- The Compare Key Figures IS and STA checkbox compares the key figures in info-structures and standard analyses. In case of difference, an error is reported.
- The Standard Default Settings field checks and reports the default user-specific settings for characteristics, key figures, and parameters.

Flexible Analysis

Select The checkbox in this frame, the Existing Flexible Analyses checkbox, when you want to see the list of existing flexible analyses for the selected info-structure.

You can use this information, for example, to find the info-structure not used in any flexible analyses and either use it or delete it.

After selecting the entire required check, press [F8] to execute the program. By default, you should select all possible checkboxes. You'll get a report like the one shown in Figure 9.31. This report will show the possible errors in the customized info-structure (or standard info-structure) for which the report was executed. The errors (and warnings) are rectified to prevent errors in flexible analyses that use the info-structure. The following SAP notes discuss some of the specific errors in customization of info-structures and how to solve them.

- Note 202631 – SIS: No Update of Individual Key Figures
- Note 430718 – LIS: Incorrect Unit Update (e.g., 10 USD + 10 EUR = 20 EUR)
- Note 434615 – LIS Objects: Field Length > 10 Not Possible
- Note 509000 – LIS: Incorrect Display of Values/Quantities in Std Analysis

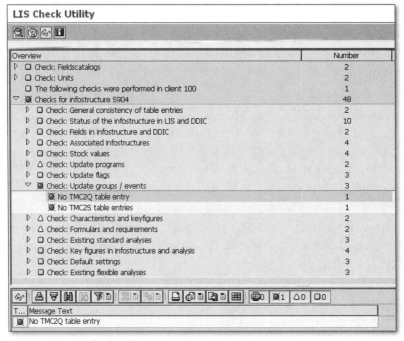

Figure 9.31 LIS Check Utility

9.3.4 Checks for SIS Info-Structures

In addition to the general checks discussed in the previous section, there are also checks performed for the info-structures created in the Sales and Distribution functionality in SAP ERP. These checks check the assignment of update groups using Transaction MCVCHECK01, shown in Figure 9.32. Note that the check is performed for both header and item levels simultaneously. However, in online mode, to avoid ABAP run-time errors, it should be run with restrictions. Running the check in the background ([F9]) for one sales organization at a time is the best solution to avoid an ABAP dump. There are two different transaction codes (MCVCHECK02 and MCVCHECK03) for checking assignments at the header and item levels, respectively. Transaction MCVCHECK02 is same as MCVCHECK01, except that the Check On Header Level checkbox is selected. Transaction MCVCHECK03 is same as MCVCHECK01, except that the Check on Item Level checkbox is selected. You should have no problem using these transactions for a consistency check, especially for online execution. These two transactions are also very helpful in helping you understand the output report.

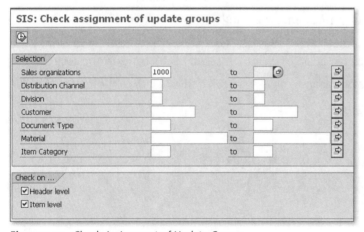

Figure 9.32 Check Assignment of Update Groups

The Check for Update Groups checkbox does the following checks at the header and item levels.

Header Level

The header level has the following checks and lists:

- All document types without an update group assigned to them.
- All customers with the Customer Statistics Group (KNVV – VERSG) field empty. The field is maintained in the customer master record (Sales tab of Sales Area data).
- All of the combinations of document type and customer for which the system will not be able to determine an update group.

Item Level

For the valid combinations at the header level, the item level check does the following checks at the item level. The missing entries are listed as warning messages (yellow triangle).

- All document types without an update group assigned to them.
- All customers with the Customer Statistics Group field empty.
- All of the item categories without an update group assigned to them.
- All materials with the Material Statistic Group (MVKE-VERSG) field blank. The field is maintained in the Sales: Sales Org.2 tab of the material master record.
- All combinations of the above four for which the system cannot determine the update group.

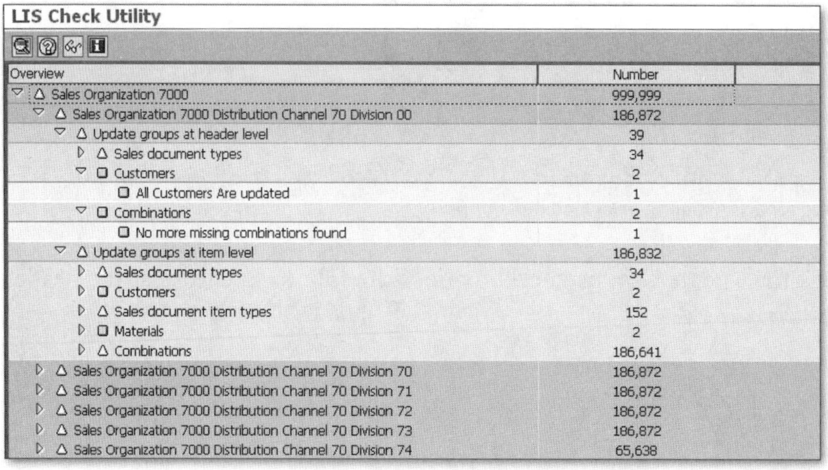

LIS Check Utility	
Overview	Number
▽ △ Sales Organization 7000	999,999
▽ △ Sales Organization 7000 Distribution Channel 70 Division 00	186,872
▽ △ Update groups at header level	39
▷ △ Sales document types	34
▽ ▢ Customers	2
▢ All Customers Are updated	1
▽ ▢ Combinations	2
▢ No more missing combinations found	1
▽ △ Update groups at item level	186,832
▷ △ Sales document types	34
▷ ▢ Customers	2
▷ △ Sales document item types	152
▷ ▢ Materials	2
▷ △ Combinations	186,641
▷ △ Sales Organization 7000 Distribution Channel 70 Division 70	186,872
▷ △ Sales Organization 7000 Distribution Channel 70 Division 71	186,872
▷ △ Sales Organization 7000 Distribution Channel 70 Division 72	186,872
▷ △ Sales Organization 7000 Distribution Channel 70 Division 73	186,872
▷ △ Sales Organization 7000 Distribution Channel 70 Division 74	65,638

Figure 9.33 Output (Online) of Assignment Check for Update Groups

When you create the output in the background (refer Figure 9.34), all data will be available. Note that for online processing, there are some limitations. For example, note the number 999999 in Figure 9.33. This is the upper limit for online processing. Also, because in a production client, it takes a lot of time and slows down the system, you should do it at night or on the weekend (or when the system is relatively less used) as a background job.

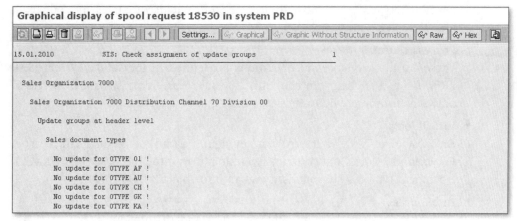

Figure 9.34 Background Processing of Assignment Check for Update Groups

9.4 Business Intelligence and Reporting

The business information warehousing software provided by SAP allows you the opportunity to extract data from both SAP and non-SAP systems, and to present it in a clear and manageable format. The performance is very fast, and when huge amounts of data needs to be analyzed, it outperforms all other options discussed in this book. The key feature of the business intelligence software offered by SAP is that it has its own database. Data is extracted from other systems, including SAP ERP and stored on its own database. This also explains the reason for better performance than *online transaction processing* (OLTP) systems such as SAP ERP. SAP NetWeaver BW is called an *online analytical processing* (OLAP) system. SAP provides an add-on called *business content* (BI content), which is preconfigured reports and objects. The objects of BI content include the following:

▶ **Extractor programs**
These programs move information from the SAP ERP system to SAP NetWeaver BW. Function module RSAX_BIW_GET_DATA_SIMPLE is one of the extractor programs available in SAP ERP.

- **DataSources**
  DataSources are delivered with BI content. They are activated in the SAP ERP (or other source) system directly or can be activated remotely from the SAP NetWeaver BW system. These DataSources structure data in the staging area in the source system. For example, DataSource 2LIS_11_VASTH extracts the sales order header status from the standard SAP ERP Table VBUK. Different fields of this table such as Billing Status (FKSTK), Delivery Status (LFSTK), Order Number (VBELN), and so on move to the DataSource fields with the same code (e.g., FKSTK, LFSTK, and so on).

- **Process chains**
  These are the sequences of operations predefined in the source system (SAP ERP). A process chain can consist of several steps. Some steps are processed only when some previous ones are successfully completed.

- **InfoObjects**
  An InfoObject is a characteristic, a key figure, a unit, or a time characteristic. For example, document currency is a unit and an InfoObject (0DOC_CURRCY). Document type is a characteristic and an InfoObject (0DOC_TYPE).

- **InfoSources**
  These consist of various InfoObjects. The standard InfoSource 2LIS_01_S260 (sales order), for example, consists of most of the fields that you find in a sales order and stored in SAP ERP Tables VBAK (header) and VBAP (items).

- **InfoCubes**
  InfoCubes take source data from one or more InfoSources. For example, InfoCube 0SD_C05 (Quotations / Orders) takes source data from InfoSources 2LIS_01_S264 (SD – Quotation), 2LIS_01_S260 (SD – Sales order), 2LIS_12_VCSCL (Schedule Line Delivery), and 2LIS_12_VCITM (Delivery Item Data). These are used for generating queries that are actual reporting tools.

- **ODS objects**
  These are database tables in the SAP NetWeaver BW system. These take source data from one or more InfoSources. Other ODS objects can also be sources of information for them. For example, ODS object 0SD_O03 (Aggregation Header Level for Sales Order) takes source information from InfoSources 2LIS_11_VAHDR (Sales Document Header Data) and 2LIS_11_VASTH (Sales Document Header Status) and ODS objects 0SD_O01 (Aggregation Order Item) and 0SD_O02 (Returns Items). ODS objects store the data at the document level (e.g., information from individual sales orders) and can be overwritten for the changes in the source system.

- **Variables**
  Variables are what make a BI report dynamic. For example, when a plant is a variable, you can restrict the output to display records for only a particular plant. There are several types of variable, for example, formula variable, text variable, and so on.

- **Data mining models**
  You can access the standard SAP-delivered data mining models by following the menu path SAP EASY ACCESS • INFORMATION SYSTEM • BUSINESS INFORMATION SYSTEM • ENHANCED ANALYTICS • DATA MINING. The transaction code is RSD-MWB. Data mining models are used to look for patterns and correlations in significantly large amount of data.

- **Queries**
  These are the actual reports. We'll discuss some queries soon.

- **Workbooks**
  Workbooks are also reporting tools. One workbook can contain several queries, for example, 0LES_C02_Q0001 (Shipment Costs by Material).

- **Crystal Reports**
  These are also highly structured reporting tools. These reports can be created using not only an SAP NetWeaver BW database, but also other sources.

- **Web templates**
  These are predesigned web pages used for reporting. They can use the information available on an SAP NetWeaver BW server to provide information interactively to the users. The Web templates delivered with SAP business (BI) content can be modified using the web application designer (WAD).

- **Roles**
  Different queries, workbooks, and other reporting tools are available to different users as per the roles assigned to them. For example, the standard role sales manager (0ROLE_0007) would monitor various aspects of sales such as incoming orders, returns, weekly deliveries, costs, and so on.

Some of the standard queries (or reports) that BI content offers are listed below. The technical name of the query is in the brackets. Figure 9.35 shows the output of the query 0SD_C03_Q003 (proportion of returns to incoming orders). Note the last row in the screen shot. With this report you can find out the returns as a percentage of incoming orders (aggregated for different months) for individual customers.

- Monthly incoming orders and revenue (0SD_C01_Q0002)
- Returns per customer (0SD_C01_Q010)

9 | Reporting and Analysis

- Product profitability analysis (0SD_C01_Q022)
- Top customers (0SD_C01_Q023)
- Incoming orders analysis (0SD_C01_Q024)
- Distribution channel analysis (0SD_C01_Q026)
- Proportion of returns to incoming orders (0SD_C03_Q003)
- Average delivery processing times (0SD_C04_Q0004)

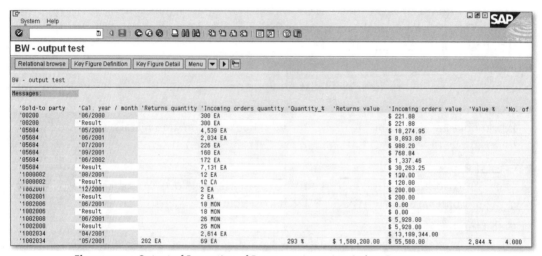

Figure 9.35 Output of Proportion of Returns to Incoming Orders Query

- Queries are based on InfoCubes. The first six items in the previous list are based on InfoCube 0SD_C01. The next two are based on 0SD_C03 and 0SD_C04. The other InfoCubes for order fulfillment are listed in Table 9.9, which also lists InfoSources that provide data to the InfoCube.

InfoCube	Technical Name	InfoSources
Quotations/Orders	0SD_C05	2LIS_01_S264
		2LIS_01_S260
		2LIS_12_VCSCL
		2LIS_12_VCITM
Shipment Cost Details	0LES_C02	2LIS_08TRFKZ

Table 9.9 InfoCubes that Source Information from Tables in the Sales and Distribution Functionality in SAP ERP

InfoCube	Technical Name	InfoSources
Shipment Cost Overview	0LES_C01	2LIS_08TRFKP
Customer	0SD_C01	2LIS_01_S001
Delivery Data of Shipment Stages	0LES_C13	2LIS_08TRTLP
Delivery Service	0SD_C05	2LIS_01_S261
Delivery	0SD_C02	2LIS_01_S005
Service Level on Order Level	0SD_C13	
Service Level on Quantity Level	0SD_C11	
Service Level on Item Level	0SD_C12	
Shipment Stage	0LES_C12	2LIS_08TRTS
Shipment Header	0LES_C11	2LIS_08TRTK
Backlogs	0SD_C14	
Sales Overview	0SD_C03	2LIS_01_S260
		2LIS_01_S261
		2LIS_01_S262
		2LIS_01_S263

Table 9.9 InfoCubes that Source Information from Tables in the Sales and Distribution Functionality in SAP ERP (Cont.)

An InfoSource contains InfoObjects that are populated by the standard SAP table fields. For example, InfoObject 0SOLD_TO (Sold-To Party) of 2LIS_01_260 (Sales Order InfoSource) is populated by the value in the KUNNR field.

The business intelligence reports using SAP systems are created using any of the following tools:

- BEx Analyzer
- BEx Query Designer
- BEx Web Application Designer

9.5 Developing ABAP Reports

ABAP (Advanced Business Application Programming) is the only programming language for the entire SAP system. Sooner or later, willingly or unwillingly, everybody interested in SAP ends up learning it. We'll discuss a few things that will help you understand the basic "grammar" of this language. We'll only discuss ABAP reporting, not dialog programs. Dialog programs are used to insert, delete, modify, or update database tables like the most standard SAP transactions. Reporting programs are used to extract information and present it. The following are the general steps for creating an ABAP report:

- Create a program specifying the program attributes.
- Write the program and activate it.
- Change text elements.
- Create documentation.
- Create variants.
- Test the program.

We'll discuss these broad steps in the following three sections

9.5.1 Create Program by Specifying Program Attributes

The transaction for creating an ABAP program is SE38 (menu path: SAP EASY ACCESS • TOOLS • ABAP WORKBENCH • DEVELOPMENT • ABAP EDITOR). The initial screen looks like the screen shown in Figure 9.36. In this screen you specify the following.

- **Program name**
  The customer program name should start with Y or Z. The next letter should identify the component for which it's created (e.g., V for Sales and Distribution), which you can enter in the Program field When you click on the Create icon next to Program field a dialog box, as shown in Figure 9.37, will appear. You specify the following program attributes in that screen.

- **Title**
  The title is a description that you give to the program.

- **Type**
  Reports must be defined as executable programs. One of the key features of executable programs is that they don't necessarily require an exclusive transaction code and can be executed using Transaction SE38. Typically, this type of program has a selection screen as the initial screen and an output screen as the last screen.

▶ **Status**
The attribute status distinguishes standard programs from customer programs. It does not indicate whether the program is active or not. This is an optional field, and you can leave it blank.

▶ **Application**
The second word of the program identifies the application for which it will be used. You can specify a program as cross-application by not specifying any application. An ABAP report for sales is represented by V.

▶ **Authorization Group**
This field is used to manage user authorization.

▶ **Logical Database**
You can use logical databases (LDBs) in executable programs by specifying the name of the logical database here. Logical databases are very similar to the database tables that physically store data. Several logical databases are available in the standard system. Refer to Figure 9.11 to see how a logical database pulls data from several database tables. To create customized LDBs, use Transaction SE36. This is an optional field, and you can leave it blank.

▶ **Selection Screen**
When you specify a logical database, you can also specify a selection screen for it. This is also an optional field.

▶ **Editor Lock**
When you select this checkbox, the program cannot be edited or downloaded by a user other than the user appearing in Last Changed By field.

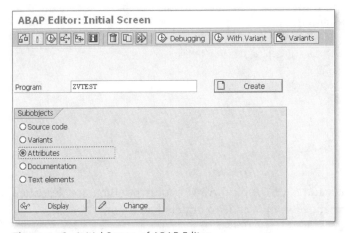

Figure 9.36 Initial Screen of ABAP Editor

▶ **Fixed Point Arithmetic**
Select this checkbox to use fixed point arithmetic in the entire program. This checkbox reduces performance but is required to avoid rounding errors.

▶ **Unicode Checks Active**
Select this checkbox to check unicode.

▶ **Start Using Variant**
Select this checkbox when the report is to start with a variant. The report will not start without a valid variant. In Section 9.5.5, we'll discuss how to create a variant.

9.5.2 Write Program and Activate

After specifying the attributes and clicking on the Save button at the bottom of the dialog box, you'll see the screen shown in Figure 9.38. This is the screen where the program codes are written. You can write the following sample code in that screen:

```
*&---------------------------------------------------------------------*
*& Report ZVTEST
*&
*&---------------------------------------------------------------------*
*& Test report for SAP Press book
*&
*&---------------------------------------------------------------------*
REPORT ZVTEST. "Name of the report is ZVTEST
TABLES VBRK.
DATA Netvalue like VBRK-NETWR.
DATA Tax like VBRK-MWSBK.
DATA Gross like VBRK-NETWR.
SELECTION-SCREEN: BEGIN OF BLOCK a WITH FRAME.
PARAMETERS: Billno(10.
SELECTION-SCREEN: END OF BLOCK a.
SELECT * FROM VBRK WHERE VBELN = Billno.
ENDSELECT.
MOVE VBRK-NETWR to Gross.
Gross = Gross + VBRK-MWSBK.
Write: / Gross.
```

Some of the important features of a typical ABAP report program are described below. We'll refer to the above sample code to understand them.

▶ **Comments**
It is a professional approach to insert comments in a program so that others who try to improve or modify it can do it faster and better. Any line starting with * becomes a comment. To comment part of a line uses quotation marks. In the sample code, note that the first seven lines are fully commented. The next line is partly commented.

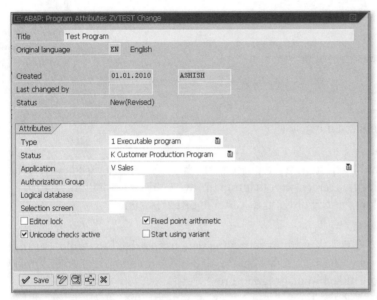

Figure 9.37 ABAP Program Attributes

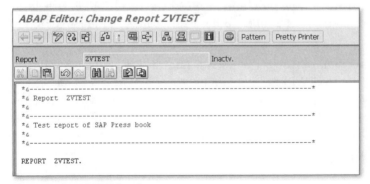

Figure 9.38 ABAP Editor Screen

- **Data declaration**

  In this section, you can define the variables to be used in the program. Some of the standard data types are listed below. You can define a variable to have the characteristics of a standard table field.

  - P: Packed numbers
  - I: Integers
  - F: Floating point number
  - N: Numeric text
  - C: Characters
  - D: Date
  - T: Time
  - X: Hexadecimal number

- **Selection screen**

  You can design the selection screen based on what the data user is likely to provide in the selection screen. In our program, we've defined "Billno," which is 10 characters long, as the only input variable or parameter.

- **Select statement**

  The statement SELECT is used for retrieving data from a database table. For this you must have declared the table in the data declaration part. For example, we'll use Table VBRK. In our program line, `SELECT * FROM VBRK WHERE VBELN = Billno.` means as per the value the user provides in the selection screen for Billno records in VBRK are selected where the VBELN field value is same as Billno. Typically, there will be only one record for particular VBELN field in VBRK table. The record contains all the other fields' values of the table VBRK.

- **Operations**

  In the sample program, our objective was to find the gross invoice value by adding the Net Value (NETWR) and Tax Amount (MWSBK) fields of Table VBRK. The user will give the invoice number and get back the gross invoice value for that invoice. We've used two simple operations, MOVE and addition, for demonstration. `MOVE VBRK-NETWR to Gross.` makes the value of Gross equal to the VBRK-NETWR field value of the selected record. `Gross = Gross + VBRK-MWSBK.` makes the value of the Gross field equal to its original value (i.e., VBRK-NETWR) plus the value of VBRK-MWSBK. So the final value is what we want in the output.

▶ **Output**

The WRITE statement is used in the sample program provided. There are different statements and function modules to present the result of a report in a list or graphically. Our program writes the value of the variable Gross. After writing the code, click on Activate to make it ready for use.

9.5.3 Change Text Elements

The text for selection parameters is done by selecting the Text Elements radio button and clicking on the Change button, in the initial screen of Transaction SE38 (see Figure 9.36). All text symbols, selection parameters, and list headings that require text will be proposed in three tabs as shown in Figure 9.39. We've defined the text element for the selection parameter Billno as Bill Number. In the selection screen, Bill Number becomes more meaningful. However, we have not saved this to check if the extended syntax check will note it. Also, note that each time you save the program, it becomes inactive, so you have to activate it again by clicking on the Activate icon.

9.5.4 Documentation

The documentation allows you to create an online user manual in different languages. In documentation, the following information about the program is provided:

▶ Purpose
▶ Integration
▶ Prerequisites
▶ Features
  ▶ Selection
  ▶ Standard variants
  ▶ Output
▶ Activities
▶ Example

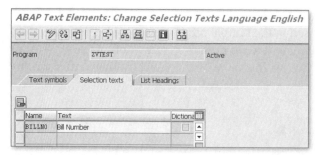

Figure 9.39 Change Text Elements

9.5.5 Create Variant

Variants are created by selecting the Variant radio button and clicking on the Change button in the initial screen of Transaction SE38. In the next screen, you enter a name for the variant. Click on Create. In the selection screen that appears, you can give default values to some of the parameters. Then you click on the Variant Attributes button in the application toolbar. You go to a screen where you can define whether some fields will be hidden, disabled, and so on.

9.5.6 Test the Program

Transaction SLIN is used for the extended syntax check of any ABAP report. You can access the selection screen for any report via the menu path PROGRAM • CHECK • EXTENDED PROGRAM CHECK from the ABAP editor screen. Figure 9.40 shows the initial screen. You can select all of the checks that you want to perform. Press [F8]. The output will list different errors, warnings, and message statements, as shown in Figure 9.41. The list of different messages for our sample program is given below. Note that the error does not mean the program cannot be executed.

- Error messages:
  - Use addition CURRENCY when outputting GROSS
  - SELECT without an INTO clause is not supported in the OO context. Use "SELECT ... INTO wa".
- Warning messages:
  - Field NETVALUE is not referenced statically in the program
  - Field TAX is not referenced statically in the program
- Information messages:
  - Selection text or parameter for selection field BILLNO is not maintained

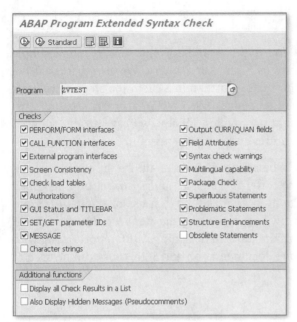

Figure 9.40 Extended Syntax Check

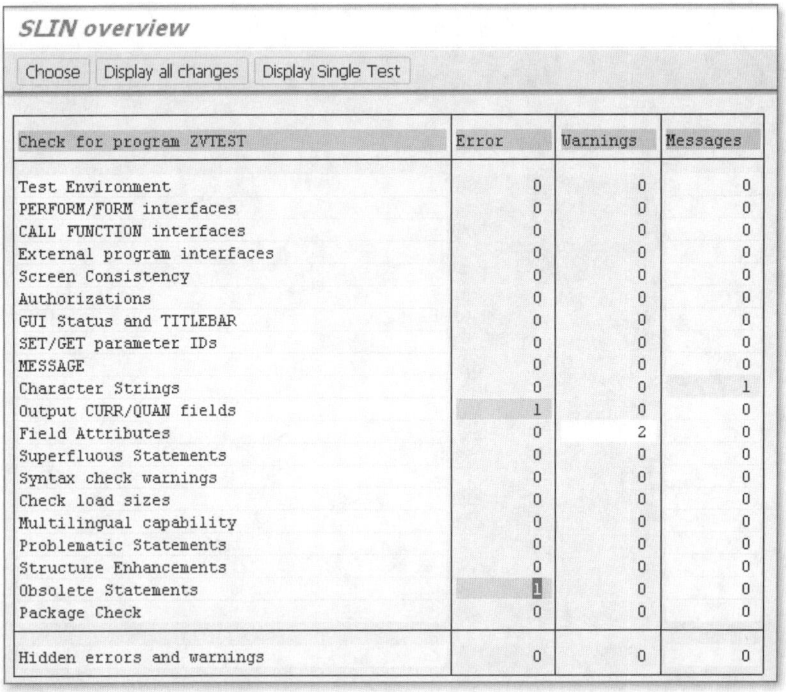

```
SLIN overview

Choose   Display all changes   Display Single Test


Check for program ZVTEST          Error    Warnings    Messages

Test Environment                    0         0           0
PERFORM/FORM interfaces             0         0           0
CALL FUNCTION interfaces            0         0           0
External program interfaces         0         0           0
Screen Consistency                  0         0           0
Authorizations                      0         0           0
GUI Status and TITLEBAR             0         0           0
SET/GET parameter IDs               0         0           0
MESSAGE                             0         0           0
Character Strings                   0         0           1
Output CURR/QUAN fields             1         0           0
Field Attributes                    0         2           0
Superfluous Statements              0         0           0
Syntax check warnings               0         0           0
Check load sizes                    0         0           0
Multilingual capability             0         0           0
Problematic Statements              0         0           0
Structure Enhancements              0         0           0
Obsolete Statements                 1         0           0
Package Check                       0         0           0

Hidden errors and warnings          0         0           0
```

Figure 9.41 SLIN Overview

9.6 Summary

In this chapter, we introduced you to SAP standard reports. We used a simple example for demonstrating the steps of an ABAP query. We also discussed the standard analyses available in the Sales Information System the steps to create a flexible analysis for your own requirement. The SAP NetWeaver BW section is just an introduction to the reports that it provides. Finally, we gave an overview of ABAP reports so you'll certain features and components of it.

With this knowledge, you should be able to help users utilize the functionalities that standard reports and analyses offer in the Sales and Distribution functionality in SAP ERP. You can motivate users to make the best use of standard SIS and BI reports. You can create your own reports using the steps we detailed for SIS and ABAP queries. You can contribute more in designing ABAP reports along with technical developers. For example, documentation and SLIN check can be used to add value to ABAP reports.

In this chapter, we'll summarize and conclude the book. You can use this chapter as a checklist and to help you review what you've learned throughout this book.

10   Summary and Conclusion

Throughout this book, we discussed the practical issues and tools that will help you address your own sales and distribution issues and processes, especially in a post-implementation scenario. We also discussed the fundamental concepts and techniques used in customization for putting the Sales and Distribution functionality in SAP ERP to optimum use. In the next section, we'll a review the important topics and information provided in each chapter.

Introduction

We started the first chapter with an introduction to SAP ERP. You learned about the different components, or functionalities, of SAP ERP (and that of Sales and Distribution). We then introduced you to the server architecture and discussed the where, how, and why of different servers (for development, quality checks, and production system). You also learned about the SAP Implementation Guide and the resources available for further learning.

In the second section, Introduction to SAP GUI, we introduced you to a typical SAP screen. You also learned about menu paths, transaction codes, icons, wild cards, and the use of function keys in SAP ERP.

The next two sections introduced you to two important project management tools: ASAP and SAP Solution Manager. Finally, we discussed how to define several organizational units including company code, company, credit control area, valuation level, and plant, which are important not only for the Sales and Distribution functionality in SAP ERP, but also in other functionalities of SAP ERP. We discussed sales organizations, divisions, distribution channels, sales offices, sales groups, storage locations, warehouse numbers, shipping points, loading points, and transport planning points. We discussed how to assign these correctly and how to check the final organizational structure.

Master Data

Chapter 2, Master Data, discussed customer master data in the first section. You learned about how to reduce the master data maintenance requirement by defining common divisions and common distribution channels. We also discussed how the customer account group is defined and how you can customize any field of the customer master data record. Finally, we went through the steps for mass maintenance using Transactions MASS and SE16N with the SAP Edit function.

In the second section, Customer Credit Master Data, we introduced you to the preliminary settings required, customizing text IDs, different groups and categories, and authorization control for customer credit master data. You also learned about the material master sales view, in the third section. There we briefly explained the fields of the three sales views in material master date (Sales: Sales Org. Data 1, Sales: Sales Org. Data 2, and Sales: General/Plant Data), and you learned how to customize some fields (including Product Hierarchy; Material Status; Material Groups 1, 2, 3, 4 and 5; and Material Commission Groups).

In the fourth section, on Batch Master Data, we explained how to define batches and how to optimize batch management using system messages, layout, DMS, batch numbers, SLED, and classification.

We also discussed customer material info records, master data records for foreign trade, vendor master records, employee master records, and general ledger and user master records.

Sales

In Chapter 3, Sales, the first three sections discussed how to optimize sales order processing through the customization of document types, item categories, and schedule line categories. We discussed different types of routines and how you can use them in copy control in next two sections. Copy control, as an optimization tool to create a document with reference to another document with a minimum of error and effort was also discussed in Chapter 2.

You also learned about the use of condition techniques in partner determination, free goods, material determination, material listing and exclusion, batch determination, and output determination. This was like a preview for the detailed discussion of condition techniques that was awaiting you in the in next chapter.

We also discussed the special functionalities SAP ERP offers for sales processes, including outline agreements and incompletion logs. You learned about how the sales process differs in some special business processes, such as consignment sales and third-party sales. We discussed how to process returns, credit memo requests, debit memo requests, and other complaint handling tools.

We touched on the common integration point of Sales and Distribution with Materials Management. You learned about the availability check, transfer of requirements, available to promise, and stock transfer processes, and in the last section, we covered the important elements of foreign trade and how to customize them for processing sales for export.

Pricing

Chapter 4 focused on condition techniques. We introduced you to the condition technique, and show you how to use it for price determination. We even discussed some suggestions for optimization in the first three sections of this chapter. In the fourth section, you learned about the customization requirements for using rebate agreements optimally, and in the fifth section, we took you through the steps for creating your own pricing reports. Finally, we discussed the steps for customizing the SAP interface for external tax software, such as Sobrix, Taxware, and Vertex.

Credit Risk Management

Chapter 5, Credit Risk Management, discussed how to manage the risk associated with credit. We discussed the settings for automatic credit checks and reviewed how to block and unblock customers for different sales operations. The chapter also covered different forms of payment and their automatic determination in sales. Finally, we took a look at some problems and their solutions in the last section in the chapter.

Logistics Management

In Chapter 6, Logistics Management, we discussed how to optimize a delivery document by the customization of delivery types and delivery item categories. You learned about the various operations carried out as part of delivery processing (including picking, packing, and goods issue). We also discussed processing deliveries in the warehouse in handling units and using a delivery due list.

The following sections included coverage of how to optimize using the route, route determination, and scheduling functionalities. You learned the steps required for stock transfers between different plants and were introduced to output in general and customization and automatic determination of shipping output in particular.

We also discussed batch management and how to optimize batch determination in a delivery document. Then we discussed processing serialized material, how it can contribute to your business, and how to configure it in SAP ERP. We reviewed the steps required for customizing the SAP interface for external carrier software such as Roadnet Transportation Suite 3.20 of UPS. Finally, you reviewed a few of the problems and their solutions that are often encountered during delivery processing.

Billing

In Chapter 7, Billing, we reviewed the principles of bill processing and discussed how to create a single or multiple invoice with and without a billing due list: how to split them, cancel them, or combine them into an invoice list. We also discussed how you can use the general billing interface optimally. In the second section, you learned how to optimize billing documents, and we discussed the complaint handling process and billing plan.

The final sections discussed the interface of Sales and Distribution with Accounting. You learned about the use of the condition technique in automatic determination of revenue GLs, reconciliation accounts, and cash accounts. We also covered how to make the accounting document number the same as the billing document number and the data transferred from billing to accounting documents and revenue recognition functionalities. The chapter closed up by reviewing common problems and their solutions.

Cross-Functional Customizing

Chapter 8 discussed how to make the best use of the text IDs available for the Sales and Distribution functionality in SAP ERP. You learned how to customize the IDoc Interface for EDI and ALE communication and how to create a Web interface. We also discussed how to optimize batch where-used lists and the batch information cockpit for reporting. In the ABAP tools section, we reviewed the three main tools (user exits, debugger, and LSMW), and finished up the chapter with coverage of how to make the best use of numbering objects and number ranges.

Reporting and Analysis

In Chapter 9, we reviewed the standard reports and analyses available in SAP ERP and SAP NetWeaver BW (business content) for the Sales and Distribution functionality in SAP ERP. You learned how you can create your own reports and analyses using the Sales Information System (SIS), ABAP queries, and ABAP reports.

Appendices

A   **Customization of Local Layout** 459

B   **List of SAP Area Menus** 475

C   **How to Initialize a Material Period** 507

D   **The Author** 511

A Customization of Local Layout

You can perform customization of local layout to suit your preferences, your screen size, your speed, and various other factors specific to you so that you are most comfortable working with it. You can customize your local layout by pressing [Alt] + [F12] or by clicking on the Customize Local Layout icon highlighted in Figure A.1. This icon is available from any SAP screen. After clicking the icon, you'll see a list of objects, shown in Figure A.2, that can be customized. Even in the login screen, when you are not logged in, you can do this customization.

Figure A.1 Icon for Customizing Local Layout

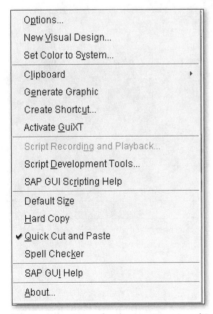

Figure A.2 Menu for Customizing Local Layout

We'll discuss the customization and tools available in the list shown in Figure A.2 in next two sections. In first section, Options, we'll discuss the features available with the first item of the drop-down list. In the second section, Other Options, we'll discuss eleven other features available on the drop-down list.

A.1 Options

The first option tool that is available is Options. This includes eight customization windows shown in Figure A.3, and later in Figures A.7, A.8, and A.11.

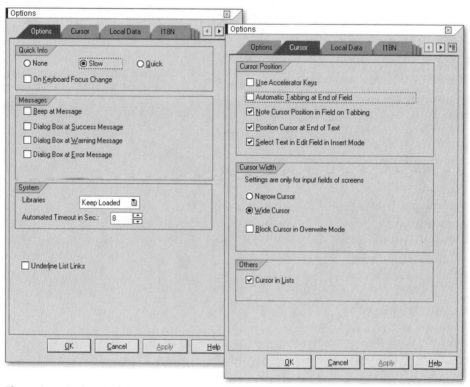

Figure A.3 Options and Cursor Screens

A.1.1 Options

In the first screen, the Options radio button for quick information has three options: None, Slow, and Quick. If you select the first option (None), when you place your cursor on any icon or tab, the name of that object does not appear. If you select the Slow option, the name appears but only after few seconds, and for the Quick option the information is available as soon as cursor is placed over the icon or tab.

The messages have four checkboxes. When you select the first checkbox (Beep at Messages), there will be beep sound for any message info, warning, or error. Select the next three checkboxes for the message to appear as a pop-up window (dialog box) in addition to appearing at the bottom of the screen in the message area for success/information message, warning, and error messages, respectively.

A.1.2 Cursor

When you select the Automatic Tabbing at the End of Field checkbox, whenever any field in any SAP screen is completely filled with data, the cursor automatically moves to the next field. It is recommended that you select this checkbox.

When you select the Position Cursor at End of Text checkbox, no matter where you click to the right of the entry of a field, the cursor moves to the right of the last character, ignoring the blank space.

When you select the Select Text in Edit Field in Insert Mode checkbox and the session is in insert (INS) mode and the field to which you go by tabbing is in edit mode, then the complete entry in the field is automatically selected, and whatever you type immediately replaces the existing entry.

You can control the cursor width by selecting the Narrow Cursor or Wide Cursor radio button. Figure A.4 shows the difference. It is recommended that you use the narrow cursor, because the wide cursor can sometimes interfere with readability.

Figure A.4 Wide and Narrow Cursors

When you select Block Cursor in Overwrite Mode, the cursor looks like the one shown in Figure A.5.

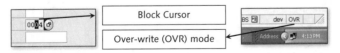

Figure A.5 Block Cursor in Overwrite Mode

Figure A.6 shows the behaviors of cursor when the Cursor in Lists option is selected and when it's not selected are shown in.

A | Customization of Local Layout

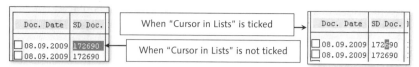

Figure A.6 Cursor in Lists

A.1.3 Local Data

When the History radio button is not selected, the previous entries to any SAP field are not stored. It is recommended that you select either the On or Immediately option. The data is stored locally, so you won't be interfering with any other user's performance. Expiration, Maximum Permitted File Size, and No of Entries are filled when you select the option On or Immediately.

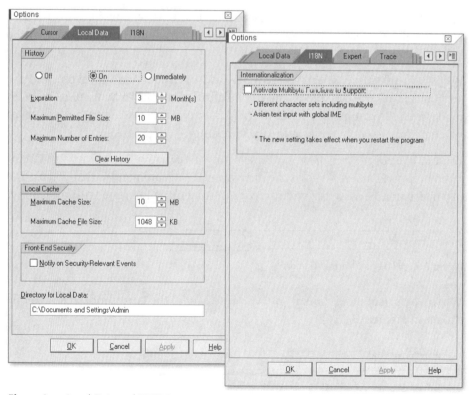

Figure A.7 Local Data and I18N Screens

You can also clear the data manually from the Clear History tab. The location where the data is to be stored is specified on the Directory for Local Data tab. The Notify on Security-Relevant Events option can be annoying if you download data regularly.

A.1.4 I18N (Internationalization)

It is recommended that you select the I18N checkbox, which is the short form for internationalization. It activates the multibyte functions.

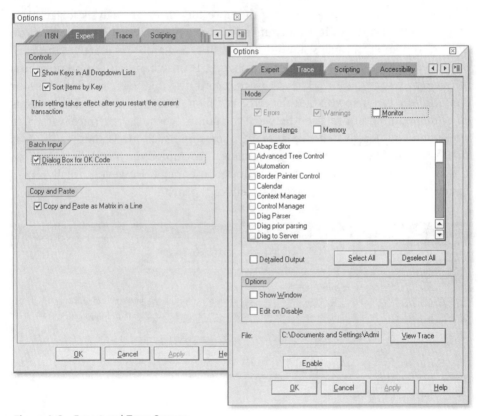

Figure A.8 Expert and Trace Screens

A.1.5 Expert

In the Expert tab, you can select the control option in the first check box. Selecting or not selecting the second checkbox depends on your preferences. Because in any drop-down list, the description can be confusing, having the key (or code) as an additional value helps and seldom annoys. The checkbox for batch input is not recommended because it delays the batch input, but occasionally (especially when testing) you may want to see the dialog box to check the code. Also, the checkbox for the copy and paste actions should be left blank. If you select them, the input you paste may go beyond the field or fields that you're trying to fill, and this will cause problems later.

A.1.6 Trace

You use the Trace tab for generating the trace file for error analysis for an error relating to the frontend. It is recommended that you activate the trace when you want to run an error analysis and deactivate it afterward. When active, the trace option will hamper your system performance. Even when you don't know how to trace the error, you must know how to record it so that you can send it to your contacts who can help you find the error and fix it. The generated text file records all of the required information between the points at which your trace was active and when you deactivated it. Figure 1.9 shows one such file is shown. The files that constitute the frontend can get damaged, corrupted, or infected quite often if your firewall or network security is not good enough. However, usually, it's is easier to reinstall the SAP GUI than to retrace the error.

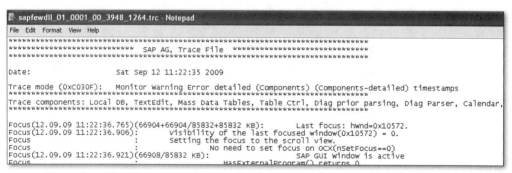

Figure A.9 Trace File

A.1.7 Scripting

You should select the Enable Scripting checkbox (see Figure A.11), but not the other two for notification hamper performance unless you have a very good reason for it. By default, these are not selected.

A.1.8 Accessibility

By default, the Accessibility option is disabled (see Figure A.11). To activate it, you can go to START • SETTING • CONTROL PANEL • SAP CONFIGURATION for changing the SAP configuration, as shown in Figure 1.10. You have the option of either selecting the Enjoy Design, which is more popular (all screen shots in this book were taken in that mode), or the Accessibility Mode.

Figure A.10 SAP Configuration for Windows

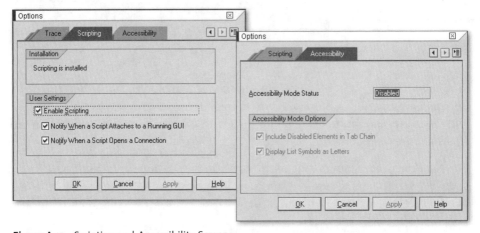

Figure A.11 Scripting and Accessibility Screens

A.2 Other Options

In this section, we'll discuss the customizing tools available at the local frontend SAP GUI and how to utilize them optimally.

A.2.1 New Visual Design

By default, the SAP GUI uses the new visual design. The other option for display is Classic design, which some people prefer. Though the new visual design is considered superior, there is no reason why you can't use the old Classic display mode. In the new visual design, you can control the color of the screen, the color contrast between different screen elements, font size, sound, and other features that typically constitute design.

The new visual setting has two tabs: General and Color, as shown in Figure A.12.

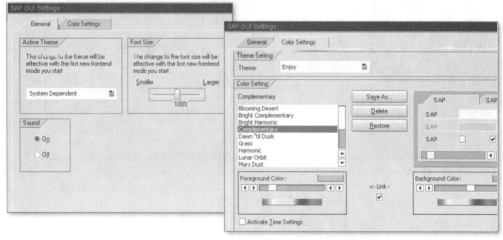

Figure A.12 New Visual Design

You have various Active Themes to chose from, including System Dependent (default), Enjoy, High Contrast Theme, Streamline, and Tradeshow. You activate and deactivate the sound using either the On or Off radio button. You can use the slider to adjust the font size.

You can change the color setting of the three themes, Enjoy, Streamline, and Tradeshow, by placing the cursor on that color setting and modifying the colors using the two sliders, with or without being linked, responsible for foreground and background colors. Then you can select the OK or Apply button. Alternatively, if you select the Save As button, you'll create a new color setting.

You can fine-tune the foreground and background color by double-clicking on the Color Picker tab shown in Figure 1.13. With the Color Picker dialog box, you can change not only the color by moving the slider, but also the *color saturation* and *luminosity*.

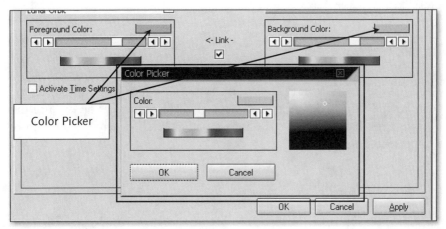

Figure A.13   Color Picker

Color Saturation refers to how vivid and intense a color is. At the lowest color saturation level, any color becomes gray (white if luminosity is highest and black if luminosity is lowest). At the highest level, there are no white (high luminosity) or blank (low luminosity) dots in the color (it is a "pure" color). Luminosity refers to the brightness of the color.

You can customize the color to gradually change with time by selecting the Activate Time Settings checkbox, as shown in Figure 1.14. You modify the default start time and end time by double-clicking on the tabs showing 09:00 and 17:00 in Figure 1.14.

A.2.2   Set Color to System

The color setting provided by SAP and those you create in the New Visual Design section will be available for selection in the Set Color to System option. You can use this to reduce stress on eyes of users who work long hours in front their SAP screen. Some colors (e.g., red) put more stress on your eyes than others (e.g., blue). Good designer use many such findings from the world of science.

A | Customization of Local Layout

Figure A.14 Activate Time Settings

A.2.3 Clipboard

The four functions for copy and paste are Select (`Ctrl` + `Y`), Cut (`Ctrl` + `X`), Copy (`Ctrl` + `C`), and Paste (`Ctrl` + `V`). With these four operations, you can copy data to and from SAP and non-SAP screens. For example, you can use this feature when you have a list of customers on an SAP report screen that is to be taken to presentation software.

A.2.4 Generate Graphic

You can use the Generate Graphic option to generate a screen shot that looks like Figure 1.15. Screen shots can be used for creating user manuals (softcopy).

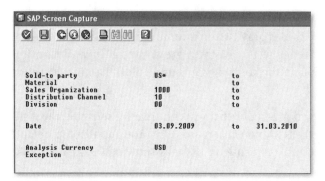

Figure A.15 SAP Screen Capture for Transaction MB52 Initial Screen

A.2.5 Create Shortcut

Creating a shortcut to a transaction code (e.g., VA01) or an area menu (e.g., VA00) will save you time every day. To create a shortcut, click on the Create Shortcut… option from the list (see Figure A.2) that appears when you click on the Customize

Local Layout icon. You'll see the screen shown in Figure 1.16, in which we show how to create a shortcut for the area menu VA00 and save it on desktop. You can create several such shortcuts. By clicking on the shortcut, you'll directly log in to the corresponding transaction or area menu.

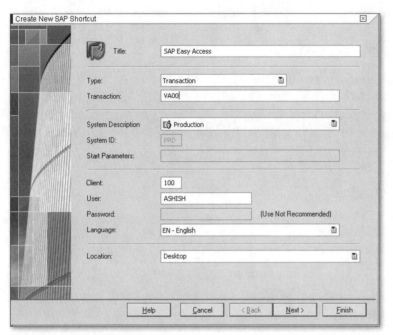

Figure A.16 Create Shortcut

A.2.6 Default Size

When you select the Default Size option, if the window is not maximized already, then it will resize itself to a pre-set default size. This feature is useful when you have a large screen and your default size is less than the screen size.

> **Double-Scroll Bar**
>
> This is a typical problem when the screen resolution is less than 1024 x 768 for New Visual design (or less than 800 x 600 for Classic design). For example, a scroll bar will appear to navigate between one item and another in a sales order overview screen (VA02 or VA03), and there will be a scroll bar outside the screen. In such a situation, you'll never able to reach the third item (or any other) of the order. This is when the font size is normal. Refer to SAP Note 26417, which specifies the system requirements for SAP GUI.

A.2.7 Hard Copy

This is the option to make a printout of the current SAP screen. You do this by pressing Alt + F12 to get the drop-down list shown in Figure A.2 from any SAP screen. Then click on the Hard Copy option. This is quite useful for creating user manuals very quickly, with a sequence of screen shots (hardcopy).

A.2.8 Quick Cut and Paste

The Quick Cut and Paste option is activated when you click once and deactivated if you click again. When this feature is active (see Figure A.2), a checkmark will appear next to the option Quick Cut and Paste. When it's active, you can select and copy texts with a left-click and paste with a right-click. This a very good example of an optimizing tool.

A.2.9 Spell Checker

You'll be surprised by SAP spell check because it will not show errors for your brand names or some of your customer's names, which you'd normally expect. This is the case because the data in the SAP database for materials and customers is taken into consideration in addition to the dictionary for spell check.

A.2.10 SAP GUI Help

SAP GUI help is a complete guide on SAP GUI. It gives you detailed help on how to use and customize the GUI and analyze errors pertaining to SAP GUI.

A.2.11 About

You can use the About option to get details about the SAP GUI version that you're using, as shown in Figure A.17. You would do this to ensure that you're running the latest version of the GUI (or as suggested by your BASIS system administrator).

> **Note**
>
> For automatic updates of your SAP GUI, use the method suggested in SAP Note 361222 – SapPatch: Importing GUI Patches.

Other Options | A.2

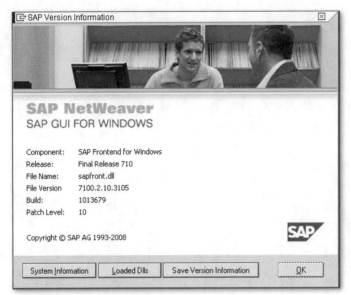

Figure A.17 About SAP GUI

B List of SAP Area Menus

Transaction	Description
0KWM	Configuration Menu for Activity-Based Costing
AC00	Service Master Data
ACCR	Accruals/Deferrals
ACE	Accrual Engine – Periodic Accruals
ADWPS_MEB	Maintenance Event Builder
ASMN	Asset Accounting
AUTH	Infosystem Authorizations
BALA	Distribution in Applications
BALD	ALE Development
BALE	ALE Administration
BALM	Master Data Distribution
BALT	IDoc/ALE Test Environment
BANK	SAP Banking
BCA_US_F9MINFO	Information System Bank Customer Accounts
BCA_US_F9MN	Customer Accounts
BCA0	Business Partner Application Development Customizing
BGMN	Guarantees
BM00	Batch Management
BPR1	Activity-Based Costing
BUMR	BP Relationships: Task Menu
BUPA_BIP_MENU	Business Information Provider Menu
BUPT	Business Partner: Task Menu
C000	Overhead Cost Controlling Information System
CA00	Routings
CA01	Cross-Application
CAC0	Master Recipe – Access Via Production Version
CACSBDT	Task Level Menu Commission Contract
CACSBDTB	Task Level Menu for Contract Bundle
CACSBDTD	Document Task Level Menu
CACSBDTI	Commission Case Task Level Menu
CACSMN	Commission System
CATI	Time Recording

B | List of SAP Area Menus

Transaction	Description
CATP	Time Sheet
CATS	Time Sheet
CBGL00	Global Label Management
CBIH	Industrial Hygiene and Safety Information System
CBIH00	Industrial Hygiene and Safety
CBP	Constraint Based Planning Workbench
CBWA00	Waste Management
CBWABDT	Waste Management: BDT Settings Complete
CBWAMD	Waste Management: Master Data
CC00	Engineering Change Management
CE00	CAPP-Based Calculation of Standard Values
CEMN	Cost and Revenue Element Accounting
CF00	Production Resources/Tools
CFM	CFM – Corporate Finance Management
CFM_BF	Corporate Finance Management: Basic Functions
CFM_CR	Credit Risk Analyzer
CFM_MR	CFM – Market Risk Analyzer
CFM_PA	CFM – Portfolio Analyzer
CFM_TM	Transaction Manager
CFM_TM_PARABB_GDDD	Parallel Valuation Areas
CFM_TM_PARABB_WP	Parallel Valuation Areas
CFM_TM_ZINSANPASSUNG	Interest Rate Adjustment
CG00	Product Safety
CIC8	CIC Customizing Menu
CICS	Customer Interaction Center
CICT	CIC Customizing Menu
CIF	Core Interface Advanced Planner and Optimizer
CIF-EA	Core Interface Advanced Planner and Optimizer
CK00	Product Cost Planning
CK90	Mixed Costing
CKML	Actual Costing/Material Ledger
CL00	Classification
CL00N	Classification

List of SAP Area Menus | B

Transaction	Description
CLOI	Production Optimization Interface
CM00	Capacity Planning
CMC0	Process planning
CML_FZM4	Drilldown Reporting
CML_PARABB_GDDD	Parallel Valuation Areas_CML
CMPP	Workforce Planning
CMRP	Material Requirements Planning
CMS_CUS_BDT	BDT Development
CMS_CUS_IMG	CMS IMG
CMS_CUS_OMS_BDT	Collateral objects
CMS_CUS_RE_BDT	BDT Development
CMS_MAIN	Main Menu
CMS_OMS_BDT_MAIN	Collateral Objects
CMS_RE_MAIN	Real Estate Add On
CN00	Notification
CO_CPROJECTS	Collaboration Projects
CO_CRM	CRM Service Processes
CO00	Shop Floor Control
CO30	CO30
COC0	Process Orders
COCB	Process Management
COFI_REP	Reports for Cost and Revenue Element Accounting (New)
COM_MDF_MENU	Master Data Framework
COND_AV	Condition Maintenance
COND_MM	Portfolio Management
CONV00	Conversion of Original Application Files
COPA	Profitability Analysis
CPE_PRICEQUOT	Price Quotations for Commodity Pricing Engine
CPMN	Activity-Based Costing
CR00	Work Centers
CRC0	Resources
CRQ0	Work Center for Quality Inspection
CS00	Bills of Material
CU00	Variant Configuration
CV00	Document Management
CVI0	Document Distribution

475

Transaction	Description
CWVT	Merchandise Distribution
CX00	Consolidation
CX000	SEM BCS – Business Consolidation
CX00BCS	Business Consolidation
CX01	Consolidation Customizing
CY00	Engineering
CY00_PPENG	Integrated Product and Process Engineering (iPPE)
DGP0	Dangerous Goods Management
DICCM	Configuration Control
DICTIONARY	SAPterm – Maintenance for Terminology and Glossary
DUMB	Premium Reserve Fund Transfer in Regulatory Reporting
DW00	
DZ00	R/2-R/3 Link
ECCS	Consolidation
EHSAMED	Occupational Health
EHSBAS	Basic Data and Tools
EHSH	Report Selection: Occupational Health
EHSH_1	Report Selection: Occupational Health
EHSHSM	Hazardous Substance Management
EIS	Report Selection for SAP-EIS
ENH_ELR	Logging
ENH_REBATE	Extended Rebate Processing
ENH_REBATE_INFO	Extended Rebate Processing – Info
EW00	EMU Local Currency Changeover
EXPORT	Export from the Data Pool
F000	Financial Accounting Information System
F8BZ	Payment Program Configuration for Payment Requests
F9L,	Settings for Additional BCA Development
F9LBDT	Development in BDT Environment
F9M1	Bank Customer Accounts: Settings
F9M3	Relationships BP-BP: Settings
F9M4	F9M4
F9MBENCH	Benchmark Customer Accounts

List of SAP Area Menus | B

Transaction	Description
F9MINFO	Information System Bank Customer Accounts
F9MINFO_IHC	Information System In-House Cash
F9MN	Customer Accounts
F9MPAYM	External Payment Transactions
FAGLINFOSYSTEM	Information System (New)
FARI	SAP Business Framework: Open FI
FBDF	BDF Reporting
FBICRC001	Intercompany Reconciliation: Open Items
FBICRC002	Intercompany Reconciliation: Accounts
FBICRC003	Intercompany Reconciliation: Open Items
FBME	Banks
FBOE	ABAP Workbench
FCHK	Check Management
FCMM	Preparations for Consolidation
FCMN	Consolidation
FCRD	FCRD
FDCU	FDCU
FDMN	Customers
FERC	Regulatory Reporting
FGM0	Special Purpose Ledger
FGRP	Report Painter
FGRW	Report Writer
FI_GL_ACAC	Manual Accruals
FI_GL_CAE_IPM	Accruals for Rights Management
FI_GL_SOA	Provisions for Awards
FIA1	Asset Accounting Information – ALT
FIAA	Asset Accounting Information System
FIAP	Reports for Accounts Payable Accounting
FIAR	Reports for Accounts Receivable Accounting
FICOMAIN	Financial Conditions
FIGL	Information System
FIGX	Flexible General Ledger
FI-LA	Lease Accounting
FILC	Consolidation
FISL	Programs for the Special Purpose Ledger
FITE_INFO	Travel Expenses Info System
FITE_TREE	Reports: Travel Expenses

Transaction	Description
FITP_INFO	Travel Planning Information System
FITP_TREE	Travel Planning Reports
FITV_INFO	Travel Management Info System
FITV_TREE	Travel Management
FKMN	Accounts Payable
FKTC	Regulatory Reporting Austria – Control Table Maintenance
FKUM	
FLQCUST	Liquidity Calculation Settings
FLQMAIN	Liquidity Calculation
FMCA	Reports for Funds Management
FMCB	Cash Budget Management
FMFGE	Additional Functions for US Federal Government
FMUSA	Functions for the US Federal Government
FMUSA2	Functions for the US Federal Government
FNBU	FNBU
FNI0	FNI0
FNMA	FNMA
FNMD	Loans: General Loans
FNME_AENDERUNGSANZEIGER	Change Pointer
FNME_CML	Loans
FNME_NEU	Loans: New
FNME_US	Loans Including U.S. Requirements
FNMEC	General Loans
FNMH	Loans: Mortgages
FNMK	Consumer Loan
FNMO	Loans: Policy Loans
FNMP	Rollover
FNMS	Loans: Borrower's Note Loans
FNUB	Data Transfer: Treasury
FO00	Real Estate Management
FO03	Rental
FO04	Settlements
FO05	Rent Adjustment
FOAR00	Application: Task Menu
FOBE	

List of SAP Area Menus | B

Transaction	Description
FOBEBEROBJ	
FOBO00	
FOFI	Rental Accounting
FOFI_CP	Rental Accounting Correspondence
FOFV	Real Estate Third-Party Management
FOI0	RE Contract: Development
FOI0SCS	RE Contract: Development/Customizing/ Service Charges
FOIC	Real Estate Controlling
FOIMGRE	Current Settings
FOIS	Real Estate Information System
FOIS_FI	Rental Accounting Information System
FOIS_SC	Info System Service Charges, Heating Expenses
FOIS_SC1	Master Data for Service Charge Settlement
FOJ0	Real Estate General Contract
FONA	Service Charge Settlement
FOST	Real Estate Management Master Data
FOTI00	Tenant Information: Task Level Menu
FOWB00	Wirtschaftlichkeitsberechnung: Arbeitsmenü
FRMN	Credit Management
FRMN1	Credit Management
FSBP	Business Partner
FSBP_FINSERV_ALL	SAP Business Partner
FSBPT	Business Partner: Tools
FSBPT_1	Application Development SAP Business Partner for Financial Services
FSBPT_2	Application Development SAP Business Partner for Financial Services: Tools
FSCM	Financial Supply Chain Management
FSCM-BD	Biller Direct
FSCM-COLM	Collection Management
FSCM-CR-AR	Integration Credit Management and FI-AR
FSCM-DM	Dispute Management
FSCM-DM-PW2	Periodic Processing in Accounting
FSCM-IHC	In-House Cash
FSMN	General Ledger

Transaction	Description
FTBPOB	Business Partner: Development of Partner-Object Relationship
FTBPT	Business Partner: Tools
FTBT	Business Partner
FTBT_ALT	Real Estate Business Partner
FTBT_CML	Business Partner (CML)
FTBT_NEU	SAP Business Partner
FTBUP1	Business Partner: Conversion Phase 1
FTBUP2	Business Partner: Conversion Phase 2
FTBUT	Business Partner: Development of Conversion Tool Control
FTR_C_MENU	Transaction: Task Menu
FTW0	Data Retention Tool
FWMY	Securities
FZ00	FZ00
FZM4	Treasury Management Information System
FZM4_PERFORMANCE	Performance
FZMN	Treasury Management Basic Functions
FZP0	Partner Management
FZT0	FZT0
GCU0	Configuration Menu: Special Purpose Ledger
GFTR_C_MENU	General Transaction Management: Task Menu
GJQ0	CRP Customizing Menu
GJVC	Joint Venture Accounting Configuration
GJVP	Joint Venture Accounting
GLFLEXCUS	Flexible General Ledger
GLFLEXMEN	Flexible General Ledger
GLFLEXSPL	Document Splitting
GLT0_SPLIT	GLT0_SPLIT
GMGMT	Grants Management
GRANT_BDT	Grant Master Development Menu
GRANT_CUSTOMIZE	Grant Master Customizing Menu
HR REPORTING TOOLS	HR Reporting Tools
HR_99	International Payroll Information System
HR_AR	Information System
HR_AT	Information System
HR_AU	Information system

Transaction	Description
HR_BE	Info system
HR_BR	Information system
HR_CA	Infosystem
HR_CH	Information System
HR_CN	Information System
HR_DE	Information System
HR_DE1	Information System
HR_DK	Infosystem
HR_ES	Information System
HR_FR	Information System
HR_GB	Infosystem
HR_HK	Information System
HR_ID	Information System
HR_IE	Infosystem
HR_IT	Information System
HR_JP	Information System
HR_KR	Information System
HR_MX	Information System
HR_MY	Information system
HR_NL	Information System
HR_NO	Infosystem
HR_NZ	Information System
HR_PA_BR	Administration BR
HR_PA_CA	Administration Canada
HR_PA_JP	Administration Japan
HR_PA_MY	Administration Malaysia
HR_PA_TW	Administration Taiwan
HR_PA_US	Administration United States
HR_PH	Information System
HR_PT	Information System
HR_SE	Infosystem
HR_SG	Information System
HR_TH	Information System
HR_TW	Information System
HR_US	Infosystem (US)
HR_VE	Information System
HR_ZA	Infosystem

Transaction	Description
HR00	Human Resources
HR21NADM	Reporting: Time Data Administration
HR21NCAT	Time Sheet
HR21NINW	Reporting: Incentive Wages
HR21NPEP	Reporting: Shift Planning
HR21NTIM	Reporting: Time Management
HR22NADM	Tools: Time Data Administration
HR22NINW	Time Management Tools: Incentive Wages
HR22NTIM	Tools: Time Management
HRAP1	Recruitment – Reports
HRBEN0000	Benefits
HRBEN00REPTREE	Benefits Reporting Tree
HRCLM0000	Claims (Asia)
HRCMP	Compensation Management Reports
HRCMP0000	Compensation Management
HRECM	Enterprise Compensation Management
HRHCP1	Data Collection Personnel Cost Planning and Simulation
HRHCP2	Cost Plans Personnel Cost Planning and Simulation
HRHCP3	Tools for Personnel Cost Planning and Simulation
HRHCP4	Settings for Personnel Cost Planning and Simulation
HRHCP5	Information System
HRJP	Administration Japan
HRMGE0000	Management of Global Employees
HROM	Organizational Management
HRPA	Personnel Administration – Reports
HRPBC	Position Budgeting and Control
HRPE	Personnel Development – Reports
HRPM	HR Funds and Position Management
HRPT	HR-FPM Tools
HRTR	Travel Expenses Information System
HUM	Handling Unit Management
HUM_CHANGE	Create and Change Handling Units
HUM_DISPLAY	Display Handling Units

List of SAP Area Menus | B

Transaction	Description
HUM_GOODS_MOVEMENT	Goods Movement Postings
HUM_INVENTORY	Handling Unit Physical Inventory
HUM_MD	Master Data
HUM_MD_NACHRICHTEN	Output Conditions
HUM_MD_PV	Packing Instructions
HUM_MD_PV_FINDUNG	Packing Instruction Determination Records
IA00	Work Scheduling
IC00	Work Centers
IDADVAT	Acquisition Tax Accruals
ID-FIGL-PP-CL-REP-GL-ACCBAL-CL	G/L Account Balance Reports (Chile)
IDFISA-FSMN-VATRETURNS-MX	VAT Returns (Mexico)
IE00	Management of Technical Objects
IECS	Management of Technical Objects
IF00	Production Resources/Tools
IHC	In-House Cash
IHC_CM	Financial Status
IHC_GUI	IHC: GUI Functions
IM00	Investment Programs
IMA0	Appropriation Requests
IMFA	Investment Management
IMFR	Appropriation Requests
INFO_PC	Product Cost Controlling
INFO_PC01	Product Cost Planning
INFO_PC03	Product Cost by Period
INFO_PC04	Product Cost by Sales Order
INFO_PC05	Costs for Intangible Goods
INFO_PC06	Product Cost by Order
INFO_PC07	Actual Costing/Material Ledger
INFO_PC2	Order-Related Production
INFO_PC2A	Order-Related Production
INFO_PC3	Make-to-Order Production
INFO_PC3A	Make-to-Order Production
INFO_PC4	Repetitive Manufacturing
INFO_PC5	Base Object Costing
INFO_PC8	Product Costing
IP00	Maintenance Planning
IPCS	Service Agreements

Transaction	Description
IPLM	Preventive Maintenance
IR00	Work Centers
IS00	Area Menu for Solution Database
ISCS	Solution Database
ISE0	Funds Management
ISISMN	Insurance Applications
ISNL	Funds Management
ISP4	Posting
ISSR	
ISSR_BASIC	
ISSR_BM_ADMIN_CUST	
ISSR_BM_CUST_MIG	
ISSR_BM_FIAA_AMORT	
ISSR_CUST	
ISSR_CUST_COPY_LISTTYP	
ISSR_CUST_OUTPUT	
ISSR_CV	
ISSR_DE_BAFIN_REP	
ISSR_EX	
ISSR_IF	
ISSR_MIG	
ISSR_MIG_TOOL	
ISSR_NB	
ISSR_OUT	
ISSR_PF	
ISSR_PR	
ISSR_RBD	
ISSR_UNTIL_2002	
ISZZ	Solution Database
IW00	Maintenance Processing
IWCS	Service Processing
J1IL	India Localization – Excise Statutory Requirements
J1ILN	India Localization Menu
J1IN-FIAP-WITHHOLDINGTAX-IN	FI-AP Withholding Tax (India)
J1IN-FIAR-WITHHOLDINGTAX-IN	FI-AR Withholding Tax (India)
JB01	Data Pool

Transaction	Description
JB02	Profitability Analysis
JB04	Market Risk Analysis
JB0B	Product Control
JB12	Default Risk and Limit System
JB14	Prototype Functions
JB19	Asset/Liability Management
JB2X	Securities
JB4X	Money Market
JB5X	Foreign Exchange
JB6X	Derivatives
JBBE	Valuation Setting
JBBM	Positions
JBD_VAR_TRANS_OLD	SEM-PA: Obsolete Transaction for Variable Transaction (Old) Area
JBDM	Loans
JBMA	EURO Changeover
JBMVT	Variable Transaction: Task Level Menu
JBMVTWORK	Variable Transaction: Task Level Menu
KAMN	Internal Orders
KAWI	KAWI
KCCF	Executive Menu
KCLA	External Data Transfer
KCMB	Executive Information System (EIS)
KCMD	Business Planning (EC-BP)
KE50	Profit Center Accounting
KEMN	Profitability Analysis
KEZZ	KEZZ
KKAM	Product Cost by Sales Order
KKMN	Reference and Simulation Costing
KKOB	Costs for Intangible Goods and Services
KKPM	Product Cost by Period
KKSM	Product Cost by Order
KLFZ	Facilities: Initial Menu
KPRO	Knowledge Provider Administration
KSMN	Cost Center Accounting
LD00	Line Design
LE_AID-BI	Auto-ID Backend Integration

Transaction	Description
LE_ANALYSIS	Analysis Tools
LE_INB	Goods Receipt
LE_INB_DELV	Goods Receipt with Inbound Delivery
LE_INB_TRQ	Goods Receipt w/o Inbound Delivery
LE_IO_TRA	Transportation
LE_IS	Information Systems
LE_IS_INB	Goods Receipt Office
LE_IS_OUTB	Shipping
LE_IS_TRA	Transportation Planning
LE_IS_WM	Warehouse
LE_MASTER	Master Data
LE_OUTB	Goods Issue
LE_OUTB_DELV	Goods Issue with Outbound Delivery
LE_OUTB_TRQ	Goods Issue for Other Transactions
LE_R2R3	R/2-R/3 Link
LE_TRA	Transportation
LE_TRA_DISP	Logistics Execution, Transportation Planning
LE_TRA_EXEC	Transportation
LE_TRA_FREIGHT	Shipment Costs
LE_WM_INT	Internal Warehouse Activities
LE01	Logistics Execution
LES	Logistics Execution
LLVS	Warehouse Management
LO01	Logistics – General
LPRO	Material Forecast
LSO_PVMN	Learning Solution
LSO_PVMN1	SAP Learning Solution – Reports
LTRM_MEN	Task and Resource Management
LVAS	Value-Added Services (VAS)
LXDOCK	Cross-Docking
LYM	Yard Management
MB00	Inventory Management
MC00	Logistics Information System (LIS)
MC6A	Sales and Operations Planning
MC6B	Flexible Planning
MCA1	Workflow Information System (WIS)
MCB1	Inventory Controlling (INVCO)

Transaction	Description
MCC1	Inventory Information System
MCC2	Inventory Information System
MCE0	Purchasing Information System (PURCHIS)
MCE9	Purchasing Information System
MCG1	MCG1
MCH0	Retail Information System (RIS)
MCI0	Plant Maintenance Information System (PMIS)
MCJE	Plant Maintenance Information System
MCK0	Service Management Information System (SMIS)
MCP0	Shop Floor Information System (PP-IS)
MCPI	Production Information System
MCT0	Sales Information System (SIS)
MCT2	Sales Information System
MCU0	Transportation Info System (TIS)
MCV0	Quality Management Information System
MCVQ	Quality Management Information System
MCVQ_INFO_1	Info System: Quality Control Key Figures
MCVQ_INFO_2	Info System: Quality Control Evaluations
MD00	Materials Requirements Planning – External Procurement
MDLP	Master Production Scheduling
MDPP	Demand Management
MDRP	Distribution Resource Planning
ME00	Purchasing
MEASURE_BDT	Measure BDT Development Menu
MEL0	Service Entry Sheet
MEMGMT_CONFIG	Device Configuration
MENU_TEST_ECKE	Corner
MEREP_TESTTOOL	Test Tool Center
MF00	Repetitive Manufacturing
MF00_OLD	Repetitive Manufacturing
MI00	Physical Inventory
MM00	Material Master
MM01	Materials Management
MR00	Invoice
MRBE	Valuation

Transaction	Description
MRM0	Logistics Invoice Verification
MS00	Long-Term Planning
MST0	Mass Maintenance Tool
OCA0	OCA0
OCH0	Batch Management
OCNG	OCNG
OCP0	OCP0
OCU0	OCU0
OFTC	Funds Management Configuration Menu
OFTD	Cash Management Configuration Menu
OFTF	Cash Budget Management Configuration
OHPS	Organizational Management Configuration (Basis System)
OIS0	Funds Management Configuration Menu
OKCM	Configuration Menu
OLI0	Configuration Menu for Master Data in Plant Maintenance
OLIA	Configuration Menu for Maintenance Processing
OLIP	Configuration Menu for Planning in Plant Maintenance
OLMS	Master Data Configuration Menu
OLPA	Settings: Sales & Operations Planning
OLQB	QM Customizing in Procurement
OLS1	Sales and Distribution Configuration Menu – Volume Based Rebate
OLVD	Customizing for Sales and Distribution: Shipping
OLVF	SD Customizing: Billing
OLVS	Customizing for Sales and Distribution: Master Data
OMO6	Maintain Applications
OMP0	Configuration Menu for Demand Management
OP01	Logistics Customizing
OPA1	Internal Orders
OPPL	OPPL
ORK0	General CO Configuration Menu
ORK3	ORK3

Transaction	Description
ORKA	Configuration Menu for Internal Orders
ORKL	Cost and Revenue Element Accounting: Configuration Menu
ORKS	Cost Center Accounting: Configuration Menu
OVPS	Document Management Configuration Menu
OWS0	Active Ingredient Management
OWV0	Customizing Pricing
P01A_M01	Company Pension Scheme Germany
P02F_M01	Pension Fund: Switzerland
P05F_M01	
PA00	Personnel Administration
PACA	Payment Cards: Task Menu
PACK	HR-CH: Pension Fund
PAW0	PAW – Performance Assessment Workbench
PB00	Recruitment
PC00	Payroll for all Countries
PC00_M01_JAHRLICHE	Subsequent Activities (Annual)
PC00_M01_PAP	Subsequent Activities – per Payroll Period
PC00_M01_PDUNABHAGIG	Subsequent Activities – Period-Independent
PC00_M01_SONSPERIOD	Subsequent Activities – Other Periods
PC00_M02	Payroll for Switzerland
PC00_M02_JAHRLICHE	Annual Subsequent Activities
PC00_M02_PAP	Subsequent Activities – per Payroll Period
PC00_M02_PDUNABHAGIG	Period-Independent Subsequent Activities
PC00_M02_SONSPERIOD	Subsequent Activities for Other Periods
PC00_M03_JAHRLICHE	Annual Subsequent Activities
PC00_M03_PAP	Subsequent Activities – per Payroll Period
PC00_M03_PDUNABHAGIG	Period-Independent Subsequent Activities
PC00_M03_SONSPERIOD	Subsequent Activities for Other Periods
PC00_M04_JAHRLICHE	Subsequent Annual Activities
PC00_M04_PAP	Subsequent Activities – per Payroll Period
PC00_M04_PDUNABHAGIG	Period-Independent Subsequent Activities
PC00_M04_SONSPERIOD	Subsequent Activities Other Periods
PC00_M05_JAHRLICHE	Annual Subsequent Activities
PC00_M05_PAP	Subsequent Activities – Per Payroll Period
PC00_M05_SONSPERIOD	Subsequent Activities for Other Periods
PC00_M06_JAHRLICHE	Annual Subsequent Activities

Transaction	Description
PC00_M06_PAP	Subsequent Activities per Payroll Period
PC00_M06_PDUNABHAGIG	Period-Independent Subsequent Activities
PC00_M06_SONSPERIOD	Subsequent Activities – Other Periods
PC00_M07_JAHRLICHE	Subsequent Activities – Annual
PC00_M07_PAP	Subsequent Activities – per Payroll Period
PC00_M07_PDUNABHAGIG	Subsequent Activities – Period-Independent
PC00_M07_SONSPERIOD	Subsequent Activities – Other Periods
PC00_M08_JAHRLICHE	Annual Subsequent Activities
PC00_M08_PAP	Subsequent Activities – per Payroll Period
PC00_M08_PDUNABHAGIG	Period-Independent Subsequent Activities
PC00_M08_SONSPERIOD	Subsequent Activities for Other Periods
PC00_M09_JAHRLICHE	Annual Subsequent Activities
PC00_M09_PAP	Subsequent Activities – per Payroll Period
PC00_M09_PDUNABHAGIG	Subsequent Activities – Period-Independent
PC00_M09_SONSPERIOD	Subsequent Activities – Other Periods
PC00_M10_JAHRLICHE	Subsequent Activities – Annual
PC00_M10_PAP	Subsequent Activities – per Payroll Period
PC00_M10_PDUNABHAGIG	Subsequent Activities – Period Independent
PC00_M10_SONSPERIOD	Subsequent Activities – Other Periods
PC00_M11_JAHRLICHE	Subs. Activities – Annual
PC00_M11_PAP	Subs. Activities – per Payroll Period
PC00_M11_PDUNABHAGIG	Subs. Activities – Period-Unrelated
PC00_M11_SONSPERIOD	Subs. Activities – Other Periods
PC00_M12_DIMONA	
PC00_M12_JAHRLICHE	Annual Subsequent Activities
PC00_M12_PAP	Subsequent Activities – per Payroll Period
PC00_M12_PDUNABHAGIG	Period-Independent Subsequent Activities
PC00_M12_SONSPERIOD	Subsequent Activities for Other Periods
PC00_M13_JAHRLICH_PS	Subsequent Activities – Annual
PC00_M13_JAHRLICHE	Subsequent Activities – Annual
PC00_M13_PAP	Subsequent Activities – Per Payroll Period
PC00_M13_PAP_PS	Subsequent Activities – per Payroll Period
PC00_M13_PDUNABHA_PS	Subsequent Activities – Period-Independent
PC00_M13_PDUNABHAGIG	Subsequent Activities – Period-Independent
PC00_M13_PIND	Subsequent Activities – Period Independent
PC00_M13_PS	Payroll for Australian Public Sector
PC00_M13_SONSPERI_PS	Subsequent Activities – Other Periods

Transaction	Description
PC00_M13_SONSPERIOD	Subsequent Activities – Other periods
PC00_M14_AWS	AWS Accounting for Malaysia
PC00_M14_FAP	FAP Accounting for Malaysia
PC00_M14_JAHRLICHE	Subsequent Activities – Annual
PC00_M14_OCWB	Off-Cycle Workbench
PC00_M14_ODS	On-Demand Payroll for Malaysia
PC00_M14_PAP	Subsequent Activities – per Payroll Period
PC00_M14_PDUNABHAGIG	Subsequent Activities – Period-Independent
PC00_M14_SONSPERIOD	Subsequent Activities – Other Periods
PC00_M15_JAHRLICHE	Payroll for Italy
PC00_M15_PAP	Payroll for Italy
PC00_M15_PDUNABHAGIG	Payroll for Italy
PC00_M15_SONSPERIOD	Payroll for Italy
PC00_M16_JAHRLICHE	Annual Subsequent Activities
PC00_M16_PAP	Subsequent Activities – per Payroll Period
PC00_M17_JAHRLICHE	Payroll Venezuela
PC00_M17_PAP	Payroll Venezuela
PC00_M17_PDUNABHAGIG	Payroll Venezuela
PC00_M17_SONSPERIOD	Payroll Venezuela
PC00_M19_JAHRLICHE	HR-PT: Subsequent Activities – Annual
PC00_M19_PAP	HR-PT: Subsequent Activities – per Payroll Period
PC00_M19_PDUNABHAGIG	HR-PT: Subsequent Activities – Period-Independent
PC00_M19_SONSPERIOD	HR-PT: Subsequent Activities – in Other Periods
PC00_M20_JAHRLICHE	Subs.activities – Annual
PC00_M20_PAP	Subs.activities – Per Payroll Period
PC00_M20_PDUNABHAGIG	Subs.activities – Period-Independent
PC00_M20_SONSPERIOD	Subs.activities – Other Periods
PC00_M22_JAHRLICHE	Subsequent Activities – Annual
PC00_M22_PAP	Subsequent Activities – per Payroll Period
PC00_M22_PDUNABHAGIG	Subsequent Activities – Period Independent
PC00_M22_RETIRE	Retirement Accounting for Japan
PC00_M22_SONSPDSI	Subsequent Activities Other Periods – Social Insurance
PC00_M22_SONSPERIOD	Subsequent Activities – Other Periods

Transaction	Description
PC00_M22_SYOYO	Shoyo Accounting for Japan
PC00_M22_YRENDADJ	Year-End Adjustment for Japan
PC00_M23_JAHRLICHE	Subsequent Activities – Annual
PC00_M23_PAP	Subsequent Activities – per Payroll Period
PC00_M23_PDUNABHAGIG	Subsequent Activities – Period-Independent
PC00_M23_SONSPERIOD	Subsequent Activities – Other Periods
PC00_M25_AWS	AWS Accounting for Singapore
PC00_M25_FAP	FAP Accounting for Singapore
PC00_M25_JAHRLICHE	Annual Subsequent Activities
PC00_M25_MID	Mid-Month Accounting for Singapore
PC00_M25_ODS	On-Demand Payroll for Singapore
PC00_M25_PAP	Subsequent Activities – per Payroll Period
PC00_M25_PDUNABHAGIG	Subsequent Activities Irrespective of Periods
PC00_M25_SONSPERIOD	Subsequent Activities for Other Periods
PC00_M26_JAHRLICHE	Subsequent Activities – Annual
PC00_M26_PAP	Subsequent Activities – per Payroll Period
PC00_M26_PDUNABHAGIG	Subsequent Activities TH Period-Independent
PC00_M26_SONSPERIOD	Subsequent Activities TH – Other Periods
PC00_M27_JAHRLICHE	Subs. Activities – Annual
PC00_M27_PAP	Subs. Activities – Per Payroll Period
PC00_M27_PDUNABHAGIG	Subs. Activities – Period-Independent
PC00_M27_SONSPERIOD	Subs. Activities – Other Periods
PC00_M28_JAHRLICHE	Subs. Activities – Annual
PC00_M28_PAP	Subsequent Activities per Payroll Period
PC00_M28_PDUNABHAGIG	Subsequent Activities – Period-Independent
PC00_M29_JAHRLICHE	Payroll Argentina
PC00_M29_MONATLICHE	Payroll Argentina
PC00_M29_PAP	Payroll Argentina
PC00_M29_PDUNABHAGIG	Payroll Argentina
PC00_M29_SONSPERIOD	Payroll Argentina
PC00_M32_JAHRLICHE	Payroll for Italy
PC00_M32_MONATLICHE	Payroll for Italy
PC00_M32_PAP	Payroll for Italy
PC00_M32_PDUNABHAGIG	Payroll for Italy
PC00_M32_SONSPERIOD	Payroll for Italy
PC00_M34_JAHRLICHE	Subs.activities – Annual
PC00_M34_PAP	Subs.activities – per Payroll Period

Transaction	Description
PC00_M34_PDUNABHAGIG	Subs.activities – Period-Unrelated
PC00_M34_SONSPERIOD	Subs.activities – Other Periods
PC00_M37_JAHRLICHE	Payroll for Italy
PC00_M37_MONATLICHE	Payroll for Italy
PC00_M37_PAP	Activity per Period
PC00_M37_PDUNABHAGIG	Payroll for Italy
PC00_M37_SONSPERIOD	Payroll for Italy
PC00_M41_BON&OFFS	Bonus & Other Off-Cycles
PC00_M41_JAHRLICHE	Subs.activities – Annual
PC00_M41_PAP	Subs.activities – per Payroll Period
PC00_M41_PDUNABHAGIG	Subs.activities – Period-Independent
PC00_M41_RETIRE	Retire Regular Payroll
PC00_M42_ADV_OCRN	Advance Payment Using Off-Cycle Reason
PC00_M42_ADV_REP	Advance Payment Using Report
PC00_M42_AWS	Bonus Accounting
PC00_M42_JAHRLICHE	Subs.activities – Annual
PC00_M42_PAP	Subs.activities – Per Payroll Period
PC00_M42_PDUNABHAGIG	Subs.activities – Period-Independent
PC00_M42_SONSPERIOD	Subs.activities – Other Periods
PC00_M43_PAP	Subsequent Activities – per Payroll Period
PC00_M44_OTHPER	Subsequent Activities in Other Periods
PC00_M44_PAP	Subsequent Activities per Payroll Period
PC00_M44_PERIND	Period Independent Subsequent Activities
PC00_M44_YEARLY	Annual Subsequent Activities
PC00_M48_13M	13th Month Pay
PC00_M48_ADV_NDED	Advance Payment without Deductions
PC00_M48_ADV_WDED	Advance Payment with Deductions
PC00_M48_BN	Bonus Payment
PC00_M48_JAHRLICHE	Subsequent Activities – Annual
PC00_M48_PAP	Subsequent Activities – per Payroll Period
PC00_M48_PDUNABHAGIG	Subsequent Activities – Period-Independent
PC00_M48_SONSPERIOD	Subsequent Activities – Other Periods
PC00_M99_PAP	Subsequent Activities per Payroll Period
PC01	Payroll for Germany
PC02	Payroll for Switzerland
PC03	Payroll Austria
PC04	Payroll Spain

Transaction	Description
PC05	Payroll Netherlands
PC06	Payroll France
PC07	Payroll Canada
PC08	Payroll Great Britain
PC09	Payroll for Denmark
PC10	(US Payroll)
PC11	Payroll Ireland
PC12	Payroll Belgium
PC13	Payroll Australia
PC14	Payroll for Malaysia
PC15	Payroll – Italy
PC16	Payroll South Africa
PC17	Payroll Venezuela
PC19	Payroll for Portugal
PC20	Payroll Norway
PC22	Payroll Japan
PC23	Payroll Sweden
PC25	Payroll Singapore
PC26	Payroll Thailand
PC27	Payroll Hong Kong
PC28	Payroll China
PC29	Payroll Argentina
PC32	Payroll Mexico
PC34	Payroll Accounting for Indonesia
PC37	Payroll for Brazil
PC40	Payroll India
PC41	Payroll Korea
PC42	Payroll Taiwan
PC43	Payroll New Zealand
PC44	Finland
PC48	Payroll Philippines
PC99	International Payroll
PC99_TOOLS	Tools
PCA0	Production Campaign
PCA1	Profit Center Accounting
PCF	Cost Object
PCI	Process Manufacturing

Transaction	Description
PCIA	Process Manufacturing
PEPMEN	Task Level Menu for the PEP
PIMN	Human Resources Information System
PK00	KANBAN
PKC1	Activity-Based Costing Information System
PM01	Plant Maintenance
PMMN	HR Funds and Position Management
PORTFOLIO	Portfolio Management
PP01	Production Planning
PP70	Organizational Management
PP72	Time Management: Shift Planning
PP74	Personnel Cost Planning
PP7S	Organizational Management
PPMM	Personnel Planning
PPPE	Personnel Development
PPSFC_INFO	Shop Floor Control
PR00	Travel Expenses
PROF	PROF
PS00	Project System
PS01	Project Information System
PS02	Project System: Basic Data
PS03	Project Planning
PS04	Project Budgeting
PS05	Project Execution
PS06	Project Cost Controlling
PS07	Project System: Financials
PS08	Project System: Dates
PS09	Project System: Resources
PS10	Project System: Material
PS11	Project System: Progress
PS12	Project System: Project
PS13	Project System: Documents
PS14	Project System: Claims
PS15	Project System: Collaboration
PS81	Individual Overviews
PS91	Project Information System (Commercial Part)
PSC_MENU	Production Sharing Accounting

Transaction	Description
PSC4	Consistency Checks
PT00	Time Management: Time Data Administration
PT00_THOMAS	Time Management: Administration
PVMN	Training and Event Management
PVMN1	Training and Event Management – Reports
PW00	Incentive Wages
PW00_THOMAS	Incentive Wages
PWB	Print Workbench
Q000	Quality Management
QA00	Quality Inspection
QA00_INFO	Info System: Quality Certificates
QE00	Quality Planning
QE00_INFO_1	Info System: Inspection Planning
QE00_INFO_2	Info System: Basic Data
QE00_INFO_3	Info System: Logistics Master Data in QM
QM00	Quality Notifications
QM00_INFO	Quality Notifications: Info System
QMU1	Quality Management
QST00	Stability Study
QT00	Test Equipment Management
QT00_INFO	Info System: Test Equipment Management
QT01	Inspection Processing
QZ00	Quality Certificate
QZ00_INFO	Info System: Quality Certificates
RCC00	Risk Object: Configuration Menu
RCL1	Reconciliation Ledger
RCPMGT	Recipe Management
RECAMENUAPPL	Flexible Real Estate Management: Application Menu
RECAMENUDEV	RE-FX (Extension): Development Menu
RECAMENUDEVCUSTTECH	RE Extension: Technical Customizing (S Tables)
REORG	Reorganization Tools in Market Risk and ALM
RKS1	Cost Center Accounting
ROLLE	Area Menu for Role Reports
RS00	SAP Business Information Warehouse
RS00_ADM	Administration
RS00_BEX	Business Explorer

Transaction	Description
RS00_BW	SAP Business Information Warehouse
RS00_BW_ONLY	SAP Business Information Warehouse (only BW)
RS00_DM	Data Mining
RS00_EI	Enhanced Analytics
RS00_MOD	Modeling
RS00_PLAN	Business Planning and Simulation
RS00_TOOL	Tools
RSW1	Standard Analyses
RTP_US_BDT	Retirement Plan Development BDT
S_TEST_WORKBENCH	Test Workbench Menu
S000	SAP R/3 System
S000_CO	Controlling
S000_CO_PC	Product Cost Controlling
S000_CO_PC_OBJ	Cost Object Controlling
S000_EC	Enterprise Controlling
S000_FI	Financial Accounting
S000_HR	Human Resources
S000_IM	Investment Management
S000_INFO_LO	Logistics Information System
S000_INFO_RW	Accounting Information System
S000_LO	Logistics
S000_OLD	SAP R/3 System
S000_PSM	Public Sector Management
S000_RW	Accounting
S000_TR	Treasury
S001	ABAP Workbench
S002	System Administration
SAP_ICC_BRASIL	Brazil
SAP_ICC_THAILAND	MENU: CHECK HANDLING THAILAND
SAP_ICC_TURKEY	Turkey
SAP_ICC_VORNUM_BELEGE	Prenumbered Forms
SAP1	Report Selection
SAP2	Info Catalog
SAPF	Forms
SASAP	Accelerated SAP
SBEA	BEAC Corporate Flight System

Transaction	Description
SBPT	Business Communication
SCC	Subcontracting with Chargeable Components
SCPI	Supply Chain Planning Interfaces
SD01	Sales and Distribution
SD01-01	Information System
SD01-02	Information System
SD01-03	Report Selection
SD01-06	Information System
SD01-07	Information System
SD01-08	Information System
SD01-09	Information System
SDAL	Sales Activity: Address Reports
SDW0	ABAP Workbench
SI00	SAP Knowledge Warehouse
SI00_DOCU	SAP Knowledge Warehouse – Documentation
SI00_OLD	SAP Knowledge Warehouse
SI00_TRAIN	SAP Knowledge Warehouse – Training
SLIS	Special Purpose Ledger: Information System
SM01	Customer Service
SOA_COPY	Business Documents Administration
SOFF	SAPoffice
SP00	Spool and Related Areas
SRZL	Test
SSUO	Structure Graphic: Settings
STTO	Test Workbench
STUN	Performance Monitoring
SWFT	Workflow: Test Suite
SWLD	SAP Business Workflow
SWUX	SAPforms Administration
SYST	SYST
TAXREPORT_PORTUGAL	Tax Reports – Portugal
TBMN	Forex Hedges
TCMK	Funds Management
TCMN	Funds Management
TDMN	Cash Management
TDMN_DIST	Distribute TR Cash Management Data
TFMN	Cash Budget Management

List of SAP Area Menus | B

Transaction	Description
TIMN	Derivative Financial Instruments
TM_HEDGE MANAGEMENT	TM_Hedge Management
TM_IMPAIRMENT	Impairments
TMMN	Money Market
TP00	Travel Planning
TP00_LFD	Current Settings for Travel Planning
TRLM	Limit Management
TRMA	Treasury
TRTC	Cash Management
TRTD	Loans
TRTG	Money Market
TRTM	Market Risk Management
TRTR	Derivatives
TRTV	Foreign Exchange
TRTW	Securities
TV00	Travel Management
TV01	HR Master Data: Travel
TVM1	Market Risk Management
TXMN	Foreign Exchange
TYMN	Treasury Information System
UCUST	Convert Treasury Partner to SAP Business Partner
UPS00	ALE Distribution Units (UOS)
VA00	Sales
VBK0	Material Grouping / Bonus Buy
VC00	Sales Support
VECN	Information System for Profitability and Sales Accounting
VF00	Billing
VI00	Shipment Costs
VI01	ROZ/IPD Reporting
VI02	Fill Again
VI03	Fill Again
VI04	Fill Again
VI05	Fill Again
VI06	Master Data/Contracts
VI07	Controlling/Settlements

499

Transaction	Description
VI08	Reports on Real Estate Management
VI09	Selection Versions
VI10	Master Data
VI11	Contracts
VI12	Overviews
VI13	Controlling RE Objects
VI14	Service/Heating Cost Settlement
VI15	Taxes
VI16	CO Third Party Management
VICP	Correspondence
VIFI	Rental Accounting
VKP0	Pricing
VL00	Shipping
VL30	Inbound Delivery
VLE1	Putaway with Warehouse Management
VLK1	Picking with Warehouse Management
VLK2	Picking with Wave Picks
VLK3	Picking w/o Warehouse Management
VS00	Sales Master Data
VT00	Transportation
VX00	Foreign Trade / Customs
VX0C	Foreign Trade
VXDG	Foreign Trade: Documentary Payments
VXDP	Foreign Trade: Cockpit
VXGK	Foreign Trade: Prohibitions and Restrictions
VXIE	Maintain Foreign Trade Data
VXKD	Foreign Trade: Communication / Printing
VXME	Foreign Trade: Periodic Declarations
VXMO	Foreign Trade: CAP – Restitution
VXPR	Foreign Trade: Preference Handling
VXSE	Foreign Trade: Service for Foreign Trade and Customs
VXSL	Foreign Trade: Sanctioned Party List Screening
W10E	Goods Receipt
W10F	Store Retailing
W10M	Retailing
W10T	SAP Retail

Transaction	Description
W10T_LO	Logistics Retail
WA00	Allocation
WAK0	Promotion
WASSO	Association Management
WB00	Subseq. Settlement, Purchasing – Vendor Rebate Arrangements
WB20	SAP Global Trade
WB20N	SAP Global Trade Management
WBST	Inventory Management
WBVK	Subsequent Settlement: Sales
WCM	Work Clearance Management
WCMCP	Category Manager Workbench (Consumer Products) PROTOTYPE
WDIS	Material Requirements Planning
WEDI	IDoc and EDI Basis
WEKF	Purchase Order
WETI	Labeling
WFIL	Store Order Online
WGCL	Class. System, Retail
WI00	Physical Inventory
WK00	Subsequent Settlement, Purchasing – Customer Arrangements
WKON	Condition/Arrangement
WKUN	Customer
WL00	Vendor
WM00	Material
WMF0	Season Management
WOB0	Plant
WOF0	Plant
WORKFLOW_SUPPORT	Business Workflow Support: Diagnosis and Help Transactions
WP00	Planning
WPDC	SAP Retail Store – PDC Processing
WPOS	POS Interface
WQ00	Value Scales and Quota Scales
WRP0	Replenishment
WRP1	Multi-Step Replenishment

Transaction	Description
WRPFMM	Replenishment: Forecast, MM-Inventory Management
WRPFSOP	Replenishment: Forecast, Replenishment-Inventory Management
WRRLE	Extended Remuneration List Creation
WRTL	Retail Ledger
WS00	Assortment
WSCM	Category Manager Workbench
WSIS	WSIS
WSMP	Merchandise Planning
WSRS_ADM	SAP Retail Store – Administration
WTAD	Additionals
WTY_FOLDER_MAIN	Warranty Claim Processing
WVEB	Valuation
WVER	Shipping
WVKF	Sales Order
WVM0	Customer Replenishment
WVTU	Sales Support
WW01	Cost Center Accounting
WWG1	Material Groups and Material Group Hierarchy
WWG2	Material Groups
WWMI	Product Catalog
WWVT	Merchandise Distribution
WXPO	Merchandise and Assortment Planning
WZR0	Agency Business
WZR01	Agency Business

C How to Initialize a Material Period

You've probably needed to reopen a closed material (also called MM) period. Especially during PGI (post goods issue) or PGR (post goods receipt), you can do the issue or receipt of materials only for the current period. A period is typically a calendar month, so January 2010 is 001/2010. When a particular period is open (e.g., 002/2010) you may be allowed to do the goods issue or receipt in its immediate previous period, 001/2010 (January 2010 or April 2010 if the accounting year is April to March). The operation of reopening an old material period is called initialization of material. The transaction that you can use to initialize a material period is MMPI. Transaction MMPV is used to close the current material period and open the next material period. Using Transaction MMRV, you can see the current period. It's often not required to reopen the previous periods in the production client, but in development and quality servers, this is often required. For example, you may want to create a material and take it through a quality check in a very old period so that it becomes available as an expired material in the current period for various kinds of testing. For reopening the closed material period, be sure to read SAP Note 487381.

The steps to initialize material period are given below:

1. Check the users that are currently active in the system, using Table USR41 (Figure C.1) or Transaction SM04 (Figure C.2). However, Transaction SM04 also shows you the individual transaction each user is doing. Figure C.1 displays Table USR41. If none of the users are expected to be doing any transaction for which material period is relevant, then you can proceed. If any user is doing any transaction relevant to material period, you have to wait. Transactions VA01 (Create Order) and VF02 (Create Bill) are not relevant, but VL02N (Change Delivery) is. The best situation is, however, to do it when nobody else is using the system.

Cl.	User Name	Term.ID	Server	Terminal	Language	Last Logon Date	LOGON_TIME
100	ASHISH	45	PRD_00	10.0.1.24-ashish	E	01.01.2010	17:28:58
100	BEL01	42	PRD_00	117.241.240.197-system	E	01.01.2010	17:09:58
100	CS01	57	PRD_00	10.0.4.5-comp1	E	01.01.2010	16:09:49
100	JAI01	46	PRD_00	59.161.126.196-soft	E	01.01.2010	17:37:02
100	MURTHY	32	PRD_00	10.0.6.28-hphyd2	E	01.01.2010	16:16:55
100	VIJ01	63	PRD_00	59.93.121.174-cpmputer-c7	E	01.01.2010	16:39:08

Figure C.1 User List (Table USR41)

C | How to Initialize a Material Period

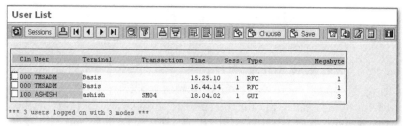

Figure C.2 User List (Transaction SM04)

2. Use Transaction SU01, SU2, or SU3 and maintain the parameter MMPI_READ_NOTE. The parameter value should be the current date (system date) in YYYYMMDD format, as shown in Figure C.3.

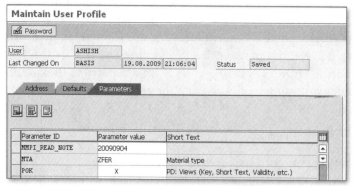

Figure C.3 Maintain Parameter MMPI_READ_NOTE

3. Check the current period of the system using Transaction MMRV.

4. Enter Transaction MMPI. Figure C.4 shows the initial screen.

5. Enter the range of company codes for which material period is to be changed.

6. Enter the period and the year you want. For example, to open the first period (January) of 2010, enter 01 in the Period field and 2010 in the Year field. In countries that follow an April to March fiscal year, period 01 means April, 02 means May, and so on. Thus, January 2010 will be period 10 of fiscal year 2009 (not 2010). This often leads to errors.

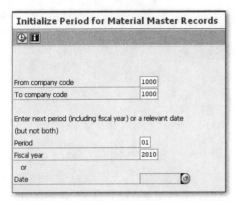

Figure C.4 Initial Screen of Transaction MMPI

7. Execute the period change by pressing F8.
8. You'll see the screen shown in Figure C.5 if the period has been changed successfully.

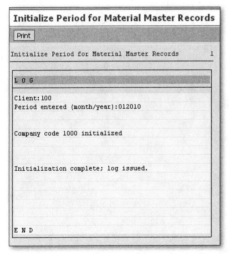

Figure C.5 Log of Material Period Initialization

D   The Author

Ashish Ranjan Mohapatra has worked with SAP software for over nine years. As team leader and assistant project manager for an implementation project, he has developed a thorough understanding of the Sales and Distribution functionality in SAP ERP and implementation and configuration pain points. As head of the Business Process Department, Ashish expanded his knowledge of other SAP software, including Materials Management, Financials and Accounting, Production Planning, and Quality Management. Ashish is an SAP SD Certified Consultant and an instructor with an SAP education partner.

Index

A

ABAP query, 399, 410
Access number, 153
Access sequence, 153, 166, 175, 320, 351
Account determination
  cash settlement, 303
  payment cards, 303
  procedure, 302, 318, 322
  reconciliation account, 302
  table, 317, 318
  type, 318, 321
Account determination analysis, 404
Accounting document, 290
  overview, 407
Accounting key, 201
Accounting period, 287
Account key, 201, 318, 323
Accounts interface, 325
Accrual period start date, 326
Additional value days, 174
Allocation number, 302, 328
Americasí SAP Usersí Group, 25
Analyses, 399
Application link enabling (ALE), 362
Application toolbar, 28
Area menu, 87
ASAP methodology, 30
Asset Management, 22
Assigning organizational units, 33, 38
Assign pricing procedure, 182
Automatic account posting, 287
Automatic credit control, 206, 210
Automatic packing, 238
Availability check, 114
Available to promise, 117

B

Backward scheduling, 264
BADI_CMP_PROCESSING, 308
Barcode, 248
Baseline date, 316
Basis for the rebate, 188
Basis mode, 410
Batch classification, 79
Batch determination, 142, 233, 276
Batch information cockpit, 371
Batch level, 72
Batch management, 367
  master data, 43
Batch master data, 70
Batch numbers, 76
Batch search procedure, 144
Batch status management, 72
Batch where-used list, 368
BDC, 57
Billing, 289
Billing block, 225
Billing documents copying requirements
routines, 105
Billing due list, 290, 295
Billing plan, 128, 289, 310, 315
  types, 310
Billing transfer routines, 106
Billing types, 298
Bill of materials, 130
Bill-to party, 112
Blocking/unblocking customers, 223
Block sales support, 224
Blueprint, 30
Bottom-up analysis, 368, 369
BSP application, 366

Business server pages (BSPs), 363
Business transaction, 278
Business transaction type, 160

C

Calculation type, 176
Cancellation invoice, 296
CarLo, 279
Cash account determination, 328
Changes, 407
Changing layout, 409
Characteristic, 79, 428
Chart of account, 201
Check customized billing types, 298, 306
Checking groups, 117
Checking rule, 118
Check purchase order no, 94
Check value, 179
Classes, 79
Classification system, 277
Collective billing document, 295
Collective requirement, 114
Comments, 447
Commodity codes, 159
Common distribution channels, 45
Common divisions, 46
Communication strategy, 154
Company, 34
Company code, 34
Complaint, 146, 289
Complaint documents, 308
Condition category, 176
Condition class, 176
Condition index, 179
Condition records, 167, 168
Condition tables, 166, 175
Condition technique, 167, 317
Condition type, 167, 176
Condition type group, 187
Condition update, 179
Configurable material, 131

Consignment
 fill-up, 129
 issue, 129
 pick-up, 129
 return, 129
 sale, 128
Consistency check, 39
Contract profile, 126
Controlling, 22
Copy control, 107
Copying requirements, 104, 301
Copy quantity, 110
Copy schedule line, 109
Correction and transportation, 24
Countries, 158
Create condition records, 182
Create query, 411
Create variant, 444, 450
Creating individual invoice, 290
Credit control area, 35, 215
Credit group, 215
Credit horizon, 213, 218
Credit limit, 209
Credit management, 205
Credit management field groups, 61
Credit manager, 210
Credit master sheet, 220
Credit memo request, 147
Credit representative, 60, 209, 210
 groups, 60, 208
Credit risk categories, 60
Critical fields, 216
Currencies, 158, 187
Currency conversion, 179
Current period, 287
Customer account groups, 47, 113
Customer analyses, 423
Customer contracts, 124
Customer credit groups, 207
Customer credit master data, 43, 58
Customer credit master records, 206, 211
Customer determination schema, 227
Customer mass maintenance, 51

Customer master data, 43
Customer master record fields, 49
Customer-material info records, 70
Customer payment guarantee procedure, 227
Customer pricing procedure, 182, 183
Customer tax classifications, 200
Customized analyses, 430
Customized info-structure, 428
Customizing specifications, 394
Customs offices, 161

D

Data declaration, 448
Data source, 410, 411
Data transfer, 104
Date categories, 310, 312
Date descriptions, 310
Date proposals, 310, 314
Days of sales outstanding, 59
Debit memo request, 147
Debugging, 374, 376
Defining organizational units, 34
Delete from database, 179
Deliveries copying requirements routines, 104
Delivery block, 224
Delivery data transfer routines, 106
Delivery document, 233
Delivery due date, 256
Delivery due list, 248, 249
Delivery item category, 234, 238
Delivery list, 256
Delivery split, 237
Delivery type, 234
Departure zones, 262
Determination procedure, 167
Development server, 23
Dispatch time, 154
Display Log, 354
Distribution channel, 36, 40
Divisions, 35, 40
Documentary payment, 225

Documentation, 444, 449
Document credit group, 207, 209
Document determination schema, 227
Document flow, 110, 407
Document management system, 75
Document payment guarantee procedure, 227
Document pricing procedure, 94, 182, 183, 302
Document statistical group, 236
Document value, 216
    classes, 211
Drill down, 409
DSO, 206, 221
Dunning levels, 217

E

Employee master data, 84
Equipment requirement, 278
Evaluation structure, 429
Execute flexible analyses, 433
Export credit insurance, 225
Export/import procedures, 159
Extended syntax check, 450
External tax document, 199

F

Field catalog, 166, 175, 317, 318
Field catalog for pricing, 66
FIFO, 248
Filter, 409
Final preparation, 31
Financial Accounting, 22
Financial document category, 226
Financial document type, 226
Fixed value days, 174
Flexible analyses, 427
Foreign trade, 157
Foreign trade master data, 82
Forms of payment guarantee, 225, 228

Index

Forward scheduling, 264
Free goods, 136
Free items, 136
Free-of-charge delivery, 146
Function code, 256, 257
   profile, 256
Function Keys, 30
Function module GN_INVOICE_CREATE, 296
Fund Management, 22

G

General billing interface, 289, 296
General ledger, 86
Golden client, 270
Go-live, 31
Goods issue, 246
Graphical presentation, 410
Group condition, 177
   routine, 177
Group header, 193
Group reference procedure, 127
Groups, 60
Group specification, 394

H

Handling unit, 244
   data transfer routines, 106
Header condition, 177
Holding company, 34

I

IDoc interface, 356
Implementation Guide, 24
Import code numbers, 159
Importing organizational units, 33
Inbound file, 358
Incompleteness analysis, 406
Incompleteness procedure, 132, 134

Incomplete text, 136
Incompletion control, 132
Incompletion fields, 135
Incompletion group, 132
Incompletion log, 135
Index list, 256
Individual billing document, 295
Individual purchase order, 131
Individual requirement, 114
InfoCubes, 442
InfoSource, 443
Infotype, 85
Initial status of a new batch, 73
Inner join, 414
Inquiry, 91
Insert tables, 412
Integration points, 150
Intercompany sales, 148
Intercompany stock transfer, 233, 266
Internal customers, 269
Internet service provider (ISP), 363
Interval characteristics, 395
Interval scale, 170
Intracompany stock transfer, 150
Invoice correction, 147
Invoice reference, 329
Invoice split, 294
IP address, 363
Item categories, 99, 100
Item category group, 100
Item conditions, 177
Item level, 193

J

JavaScripts, 364
Join tables, 411

K

Key field, 194
Key figures, 428

L

Layout mode, 411
Layout of batch master records, 74
Lead time, 97
Left-outer join, 414
Letter of credit, 225
List fields, 416
Listing/execution analysis, 407
List profile, 252
Lists, 399, 400
Loading point, 38
Loading time, 264, 265
Location master data, 284
Logical database, 412
Logistics Execution, 22
Logistics Information System, 66
LSMW, 57, 374
LVKMPFZ1, 216, 376
LVKMPFZZ2, 216, 376
LVKMPFZZ3, 216
LVKMPTZZ, 216, 376

M

Make-to-order production, 130
Manual entry, 177
Master contract, 124
Master data, 43, 453
Material analyses, 426
Material commission groups, 69
Material determination, 140
Material determination analysis, 407
Material for settlement, 188
Material listing/exclusion, 140
Material master, 62
Material master data, 43
Material period, 287
Material-related value contract, 125
Materials Management, 22
Material status, 67
Material tax indicators, 201

Max tax, 202
MCSCHECK, 433
MCVCHECK01, 437
Menu bar, 27
Message control, 355
Method of payment, 187
Milestone billing, 310
MIME object, 366
Mode of transport, 161
 category, 260
Modes of transport, 260
Movement type, 78, 148
MRP type, 102, 115
Multiple reference, 147

N

Negative posting, 300
Next internal review date, 216
Next review date, 222
NOK, 219

O

Oldest open item, 217
Online Support System, 25
Online transaction processing, 439
Open items, 216
Operations, 448
Order block, 224
Order confirmation, 154
Order data transfer routines, 106
Order fulfillment, 22
Order reason, 98
Order reference, 235
Orders copying requirements routines, 104
Organizational structure, 33
Organizational units, 33
Outbound trigger, 358
Outline agreements, 124
Output determination analysis, 404

Output determination procedure, 236
Output processing analysis, 404, 405
Outputs, 152
Output type, 153, 236

P

Packaging materials, 244
Packing, 245
Page header, 193
Parameter LE_VL10_USER_VARIANT, 253
Parameter rdisp/max_wprun_time, 329
Parameters, 88
Partner determination, 112
Partner determination procedure, 210, 237
Partner function, 154
Payer, 112
Payment cards, 225
Payment guarantee, 205, 225
  category, 225
  determination procedure, 226
  procedures, 227
  schema, 228, 229
Payment History, 212
Payroll, 22
Periodic billing, 310
Period indicator, 77
Personnel Management, 22
Picking, 242
Picking lists, 275
Pick/pack time, 264, 265
Planned goods issue date, 256
Planning, 117
Plant, 35
Plant Maintenance, 22
Post goods issue, 215
Posting block, 223, 299
Previous period, 287
Pricing, 165
Pricing analysis, 403
Pricing procedure, 179, 180
Pricing type, 110

Print, 410
Processing status, 172
Process key, 201
Product allocation, 117
Product hierarchy, 65
  structure, 66
Production Planning, 22
Production server, 23, 270
Pro forma billing type, 307
Pro forma invoice, 289
Program
  attributes, 444
  name, 444
  LV07A111, 244
  LV50R_VIEWG09, 251
  MV45AFZZ, 332
  MV50AFZ1, 234
  MV50AFZ3, 243
  MV50AFZZ, 236
  MV60ATOP, 293
  RFYTXDISPLAY, 202
  RM07CHDX, 72
  RV15B003, 191
  RV60AFZZ, 303, 332
  RVKRED08, 216, 218
  RVKRED77, 332
  RVV05IVB, 191
Project preparation, 30
Proposed delivery date, 97
Proposed PO date, 97
Proposed pricing date, 97
Proposed valid-from date, 97

Q

Qty Proposal, 144
Quality Management, 22
Quality server, 23
Quant, 248
Quantity contract, 124
Quantity scale, 170
Quotation, 91

R

Realization, 31
Rebate agreement, 186
  type, 188
Rebate recipient, 187
Rebate settlement, 289
Reconciliation account determination, 327
Record type, 297
Reference application, 178
Reference condition type, 178
Reference mandatory, 93
Reference number, 302, 328
Releasing blocked document, 219
Relevant for account assignment, 179
Remote function call (RFC), 361
Rental contract, 125
Report in Excel/Lotus, 410
Report RFDKLI20, 286
Request of quotation, 90
Requirement routine 104, 113, 210, 211
Requirements, 104
  formulas, 104
Requirements class, 115, 118
Requirement type, 115, 119
Returnable packaging, 129
Returns, 146, 147
Revenue account determination, 317
Revenue distribution type, 326
Revenue event, 327
Revenue recognition, 325
  category, 326
RFID, 248
Risk categories, 208, 215
ROADNET, 279
Rounding difference comparison, 177
Rounding rule, 177
Route determination, 233, 237, 259, 262
Routes, 259
Route schedule, 256
Route stages, 262
Rule MALA, 235
Rule MARE, 236

Rule RETA, 236
Rules for determining dates, 316

S

Sabrix, 197
Sales, 89
Sales activity
  copying requirements routines, 105
  data transfer routines, 106
Sales and Distribution, 22
Sales and Operation Planning (SOP), 151
Sales area, 36, 38, 44, 182, 224, 269
Sales document, 91
Sales group, 37, 40
Sales Information System, 399
Sales office, 36, 40
  analyses, 425
Sales organization, 36, 39
Sales organization analyses, 426
SAP Advanced Planner and Optimizer (APO), 98, 123
SAP Central Process Scheduling, 33
SAP Developers Network, 25
SAP Easy Access Menu Paths, 28
SAP edit function, 55
SAP Education, 25
SAP ERP Operations, 22
SAP GUI, 25
SAP icons, 29
SAP NetWeaver BW
  reporting, 399
SAP Notes, 25
SAPPHIRE, 25
SAP PRESS, 25
SAP Quality Center by HP, 33
SAP query infoset, 412
SAP Safeguarding, 32
SAP Service Marketplace, 25
SAP Solution Manager, 31
SAP tax interface, 199
Scale basis, 179

Scale formula, 179
Scales, 170
Scale type, 179
Scheduling agreements, 127
SD document category, 92
SD TPS 4.0, 279
SD User exits, 374
Search, 409
Selection fields, 411, 416
Selection screen, 448
Select list, 411
Select statement, 448
Serialization, 233
Serialization procedure, 278
Serial number, 233, 277
Service and maintenance contract, 125
Shelf life expiration date, 77, 367
Shifts, 264
Shipment data transfer routines, 107
Shipping condition, 263
Shipping point, 37, 40
Shipping point analyses, 426
Shipping type procedure group, 260
Shipping types, 260
Ship-to party, 112
Simple credit limit check, 209
SLIN Overview, 451
Sold-to party, 112
Sort, 409
Split analysis, 294
Standard analyses, 423
Static check, 216
Status, 187
Status bar, 28
Status file, 359
Status groups, 132
Status overview, 407
Stock overview, 408
Stock transfer, 233, 266
Storage bin, 248
Storage location, 37
Storage location rule, 235
Storage types, 248

Strategy, 120
  group, 119
  type, 143
Structure condition, 177
Subtotal A, 218
Supplement conditions, 172
System messages, 74
System status bar, 27

T

Table join, 412
Table view, 412
Tax category, 200
Tax codes, 201
  juristiction, 200
Tax determination rule, 200
Tax type, 201
Taxware, 197
TechEd, 25
Terms of payment, 174
Text data transfer routines, 107
Text determination
  analysis, 353
  procedure, 236, 348
Text elements, 444, 449
Text group, 345, 349
Text ID, 348
Text name data transfer routines, 107
Text objects, 345
Texts copying requirements routines, 105
Text specifications, 394
Third-party order, 131
Title bar, 28
Top-down analysis, 368, 369
To scale, 170
Total and subtotal, 409
Transaction, 28
  MASS, 51
  NACE, 154, 273, 355
  SE16N, 55
Transaction keys, 202

Transaction variant, 94
Transfer of requirements, 114, 123
Transfer order, 247
Transfer posting, 267
Transit time, 264, 266
Transmission medium, 154
Transportation connection points, 260
Transportation group, 262, 263
Transportation Management, 38
Transportation planning time, 264
Transport planning point, 38
Transport scheduling time, 266
Traveling time, 266
Two-step stock transfer, 267

U

Update condition, 174
Update group, 35
USEREXIT_LIPS-KOQUI_DETERMINE, 243
USEREXIT_NUMBER_RANGE, 234
USEREXIT_PRICING_PREPARE_TKOMP, 332
User master data, 86

V

Validity period, 172, 187
Valuation level, 35
Value contract, 125
Value scale, 170
Vendor master data, 82
Vertex, 197
VOFM routines, 103, 345
VOTXN, 345

W

Warehouse Management, 22, 247
Warehouse number, 37, 248
Web Interface, 362
    Builder, 364
Weight groups, 263
Wild Cards, 29
Working hours, 264
Work lists, 399, 402

www.sap-press.com

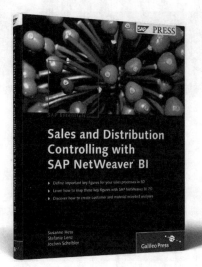

Teaches how to identify and assess key figures for your sales processes in SD

Provides step-by-step instructions for creating customer and material oriented analysis

Contains practical tips on how to create effective, useful data and analysis

Susanne Hess, Stefanie Lenz, Jochen Scheibler

Sales and Distribution Controlling with SAP NetWeaver BI

This book teaches users how to define, evaluate, and report key figures for sales and distribution controlling in SD (SAP ERP 6.0) using SAP NetWeaver BI 7.0. It starts with an overview of essential key figures in SD controlling and explains their business background. From there, it details the sales processes, and provides an overview of how raw data is created. Users learn how to map key figures for business controlling in a business warehouse, and how to use key figures in various analysis tools.

250 pp., 2009, 68,– Euro / US$ 85
ISBN 978-1-59229-266-0

>> www.sap-press.com

Your SAP Library is just a click away

www.sap-press.com

- ✓ Easy and intuitive navigation
- ✓ Bookmarking
- ✓ Searching within the full text of all our books
- ✓ 24/7 access
- ✓ Printing capability

Interested in reading more?

Please visit our Web site for all
new book releases from SAP PRESS.

www.sap-press.com